FREEMASONRY IN
AMERICAN HISTORY

D1521983

Books By The Same Author

"A Daughter of the Grand Lodge of Virginia," the formation of the Grand Lodge of West Virginia, 1959

House Undivided: The Story of Freemasonry and the Civil War, 1961

Freemasonry in Highland Springs, A history of Babcock Lodge No. 322, Virginia

Sword and Trowel (with John Black Vrooman), Military Lodges, 1964

Masonry Under Two Flags, 1968

Key to Freemasonry's Growth, 1969

Freemasonry's Servant: Fifty years with The Masonic Service Association, 1969

How to Conduct a Successful Leadership Seminar, 1970

Fifty Golden Years, 1971

Brotherhood in Action, the history of the Virginia Craftsmen, 1971; 1977

The Craft and Its Symbols, 1974

G. Washington: Master Mason, 1976

A Chronicle of Virginia Research Lodge, 1980

Frontier Cornerstone, the history of the Grand Lodge of Ohio, 1980

Motion Pictures Written, Produced and Directed

The Pilot, 1968

Growing the Leader, 1969

Breaking Barriers to Communication, 1970

Planning Unlocks the Door, 1971

People Make the Difference, 1972

The Saga of the Holy Royal Arch of Freemasonry, 1974

The Brotherhood of Man. . ., 1975

Challenge!, 1977

Precious Heritage, 1978

Lonely World, 1979

Fraternally Yours, 1980

Virtue Will Triumph, 1982

1. Freemasonry - U.S. - History

Freemasonry
in American History

Allen E. Roberts

MACOY PUBLISHING & MASONIC SUPPLY CO., INC.
Richmond, Virginia

PRINTED IN THE UNITED STATES OF AMERICA

Dedicated to...

those men of yesteryear who practice the principles of Freemasonry in their everyday lives, thereby making this a better world than it might have been, and those men of today who are doing the same, this work is greatfully dedicated.

May the men of this and future generations dedicate themselves to live according to the tenents of Freemasonry, and in so doing help bring the peoples of the world close to the day when the brotherhood of man under the fatherhood of God, by whatever name He may be called, becomes a reality.

FOREWORD

IN 1963 I first heard of, and joined, The Philalethes Society. I was a brand new York Rite member and had been a Mason for only five years. I had trouble waiting for the April issue of *The Philalethes* magazine. Like most other people, I wanted to see my name in print.

In that April issue a short article announced that, in February, Jerry Erikson of California and some fellow named Allen Earl Roberts had been elected Fellows of the Philalethes Society. The article mentioned that Roberts was the author of *House Undivided*, a story of Freemasonry and the Civil War, which had been published by the Missouri Lodge of Research. I hadn't heard of the Missouri Lodge of Research at the time, even though I was living in Trenton, Missouri. I soon rectified that. I purchased a copy of the book and settled down to a couple of evenings of the most enjoyable Masonic reading I had ever had.

I even did something I hadn't done before. I sat down and wrote the author of the book, and told him how much I liked it. I expected that I would get the usual terse note from him that my fan letters usually get. I was surpised when I got a lengthy and a very brotherly and informative letter. Correspondence continued through the years and I have always made it a point to read each of Al's books as they have come out. I have read them all. I have seen all of his films and have followed his leadership courses with interest.

In my opinion, Allen Roberts is the most knowledgeable Masonic educator of the present day. He has taken contemporary management techniques and has applied them to Freemasonry. Naturally, he isn't universally popular. Men of little minds and big egos take strong exception when someone shows them what they have been doing wrong. The one strident voice, crying in the wilderness (or perhaps whimpering in the back pasture), making itself heard over the sounds of the general acclaim, is ignored as much as possible.

Al Roberts has taken his lumps. "The honors so justly his due have never been paid him."

As a professional editor, not a Masonic editor, but a professional, I am appalled at the amount of work which Allen puts in on each project and the small amount of profit he has ever made. If he were to apply the same amount of energy and time to some professional endeavor, he would become independently wealthy. Instead he works for the Fraternity which he loves. He never knows until a film or other project ends whether he will lose money on it.

Fortunately he has Dottie, his wife. Were it not for her strong support, Al wouldn't have been able to do half as much as he does. Most women wouldn't tolerate the amount of work Al does for the Masonic Order without reward. Dottie encourages him to do more. Allen is fortunate in his home and family life, and the Fraternity is fortunate that Dottie will keep him working.

For the last few years I have missed new books by Al Roberts. He's been making films. His newsletter, *The Altar Light*, gave me much enjoyable reading, but finances caused its demise, as they have done for many other publications. It was not a good day when the publication succumbed, but it did give me "Through Masonic Windows," one of the most popular features of *The Philalethes* magazine.

We have long needed a good one volume Masonic history of Freemasonry. Most of the histories which we have are a collection of names and dates, sometimes in subject outline, but far too many times in straight chronological order. Few of us would want to try to condense the history of Freemasonry in the United States of America into one single volume. Even less would any of us want to write the history of Freemasonry in the context of the part it played in the growth of America. Sociological histories, though popular in academic circles, are practically unheard of in Freemasonry. Most of our histories treat Freemasonry as if it were a phenomenon apart which had no relation to the time in which it existed.

James Craig and H. L. Haywood wrote a one volume history of Freemasonry. It was not a good book. It treats Freemasonry as a thing apart.

Whatever faults a person can find in *Freemasonry in American History*, separation of Masonry from the general history is not one of them. Allen Roberts has taken the history of Freemasonry and the history of the United States and woven them tightly together. He hasn't fallen into any of the traps which so many inexperienced Masonic historians do, such as trying to make our Fraternity the prime mover of all that is good in our country. He has worked the history of Freemasonry into the actual history of the United States.

This is not a totally objective book. It is not a history, written by a historian for other historians. It is an easily readable book about Freemasonry, written by a Freemason for the benefit of other Freemasons. It is not without its faults. One of these, in my opinion, is that Allen has spent far too much time on the beginnings of Freemasonry in Massachusetts and Virginia; and has slighted much of the Masonic history of the western states. Some of his conclusions, especially about the Morgan incident and the Mormon problems, seem to me to be too simplistic. But the book gives an overview of both the history of the country and the Fraternity. Much more could be done. Each of Allen's chapters could be expanded into an entire book.

What Allen Roberts has done here is to give us the skeleton of a complete history of Masonry in America. It remains for him, or perhaps others, to finish out that skeleton.

But Allen has done one thing. He has written the first sociological history of Masonry which we have. This book is valuable to the Masonic student and will become more valuable in the years to come. It is valuable to the general reader and to the newly made Mason who wishes to receive more light about the Order to which he belongs. This book should be the first of a number of volumes dealing with Masonry and its place in history. Hopefully, Allen will consider this book a beginning and will write more and more sociological history.

If he does not, I hope someone else will. This is a book which has been badly needed and which should add to our understanding of our Fraternity's place in the history of our country. We can be grateful to Allen for taking the time and for doing the vast amount of research needed to produce this unique book. Regardless of what faults some reviewer may find, and having reviewed a number of books myself, I have a jaundiced eye for faults, the virtues of this book far outweigh any errors.

I am grateful to Allen Roberts for many things. They would require too much time to mention. I am especially grateful and proud to be asked to read, and criticize, the advance copy. I am proud to be allowed to have a small part in introducing this much needed book to the fraternity.

JERRY MARSENGILL, P.G.H.P.
Editor, The Philalethes

AUTHOR'S PREFACE

HISTORIANS have ignored the contributions of Freemasons and Freemasonry in their accounts of the happenings in the world. Even those men who were, or are, Freemasons haven't, for the most part, credited the part Freemasonry has played in their lives. This book is an attempt to bring the history of America and Freemasonry into focus.

History is made by men and women. Freemasonry is composed of men; women comprise some of its appendant bodies. Although it's impossible to relate the full influence the teachings of Masonry have had on the history-makers, it has been considerable. In some instances this influence is related in this story by those involved. In other cases we can assume the work of many of those noted was favorably influenced by the teachings of the Craft.

Over the years millions upon millions of men have received the degrees as conferred in Masonic lodges throughout the free world. Many of these men have played vital roles in the history of the world. Only a few, too few, could be mentioned in a book of this size. As an example, William Denslow's *10,000 Famous Freemasons* measures over six inches deep; the books studied for this volume take up over fifteen feet on my book shelves. The Grand Lodge histories that have been written measure more then four feet. Thousands of other volumes have been written on or about Freemasonry.

Even so, this is the first attempt to weave the history of the United States with that of Freemasonry. It is the first general history of Freemasonry in America. It is the basis on which some other Masonic historian can build.

This book is an attempt, in a small way, to cover the history of America in a concise manner, and to show in some measure the influence Freemasonry had in making this the greatest country the world has ever known.

There were disappointments encountered in searching for the material necessary to make this as accurate an account as possible. One disappointment was failure to get access to the manuscript of the early years of Freemasonry in Virginia as written by Archer B. Gay before his death. I wanted to record his reasoning for believing Masonry was active in Virginia around 1733, even though he had no concrete proof. I have told the truth as I found it concerning the early days of the Craft in Virginia. There will be those who will disagree, perhaps some future historian will be able to produce information I could not find.

Melvin M. Johnson of Massachusetts did a monumental job of recreating the early history of Freemasonry in that colony. Much of what he wrote becomes suspect when the reader recognizes that he attempted to make Massachusetts first, Masonically, in everything. This is obviously false. The *Proceedings* of the 19th and 20th centuries, useless as historical references, were cited as documenting his statements. Again, I have recorded the truth as I found it.

More of the history of Canada and Mexico could have been incorporated into this work had information not been lacking. This is also true concerning the early days of Freemasonry in the West. Some areas are covered in some depth. The efforts of the Freemasons noted in these, really serve to tell the story of our wilderness brethren. Frontier Pennsylvania Masonry was duplicated, to some extent, as civilization moved westward.

To those Grand Secretaries and others who cheerfully answered my plea for information, I owe a debt of gratitude. To all those historians noted in the bibliography, I'll always be indebted.

To Vee Hansen and H. Paul Scholte of Macoy Publishing and Masonic Supply Co., Inc. I am grateful. They asked that this book be expanded way beyond its original intent. This caused me to learn more about the history of this great country of ours. It also caused me to "discover" many more truly great Freemasons.

No historical work should be published without having searching, critical, and knowledgeable eyes check it for inaccuracies. In Freemasonry there are few historians left. One came readily to mind—Jerry Marsengill. He is a Freemason who knows and understands Freemasonry. He's not merely a Masonic editor; he's a professional editor, writer and author. He edits *The Philalethes* and *Royal Arch Mason* magazines, plus *The Advance*, a newsletter for the leadership of Royal Arch Masonry.

His editing, writing and Masonic knowledge have long been the mainstay of two Iowa Research lodges. He owns his own company which specializes in writing. He graduated *summa cum laude* with a 4.0 grade in journalism from Drake University. His background was what I needed to check the manuscript for this book. I also hoped he would agree to write the Foreword. He did.

With this background I started using a modern innovation—word processing—along with its "dictionaries" and "grammar-checkers." Mistakes still sneaked through. My friend and Brother, Edward R. Schmidt, helped catch many of them.

As always, my good wife Dottie had to spend many lonely evenings while I again attempted to produce another book. Her understanding, patience and encouragement made it much easier for me to do the painstaking research and writing necessary.

Above all I must continue to thank the many friends and brothers I've found in Freemasonry throughout the years. Those who continue to practice outside their lodges the lessons they have learned within, have proven a tower of strength to me. I'll always be greatful for being permitted to become a Freemason.

To those Freemasons of today and yesteryear, known and unknown, who worked and fought to make this a better world, we all owe a debt of gratitude. I hope this book will repay many of them.

Highland Springs, Virginia   ALLEN E. ROBERTS
July 4, 1983

CONTENTS

ILLUSTRATIONS

FREEMASONRY IN
AMERICAN HISTORY

DANIEL COXE

First Deputized Grand Master of the North American Colonies, 1730.

The first official act of the Grand Lodge of England respecting the American Colonies was the deputation issued June 5, 1730 by the Grand Master, the Duke of Norfolk, to Daniel Coxe as Provincial Grand Master for New York, New Jersey, and Pennsylvania.

Coil's Masonic Encyclopedia

One

THE OLD WORLD

THE beginning of the organization known as Freemasonry is hidden by the mists of time. No living person has even the remotest idea about when it started. There has been plenty of speculation. There always will be.

For centuries after the start of civilization, as we think we know it, there are no records to be found. For more centuries, a few accounts are known to exist. Many more centuries were to pass before recorded history could be relied upon to any extent.

It's impossible to imagine how many valuable accounts of man's progress have been destroyed. Barbarians, natural calamities, and ignorance took their toll. They always will. Even in this "enlightened" age historical records find their way to destruction. There always has been, and there always will be, censorship in varying forms.

Freemasons have been notorious for poor record-keeping. This can be contributed to laziness, ignorance, or just plain fear. Fear of revealing "secrets" has been with us since the beginning of Freemasony as we know it. This is unfortunate. There *are no secrets in Freemasonry.* There never have been.

Soon after the formation of a Grand Lodge in England expose's appeared in newspapers, tracts, books, and by other means of disseminating information. Thanks to one of these early expose's we know something about the early ritual. Samuel Pritchard's *Masonry Dissected* was published on October 20, 1730. The next day a second edition was off the presses. Two days later a third edition was available. It was stolen by newspapers and illegitimate publishers immediately. In all, there may have been as many as 30 editions of the book before the end of the century.

It's difficult to believe that Pritchard's book sold so widely to the uninitiated. Freemasons have always been "hungry" for Masonic literature they could understand. With nothing being printed that would reveal the "secrets" of the Order, it's likely most of *Masonry Dissected* found its way into the hands of legitimate Masons. Pritchard claimed his book was the result of "the Request of several Masons." There may be truth there.

Not an expose, but certainly a valuable account of Freemasonry, is *The Regius Poem*, also known as "The Regius Manuscript" or the "Halliwell Manuscript." It was written about 1390 and, as noted in the poem, it was copied from an older document. Its Masonic content wasn't discovered until 1838 (some claim it was 1849), and then by a non-Mason, James O. Halliwell.

It is interesting to note the date of the discovery—1838. It's the oldest known Masonic document. Yet, in 1723 Dr. James Anderson's *The Constitutions of the Free-Masons* was published. A large portion that's in *The Regius Poem* this much disparaged man put into his *Constitutions*. Where did he obtain his information? Other old manuscripts discovered over the years suggest there were other "Gothic Manuscripts." Many of these were probably destroyed to keep them from falling into the hands of the "upstarts" who had formed a Grand Lodge.

The Regius Poem, a beautifully printed book, proves that Freemasonry has changed but little over the centuries. It's still an organization that believes morality is all important. It still believes in the Brotherhood of Man under the Fatherhood of God. It's still a Way of Life for the moral man. Its fifteen articles and fifteen points prove the changes in the laws of Freemasonry have been few.

For example, the first article says: "Pay the Craft their wages if aught be due." The first point states: "Love of God and Brethren is obligatory." (For a further condensation of these articles and points see *Key to Freemasonry's Growth*, page 24.)

The poem is written, naturally, in what we call "Old English." This is as difficult to read as any foreign language. There are a few people who can interpret this writing. One of them is Roderick H. Baxter. This interpretation, early in the Poem, is of historical interest. It points out how old the author of the document believes Masonry to be:

> This craft came into England, as I you say,
> In time of good King Athelstan's day;
> He made then both hall and even bower,
> And high temples of great honour,
> To disport him in both day and night,
> And to worship his God with all his might.

King Athelstan ruled from 926 to 933 A.D. Did he, as legend has it, hold a meeting of all Masons at York? *The Regius Poem* would indicate he did. If so, this would make "organized" Masonry over 1,000 years old—not merely the six hundred claimed by Harry Carr and Henry Wilson Coil.

Coil was an eminent Masonic scholar, lawyer, researcher, writer and author and is now deceased. Carr (died in 1983) was for many years the Secretary and Editor for Quatuor Coronati Lodge No. 2076, London, England. The words of both should command the respect of all Freemasons who are seeking truth.

Coil, the lawyer-Freemason, analyzed the various theories concerning the beginnings of Freemasonry. These range from the creation of the world, the period of Pythagoras, the building of King Solomon's Temple, by Sir Christoper Wren at the building of St. Paul's Cathedral, and the English and Scots operative Freemasons of the Middle Ages.

"Evidently," wrote Coil in his *Freemasonry Through Six Centuries*, "most of these theories must be false. An hypothesis, in order to ripen into a valid conclusion must be supported not merely by some fact, but by sufficient fact to carry moral conviction and remove it from the realm of conjecture, and, moreover, it must be consistent with all other known facts. Truth is an entire fabric; anything that is true will conform to every other thing that is true; what is false will not match what is true."

He notes that those who believe Freemasonry didn't come into being until the formation of the Grand Lodge of England in 1717 are wrong. There are facts, even though records are scarce, to prove Masonry was alive long before the beginning of the 18th Century. And indeed it was. But how far before the 18th Century is still open for discussion.

The Regius Poem claims there was a meeting of Masons called by King Athelstan. That would have been around 930 A.D. The script of *The Saga of the Holy Royal Arch of Freemasonry*, an award-winning motion picture, points out several facts, and asks an important question:

> From the middle of the 14th Century the record of Craft Masonry is constant. In 1356 a Code of Mason Regulations was drawn up in Guildhall in London. In the German City of Cologne, a seal was granted the Masons in 1396. Arms were granted the Masons Company of London in 1472.

> Was there a central head in Masonry during those early days? Was there a nation-wide method of teaching Masons? Possibly. There was a striking similarity of rules, regulations, customs, and architectural practices leading to a belief that there was some kind of an association almost from the time of the Norman conquest in 1066 A.D., and Medieval England was an age of cathedral building.

"The period of Gothic architecture extended from about A.D. 1150 to 1550, and, unless we are prepared to believe that those remarkable Gothic edifices were erected by stonemasons and architects who sprang to the work without prior experience or any long period of developing art, we must presume some organization prior to the twelfth century," writes Coil.

Coil adds two other important dates not mentioned in *The Saga*—"the first Statute of Laborers in 1349 expressly applied to the Masons; the Fabric Rolls of York Minister date from 1355."

The Saga took note of the building of York Minister with graphic pictures to go along with this dialogue:

> No work of the building art means more to Masons than does the monumental structure of York Minister, begun in 1227 and not finished until 230 years later. In the crypt of

this cathedral, the Masons of York held many of their meetings. It is not only a monument to operative handiwork and continuity, but is the motivating force that produced the Fraternity of Speculative Freemasons.

Strange how the name of this beautiful, enduring Gothic architecture came to be, no one can determine. Or is it possible to be certain how the name "Freemason" was arrived at. Again, there has been much speculation, but that's all it has been—speculation.

So, it's really not so strange that we can't pinpoint the exact date Freemasons, and Freemasonry, came to the New World.

Two

BEGINNINGS IN AMERICA

FREEMASONS came to North America in the 17th century. But as we've seen, it had been active to some extent for centuries in other parts of the world.

No one knows the exact date a Freemason stepped ashore in the new world. There have been many positive statements made, and there probably will be more. There could have been Masons among the handful of men who stepped ashore at Jamestown in 1607, in what was to become the Colony of Virginia. There could have been Masons among the Pilgrims who reached Massachusetts in 1620. If so, there are no records existing for such proof.

There may have been a Masonic record left in Nova Scotia as early as 1606. It concerns a stone discoverd by Dr. Charles T. Jackson of Boston. He wrote about it, and his other findings, in his "Historical and Statistical Account of Nova Scotia" in 1829. He called it the "Annapolis stone."

This stone was found on a peninsula separating Annapolis Basin from Digby. It was described as being almost two and one-half feet long by two feet broad, and composed of material which forms the substratum of Granville Mountain. "On the upper part are engraved the square and compass of the Free Mason." In the center appeared "in large and deep Arabic figures, the date 1606."

This "Annapolis stone" proves only one thing, unfortunately: white men occupied the area early in the 17th century. There's no way to determine when the stone was placed where it was found. There's no way to positively connect it with Freemasonry.

This stone was presented to the Canadian Institute at Toronto about 1887. It became a part of the wall of a new building. The carving was left for anyone to see. But, some workman, not realizing its importance, covered it with cement. It has never been found again.

Let's look into the early days of Nova Scotia a little further. We'll speculate, along with Henry W. Rugg, D.D., who wrote *History of Freemasonry in Rhode Island* in 1895. According to Dr. Rugg, Sir William Alexander of Scotland established a colony at Port Royal, Nova Scotia, in 1628. Sir William Alexander, Jr., his son, was the head of the colony for years. On July 3, 1634, the son was *admitted* a "Fellow of the Craft" in the Lodge at Edinburgh, Scotland. Note the word "admitted." And note he received the *seond degree in Masonry.*

There's certainly room for error, human or typographical, in such a statement. But the writer was David M. Lyon who was initiated into Lodge Ayr Saint Paul No. 204, in 1856. Among his works was the *History of the Lodge of Edinburgh No. 1.* He relied on the excellent records of the Lodge for his account.

Sir Alexander became Lord Alexander and didn't return to North America. But where did he receive the First Degree in Freemasonry? Was he initiated by some brethren he found at or near Annapolis? Why did the Lodge at Edinburgh recognize him as an Entered Apprentice? It certainly wouldn't have done this lightly. We might have the answer to this and many other questions if records had been kept everywhere as they were by the Lodge at Edinburgh.

Who was the first known Freemason to settle in America? No one can be certain. John Skene was a member of Aberdeen Lodge No. 1, Aberdeen, Scotland. He became the 27th on its roll in 1682. In October of the same year he came to America. He settled at Burlington, New Jersey, and was deputy governor of West Jersey from 1685 until his death in 1690.

Melvin Maynard Johnson of Massachusetts makes no mention of Skene in his *Freemasonry in America Prior to 1750,* originally an address when he was Grand Master, to the Grand Lodge of Massachusetts. Or does he mention Skene in his much larger work, *The Beginnings of Freemasonry in America,* a publication of The Masonic Service Association in 1924. It is apparent in both that he was primarily interested in making a case for Masschusetts as being first, Masonically, in every instance.

Historians do agree with Johnson that Jonathan Belcher was one of the earliest Freemasons in America. Johnston claims he was the first. Belcher was born January 8, 1681 at Boston. While he was in England in 1704, he was evidently made a Mason in an old "Guilde Lodge." This is the belief because in reply to congratulations on September 25, 1741, from the "First Lodge of Boston,"Belcher stated:

> Worthy Brothers:
>   I take very kindly this mark of your Respect. It is now Thirty Seven years since I was admitted into the Ancient and Hon'ble Society of Free and accepted Masons, to whom I have been a faithful Brother, & well-wisher to the Art of Masonry.
>   I shall ever maintain a strict friendship for the whole Fraternity; and always be glad when it may fall in my power to do them any service.
>
> J. BELCHER

Belcher had graduated from Harvard in 1699, and had immediately gone to England. He remained there until 1705. He returned to England as an agent for the Colony of Massachusetts in 1729. While there this time he managed to secure the position of Royal Governor of Massachusetts. He held this office until 1741. Then, in 1745, he became Royal Governor of New Jersey. He died on August 31, 1757.

Belcher had affiliated with St. John's Lodge in Boston. So, it was well-known that he was a Mason. That's probably why, when the trustees of Princeton University wanted to name Nassau Hall after him they said: "When your Excellency is translated to a house not made with hands, eternal in the Heavens, let Belcher Hall proclaim your beneficent acts."

June 24, 1721, was an historical day as far as Johnson was concerned. It was the day "the Mother Grand Lodge of the Masonic world, that at London, adopted a regulation...[that] has ever since been the law forbidding the formation of a Lodge without a Grand Master's Warrant. This Mother Grand Lodge acquired jurisdiction over the new world and every Regular and Duly Constituted Lodge which existed in America during the period with which we are dealing."

A thorough search of Johnson's works to learn how he dealt with the formation of St. Andrew's Lodge in Boston reveals he ignored it. Why?

He ignored it because the Grand Lodge of England adopted no law as broad as Johnson claimed. It sought to rule its own members. It had absolutely no authority over those not under its control. And Massachusetts knew this. It recognized this. It still does. It's not uncommon today to find lodges of English, Irish, and Scottish Constitutions meeting in the same country, in the same cities, in complete harmony.

"The so-called Lodges in the Colonies, therefore, meeting without warrant after 1723 are no part of legitimate Masonic history until they 'humbled themselves' as did the Masons of Pennsylvania when they applied for and received recognition from Provincial Grand Master Henry Price, in 1734/5," wrote Johnson. "Until then, under the law quoted they were 'rebels.' And never in any phase of the life of the world have rebels obtained the rights of legitimacy unless the rebellion was successful."

By this thinking, many of the Founding Fathers of this country were "Rebels"—illegitimate Masons. The enemies of Freemasonry can be happy to learn that the First President of the United States was an irregular Mason!—Or was he?

If he was, so were Freemasons who came under the jurisdiction of Scotland. And Ireland. And the English men who belonged to the Lodge at York who even formed their own Grand Lodge—Grand Lodge of England South of the River Trent. Then, in 1751, a year before the Lodge at Fredericksburg in Virginia was known to exist, six lodges formed the Grand Lodge of the Antients in England. This Grand Lodge authorized dozens of lodges throughout the world before it merged with the "Moderns" in 1813 to become the United Grand Lodge of England.

Coil wrote of Johnson's claim: "How queer it sounds to hear one living within the purlieus of Boston, Bunker Hill, Lexington, and Concord expound the theory of government without representation! If the Grand Lodge of England could thus make regulations governing lodges acting under immemorial custom, it could have required them to pay dues to the Grand Lodge." Later Coil wrote: "This is the language of an advocate; not a mere recorder of facts."

It would appear that Johnson had but one goal in mind: to prove that organized, legitimate, Freemasonry in America commenced in Massachusetts. But it would appear that it actually began in Pennsylvania.

The pages of the *Pennsylvania Gazette* for December 5-8, 1730, published by Benjamin Franklin, had this item:

> "As there are several Lodges of Free-Masons erected in this Province, and People have lately been much amus'd with Conjectures concerning them; we think the following Account of Free Masonry from London, will not be unacceptable to our Readers."

The story is interesting:

London, August 12.

By the Death of a Gentleman who was one of the Brotherhood of Free-Masons, there has lately happen'd a Discovery of abundance of their secret Signs and Wonders, with the mysterious Manner of their admission into that Fraternity. The Following is a true Copy of a Manuscript which the Deceased had written for the Benefit of his own private Remembrance, and which was found conceal'd among his choicest Papers in the Most hidden Part of his Cabinet. The World has long Admir'd, that in such a numerous Còmpany, many of them not remarkable for Taciturnity, there has been no one found, that in his Cups, or in any other Circumstances, would discover their Mysteries: But the whole appears so childish and ridiculous that this is probably the case, their Grand Secret is that they have no Secret at all; and when once a man is entered, he finds himself obliged *se defendendo* to carry the Jest with as solemn a face as the rest. We shall not use many Words to persuade the Public that the following Piece is genuine; it carries all the Marks of Truth in itself: We would only refer the Reader to the Conduct of the Brotherhood upon this Occasion; if they ridicule it, or look very grave upon it, or if they are very angry and endeavor to decry it, he many be satisfied it is the real Truth.

This satirical article just may have helped Benjamin Franklin to decide he wanted to become a member of the Craft. It may have convinced others, also. Many good men fear "secret" societies, and with good reason. The inquisitions conducted in the name of religion must have been vivid in the minds of most men in the Colonies. Even more recent were the "witch-burnings" and other atrocities conducted in secrecy, also in the guise of religion. "Justice" overseas and in the Colonies was often dispensed secretly. No man should have then, or now, become involved in something completely unknown.

The satirist from London had revealed the truth, even though he may not have suspected it. "Their Grand Secret is that they have no Secret at all." He had shown the good men in the Colonies they really had nothing to fear if they associated with Freemasonry. If only this truth had been realized throughout the ages, the historian's lot would have been much simpler. We would know the answers to the questions on which we can only speculate. The answers to how, when, and where Freemasonry started in the new world would be clear.

Some answers are clear, however. We do know who received the first commission as Provincial Grand Master in a Colony in America.

Three

DANIEL COXE AND PHILADELPHIA

MELVIN JOHNSON wrote in his first work: "The Duke of Norfolk appointed Daniel Coxe, Pro. G. M. of New York, New Jersey, and Pennsylvania for two years. There has appeared no evidence, however, that he exercised this deputation. There is evidence that he did not and that he remained in England during its term." Johnson pointed out that his theory was correct in that "Regular and Duly Constituted lodges could exist in the Colonies only through the authority of a Pro. G. M. appointed by the Grand Master of England."

In his 1924 update Johnson wrote of the Coxe appointment: "There is no evidence, however, that he exercised this deputation or even that he was on this side of the Ocean during the said two years. The fact is that during that period he remained in England endeavoring to perfect his title to nearly half of the Continent of North America..."

Johnson claims there's no evidence Coxe was in America "between 1728 and 1734."

Grand Lodge 1717-1967 is the official history of the United Grand Lodge of England. Its various sections were written by well-versed English Masonic historians. "Overseas Development and the Military Lodges" was written by A. J. B. Milborne. Concerning Coxe, he wrote: "A Patent of Appointment as P. G. M. of New York, New Jersey, and Pennsylvania was granted to Daniel Coxe in 1730. Coxe appears in the Return made in 1730 of the Lodge at Devil Tavern within Temple Bar.

The full text of his Patent follows the Minutes of the meeting of Grand Lodge held on 21 April 1730. The appointment was for two years, and the election of a P. G. M. every other year was authorized. There is no evidence that Coxe exercised his authority. He attended Grand Lodge on 29 January 1731. He died in 1739."

Without question, Daniel Coxe was appointed the first Provincial Grand Master in North America.

Because this has been questioned, the record should be set straight. If the quotation from *Grand Lodge* doesn't do that, this passage from the *Proceedings of the United Grand Lodge of Ancient, Free & Accepted Masons of England* for June 4, 1930, should:

REPORT OF THE BOARD OF GENERAL PURPOSES

To the United Grand Lodge of Ancient, Free and
    Accepted Masons of England.
Bi-Centenary of American Freemasonry.

The Board desires to place on record the fact that June 5th, 1930, will mark a most important bi-centenary in the history of Freemasonry. It was on June 5th, 1730, that the then Grand Master (Duke of Norfolk) signed in London a Warrant which for the first time recognized on behalf of Grand Lodge the existence of Freemasonry in the American Colonies, which formed the nucleus of the present United States. By this Warrant a prominent American Freemason of the time, who appears also to have been a member of a London Lodge, was empowered to constitute what was then termed a Provincial Grand Lodge, which embrased Massachusetts, Pennsylvania, New Jersey and New York. Fully empowered Grand Lodges were later constituted in each of these Provinces, as well as in every other State in the Union, and our Brethren of today, knowing the momentous consequences to Freemasonry which have flowed from the great spread of English-speaking Freemasonry in the United States and the splendid efforts continuing with increasing strength to be put forth by the American Brethren, will desire to congratulate them all on the progress thus made, and to express the earnest prayer that happiness and success will for all time attend them.

After this report was read by the Board of General Purposes, which actually controls the actions of the Grand Lodge of England, His Royal Highness, the Grand Master, had a telegram he was sending to all 49 Grand Lodges in the United States, read:

> On the eve of the two-hundredth anniversary of the first Grand Lodge recognition of American Freemasonry by constituting a Provincial Grand Lodge for New England, I wish to congratulate all our Brethren in the United States on the great Masonic progress they have made. I reiterate my fraternal good wishes and sincere desire for their continued happiness and prosperity. It remains my earnest hope that the tenets of our Order may assist still further to strengthen the bond of friendship and goodwill which so happily exists between our two Nations. And I shall continue to watch with sympathy every endeavor on both sides of the Atlantic to promote those feelings by the development of Freemasonry in its purest and highest form.

The reading of the telegram was greeted with "loud applause." It's interesting to note that the Board added Massachusetts to Coxe's domain, and the Grand Master gave him the Provincial Grand for New England. His Warrant didn't go quite that far.

It is evident that Daniel Coxe was appointed Provincial Grand Master on June 5, 1730. However, this notation is interesting:

> At a Quarterly Communication held at the Devil Tavern within Temple Bar the 29th of January 1730/1. Present Nathaniel Blackerby Esqr. D. G. M.... Daniel Coxe Esqr. Provincial Grand Master of North America.

The minutes later stated:

> The minutes of the last Quarterly Communication were read.
> And after the general Healths were drank the Deputy Grand Master proposed the Health of Br. Cox Provincial Grand Master of North America which were drank accordingly.

Coxe had attended a meeting of the Council of Proprietors in Burlington, New Jersey, on December 9, 1730. On January

29th he was with the Grand Lodge of England. Those who argue that Coxe didn't use his Masonic powers in America, claim he couldn't have been in those two places on those two dates. The time was too short for the old sailing vessels. That argument in easily destroyed. Dozens of records exist to prove vessels made the journey in much shorter time.

Then, there are those who claim Coxe wasn't in America during the period of his Warrant. Henry S. Borneman did a mammoth job of research for his publication *Early Freemasonry in Pennsylvania.* This was published in 1931. His exhaustive research proves Coxe was out of the Colonies for no more than five months.

On December 9, 1730, Coxe attended a meeting in Burlington, New Jersey. On January 29, 1731, he was at a communication of the Grand Lodge of England. The Council of Proprietors of West Jersey had a meeting scheduled for February 3, 1731, and this was the only one he missed. He was present at the May meeting, and again he presided as President on August 4, 1731.

Borneman notes: "The Council of Proprietors for the Western Division of New Jersey is still in existence... Its records are kept in a building devoted entirely to the uses of the Council... The original Minute Books from which the foregoing abstracts were made are part of the records of the Council."

Coxe executed a deed to James Hyde, Jr., on April 8, 1731, conveying 67 acres in Hopewell County, New Jersey. The records show he was present for the transaction.

The next question raised concerning Coxe as Provincial Grand Master is that he did not exercise his authority. Proof of this supposedly rests in the fact he made no returns to the Grand Lodge of England. The Grand Secretary of the Grand Lodge of England agreed that this was so in 1870. He added: "At the period when he was appointed, it was a rare thing for any reports to be made by the Provincial Grand Masters abroad of their doings. Brief details came in once or twice from Bengal, but I find none from any other foreign country."

Even if Coxe didn't exercise his powers and form the Lodge in Philadelphia, was it illegal? Johnson said it, and all other lodges like it, was illegal. Sir Alfred Robbins didn't agree. He wrote in his *English-speaking Freemasonry* in 1930: "Freemasonry was brought into the colonies of North America at a very early period in the eighteenth century and the immigrating freemasons soon established lodges in various places where they worked without the sanction of warrants. This was in accordance with the then general custom. Warrants for lodges were nonexistent, as there was no controlling organization which could grant them, every lodge being a separate and self-created entity... Even as late as 1734, the Grand Lodge of England had explicitly limited its disciplinary powers to any place within ten miles of London and this remains two hundred years after, precisely the area of direct exercising of Grand Lodge discipline over ordinary lodges."

Henry Wilson Coil wrote in 1967:

> Brother Johnson, carrying out his theory designed to give priority to Boston, takes the position (p. 57) that Coxe's deputation of June 5, 1730 established 1) that the Grand Lodge claimed jurisdiction over the Colonies, 2) that, only through its authority, could regular and duly constituted lodges exist in the Colonies, and 3) that the Grand Lodge having assumed jurisdiction in New York, New Jersey and Pennsylvania, no other authority could establish lodges there during the term of the deposition, and that, since no lodge was established thereunder, any lodge formed during this two-year period was clandestine.

> Of course, the document states no such thing and leads to no such conclusion. There is nothing in it claiming any degree of exclusiveness and, if there were, it would not be binding upon those not parties to it...

> Brother Johnson's ideas reflect confusion between the rules of law governing private unincorporated associations where consent and agreement is the only binding force, and the rules of international law whereby a nation may seize territory, particularly, if unoccupied or occupied only by savages, and subject that land and its inhabitants to its will sanctioned by force of arms. Or he may have indulged, unconsciously, in retroactive application of the rule of exclusive jurisdiction later generally concurred in

by all Grand Lodges. But that rule did not develop until more than half a century after the period of which we are speaking.

Later Coil added:

> There is one way and only one way by which illegitimacy in The Philadelphia Lodge could be shown, and that is by demonstrating that all those who first formed the Lodge were or had been members of lodges under the Grand Lodge of England. Then, their action would be wrongful and their lodge clandestine, not by reason of Coxe's or any other deputation, but because those Masons had breeched their covenant made when they accepted and agreed to the Regulations of 1721. But, that cannot be shown; they may have been made Masons in Irish or Scots lodges or even English lodges not under the Grand Lodge or even before the Grand Lodge was founded. The later body was only fourteen years old in 1731, and it is not at all certain that even a majority of Freemasons were then of Grand Lodge obedience.
>
> It is not true, therefore, that the Coxe deputation or that of Price had or was expected to have any effect upon the immemorial rights of the Lodge at Philadelphia or any other similar lodge.

Subsequent actions by Freemasons in England prove the majority of them didn't hold allegiance to the Grand Lodge formed in 1717. This would change during the next century. Too often people look at conditions of today and apply them to those existing in prior years. This was noted by John Heron Lepper who reviewed J. Hugo Tatsch's *Freemasonry in the Thirteen Colonies* for the *Transactions* of Quatuor Coronati Lodge No. 2076, London:

> What can be more certain than that where a few freemasons were gathered together in New England, they should form themselves into a lodge according to English custom? Who are we to dub these non-regular or even clandestine meetings? It is essential that we should cast off our present-day conceptions of Masonic Jurisprudence, if we are going to look upon the Colonial Freemasonry of two centuries ago with any clearness of vision or judgement.

There is another point that we should bear in mind
when estimating the probable or possible antiquity of some
of the American lodges. The Warrant, as we know it today, did not exist in the Grand Lodge of England till the
sixth decade of the eighteenth century. Therefore, all
English lodges, regularly constituted, either at home or in
the colonies before this date, would come into being by virtue of a "Deputation," an authority to some person or persons to install a new Masonic body under the aegis of the
Grand Lodge in London.

This document might or might not be preserved by the
new lodge; in the vast majority of cases it was not preserved
and its actual preservation was unnecessary as a certificate
of regularity... So to my mind there is more than a little to
be said before rejecting such early traditional dates as attach
to some of the old American lodges, for example to the
Lodge of Norfolk, in Virginia.

Was the first Lodge meeting in the Colonies approved by
anyone in "authority"? It's highly doubtful. Even the exact date
of the first meeting can't be determined. That it took place in
Philadelphia is definite. Even Melvin Johnson agrees. However,
he claims: "but like all meetings in Philadelphia prior to
February 21, 1734/5, the Lodge was neither 'Regular' nor 'Duly
Constituted.' " Other authorities disagree with his conclusions.

The first record of a lodge actually meeting in the Colonies is
found in "Liber B", an account book of the secretary. On the
front cover it reads: "Philadelphia City, St. John's Lodge, Liber
B." (If the first book could be found, what light it could shed on
early Freemasonry!) It begins with entries on June 24, 1731,
and ends on June 24, 1738. Its first entries show that the
brethren met before 1731. The Lodge met on the first Monday
of each month. It had been constituted with 13 members.
William Allen was the "Grand Master" and he was continued in
office in 1732. It should be noted that he was Grand Master of a
Grand Lodge that had been formed according to the custom
then prevailing. It was a general communication of Brethren.
It's highly probable that the only time it met was to celebrate
the Festivals of the Sts. John. Entries show that the Lodge and
Grand Lodge were one and the same.

Did Daniel Coxe approve the formation of this Lodge? At least one historian believed he did. Wilhelm Begeman, a German Masonic historian, wrote in his *Beginnings of Freemasonry in England:*

> Those who deny Coxe's activity must naturally assume the Provincial Grand Lodge established itself through its own power, which is much less probable than the legal action of Coxe. On January 29, 1731, naturally he related the results achieved in Philadelphia; therefore a special toast greeted him. That his home was in Trenton, was no serious obstacle, for the London Grand Masters nearly all lived at a distance from London, Lord Kingston, for instance, in Ireland. I note also that Benjamin Franklin, 1734-5, was Grand Master of the Province, and again later, November 17, 1760, he visited the Grand Lodge in London and was entered a "Provincial Grand Master of Philadelphia." From the beginning the Grand Masters of the Province, as they were termed in newspaper reports, regarded themselves as members of the London Grand Lodge, and in 1734 Franklin published a reprint of the first Constitution Book, adding to the line, "London, printed anno 1723," the words, "Re-printed in Philadelphia by Special Order, for the Use of the Brethren in NORTH-AMERICA."
>
> This speaks against the independence of the then Grand Lodge of the Province.

Begeman may have an excellent supposition there. A reprint of Benjamin Franklin's copy of *The Constitutions* by the Masonic Book Club illustrates what Begeman claims.

Henry S. Borneman of Pennsylvania gives this brief account of the life of Daniel Coxe:

> Daniel Coxe was a man of strong purpose and intense activity.
>
> He adopted America as his domicile as early as 1707. He began his married lfe with a romantic elopement and, when his wife died in 1725, there were, at least, four children, the oldest of whom was seventeen years of age and the youngest three. He was the ancestor of a family that became distinguished in American life.
>
> As a Churchman, he was allied with the Church of England. He procured a Charter for St. Mary's Church,

Burlington, and contributed largely to its maintenance.
He was a generous and loyal supporter of the Church in all
its activities and was buried in front of the chancel in the
Church.

His religious beliefs were those of the Episcopal Church
and in strong opposition to the Quakers. He used his influence with the Crown in securing the repeal by Queen
Anne of an Act which gave the Quakers in Pennsylvania
the right to make an affirmation instead of taking an
oath...

He was twice appointed in command of the Militia,
with the rank of Colonel in West Jersey. This was an of-
fence to the non-resistant Quakers.

Coxe's father acquired patents and grants of large ex-
panses of American territory. Col. Coxe made it his
business to acquire an absolute owner title to thousands of
acres of land in New Jersey. He, therefore, became a
member of the "Council of Proprietors" and so remained
for the last sixteen years of his life, most of the time serving
as its President.

He traveled in the Colonies; studied the political needs
of the country; and drafted a Plan of Union for the colonies
as early as 1722.

In the Province of New Jersey, he was a Member of the
Governor's Council; a Member of the Assembly, in which
he served as Speaker,and the last years of his life were
spent as a Judge of the Supreme Court of the Province of
New Jersey.

He used his influence to procure the building of a college
at Burlington.

He was in close touch with the ruling Sovereigns of
England, an influence which he never hesitated to use.

As a Mason he was described by the Grand Lodge of
England in his Deputation as a "Right Worshipful and
well beloved Brother, Free and Accepted Mason," and his
Deputation as Provincial Grand Master contained powers
and privileges which were never again contained in any
deputation by the Grand Master of England.

The "Plan of Union" described was contained in "Carolana,"
published by Coxe in 1722. He proposed that the Colonies "be
united under a lawful, regular and firm establishment." He
wanted a "Supreme Governor" to whom all other governors

would be subordinate; two deputies to be elected by each province to meet "together, consult and advise for the good of the whole, settle and appoint particular quotas or proportions of money, men, provisions, that each respective government is to raise for their mutual defence and safety."

Twenty-five delegates from seven northern Colonies met at Albany on June 19, 1754. Among them was Benjamin Franklin. They were there to determine a "plan of union" for defending their frontiers as the French and Indian War was about to begin.

James Bach McMaster, in writing of the life of Franklin, said:

> The idea of union had long been in his mind, and to the conference which gathered at Albany he brought a carefully drawn plan. The credit of that plan is commonly given him. But it ought in justice never to be mentioned without a reference to the name of Daniel Coxe... So early as 1722 Coxe foresaw the French aggression, called on the colonies to unite to prevent it, and drew up the heads of a scheme for united action. Coxe proposed a governor-general appointed by the Crown and a congress of delegates chosen by the assemblies of the colonies. Franklin proposed the very same thing. Coxe would have each colony send two delegates annually elected. Franklin would have two to seven delegates triannually elected. By each the grand council, with consent of the governor-general, was to determine the quotas of men, money, and provisions the colonies should contribute to the common defense. The difference between them is a difference in detail, not in plan. The detail belongs to Franklin. The plan must be ascribed to Coxe.

Daniel Coxe died on April 25, 1739, at Trenton, New Jersey. He was buried beside his wife in St. Mary's Church, Burlington.

Benjamin Franklin became a Freemason in February, 1731, while William Allen was "Grand Master." Who was William Allen?

William Allen, the first Grand Master of Masons in Pennsylvania (that we know about) was born in Philadelphia on August 5, 1704. He studied law at the Temple in London, and returned to Philadelphia in 1726. Shortly after this he was elected to the Common Council. He became a member of the Assembly in 1731 and served until 1739. In October 1735 he was chosen Mayor of the city.

Allen served as Judge of the Orphan's Court and the Court of Common Pleas. He succeeded his father-in-law, Andrew Hamilton, as Recorder in 1741, serving until 1750, when, on October 2, he was appointed Chief Justice of the Province. He held this office until 1774 when he went to England. While there he published "The American Crisis." This was a plan for restoring the dependence of the American Colonies.

Where and when Allen became a Freemason is not known. He is listed as Grand Master in Liber B on June 24, 1731. He held this office for another year. In 1750 Lord Byron, Grand Master of Masons in England, appointed him Provincial Grand Master. This office he held for several years.

Allen returned to Philadelphia after the Revolution and ended his days at Mount Airy. He died on September 6, 1780.

Humphrey Murray was Grand Master in 1733; Benjamin Franklin, of whom much more is to be heard, became Grand Master for the first time on June 24, 1734.

Freemasonry was becoming an honored institution in the Colonies of the New World.

Four

HENRY PRICE AND BOSTON

THE FREEMASONS living in the Colony of Massachusetts, and other places, were not standing still. Members of the Craft were undoubtedly meeting in Boston and vicinity, although no record exists. But this is more than a supposition. In April, 1733 (13th or 30th), Johnson claims Henry Price was appointed Provincial Grand Master "of New England and Dominions and Territories thereunto belonging." On July 30, 1733, he formed a Grand Lodge in Boston.

One of Price's first acts was to appoint Andrew Belcher, son of the governor, as his deputy. His second act was to answer the plea of 18 Masons who desired to form a lodge in Boston. "Ten, at least, of the petitoners had been 'made here,' i.e., had been made in Boston in some of the earlier meetings held," wrote Melvin Johnson, "like those in Philadelphia and elsewhere perhaps, without charter or warrant but according to the 'Old Customs.' Thereupon he granted the prayer thereof and did then and there in the most solemn manner according to ancient custom and form as prescribed by the book of Constitutions, constitute them into a regular Lodge."

It's interesting to note that Johnson didn't call these ten Masons "rebels" or "illegal."

This Lodge became No. 126 on the 1734 engraved list of English Lodges. "*No other Lodge in America*, however, appears on this list, which closed with No. 128, constituted in 1734," Johnson wrote. The emphasis is his. Its number decreased over the years to 110, 65, 54, 42 and 39. With the union of the two Grand Lodges in England in 1813, it, like all other lodges in the United States, was erased from the roster of English lodges. But, it must be remembered that there were several different lists of lodges published over the years.

The First Lodge held its first meeting "at the houfe of Edwd Lutwych at the Sign of the Bunch of grapes in King Street Boston, N.Engld on Monday July the 30th A.D. & of Mafonry A: 5733," the minutes state. Henry Hope was elected Worshipful Master. He appointed Frederick Hamilton and James Gordon as Wardens. The officers were invested "with the Implements of their Offices."

The fact that the officers' jewels were available would indicate these brethren had been meeting as a Lodge earlier. Or, less likely, they had prepared these jewels for this occasion within an extremely short period.

The Lodge lost no time in going to work. On August 3, 1733, John Smith was made a Freemason. On September 12, Moses Slaughter and Thomas Phillips were "made."

Benjamin Franklin visited Boston in the autumn of 1733, and it is said he met Henry Price. There is no record that he attended any meeting of the First Lodge. The only "proof" that Franklin met Price is Josiah H. Drummond's account in Gould's *The History of Freemasonry*. But when the letter Franklin wrote to Price in 1734 is read, it would appear they were strangers:

> RIGHT WORSHIPFUL GRAND MASTER AND MOST WORTHY AND DEAR BRETHREN: We acknowledge your favor of 23rd of October past, and rejoice that the Grand Master (whom God bless) hath so happily recovered from his late indisposition; and we now, glass in hand, drink to the establishment of his health, and the prosperity of your whole Lodge.
>
> We have seen in the Boston prints and article of news from London, importing that a Grand Lodge held there in August last, Mr. Price's deputation and power was extended over all America, which advice we hope is true, and we heartily congratulate him thereupon, and though this has not been as yet regularly signified to us by you, yet, giving credit thereto, we think it our duty to lay before your

Lodge what we apprehend needful to be done for us, in
order to promote and strengthen the interest of Masonry in
this Province (which seems to want the sanction of some
authority derived from home, to give the proceedings and
determinations of our Lodge their due weight), to wit, a
Deputation or Charter granted by the Right Worshipful
Mr. Price, by virtue of his commission from Britain, con-
firming the Brethren of Pennsylvania in the privileges they
at present enjoy of holding annually their Grand Lodge,
choosing their Grand Master, Wardens and other officers,
who may manage all affairs relating to the Brethren here
with full power and authority, according to the customs
and usages of Masons, the said Grand Master of Pennsylvania only yielding his chair when the Grand Master of
all America shall be in place. This, if it seems good and
reasonable to you to grant, will not only be extremely
agreeable to us, but will also, we are confident, conduce
much to the welfare, establishment, and reputation of
Masonry in these parts.

We therefore submit it for your consideration, and, we
hope our request will be complied with, we desire that it
may be done as soon as possible, and also accompanied
with a copy of the R. W. Grand Master's first Deputation,
and of the instrument by which it appears to be enlarged
as above mentioned, witnessed by your Wardens, and
signed by the Secretary; for which favors this Lodge doubt
not of being able to behave so as not to be thought
ungrateful.

We are, Right Worshipful Grand Master and Most Worthy Brethren, Your Affectionate Brethren and obliged
humble Servts.

Signed at the request of the Lodge,
B. FRANKLIN, G. M.

Philadelphia, Nov. 28, 1734

As with every publication of this nature, several interpreta-
tions can be made. Johnson said it proved the Philadelphia
brethren "humbled themselves" so they could become legitimate. Drummond claims it proves "the Masonic body over
which Franklin presided had not received a warrant from either
Coxe or Price." But, Drummond adds: "It will be observed,
moreover, that a confirmation of privileges already existing is
all that is solicited." How can Drummond have it both ways?

It would appear that Franklin was concerned about who really was in authority in the New World. Here he was Grand Master in Pennsylvania, yet in the press he learns one Henry Price has had his "power extended over all America." If this was so, the Masons in Pennsylvania had better do something, especially when there are "false and Rebel Brethren" about to form a lodge in the area. Even so, he's not certain what he has read is correct. He wants his Grand Lodge's request answered—"accompanied with a copy of the R. W. Grand Master's first Deputation, and of the instrument by which it appears to be enlarged as above mentioned."

Price's authority didn't extend throughout America. This may be the reason he didn't answer Franklin's letter. It wasn't until 1749 that anything was sent from Massachusetts to Pennsylvania. Then, on July 10, Thomas Oxnard appointed Benjamin Franklin Provincial Grand Master.

Drummond (in Gould's *History*) notes that going back to the year 1731, "we shall do well to reflect that the sovereignty of Grand Lodges was then only on its trial. Such bodies had been formed, it is true, at London, York, and Dublin, though we should be careful to remember that the latter towns were as much under *English* government as Philadelphia. But in Scotland—the most ancient home of Masonic precedent—there were as yet no chartered lodges, and assemblies of brethren, formed as in Philadelphia, were the only Masonic associations existing in that country. Brethren united to form lodges in neighborhoods where there were fair chances of their continuance, and such assemblies, though without any other sanction, were not styled irregular when the Grand Lodge of Scotland was erected in 1736, the old lodges, whether offshoots of 'Mother Kilwinning,' or other ancient courts of Operative Masonry, or simply the results of local combinations, uniting to form that organization which has happily continued to this day."

So, according to Drummond, Gould, others, and actually all the evidence available, no lodge formed in the New World can in any way be considered illegal.

Without question, Henry Price was an active and interested Freemason. He was born in London about 1697. (This statement by Tatsch sent me on a long search: "The vacancy caused by Oxnard's death brought Jeremy Gridley into the highest office. He, like Price, was also a native Bostonian.) Tatsch was incorrect. In 1730 Price was listed as a member of Lodge No. 75, meeting at the Rainbow Coffee House in York Buildings, London.

Price moved to Boston in 1723 where he was listed as a tailor, and the keeper of a drygoods and clothing establishment. He was made a "Cornet" by Governor Jonathan Belcher in 1733. This gave him the rank of Major, and this is what he was called for the rest of his life. He formed a partnership with Francis Beteilhe, who would later become Secretary of the First Lodge of Boston. This partnership would extend to the Provincial Grand Lodge, and the Master's Lodge.

On April 13, 1733, Price was in London, according to Johnson, who relied on a letter written by Price on January 27, 1768, to the Grand Lodge of England. In it he stated: "I myself paid three guineas therefor to Thomas Batson, Esquire, the Deputy Grand Master who with the Grand Wardens then in being signed my said deputation." Price returned to Boston to carry on his business at the "sign of the Brazen Head on Cornhill."

In the fall of 1737 Price married Mary Townsend over the strong objections of her uncle James who disinherited her. In October, 1738, a daughter was born to the Prices. Sometime in 1751 Mary died. He married another Mary, this one a Tilden, on May 25, 1753. Only six or seven years later his second wife died. This was followed by the death of his daughter on October 8, 1760. He appeared to lose interest in many things after these tragedies, but later moved to Townsend. There he was chosen to represent the town in the Provincial Legislature in 1764-65. He was married again September 17, 1771, to Lydia Randall, a widow with a minor son. They were to have two children, Mary and Rebecca.

At the age of 83 Henry Price was fatally injured. While splitting logs on May 14, 1780, his ax slipped and struck his abdomen. On the 20th he died.

Price remained active in Masonry until his death. He served as Provincial Grand Master from 1733 to 1737; again from 1740 to 1744; and from 1754 to 1755; and finally from October, 1767, to November, 1768. He was charter Master of Masters' Lodge as well as the Second Lodge in Boston. He served as Worshipful Master of the First Lodge. At the age of 76 he presided over the Provincial Grand Lodge on April 30, 1773, during the absence of John Rowe. Price attended the Provincial Grand Lodge for the last time on January 28, 1774.

Five

THE BUFFER COLONY— GEORGIA

THE Grand Lodge of England, having found a firm footing for Freemasonry in the New World, extended it further, *Grand Lodge 1717-1767* states:

> A Royal Charter for the colonization of Georgia was granted in 1732. Many of the grantees were Masons, and among them was James Edward Oglethorpe. In 1733 it was recommended in Grand Lodge that the Masters and Wardens of the regular Lodges make a generous collection amongst their members to assist the Trustees who had been appointed "to send distressed Brethren to Georgia where they may be comfortably provided for." These distressed Brethren were probably those committed to Debtors' Prisons, for it is known that Oglethorpe took a great interest in the amelioration of their lot.
>
> Roger Lacy was appointed P.G.M. for Georgia in 1735. He was a member of the Lodge at the Swan, Long Acre, in 1730, and one of the original members of the Lodge at Savannah, of which Oglethorpe was the first Master in 1734. In 1735 the Lodge was registered under the No. 139, and was known later as Solomon's Lodge, No. 1.
>
> Lacy died in 1738, and Grey (or Gray) Elliot was appointed P.G.M. in 1760. Dr. Noble Jones, initiated in Solomon's Lodge in 1734, succeeded Elliot as P.G.M. in 1774, followed by Samuel Elbert in 1776, who continued in office until 1786 when the present G.L. of Georgia was formed.

Melvin Johnson records under the date of February 10, 1733/4: "A Lodge met in Georgia, probably, for the first time this day." He also noted that on March 18, 1733/4: "The following was this day adopted by the Grand Lodge of England: 'Resolved that all the Masters of all regular Lodges who shall not bring in their contribution of charity, do at the next quarterly communication give the reasons why their respective Lodges do not contribute to the settlement of Georgia.' "

The action by the Grand Lodge of England, and the statement of its official history concerning contributions are strange. Why the strong request—rather *demand*—for aid for the Georgia brethren? Why was Oglethorpe so interested in those confined to debtors' prisons?

Harry Leroy Haywood found the answers! Oglethorpe, a professional soldier, returned to England and was elected to Parliament in 1722. For 32 years he was re-elected. He learned that a close friend of his had been thrown into prison for bills he couldn't pay. He caught smallpox from the inmates and died. Oglethorpe investigated and found many suffering cruel and unusual punishment. So, he proposed a colony be established in North America for the poor.

King George approved, and in 1732 granted a charter to establish such a colony to be known as "Georgia." Savannah was the site for the first settlement which was established February 12, 1733. It didn't take long for the Freemasons to hold an outdoor meeting. On February 21, 1734, the first Masonic lodge was organized. And Oglethorpe became twice a father—of Georgia, and of Freemasonry in the Colony.

The following year the Lodge at Savannah received a warrant from England and Roger Lacy with a deputation *for constituting a Lodge at Savannah of Georgia in America.* A list in 1736 shows "Savannah in ye Province of Georgia" as No. 139. It is only the second Lodge in the New World on the list, the other being the Lodge at Boston.

The Lodge at Savannah remained the only non-military one in the Colony until 1784. Then several brethren who believed the "Antients" were better, applied to the Provincial Grand

Lodge of Pennsylvania for a charter. It was granted on October 29. This became Hiram Lodge No. 42 on the roster of Pennsylvania.

Not surprisingly, the members of Solomon's Lodge resented this new Lodge. Under the severest of conditions the members of the first Lodge had kept the light of Freemasonry gleaming for 50 years. They had made it possible for another lodge to be even considered.

It would take a volume, at least, to cover the trials the settlers in the Colony of Georgia suffered. They lived continuously under the threat of extinction. To their south was Florida, controlled by the Spaniards. To the southwest was Louisianna under the domination of the French. Both powers looked toward the conquering of the Colonies in the north. Georgia was in the way.

To Oglethorpe and his determined men go the credit for stopping the Spaniards and the French. Many a forest was left with the blood of Georgians and their enemies.

William B. Clarke, in *Leaves From Georgia Masonry*, in the section titled "History of Freemasonry in Georgia," describes a crucial time in Georgia's survival:

> ...There were less than five hundred people in the colony at the time of the Spanish attack. This took place in 1742 and was the crisis in Georgia history as well as being the crisis in the history of the English colonies in America.
>
> The battle of Bloody Marsh is one of the great epics in the military history of America. The strategy and skill of Oglethorpe in outwitting the Spanish reads like a romance. The Spanish had more than four thousand men and at least thirty-six ships of various types supporting this military force. Pitted against them was a force of less than six hundred English and Scotch assisted by the Yamacraw Indians under Tomochichi, their loyal chief.
>
> The strategy and daring of the colonists under the inspiring leadership and military knowledge of Oglethorpe completely annihilated the Spanish force and many of them perished in the marshes after the battle. Skeletons of dead Spaniards were found for many years after to mark the scene of conflict. Had the Spaniards succeeded,

Georgia would have perished and the Spaniards would
have overrun the prosperous English colonies to the north.
The whole course of American history might have been
changed. This battle has rightly been called "the Ther-
mopylae of America." Shortly after this battle, Oglethorpe
returned to England, never again to return to America
although his sympathies were always with the colonies in
their struggles with the mother country.

Although Freemasonry grew slowly in Georgia, it did grow.
And a year after the formation of Hiram Lodge, the members of
Solomon's Lodge greeted its members as brothers. The two joined together to form the Grand Lodge of Georgia on December
16, 1786.

The Colony of Georgia, and Freemasonry there, must be
credited to one man—General James Edward Oglethorpe. It
was he who fought for a place where the down-trodden could
live in peace. Although the politics of the period didn't help the
promise of peace, they did find freedom; a freedom they found
worth working, fighting and dying for.

When Oglethorpe and his 35 families, consisting of about 150
people, settled at the mouth of the Savannah River, they believed
their dreams had come true. What a contrast to what they had
left! Oglethorpe quickly met with the Indians, and then laid out
the village of Savannah. As the first governor he was called upon
to supervise all activities.

In 1734 he returned to England, taking the Yamacraw Indian
Chief with him. He brought 300 more people with him when he
returned to Georgia a year later. He found many German Pro-
testants had joined the Colony. Then he had to hurry back to
England to raise a fighting force to hold the Spaniards in check.

He returned to Georgia in 1738 to hold the frontier. In 1742
he fought back a full-scale Spanish attack that was designed to
throw the English out of North America. He continued to successfully defend the Colony, and in so doing, his more prosperous neighbors to the north.

Oglethorpe retired from Parliament in 1754. When the
America Revolution began he was offered supreme command of

British forces. He refused, at least until he could attempt to reconcile the differences. This wasn't permitted by the British.

He died in 1785 in England.

It is said the Lodge at Savannah was formed "in a low vale under the spreading branches of an oak, in February, 1734." A chair was made from this oak tree and presented to the Lodge on June 21, 1866. This chair now occupies the East in the Lodge over which Oglethorpe is believed to have presided as Worshipful Master for nine years.

Dr. Noble Jones succeeded Oglethorpe as Master in 1743. He was the first applicant to be initiated in the Lodge at Savannah. He was also the first medical doctor in Georgia. And he had arrived there with the first group of settlers.

Jones was a remarkable man. He was captain of the militia company which still exists as the "Georgia Hussars of Savannah." In 1757 he became a colonel and commanded the Georgia troops. He also was chosen as a member of the first King's Council, later becoming its president. He presided over the first General Court of Georgia.

His son, Noble Wimberly Jones, also a Mason, became Speaker of the Assembly and an active member of the Sons of Liberty. His son, George, also was a member of Solomon's Lodge. Both were medical doctors.

Roger Hugh Lacy was not a Provincial Grand Master, Walter M. Callaway, Jr., informs us in *Colonial Masonry*, so there was no authority in Georgia until October 20, 1760, when Gray Elliott was appointed. In 1774 Noble Jones became the second Provincial Grand Master. But he didn't serve long. He died on November 3, 1775.

Although *Grand Lodge* does claim Lacy was appointed a Provincial Grand Master, Callaway claims he wasn't. Callaway was long a staunch supporter of Georgia Freemasonry, and a meticulous historian. He would not have made a statement such as the above without conclusive evidence.

The Library of Congress had purchased a large collection of manuscripts from a Peter Force. Within this collection were minutes of Solomon's Lodge for 1756 and 1757. In 1926, by an act of Congress, these minutes were returned to the Lodge. A roster of the membership was found in them. And we learn for certain that Noble Jones was the first Mason initiated in Georgia.

Another Freemason initiated in 1733/4 was Moses Nunis. He may have been the first Jew to become a Mason in the New World. This is true insofar as Georgia is concerned, because Jews and Catholics were prohibited from settling there. This prohibition didn't last long. His father was a doctor whose service to the Colony was outstanding. Oglethorpe was able to use him as an example as to why Jews shouldn't be excluded. When Nunis died at the age of 82 on September 5, 1787, he was buried in the Jewish Cemetery with Masonic rites.

Oglethorpe's secretary, William Stephens, not a Mason, kept a journal. In it for the year 1739 he wrote of a Masonic procession in Savannah. The Lodge, led by the Senior Warden, marched to church dressed in Masonic regalia, while the people along the way jeered the Masons.

The people may have jeered because of what they believed the Freemasons were causing. Walter Callaway writes:

> A great complaint went up among the colonists about the inflated prices for vegetables being charged by the Carolina merchants. It was suggested by some that the exorbitant prices were due mostly to the high and profligate living in the Savannah clubs and by Freemasons at their banquets. Robert Parker complained: "We have about 30 or 40 Free Masons; they have fine Supper every Saturday Night and often 2 or 3 in the Week besides where such an expence can be born I am at a loss to know, one Night amongst other Disorders they went to the Guard Cut the Capt. down the Head & Disarm'd the rest by carrying the arms away. Wn they came to reflect On't on the Morrow to make things up they Call'd a Lodge at Night and admitted Goff the Capt a Free Mason, so I suppose the thing Dropt."

Throughout the years before the struggle for freedom of the Colonies was accomplished, members of Solomon's Lodge were in the fore-front of those fighting against tyranny. When the fighting reached Savannah in 1778, the Patriots were led by Georgia Freemasons. William B. Clarke tells part of the story:

> The siege of Savannah by the British took place on December 27, 1778. The patriots were under command of General Howe. He failed to take the advice of Brother George Walton, Colonel, and defend a path across the marsh in the rear. The British found this path. The line troops were under command of Brother Samuel Elbert, Colonel. Although greatly outnumbered, the Americans ably defended the city until the British attacked over the unprotected path across the marsh. The resulting conflict would have been a rout had it not been for the bravery and strategy of Brothers Samuel Elbert, George Walton and Joseph Habersham. Brother Elbert held his troops in line until the Americans on the right and center had retreated to safety. Brother Joseph Habersham and the men under him fought their guns until every man had been killed or wounded. Brother Walton and his troops held the rear under heavy losses. All three of these brethren were severely wounded and Brother Walton received a grape shot in the thigh. Later, when his remains were to be removed some years after the Revolution to be reinterred in Augusta under the monument of the Signers of the Declaration of Independence, his remains were identified by the presence of this grape shot in the thigh of the skeleton.
>
> After the capture of Savannah, the British published a list of prominent patriots whose capture was desired and for whom rewards were offered... On this list of patriots appear the names of brethren who, five years later, are known to have been the officers of the Grand Lodge of Georgia. They were probably the officers at the time of the siege of Savannah and the list thus contains the names of Samuel Elbert, Grand Master; William Stephens, Deputy Grand Master; Mordecai Sheftall, Senior Grand Warden; James Jackson, Junior Grand Warden; Joseph Habersham, Grand Secretary; James Habersham, Grand Treasurer; John Martin, Oliver Brown, Grand Stewards. It is readily seen who were leading patriots in Georgia in their struggle for liberty.

The Grand Lodge of Georgia dates its birth as December 2, 1735, when Roger Lacy was appointed to form a lodge in Georgia. The present Grand Lodge was established on December 16, 1786.

Six

THE ANTIENT INFLUENCE
IN SOUTH CAROLINA

GRAND Lodge 1717-1967 reported on the Colony of South Carolina briefly:

> The *South Carolina Gazette* of 29 October 1736 contained a report of a meeting of a Lodge at Charleston, at which John Hammerton, the Secretary and Receiver-General of the Province, was chosen Master. This was Solomon's Lodge, for which the Moderns had issued a Warrant the previous year originally numbered 251. The Lodge did not appear in the List until much later, and was then allotted the vacant number 74. John Hammerton was formerly a member of the Lodge at the Horn, and had offered to serve as Grand Steward in 1730. He received a Patent of Appointment as P.G.M., [Provincial Grand Master] of South Carolina in 1736. He resigned from the Mastership of Solomon's Lodge in 1737 on returning to England, and was present at Grand Lodge in 1738 and in 1739. James Graeme was elected Master of the Lodge in his stead, and he also received a Patent of Appointment as P.G.M. of South Carolina in 1737.
>
> The office of P.G.M. was filled, either by election or appointment, until 1783, when the P.G.L. [Provincial Grand Lodge] declared its independence.

The article in the *Gazette* referred to stated: "Last night a Lodge of the Ancient and Honorable Society of Free and Accepted Masons, was held, for the first time, at Mr. Charles Shephard's on Broad Street, when John Hammerton... was unanimously chosen Master." How long before this the Freemasons in the area had met informally, or even formally, cannot be determined.

The *Gazette* carried another story on December 29, 1737:

> On Tuesday last, being St. John's Day, all the members of the Ancient and Honorable Society of Free and Accepted Masons in this place met at Mr. Seaman's, Master of Solomon's Lodge, from whence they proceeded, all properly clothed, under the sound of French horns, to wait on James Graeme, Esq., Provincial Grand Master, at his house on Broad St., where they were received by all the members of the Grand Lodge. After a short stay there, they all went in procession and with the ensign of their Order into the Court room at Mr. Charles Shepheards's house, making a very grand show. Here, to a numerous audience of Ladies and Gentlemen, who were admitted by tickets, the Grand Master made a very elegant speech in praise of Masonry, which we hear was universally applauded. Then the Grand Master withdrew in order to proceed to the election of a Grand Master for the ensuing year, when James Graeme, Esq., was unanimously rechosen Grand Master, who appointed James Wright, Esq., Deputy Grand Master...
>
> The same day Mr. James Crokett was unanimously chosen Master of Solomon's Lodge.

This article makes interesting reading, and each reader will find something different in it. Contrary to many reports in current years, the ladies *were* considered an important part in the activities of the Freemasons of yesteryear. And, as in Boston, one Lodge considered itself both a Grand Lodge and a Subordinate Lodge. The Masons of the period evidently knew much more about Freemasonry than for which we've given them credit. They were following the practice of Mother Kilwinning Lodge in Scotland. For many years the latter considered itself subordinate to no other Masonic body.

Henry Collins in *Colonial Masonry* writes more about the early days of Freemasonry in South Carolina:

> Each year the celebration on December 27 of the Festival of St. John the Evangelist was an elaborate affair, generally beginning at sunrise, with the firing of guns in the harbor, and concluding around midnight with a banquet and ball. The general program seems very similar each year. There was a procession to church for divine

service, the return to the lodge room, election and installation of officers, a banquet and a ball.

The following item appearing in the *South Carolina
Gazette* on January 26, 1738, is of interest:

"We hear that at Mr. William Flud's at the sign of the
Harp and Crown, is held a Lodge of the Ancient and
Honorable Society of Free and Accepted Masons, belonging to the Lodge of St. John, Doct. Newman Oglethorpe
being chosen Master."

It is generally understood that this lodge was the child of
the Provincial Grand Lodge of Massachusetts.

Just what became of it we have been unable to learn, for
only a few references are to be found to it, and then it
drops out of existence.

Albert Mackey, in his *History of Freemasonry in South
Carolina*, believed this Lodge was authorized by Henry Price.
"But as its Constitution was manifestly an interference with the
prerogatives and jurisdiction of the Provincial Grand Lodge, it
must have been soon abandoned, and hence it is that we find no
further account of it in the subsequent Masonic proceedings of
the Province," he wrote.

Prerogatives and jurisdiction were "inventions" in Mackey's
day. They were not considered in the 1700s anywhere, not even
in England and Scotland where there was some form of organized Freemasonry. Some other reason for the demise of St.
John's Lodge will have to be found.

The Grand Historian in South Carolina, Wm. G. Mazych,
wrote to Bro. J. Hugo Tatsch: "I have found no further information of this Lodge than is given in this item in the 'Gazette.'
None of the old city directories in the Charleston Library mentions the name of either Newman Oglethorpe or William Flud,
nor can I find any mention of the 'Harp and Crown' tavern. My
opinion is that this Lodge was located at Savannah, Georgia, as
both the names, Oglethorpe and Flud, are prominent in Savannah's history." Walter Callaway, in his account on Georgia,
makes no mention of this Lodge.

Charles Pelham, the Grand Secretary of the Provincial
Grand Lodge of Massachusetts, wrote a letter on December 27,
1735. Within it he claimed: "... about this time sundry Brethren
going to South Carolina met with some Masons in Charleston

who thereupon went to work, from which sprung Masonry in those parts." Actually, Freemasonry was already there. Johnson indicates a Warrant for South Carolina was granted by Price.

About all that's known of Freemasonry in this Colony, and others, is what's noted in the press. And for over a decade nothing appeared in newspapers about the Craft. This may have been due to a prohibition by the Grand Lodge of England against anything taking place in Freemasonry being made public. "Mock Masons" were ridiculing legitimate Masonry in public. (Much the same thing would happen in the United States for a decade beginning in 1826.)

An example appeared in the *Boston Evening Post* on June 15, 1741 (reprinted from a London paper):

> *March 28. By the Right Worshipful the* Grand Master, Grand Officers, Stewards, *and* Brethren *of the* SCALD MISERABLE MASONS.
>
> ### A MANIFESTO
>
> WHEREAS it hath been maliciously and impudently insinuated that *Our Procession* of the 19th Instant, was intended as an unkind and ungenerous Reflection on the *Cavalcade of Our younger Brethren* the *Free Masons.* Let this satisfy the Public, that We had no such Intention, bearing always the greatest *Brotherly Love* and *Friendship* towards Our separated Brethren. But our Reasons are.
>
> *Primo,* That We are the True Original SCALD MISERABLE MASONS, as We can prove by the Records of the *Ancient Lodges of RAGG-FAIR, HOCKLEY in the HOLE, St. GILES'S, BRICK-STREET,* and the GOOSE and GRIDIRON in St. Paul's Church-Yard.
>
> *Secundo,* That we were incontestibly one Body at the AERA of the *Grand Mastership* of Mr. A-YER now *Tyler,* or Porter to their Grand and several other of their Lodges,
>
> *Tertio,* Because several of the *Gentry,* without our Privity, have crept in among Us who had more *Money* than *Wit,* and more *Nicety* than *Good Fellowship,* and have set up, themselves as a distinct Body, under the Name of FREE MASONS, in open Violation of our Ancient Constitution.
>
> *Quarto,* Because We have heard it insinuated, that our discontinuing the *Annual Procession* was urged as a proof

of our Non Existence; or, at least, was a Tacit Resignation
of Right of Eldership to our *Younger-Brothers*, the FREE
MASONS.

Wherefore, We have at this time thought fit, according
to the *known Constitutions* of the above *ancient Lodges*, to
re-assume our *Processional Ceremony*.

And that All whom it may concern may Judge of the
Justness of our Pretensions, We have annexed a Scheme of
our *Procession*, and their *Cavalcade*, and submit to the
Public which wa' most becoming the *Dignity* and *Solemni-
ty* of so *Ancient* and so *Venerable a Society*.

PROCESSION of the SCALD MISERABLE MASONS.

Two *Sackbutts*, vulgarly call'd *Cow's Horns*, in Liveries.

An Ass, in proper Habilments, led by two Pages in the
Liveries and Ribbons of the *Stewards* Colour; carrying a
Pair of *Butter Firkins*, on which Youth in a neat Attire
beat, with a Pair of *Marrow-Bones*.

A dextrous one legged Man riding on an *Ass*, and playing on a *Tinkling Cymbal*, viz. a *Salt Box*.

THE TYLER, in a long Robe or Vestment, completely
arm'd; on his Head a Cap of Maintenance, on which was
Hieroglyphically depicted the mystical Emblems of the
CRAFT; in his Hand a wooden Sword, riding on a *Lean,
Lame*, cropt Sorrel Nagg.

Three Stewards in *Proper Cloathing*, with *Jewels* and
Wands, in a GUTT CART, drawn by Three Asses
beautifully adorned, with Ribbons and Cockades. A
Postilion on the first, which was led by two *Pages*.

Three more *Stewards* in a SAND CART, drawn as
before.

GRAND GARDER, or *Tyler*, to the Grand Lodge, in a
Huge Cap of Skins, in his Hand a Truncheon; his
Shoulders from both Sides *ornamented* with LAYBANDS,
like a *Hamlet Collonel*, riding on a *Fine* prancing Steed,
well managed *in a Grain Cart*.

RAGGED BRETHREN in proper Cloathing, walking
according to the Ancient Constitutions, THREE, THREE
and THREE.

The Right Worshipful *GRAND MASTER* with his
GRAND OFFICERS in a *superb magnificent, sable State
Coach*, drawn by *Spavin Splint, Swishtail, Bobtail, One
eye*, and *None-eye*, all of various Colours, and bedecked
with *Azure Ribbons*.

SCALD MISERABLE MASONS

Burlesque Procession of Scald Miserables in 1741 parading in front of the Apple-Tree Tavern.

This *Grand* and *Illustrious* Procession, was finish'd by vast Numbers of different Instruments, which all together composed a *detectable* Symphony of ROUGH MUSICK.

The—Mark of the right worshipful

PONEY

Grand Master

Only the old-time "s" shaped like an "f" has been changed in the above to make it easier to read.

But even before there were any recorded items there must have been Freemasons in the Colony. Benjamin Franklin had reprinted Anderson's *Constitutions* of 1723—the first Masonic book ever printed in the Colonies—and advertised its availability. In his journal for August 15, 1734, he recorded a charge for 25 copies sent to South Carolina.

The charitable work of Freemasons was evident, even in the early days of the Craft in the New World. Every house between Church and East Bay Streets in Charleston was destroyed by fire in November, 1740, Collins notes. The *South Carolina Gazette* reported, "The Ancient and Honorable Society of Free and Accepted Masons contributed the sum of two hundred and fifty pounds." This sum, estimated to amount to $25 per Mason, went to the relief of the victims of the catastrophe.

Collins notes: "For several years the Provincial Grand Lodge was so inactive that in 1754 it became necessary to effect a complete reorganization. Peter Leigh, Chief Justice of South Carolina, was elected Grand Master, and the other offices were filled by some of the most distinguished men of the time."

It worked. In two years the Provincial Grand Lodge could claim six lodges on its roster: Solomon's at Charleston; Prince George's at Georgetown; Port Royal at Beaufort; St. George's at Dorchester; Union at Charleston; and The Masters' at Charleston.

According to Drummond in Gould's *History*, five of these were on the English list of 1760: Solomon's, 1735; Prince George, 1743; Union, 1755; Masters', 1756; Port Royal, 1756. St. Mark's Lodge was added in 1763.

Why a "Masters' Lodge"? It is presumed by Coil, and many others, that in the early years lodges conferred but two degrees. The ultimate, and final degree, that of Master Mason, was reserved for a special lodge. This was true in Philadelphia and Boston, and probably Charleston as well.

Drummond also stated: "This State was the battle-ground of the fiercest contest between the 'Ancients' and the 'Moderns.' For nearly twenty years each party had a Grand Lodge in active operation, and the contest was maintained for many years after it had ceased elsewhere in this country, and after the union had taken place in England."

"Antients" or "Ancients"

There is little information about the formation in England of the "Most Ancient and Honourable Society of Free and Accepted Masons according to the Old Institutions." It has been called the "Antients" or "Ancients" ever since the formation on July 17, 1751. Its first Secretary, John Morgan, evidently didn't keep good records. This changed the following year when he resigned because he had been "lately appointed to an office on board one of His Majesty's ships," and had received "orders to prepare for his departure." Laurence Dermott was "Unanimously chosen Grand Secretary; and accordingly he was installed (in the Ancient Manner) by Worshipful Mr. James Hagarty, Master of No. 4, then presiding officer."

Gould called this body "Schismatic," and "commonly, but erroneously, termed the 'Ancient Masons.' " Of Laurence Dermott he wrote: "It may be said, without erring on the side of panegyric, that he was the most remarkable Mason that ever existed." Gould felt he was an "unscrupulous writer" and a "matchless administrator." And "he displayed qualities which we find united in no other member of the Craft, who came either before or after him."

Present at this second meeting were officers of "Nos. 2, 3, 4, 5, 6, 7, 8, 9, and 10, being the representatives of all the Ancient Masons in and adjacent to London." Gould writes of Dermott:

Laurence Dermott was born in Ireland, 1720; initiated into Masonry, 1740; installed as Master of No. 26, Dublin, June 24, 1746; and in the same year became a Royal Arch Mason. Shortly after this, he came to England; and in 1748, joined a lodge under the *regular* establishment, but had shifted his allegiance, and become a member of Nos. 9 and 10, on the Roll of the Schismatics, when elected Grand Secretary by the latter, February 5, 1752. This office he laid down in 1771; and on March 27, that year, was appointed Deputy Grand Master, being succeeded, at his own request, by William Dickey, December 1777. He was again "Deputy" from December 27, 1783, until the recurrence of the same festival in 1787, when—also at his own request—he was succeeded by James Perry. His last attendance at Grand Lodge occurred June 3, 1789, and he died in June 1791...

His attainments were of no mean order. The Minutes of the Steward's Lodge—March 21, 1764—informs us that, an "Arabian Mason having petitioned for relief, the Grand Secretary conversed with him in the Hebrew language."...

In addition to his manifold labors as Secretary, he took upon himself the task of compiling a "Book of Constitutions" for the Seceders. This work...passed through no less than four editions during the author's lifetime, and if his fame rested on nothing else, would alone serve as a lasting monument of his zeal and ability...

In "Ahiman Rezon," 1764, whilst explaining the difference between "Antient and Modern" Masonry, the author [Dermott] says: "I think it my duty to declare solemnly, before God and man, that I have not the least antipathy against the gentlemen, members of the Modern Society; but on the contrary, love and respect them." "Such," he adds, fourteen years later, "was my declaration in the second edition of this book; nevertheless, some of the Modern Society have been extremely malapert of late. Not satisfied with saying the Ancient Masons in England had no Grand Master, some of them descended so far from truth as to report the author had forged the Grand Master's hand-writing to Masonic warrants, etc."... He then goes on to say, "As they differ in matters of Masonry, so they did in matters of calumny; for while some were charging me with forgery, others said, that I was so illiterate as not to know how to write my name. But what

may appear more strange is, that some insisted that I had
neither father nor mother; but that I grew up spontaneous-
ly in the corner of a potatoe garden in Ireland."

Many were the changes made by the "Modern" Grand Lodge
in the old customs and laws of the Craft. These were made
because of the "Mock Masons" and other anti-Masons of the
period. But those changes are what caused many of the "old-
timers" to stay away, or break away, from the Grand Lodge.
These were the Masons who formed the "Ancient" Grand
Lodge.

One of these changes concerned the wearing of the apron.
Many in the older Grand Lodge wanted to do away with the
wearing of aprons all together. Others claimed, successfully,
that this was the only sign left to show they were Masons. It was
then decided the apron should be worn upside down! "It was
attended with an ugly circumstance," said Dermott, "for in
traversing the lodge, the brethren were subject to tread upon
the strings, which often caused them to fall with great violence,
so that it was thought necessary to invent several methods of
walking, in order to avoid treading upon the strings.

"After many years' observations on these ingenious methods
of walking, I conceive that the first was invented by a man
grievously afflicted with the sciatica. The second by a sailor,
much accustomed to the rolling of a ship. And the third by a
man who, for recreation, or through excess of strong liquors,
was wont to dance the drunken peasant."

The "Antient" Grand Lodge chartered three lodges in
Charleston, claims Gould (Collins said two). A list of lodges,
their numbers, and who chartered, or warranted, them does
show three: No. 92 in 1761; No. 190 in 1774; and No. 236 in
1786. The Provincial Grand Lodge of Pennsylvania, which was
then adhering to the "Ancients," chartered three: No. 38 on
December 23, 1782; No. 40, July 12, 1783; and No. 47,
November 22, 1786. It was noted publicly that Lodge No. 190
celebrated St. John's Day in 1777.

On December 27, 1777, the lodges holding allegiance to the
"Modern" thinking, met and formed a Grand Lodge. The

"Ancient" lodges stayed away. It is claimed the "Antients" later proposed terms for joining the "Moderns" but to no avail. So, on January 1, 1787, Lodges No. 190, 38, 40, 47, and 236 sent their Masters, Wardens, and Past Masters to meet in a convention. It was voted to form a Grand Lodge, and on February 5 the lodges again met to elect officers and form a Grand Lodge. The officers were installed on March 24, 1787, and the Grand Lodge was formally organized.

There was "confusion among the Craft." Pennsylvania, in order to bring about harmony, dropped the word "Ancient" from its title, sent out a letter requesting unity throughout Freemasonry. It set an example by inviting to its feasts "all Free and Accepted Masons."

If the Masons of South Carolina received this message, they ignored it. The "Ancients" grew rapidly. Drummond claims that in four years the six "Ancient" lodges had grown to 35; the "Moderns" had but 12. He also notes, as do others, that little is known about what really did happen among the Craft for 20 years. Nothing was published. In 1807 there were over 50 lodges in the "Ancient" Grand Lodge; about 15 in the "Moderns." Then wisdom prevailed—almost.

A series of meetings were held between representatives of the two rival bodies commencing in 1807. Formal committees met during the later part of 1808. But, the leaders of St. John's Lodge in Charleston weren't happy. They revived the "Ancient" Grand Lodge, and 34 other lodges joined them. The rivalry continued until 1817. Then on December 27 officers of the "Grand Lodge of Ancient Freemasons of South Carolina" came into being with the installation of Grand Lodge officers. Today it's still "Ancient Free Masons."

Seven

HARNETT AND
NORTH CAROLINA

THE record for North Carolina in the official history of the United Grand Lodge of England, *Grand Lodge 1717-1967*, is brief:

> In 1735 some Masons assembled at the Cape Fear settlement (now Wilmington) to form a Lodge. This is believed to be a forerunner of the Lodge which received a Warrant from the premier G. L. in 1754 (No. 213) and which was later named St. John's Lodge.
>
> Henry Price, P.G.M. of Massachusetts, issued a Patent of Appointment to Thomas Cooper as Deputy G.M. of North Carolina in 1767. In 1771 the Duke of Beaufort appointed Colonel Joseph Montfort, P.G.M. of and for America, according to the Patent, but the Minutes of G.L. of 1771 read: *Joseph Montfort, Esq., on being appointed Provincial G. M. for North Carolina 10: 10:0.*
>
> The G.L. of North Carolina was formed in 1787.

Early writers claimed Freemasonry began in North Carolina before 1735. They produce "evidence" to substantiate this claim. J. Hugo Tatsch in his *Freemasonry in the Thirteen Colonies*, took a dim view of the evidence. John Edward Allen, writing in *Colonial Fremasonry*, goes along with the early writers. He, and they, believed a lodge was formed near Cape Fear.

Thomas C. Parramore in the 1975 history of North Carolina Freemasonry, *Launching the Craft*, said this Lodge was supposed to have been named "Solomon's", and "more recent study, alas! has cast over the legend of Solomon Lodge a dark shadow of skepticism." He also notes legend has placed another lodge close to where Solomon's was supposed to have been. It was called "Hanover Lodge" and was supposed to have been formed by veterans of the French and Indian War. Parramore discounts this report as a myth.

It's difficult indeed to account for "time immemorial Lodges." There really can be little question but that when a group of Freemasons met, they held a meeting. Whether these meetings can be considered "lodges" or not the individual may decide for himself. It's difficult to let our minds travel back to the days before the present laws, rules and regulations that control all of Freemasonry. But one must remember that the idea of Grand Lodges was new. And more legitimate Masons ignored the Grand Lodges then in existence than supported them. It took many years in the New World before all Masons gave their allegiance to one Grand Lodge. Witness Massachusetts, South Carolina, and New York. And even England until 1813. And it was years before Mother Kilwinning Lodge would give up its authority to the Grand Lodge of Scotland.

The historian must look for, and report, hard, cold facts. But there must also be reason along with the facts. And one central fact throughout the history of Freemasonry is that Freemasons *will meet as Freemasons* whenever and wherever they can.

Throughout every war in modern times Masonic meetings have been held. These have been called "Masonic Clubs," "Study Groups," "Ritual classes," and dozens of other names. From many of these groups have come lodges. The historian who isn't a Mason is not aware of the peculiarities within the Craft.

A personal note: During the last days of World War II, I was a Chief Petty Officer aboard an LST. Two other chiefs shared my quarters with me. Often I would walk into the quarters and find them talking. Nothing unusual about that—except they would stop as soon as I walked in. One day I asked them if they were Masons. They said they were. I wasn't. But I told them I was going to be one as soon as the war was over. They looked strange. A couple of years later I knew why.

Even today where two or more *interested* Freemasons get together they hold a "meeting." These meetings are informal. Even so, there are many Masonic clubs of varying descriptions in almost every jurisdiction in the United States. These range from small groups such as Chapters of the Allied Masonic Degrees, Chapters of The Philalethes Society, to large groups of Scottish Rite Masons. For twenty years a small organization known as the "Virginia Craftsmen" has met and traveled throughout the world spreading Freemasonry's first tenet, Brotherly Love.

We can't brush aside the stories of Freemasons meeting, formally or informally, in small communities in North Carolina— or in any other colony. There have been indications of this throughout this book; there will be more in the pages to follow.

But, if the historian is to be trusted, he must adhere to an unbiased account of the written record as he finds it. The written record for North Carolina shows that a Lodge was formed in 1754 in Wilmington. It became No. 213 on the roster of the Grand Lodge of England, and was known as St. John's. Tatsch, Allen, and Parramore say England acknowledged receipt of the payment for the Warrant on June 27, 1754. Drummond, writing in Gould's *History*, has little to say about North Carolina.

What this Lodge did during its early years is unknown. But it is known that Cornelius Harnett was its Worshipful Master for many years. Harnett was also to become an outstanding Patriot, and "long before it became fashionable to be one," wrote Parramore.

As President of the Sons of Liberty, Harnett led the fight against the British taxes. He was bitterly opposed to the Stamp Act. He was a member of the assembly "that defied the governor by adopting the 'Non-Importation Association' and was chairman of the committee charged with enforcing it."

His continuing defiance of Great Britain earned him the honor of being "with Robert Howe, the King's most dangerous enemy in North Carolina." He would continue to be until his death in 1781.

William Moseley Brown in his *Freemasonry in Virginia,* believed it was Harnett's influence as Deputy to Joseph Montfort, Provincial Grand Master for North Carolina, that caused him to issue a charter for the formation of Cabin Point Royal Arch Lodge in Virginia.

Parramore unearthed an interesting document. It's a pamphlet showing that a sermon was preached in New Bern on St. John the Evangelist Day, December 27, 1755. It was "Published at the Request of the Master, Wardens, and Brethren of the LODGE." Dr. Andrew Scott was the Master; John Clitherall and Joseph Carruthers were the Wardens. Parramore covers the background of these men, but has nothing further to say about the Lodge.

John Edward Allen, however, said "it has been definitely learned that there was a Masonic Lodge here as early as 1764." He was quoting from the history of St. John's No. 3 written in 1944. It quoted a story printed in "the *North Carolina Magazine or Universal Intelligencer,* dated December 21, 1764. Within the story quoted was: "Thursday, being the Feast of St. John the Baptist, the Members of the Ancient and Honourable Society of FREE AND ACCEPTED MASONS, belonging to the Lodge in this town, met in their Lodge Room; and, after going through the necessary Business of the Day, retired to the Long Room in the Courthouse, to dine, where was served up an elegant dinner; the Lieutenant Governor honored them with his company; where also dined many other Gentlemen. The usual and proper healths were drank; and at drinking 'The King and the Craft,' the Artillery fired 3, 3, 3."

As with many newspaper accounts of Freemasonry, this one had the name of the Festival wrong. It would be the Evangelist (the Baptist is on June 24), and the brethren must have celebrated the Festival early, which is still not uncommon.

Allen continues: "We learn that upon proper petition of Masons to Provincial Grand Master Montfort, led by Martin Howard, the first charter of a new lodge in New Bern was granted with date January 10, 1772, and the name St. John's

No. 2." Since the 1975 printing of *Launching the Craft,* the New Bern brethren will be able to claim a much earlier date for a Masonic meeting.

Drummond records that through 1766 Jeremy Gridley had granted warrants for 30 lodges, including one in Pitt County, North Carolina. He has nothing further to say about this Lodge. Neither does Allen. Parramore writes that "Crown Point Lodge," also "called 'the First Lodge of Pitt County,' " had its payment for its "constitution" recorded in Massachusetts on December 10, 1764. It didn't hold its first meeting "until June 24, 1767."

Parramore cites Tatsch as his authority for stating "the present Lodge at Halifax was warranted by Cornelius Harnett, 'Grand Master' of St. John's in Wilmington, on November 1, 1764." Actually Tatsch wrote: "The record of this famous lodge does not show by what authority it was originally established." It did begin work, however. It became No. 413 on the list of Lodges warranted by the Grand Lodge of England ("Moderns") in 1767.

For years this Lodge, Royal White Hart, claimed to own the oldest Masonic Temple in the country still in actual use. The same claim was made by another Lodge, Richmond Randolph, in Richmond, Virginia, meeting in "Masons Hall." Both couldn't be correct. Continual requests for several years for factual information from North Carolina proved fruitless. With the publication of *Launching the Craft,* North Carolina's official history, in 1975, the answer has been found. The tale of two Temples is interesting.

The tale of one Temple begins with the chartering of Richmond Lodge in 1780. It was the first new Lodge chartered by the new Grand Lodge of Virginia, which was meeting in Raleigh Tavern in Williamsburg. This would be its last meeting there. It had voted to move to Richmond the following year.

The Grand Lodge needed a home, so did Richmond Lodge. On August 18, 1785, the Lodge: "*Resolved,* That it is the sense of the Lodge that an advertisement be inserted in the papers to

ROYAL WHITE HART LODGE, HALIFAX, N.C.
One of the oldest Masonic Temples in the World.

petition the Assembly at their next meeting for leave to raise a Sum of money by Lottery."

The historian of Richmond Lodge wrote 83 years ago: "This scheme was devised in order to build the old Masonic Hall on Franklin Street near Eighteenth... the early history of the Lodge would have been far more happy and conditions greatly more prosperous, Masonically, had the Lodge not undertaken this work." He believed this project caused so much dissension, many members dropped out of Masonry, or formed two other lodges.

The cornerstone of Masons Hall was laid on October 12, 1785. The ritual had to be improvised. It must have been a good one, as the minutes note: "Alexr. Montgomery, Master, in festive procession, went forth to lay their foundations with songs, and, the command being given, James Mercer, the Most Worshipful Grand Master of the Virginia Brethren, having performed the proper rites, laid the first stone. —Far hence, O be far hence, ye profane."

The first meeting held by the Lodge took place on July 11, 1786. Later in the year the Grand Lodge met in Masons Hall, as it would for many years. Masonic lodges and Royal Arch chapters have been meeting in it continually. It has been the site for many historical moments.

The tale of the Masonic Temple in Halifax, North Carolina, is also fascinating. Parramore recorded:

> Royal White Hart Lodge in Halifax, like virtually all of North Carolina's 18th century lodges, held its meetings in rooms rented from local inn-keepers or in private homes. From its first meetings in April 1765, and for three years afterward, this lodge met at Anthony Troughton's tavern, Peter Copeland's, Daniel Lovel's, and Thomas Wild's before finally settling for a long stay at William Martin's Ordinary. Martin had a large two-story house, built and formerly owned by legislator Alexander Elmsley as his place of residence. Here, at the sign of the Thistle, the lodge was convening in late 1772 when a gap first appears in the lodge-minutes, and here the brethren were still in session when the minutes resume in 1783. Thus, it seems

that all meetings of the lodge for a period of fifteen years—less an interruption during the latter part of the Revolutionary War—were held at Martin's.

There is, however, a remarkable story—one hesitates to label as a legend what is really a simple mistake—that Royal White Hart from its earliest days has always met in the present lodge-building in Halifax. This notion, unfortunately, has been parlayed into the claim that the present hall is "the oldest Masonic building in the world."

Parramore claims the mistake was made by a "misreading of early minutes of the lodge." Attempts were made to build a Temple, but they were doomed to failure. Then they succeeded, and "on December 15, 1821, the brethren of Royal White Hart finally convened 'at their new hall.' ...It is this hall, now more than 150 years old, in which the lodge has met ever since."

The North Carolina historian found what all historians of the early days of Freemasonry find:

Lodge meetings in those free-wheeling days of "Tom Jones" and "Moll Flanders" were not all somber speeches and pious ceremonies; they included a generous portion of merriment as well. It need not surprise us, therefore, that the most impressive order placed by Royal White Hart in these early years was one that was agreed upon at the St. John's Day Festival on December 27, 1767. The Treasurer was ordered at this meeting to send to England for six dozen pint glasses, all with "worm's stalks", three dozen punch glasses, three and a half dozen quarter-decanters, three two-quart decanters, and four one-gallon bowls of Bow China, all items to have enameled upon them the words: "Halifax Lodge No. Carolina." The mind's eye conjures up visions of many a quiet night in old Halifax stirred by the exuberant melody of the brethren departing homeward from Brother Martin's tavern.

One of the Bow China bowls is still in existence.

Provincial Grand Master Montfort issued a warrant on January 10, 1772, for St. John's Lodge at New Bern. Martin Howard, Chief Justice of the Colony, was named as Worshipful Master. He was an ardent Loyalist, and later refused to take an oath of allegiance to North Carolina. The Lodge met fairly regularly during its first two years, but for 14 years it was silent. In 1787 it was "reorganized."

Parramore records another lodge that previously had been lost in the midst of time. It was "Buffalo Lodge" located "on Buffalo Creek in what is now Warren (then Bute) County." It was the "forerunner of Johnston-Caswell Lodge." It is believed to have been formed in 1766 by Masons from Blandford Lodge in Petersburg, Virginia, and other older North Carolina lodges. The first minutes of this Lodge were, luckily, saved from the debris in an old barn in 1916.

William Moseley Brown, in his history *Blandford Lodge No. 3, A. F. & A. M.*, of Petersburg, Virginia, writes: "One of the most famous of the 'daughters' of Blandford Lodge No. 3 is know known to but few Virginia Masons. It was organized on April 29, 1766 in Bute County, North Carolina and was chartered as Blandford Bute Lodge by the Grand Master of Virginia on December 23rd of the same year." Brown knew Virginia had no Grand Master until 1778. In his *Freemasonry in Virginia* he records H. P. Thornton as having been appointed Provincial Grand Master for Virginia about 1764 and Peyton Randolph about ten years later. He has nothing further to say about them in this capacity. He attributes the "Grand Master" statement to the *Constitutions* of the Grand Lodge of North Carolina for 1924.

Brown quotes J. Edward Allen's article in *Nocalore*, Vol. VI:

> There seems to be little doubt concerning the origin of the name "Blandford Bute." A number of these men came from the vicinity of Petersburg, VA. down the old Stage Road which went to the far South. They were probably members of Blandford Lodge in Petersburg, which was formed in or about 1756. It is interesting to note that the list of Charter Members of Blandford Lodge contains several family names identical with those of the men who later formed Blandford Bute Lodge. ...
>
> The record of Blandford Bute Lodge disappears with the beginning of the Revolution and at its end Johnston Caswell springs up. The records of the two were kept together. What these Brethren did during the Revolution will never be known.

"The date of Blandford Bute Lodge's first meeting is given as April 9, 1766," writes Brown. "It was already in operation at that time. Six officers are listed as being present at this meeting and four petitioners for initiation were elected and 'received into the Lodge accordingly.' The last recorded meeting was held 'at high 12 the 10th of July, 1767.' "

One man stands out in the early history of North Carolina Freemasonry—Joseph Montfort. He had probably been made a Mason in England, but nothing concerning his early life is known. But there's no question that he took an extremely active part in Masonry. He was Master of Royal White Hart Lodge, Provincial Grand Master for North Carolina (not America, as some claim), in which capacity he worked for the Craft. He was a long-time member of the Colonial Assembly, and a Colonel of Provincial troops.

Montfort died on March 25, 1776. Cornelius Harnett was Montfort's Deputy, but it appears he did not assume the office of Provincial Grand Master when Montfort died. Where and when Harnett was made a Mason is not known. It is presumed Harnett was a member of St. John's Lodge (now No. 1). Allen claims he "became a martyr in the cause of a free America" and had little time for anything else.

Joseph Hewes, a Signer of the Declaration of Independence, is considered a North Carolina Freemason by Ronald Heaton in his *Masonic Membership of the Founding Fathers*. But where and when he was made a Mason isn't known. Unanimity Lodge No. 7 of North Carolina believes he became a member after visiting the Lodge on December 27, 1776.

Samuel Johnston, who was to be elected the first Grand Master on December 10, 1787, was active in the politics of the Colony. When North Carolina became a State, he became the first United States Senator. In 1787 he became Governor.

Richard Caswell, the first Deputy Grand Master and second Grand Master, was considered "one of the most powerful men that ever lived in this or any other country," by Nathaniel Macon. He was a member of St. John's No. 1. He became a Major General in 1780. He was twice Governor of the State. Heaton records him as one of the Signers of the Articles of Association.

Masonry was in its infancy in North Carolina, as it was in the other colonies, when the Revolution erupted. With the war, records were wiped out. Consequently, much of the early history of this and other colonies may never be learned. But there is always hope. Perhaps in the rubbish of other barns and attics more Masonic records will be rescued.

Eight

THE OLD DOMINION

THE briefest account of Freemasonry in the New World that appears in *Grand Lodge 1717-1967* is that of Virginia:

> The Moderns issued a Warrant No. 236, dated 20 December 1753, to establish a Lodge which met at Royal Exchange, Norfolk, but it appears in Cole's List of 1764 with the date 20 December 1733, an error which has given rise to much speculation. The Hon. Presley Thornton was appointed P.G.M. of Virginia in 1766, but he constituted no Lodges, and does not appear to have exercised any of the powers conferred upon him. The G.L. of Virginia was formed in 1778.

The speculation mentioned has become chaotic over the years. The differing opinions about the Lodge warranted by the "Moderns" in 1753 have at times been alarming.

The Worshipful Master of what is now Norfolk No. 1 began a long search before he assumed office for 1982 to try to find evidence that his Lodge dates back to 1732. He didn't find it, but he celebrated the year as the 250th in the life of the Lodge.

Earlier historians didn't have the official statement of the United Grand Lodge concerning the date. However, they did have what evidence that was available. What they had then is all that can be found today. For the sake of accuracy, some of what was, and is, known is recorded here.

The major proponent for the date of 1733 for the Lodge of Norfolk was John Dove who was Grand Secretary of the Grand Lodge of Virginia from 1835 to 1876. On December 11, 1872, the Grand Lodge ordered a reprint of its *Proceedings* from its organization to date. No mean undertaking. It fell to the lot of Dove to do the job. He did it within two years.

What he had to work with is not known. He did note that records were scarce. But he starts his introduction with an error. He said Cornelius Harnett had been appointed Provincial Grand Master for Virginia; it was Presley Thornton, and he wasn't appointed until 1766. Dove then claimed the *Freemasons' Pocket Companion* had "No. 172. The Royal Exchange, in the Borough of Norfolk, in Virginia; 1st Thursday; Dec. 1733. No. 204. In Yorktown, Virginia; 1st and 3rd Wednesday; August 1, 1755."

Strangely, Dove notes in October 1786 a Grand Lodge committee was appointed to "regulate the rank of the several Lodges then under the jurisdiction of the Grand Lodge of Virginia." The result was:

"No. 1 Norfolk, Constituted June 1, 5741.
2. Port Royal Kilwinning Crosse, Constituted December 1, 5755.
3. Blandford, Constituted September 9, 5757.
4. Fredericksburg, Constituted July 21, 5758.
5. Hampton Saint Tammany, Constituted February 2, 5759.
6. Williamsburg, Constituted November 6, 5773.
7. Botetourt, Constituted November 6, 5773.
8. Cabin Point Royal Arch, Constituted April 15, 5775.
9. York, Constituted February 22, 5780."

The list goes through number 19. The curious dates for two of these Lodges are explained by Dove:

By reference to the aforementioned Freemasons' Pocket Companion, by Auld & Smellie, of Edinburgh, it will be found that York Lodge, No. 204, was Chartered for York Town, Virginia; 1st and 3d Wednesday; August 1, 1755; and we are left to the conclusion that it became dormant, (and was revived in 1780, twenty-five years after its first Charter,) as was undoubtedly the case with the Royal Exchange, No. 172, of the date December, 1733, which became No. 1, of the date June 1741.

There are now three dates cited for the formation of the Lodge at Norfolk: *Grand Lodge* says, 20 December 1753; Dove says, Dec. 1733, and June 1, 1741. Which is correct?

Henry Wilson Coil, a lawyer-Mason, an unbiased Californian, untiring researcher, and an excellent historian, writes in *Freemasonry Through Six Centuries:*

> W. Bro. Dove, historian of the Grand Lodge of Virginia, quite innocently, fell into the error of stating that the formation of a lodge at Norfolk occurred on December 22, 1733 as *Royal Exchange* No. 172. That date does appear on the official list of the Grand Lodge of England, but the Lodge is there numbered 236 and follows No. 235, chartered December 20, 1753 and precedes No. 237, chartered February 9, 1754. Accordingly, its date must have been December 22, 1753.

"The reproduction herewith shows Lodge No. 173, the Royal Exchange in the Borough of Norfolk in Virginia, meeting the first Thursday of each month, and chartered Dec. 22, 1733."

Freemasonry in the Thirteen Colonies
Jacob Hugo Tatsch

Several historians record the chartering of *St. John's Lodge* at Norfolk by the Grand Lodge of Scotland, June 1, 1741. The fact is that it appeared on the Scots list only as No. 117, chartered in 1763. No Lodge in America appears on the Scots list or in the records of the Grand Lodge of Scotland prior to *St. Andrew's Lodge* at Boston in 1756.

Confusing? Perhaps the reproduction of the authority cited by Dove will help. It's from *A List of Regular Lodges, according to their Seniority & Constitution, by Order of the Grand Master.* It was published in 1764, and is one of Cole's engraved lists.

No. 173 and "The Royal Exchange" appear between No. 172, Dec. 20, 1753, and No. 174, Jan. 31, 1754. Can the "1733" be considered anything but a typographical error? William James Hughan, an English Masonic historian, believed it was an error, and goes deeply into showing it is. J. Hugo Tatsch, an American Masonic historian, believed it was an error. So does every Masonic historian outside of Virginia.

William Moseley Brown wrote the history of several Virginia lodges. He also wrote the only history of Freemasonry in Virginia. In his *Freemasonry in Virginia* he wrote: "Doubtless every one of the early American Grand Lodges has its controversial points so far as the Masonic historian is concerned. And Virginia is no exception."

Brown rightly claims: "In order to understand the story of early Freemasonry in America, the reader must divest himself of all preconceived notions and prejudices, and must approach the facts in an open-minded fashion. For they cannot be interpreted as we would interpret the same events, if these happenings were taking place today."

Brown, the Virginia historian, argues that the date of 1733 is correct; that not all involved could have overlooked a "3" being substituted for a "5". If true, this would mean the Lodge at Norfolk applied for a charter from the Grand Lodge of England sometime prior to 1733. Yet, in a footnote on page 6 Brown writes:

[3] No Virginia Lodge is known to have written to any Grand Lodge for a warrant of constitution, or charter,

prior to 1757. All requests were addressed to a LODGE. Kilwinning Port Royal Crosse Lodge wrote to Kilwinning Lodge in Edinburgh for a charter May 10, 1755; the request was presented in the Grand Lodge of Scotland by Kilwinning Lodge and the charter was issued Dec. 1, 1755. The Port Royal Lodge was working as a regular Lodge from April 12, 1754.

The only way any lodge could have made the "list of Lodges" would have been to request a warrant or charter from the Grand Lodge. If none did prior to 1757, how could one be listed for 1733?

In 1934 Brown visited London. He spoke to officials at the United Grand Lodge about Royal Exchange. He was given access to the engraved lists "and the like." He asked "Brother Gordon P. G. Hills, P.A.G. Supt. Wks., who was then Grand Lodge Librarian, to make a thorough search of all his records and communicate the results to me." He did. On September 27, 1934, Hills wrote:

> I have looked up the subject of your query about early Lodges in Virginia. Our information here is, that the earliest Lodge in Virginia, recorded in our Registers, is *'The Royal Exchange, Borough of Norfolk, Virginia, warranted 22 Dec. 1753'*. We have no correspondence or papers relating to this Lodge.

Brown insisted in his closing statement that "I am compelled, therefore, in the light of all the available facts, to assign the earlier date (1733) to the Royal Exchange (Norfolk) Lodge."

The available facts indicate otherwise. The earliest date for the *charter, or warrant,* for the Lodge at Norfolk has to be December 20, 1753, as recorded by the Grand Lodge of England, "Moderns." No other record can be found. And Brown noted that "no Virginia Lodge is known to have written to any Grand Lodge for a warrant of constitution, or charter, prior to 1757." If so, how did the Lodge at Norfolk receive warrant No. 236 on December 20, 1753? Somehow it did.

Actually, the *official* date of the warranting of a lodge should not be that important. It is known that "Immemorial Lodges" were formed for many years after the Grand Lodge system came into reality. It is known that wherever interested Freemasons were, they held meetings of some description. It is unrealistic to believe Freemasons didn't meet in as busy a seaport as Norfolk until 1753.

The first *recorded* date found that speaks of Freemasons meeting in the Colony of Virginia is April 5, 1751. On this date the *Virginia Gazette* of Williamsburg published this notice:

Sir: you are desired by some of your subscribers to insert the following in your paper.

FABRICANDO FABRI SUMUS

The ancient and loyall Society of free and accepted Masons made a Figure in this City some time ago like a Meteor whose exquisite Brightness portended a happy Influence; but lavish of its Fires was soon extinguished. So the Society was too soon dispersed and no more Lodges held of Gentlemen of the strictest Honor and Probity who were initiated therein; whose act of benevolence performed to a person (tho' not their Brother) shew'd their inimitable Goodness and compassion for those in Distress. It is to be hoped that Men of their Principles will not obliterate from their Minds the Practice of Associating in the most ancient con-fraternity in the World; which has been traditionally handed down to Posterity these several Thousand years; and its Dignity is now supported by the Greatest Monarchs on Earth and was always observed as the most inviolable ever introduced among men . . .

An ode in four stanzas follows the above. It is signed by "N. S." *Fabricando Fabri Sumus* and is translated to mean, "We are builders by building."

This is an important publication. It proves what many Masonic historians have claimed throughout the years. Freemasons did form occasional lodges. They did meet. They did take "Gentlemen of the strictest Honor and Probity" and they "were initiated therein."

Was it through these unknown Masons and this unknown Lodge that at least one young man learned about Freemasonry? It was just a little over a year later "Mr. Geo. Washington" paid his entrance fee and received the First Degree in Freemasonry. The date was November 4, 1752, in the "Lodge at

Fredericksburgh" in the Colony of Virginia. [Note: *The charter reads Fredericksburgh. The spelling later has been without the "h."]*

The first recorded minutes of any Masonic meeting held in the Colony of Virginia is that for the Lodge of Fredericksburg. The record is dated September 1, 1752. A full slate of officers is listed on this date. This has to indicate this wasn't the first meeting of the Lodge. But when and where they were elected is not known.

An excellent example of how Masonic lodges operated in the New World in the colonial days is recorded by Ronald E. Heaton and James R. Case in *The Lodge at Fredericksburgh:*

> For the first few years the minutes show little more than the names of officers, members, and visitors present, and the degrees conferred, if any. For the first five years only sixteen Entered Apprentices were initiated, but no less than thirty-two were "admitted", "admitted a member", "admitted and made member", or "ordered a member." The Lodge appears to have been a social group which came together for a dinner and good time, but did little Masonic or degree work.
>
> From 1759 to 1764 no more than four meetings per year are recorded. Presumably meetings were held every month but only in 1753 was a full series recorded. St. John's Day in December seems to have been observed regularly and religiously. There are only four years when minutes of that day are missing. St. John's Day in June is mentioned in only one third of the years.
>
> Any acceptable applicant or candidate could be made a Mason, but he became a member only after he passed the ballot, was initiated, and agreed to pay his dues or quarterly contributions. Many Masons were made who never became members but who appear later as visitors. A few names are found once but never mentioned again.

The life-work of some of the members include: "One President of the United States, 1 member Continental Congress, 13 preachers, 17 merchants, 30 officers in the Continental Army, 17 planters, 10 doctors, 15 officers in Virginia Militia, 11 in public service of various kinds, 6 lawyers, 1 tavern keeper, and 1 shipmaster."

RISING SUN TAVERN

Where "The Lodge of Fredericksburg" was held after the Market House was torn down.

Another indication that Freemasonry was known in Williamsburg during the 1750's occured when Simon Frazier arrived there. He advertised himself as an instructor in "the latest methods of military science and tactics." Then he visited the Lodge at "Fredericksburgh" on December 20, 1753. Two days later (December 22, 1753) he presided as Grand Master "of a Royal Arch Lodge." For the first time in the history of this degree minutes are recorded of its conferment. There were three sitting officers and three candidates were "Raised to the Degree of Royal Arch Mason."

After this conferment, the "Royal Arch Lodge being Shutt: Entered Apprentices Lodge opened" and members of the Lodge and visitors were admitted.

In this Lodge George Washington was "Pass'd Fellowcraft" on March 3, 1753; and "rais'd Master Mason" on August 4, 1753. He was the first to be Raised in this Lodge.

Williamsburg is noted again: "Alex. Finnie: from the Williamsburg Lodge" was listed as a visitor to the second meeting of the Lodge at Fredericksburg on October 21, 1752.

A charter was granted "Fredericksburgh" Lodge on July 21, 1758, by the Grand Lodge of Scotland. Within the wording of the charter is an important provision: Members are "not to desert their said Lodge here Constituted or form themselves into separate meetings without the Consent and Approbation of their Master and Wardens for the time being."

Legally, Fredericksburgh Lodge, as well as Port Royal Kilwinning Crosse Lodge, which had received a charter from the same source dated December 1, 1755, could charter other lodges. This they did.

The minutes of February 28, 1768, for Fredericksburgh, read:

> A petition being read from the Brethren in Falmouth to Erect and Constitute a Lodge there, it being inconvenient for them to attend this Lodge, it was unanimously agreed to and ordered when the Said Brethren should give us notice that we wait upon them and Constitute a Lodge there in due form.—Ordered that the petition be recorded at full Length which is according done, viz:

On Wednesday, March 30, 1768, Falmouth Lodge was constituted by the officers of Fredericksburgh Lodge.

Fredericksburgh agreed to warrant a lodge at Gloucester on October 10, 1770. The Lodge was constituted and immediately applied to the Grand Lodge of England ("Moderns") for a charter. It was granted on November 6, 1773; so was one for Williamsburg Lodge on the same date.

The Lodges at "Pt. Royal and Hobs Hole" asked to join with Fredericksburgh Lodge in celebrating St. John's Day. The Lodge agreed, and the three held the celebration on December 28, 1767.

Port Royal Kilwinning Crosse Lodge (now Kilwinning Crosse No. 2-237 at Bowling Green) has had a turbulent history. It was formed at Port Royal on the Rappahanock River on April 12, 1754. A year later it asked Kilwinning Lodge, Scotland, for a charter. This was granted by the Grand Lodge of Scotland on December 1, 1755.

The Lodge was represented on May 6, 1777, for the first convention held for the purpose of deciding whether or not to form a Grand Lodge. Representatives were also present from Norfolk, Blandford, Williamsburg, and Cabin Point Royal Arch Lodges. Kilwinning was also represented on June 23, as were Fredericksburg, Blandford, Cabin Point Royal Arch, and Williamsburg. Kilwinning was present for the election of John Blair, Jr., as Grand Master on October 13, 1778, and again for his installation on October 30.

Port Royal Kilwinning told the Grand Lodge of Virginia on November 30, 1796, that "their Lodge had never received the Charter heretofore issued for them from the Grand Lodge of Virginia, but since that period and previous thereto, they have continued to work under the Grand Lodge of Scotland." A charter was requested and granted on December 3, 1796. The Lodge received another charter from Virginia on December 12, 1855. About 1862, because of the War between the States, it ceased its work. On December 14, 1881, it again received a charter. In the meantime, No. 2 had been given to Atlantic

Lodge in Norfolk, so the Grand Lodge graciously ordered it numbered 237, BUT with a "2" preceding it. It then became the only Lodge in Virginia to hold two numbers: 2-237.

Blandford Lodge held its first meeting in a private home on November 16, 1755. It applied to the Grand Lodge of Scotland, through Captain Peter Thompson of Aberdeen Lodge, for a charter. It was granted on September 9, 1757. One of its most famous members was Duncan Rose who became the first Grand Secretary of the Grand Lodge.

St. Tammany Lodge (often spelled "Taminy" or "Tamany" in the early days) became No. 5 on the roster of the Grand Lodge of Virginia. It received a charter from the Grand Lodge of England on February 2, 1759, according to Brown. However, Gould doesn't list this as one of the early lodges on the roster of England. Because of its location on the Chesapeake Bay (Hampton), the Lodge was burned out during three wars. Yet it has continued to be active.

Notably, Williamsburg Lodge has made no claim concerning an early date for the beginning of Freemasonry in the city. It became No. 457 on the roster of the Grand Lodge of England ("Moderns") on November 6, 1773. Yet it is known from the *Virginia Gazette* account of April 5, 1751, that a Lodge had met, at least for a moment, in the capital of the Colony. Another account in the *Gazette* for September 17, 1767, indicates Masons were in the city. William Waddill, a Goldsmith and Engraver, advertised, among other items for sale: "Masons medals, and Mourning rings of all sorts."

On August 26, 1773, shortly before the English charter was granted, the *Virginia Gazette* published:

On Thursday the 19th Instant, after a lingering Illness, died Mr. WILLIAM RIND, Publick Printer to the Colony
. . .

His remains were interred; and, being one of the ancient and honourable Fraternity of Free and Accepted Masons, the Worshipful Master, the Wardens, and other officers and Brethren of the Lodge of this City, met at their Lodge at 3 o'clock to prepare themselves for expressing a proper Respect to the Memory of their deceased Brother, from whence they soon after proceeded, in the Order and with the Formalities usual on such Occasions, to the House of the Deceased . . . The Service in the Church, and at the Grave, was performed by the Reverend John Dixon, one of the Brethren, and Professor of Divinity in William & Mary College and a solemn Dirge, suitable to the Occasion, was performed on the Organ, by Mr. Peter Pelham, a Brother likewise. . . .

The Lodge may have received its charter by the time this announcement appeared in the *Gazette* on August 26, 1773:

Last Monday being the anniversary of St. John the Evangelist, the antient and honourable fraternity of FREE AND ACCEPTED Masons celebrated it in the following manner: About ten in the forenoon they repaired to the Lodge in this city, from whence, after staying some time, they proceeded to Church, each brother walking in his proper rank, agreeable to his achievement in the royal art, where the Reverend Mr. ANDREWS, one of the Brethren, favoured them, and a Considerable number of the respectable inhabitants of this City, with a most excellent sermon, adapted to all ranks of people, and to every society. After the service was ended, they returned to the Lodge, in the Same order, where they dined, And in the evening gave an elegant ball to the ladies.

The Reverend Andrews mentioned was the Robert Andrews who presided over the Conventions for the formation of the Grand Lodge and who installed the Grand Master.

Other notices appeared in the *Gazette* but two of the most important ones, Masonically, were those that appeared on November 10 and November 29, 1775:

WILLIAMSBURG LODGE, November 6, 1775.
Ordered. THAT the members of this Lodge go into mourning, for six weeks, for the late honourable and worthy provincial grand master, PEYTON RANDOLPH, esquire.

GEORGE REID, Secretary

On Tuesday last the remains of our late amiable and beloved fellow citizen, the Hon. PEYTON RANDOLPH, Esq. were conveyed in a hearse to the College chapel attended by the worshipful brotherhood of Freemasons, both Houses of Assembly, a number of other gentlemen, and the inhabitants of this city. The body was received from the hearse by six gentlemen of the House of Delegates, who conveyed it to the family vault in the chapel, after which an excellent oration was pronounced from the pulpit by the reverend Thomas Davis. . The oration being ended, the body was deposited in the vault, when every spectator payed their last tribute of tears to the Memory of their departed and much honoured friend. . . The remains of this worthy man were brought thither from Philadelphia by Edmund Randolph, Esq.; at the earnest request of his uncle's afflicted and inconsolable widow. . .

The first President of the Continental Congress was laid to rest among his friends in Williamsburg.

The *Proceedings* of the Grand Lodge of Virginia for 1882 contains a brief history of Botetourt Lodge No. 7. It's based on an address made by John B. Donovan on June 24, 1871, and contains a curious statement:

Shortly after the revival of this Lodge in 1857, a gentleman of this county presented it the original Dispensation for its formation. It was said by him to have been picked up by a negro in the street at this place, and was carefully preserved in the archives until the late war, and then unfortunately lost. It threw a flood of light upon the Masonic history of that period. Often and carefully have I examined that curious relic of antiquity. It was granted neither by a Grand Lodge nor by a Grand Master, but by Fredericksburg Lodge, which was therein said to have been regularly chartered by the Grand Lodge of Scotland. . . It was dated in 1757. It is highly improbable that a Lodge that had never been chartered, would attempt the exercise of the high prerogative of issuing a Dispensation for the formation of a new Lodge. This fact, taken in connection with my recollection of the contents of the document, convinces me that Fredericksburg Lodge was chartered anterior to 1758.

Something is amiss. The minutes of Fredericksburg Lodge which records the authorization for Botetourt, the Lodge at Glouchester, to be constituted are dated October 10, 1770. Nothing appears in the minutes earlier. At any rate, this Lodge became No. 458 on the roster of the Grand Lodge of England on November 6, 1773.

Why did Botetourt Lodge apply for a charter to the "Modern" Grand Lodge? Why did Warner Lewis refuse the nomination to become the first Grand Master in Virginia? There has been much speculation over the years. Perhaps a portion of this letter sent to the Convention in Williamsburg on April 30, 1777, will provide some answers:

> . . . notwithstanding, as members of the body-politick, we have renounced all dependence upon the kingdom of Great Britain, yet, as Masons, our relation to the Grand Master of England remains indefeasible. From him we derived our Constitution, which he *cannot* revoke, on account of our being termed rebels by his State. That we cannot be rejected, on the pretext of rebellion, may be, by parity of reasons, . . . Lord Petre, therefore, or his successor, is still our Supreme; and to his power alone can we have recourse for the appointment of an officer, who acts by deputation, and is amenable, by the Constitution of Masonry, to the G. M. of England. . . Our Lodges are now held in *due,* tho' not in *ample* form; and if any abuses should arise, we apprehend, upon the principle of necessity, a Convention of the Craft might regulate them; or, should any number of Masons chuse to form a new Lodge, the power of deputation is conferred, by proper authority upon the Lodge at Fredericksburgh.

St. John's Lodge in Norfolk (not to be confused with later lodges of the same name) was chartered by the Grand Lodge of Scotland in 1762 as No. 117 on its roster. For some reason this Lodge is unknown in Virginia. Falmouth Lodge, originally warranted by Fredericksburg, received a warrant from Kilwinning Lodge, Scotland, in 1775. Nothing is known about this Lodge, either.

Cabin Point Royal Arch Lodge, which received its warrant from Joseph Montfort of North Carolina, evidently faded away shortly after the Grand Lodge was formed. Brown believes it was composed of Scots who were loyal to Great Britain.

The Lodge that became No. 9 on the English list of Lodges for Virginia was recorded by Gould as "205, Swan, Yorktown, Virginia, 1755-56" on the list of the "Moderns." It didn't take part in the formation of the Virginia Grand Lodge. It did, however, receive a charter from Virginia dated February 22, 1780. It again became dormant and wasn't revived until February 12, 1925, when it received another charter from the Grand Lodge of Virginia. It is now Yorktown Lodge No. 205 at Yorktown.

The Provincial Grand Lodge of Pennsylvania chartered a Lodge at Winchester, Virginia, in 1768. This Lodge, being closer to Philadelphia, than Williamsburg and Richmond, refused to join the Grand Lodge of Virginia until December 10, 1807. On May 1, 2, and 3, Major William McKinley, a future President of the United States, received the three degrees in Masonry in this Lodge.

It's surprising to note the area in which these early lodges were located, especially so when the vast territory that comprised the Colony of Virginia is considered. When Freemasonry began to evolve in the New World, its territory extended from the Potomac River into the far west. After the French and Indian War ended, it still claimed the Northwest Territory. This included all, or portions of Ohio, Illinois, Indiana, Michigan, Wisconsin, Minnesota, Kentucky and West Virginia. Yet, all of its known lodges were close to Williamsburg. All had easy access to rivers or the ocean.

For 200 years from 1610 Virginia ranked first in population, as well as size. But Freemasonry grew faster in the Northeast. The Provincial Grand Lodges of Pennsylvania and Massachusetts were agressive. Virginia had no Masonic leadership. As conditions developed, this may have been beneficial. When it formed its Grand Lodge there was no concerted opposition. This was far from true in Massachusetts. New York, South Carolina, and to a lesser extent, Pennsylvania. "Ancients" and "Moderns" vied for control. Then, too, as in New York, there were other factions.

With the end of the war for American Independence, Freemasonry began to move westward along with American troops.

Nine

MARYLAND AND DELAWARE

THE minutes of the Provincial Grand Lodge of Massachu-setts state: "5750, Aug. 12. At the Petition of Sundry Brethren at Annapolis in Mary Land, Our Rt. Wors'l Grand Master, Bro. Thos. Oxnard, Esqr. Granted a Constitution for a Lodge to be held there. . .

"Fryday, July the 13th, 1750. For the Lodge at Mary Land, Bro. McDaniel, D.G.M. app'd & pd. for their Constitu'n."

Tatsch notes that the *Maryland Gazette* contained items about this Lodge on June 25, 1761, December 26, 1763, and June 24, 1764. This would certainly indicate the Lodge celebrated the Festivals of the Sts. John. No trace of the Lodge can be found after 1764.

A Lodge was warranted in "Charles County, at Port Tobac-co, some time prior to 1759," by the Provincial Grand Lodge of Massachusetts, Tatsch writes. But Gould's *History* which lists the lodges warranted by Massachusetts doesn't mention this. Both Tatsch and Alphonse Cerza (writing in *Colonial Free-masonry)* state there was a lodge working in Leonardtown about 1759. Tatsch records this from the minutes of the Lodge for June 25, 1759:

> . . .Being assembled, after hearing a Polite, Acurate, and most Edifying discourse delivered by our Rev'd Brother, John McPherson, we returned to the Lodge Room in the above order. In the evening was a Genteel Ball, At the opening of which was sung by the Members of the Lodge, Locked in a Circle, the Entered Apprentices' Song. In the morning of the 26th the members again repaired to the Lodge Room where it was ordered that the money due to

the Lodge be applied towards the expences of the Ball, and what may remain undischarged to be collected from the members.

On other occasions, writes Tatsch, the members were "admonished to be home by nine o'clock!" On St. John's Day in 1761, the minutes have a somewhat sorrowful note:

As there is at present no Jewells belonging to this Lodge, and as there is no Clergyman to perform divine Service on the occasion, there cannot be any procession, nevertheless it is ordered that the Clerk of the Parish read the Evening Service and that Brother Bate thereafter read the Mason's Charge.

There was a ball, however, following this ceremony, and the Lodge wasn't closed until the members returned the next morning to do so.

A warrant was issued on August 8, 1765, by Lord Blaney, Grand Master of the Grand Lodge of England, "Moderns." Joppa Lodge became No. 346 on the roster. But, according to Gould, those who applied for the warrant made a mistake:

Curiously enough this Lodge supposed itself an "Ancient" Lodge, and adopted a By-Law that no one, who had been admitted in any Modern Lodge should be admitted a member of that Lodge "without taking the respective obligations peculiar to 'Ancient Masons.' " The explanation probably is that the first members were made in the Ancient Lodge in Philadelphia, and, by mistake, applied to the other Grand Lodge for a charter. Two Brethren were complained of for attending the work of an "unconstituted and unwarranted Lodge." A committee was appointed to confer with them and report to the Lodge. One of the brethren promised to abstain from attending any such Lodge, the other said he was not convinced that he had "made any breach in our law;" the Lodge concluded that the matter should be "considered in full Lodge," but nothing further appears in relation to it. This shows that it was not then fully settled that voluntary Lodges were illegal.

In March 1766, an invitation was received from Lodge No. 3, Ancient York Masons, "Held at John Kelley's, in Pewter Platter Alley in Philadelphia," to open a regular correspondence, "which desire was immediately agreed to." The Ancient Provincial Grand Lodge of Pennsylvania refused to recognize this Lodge as an Ancient Lodge, and in consequence, in 1782 it took a charter from that body. It took part in the formation of the Grand Lodge of Maryland, and seems to have become dormant about ten years after it received its second charter.

The Provincial Grand Lodge of Pennsylvania was, and would be, closely associated with Freemasonry in Maryland. In fact, all of its lodges prior to the formation of the Grand Lodge of Maryland were chartered by Pennsylvania. These lodges were all "Ancient" bodies, because Pennsylvania had become "Ancient."

This happened on June 7, 1758, when the Grand Lodge of England, "Ancients," warranted Lodge No. 69, at Philadelphia. With this the Provincial Grand Lodge, organized in 1731, voluntarily withdrew. So did the "Franklin-Allen Grand Lodge, organized in 1749," said Gould. Then the brethren of Philadelphia applied to the "Ancient" Grand Lodge for a warrant to organize a Provincial Grand Lodge. This was granted on July 15, 1761. However, it didn't arrive until after a third one had been dated June 20, 1764. Gould tells the story:

> . . .The Grand Secretary, Dermott, wrote that he had actually issued three: the first, which, according to the Grand Lodge record, was dated July 15, 1761, was sent by a vessel which was taken by the French; the next was lost in some unknown manner; the third dated June 20, 1764, was safely received; while it bore a later date, in fact, by a memorandum upon it, it seems that it was entitled to date from July 15, 1761, the date borne by the record of it in the Grand Lodge books.

In 1766 Pennsylvania warranted two lodges in Maryland: at "Georgetown on the Sassafras River, Kent County"; and to another lodge in Kent County, at Chestertown. A Lodge located at Fell's Point, Baltimore, was warranted on June 28, 1770; on September 21, what was to become St. John's Lodge No. 20, received a warrant. A Lodge located at Queenstown was warranted on September 16, 1773. Cerza notes that John

Coats was the first Master of this Lodge, and would later become Deputy Grand Master of the Grand Lodge of Pennsylvania, and then the first Grand Master of Masons in Maryland.

Coats was elected Grand Master of Masons in Maryland on July 31, 1783. The Reverend Dr. William Smith, Grand Secretary of the Provincial Grand Lodge of Pennsylvania, presided over the convention. It was resolved to ask Pennsylvania for "a warrant to constitute ourselves into a Grand Lodge." But Coats had second thoughts. He visited the Grand Lodge of Pennsylvania and explained Maryland's position. He told his brethren:

> I then enlarged upon our situation as Freemasons, and free men of a State, independent and sufficiently numerous to form a constitution, and at the same time wishing to promote the most brotherly intercourse with the craft, not only in Pennsylvania, but through the globe. I wanted to know where we were to receive our authority. If your Grand Lodge gives us a warrant, we must demean ourselves to it, otherwise it will be of no force or virtue, consequently void. Pray do you think yourselves bound to pay that obedience to the Grand Lodge of London, from whence you originate? Are you, the representatives of Pennsylvania, dependent upon them? If you are, I, for one as a member, as a Past Master of this Grand Lodge, protest against it. Who formed a Grand Lodge in England, Scotland, and Ireland, or any other state blessed with a Grand Ldoge? their own independence. They owe no subjection, but are always happy in meeting and acknowledging their brethren, wheresoever they come, upon equal terms.

The Grand Lodge of Maryland did not meet again until April 19, 1787. Evidently Pennsylvania was still not convinced the new Grand Lodge had a right to existence. The action previously taken was reaffirmed. It didn't formally dissolve, but it went through the motions again, established a Grand Lodge and re-elected the Grand Master and Grand Secretary.

Gould states: "So that although the Grand Lodge did not meet for nearly three years and although it celebrated its centennial anniversary in 1787, it really dates from 1783."

The early lodges in Delaware also owed their allegiance to the Provincial Grand Lodge of Pennsylvania. On June 24, 1765, it warranted a Lodge at Cantwell's Bridge, about half way between Dover and Wilmington. Charles E. Green, writing about Delaware in *Colonial Freemasonry*, states: "This small country lodge from 1765 to 1779 appended ninety names to its By-Laws. That these Brethren were devoted to the cause of the Colonies is demonstrated by the many emergency meetings held in order to confer the degrees upon men about to leave for Washington's Armies, two were colonels, nine were captains, and seven, lieutenants."

Green cites the bravey of Colonel Charles Pope, and the services of Archibald Alexander, a surgeon "with the 10th Virginia Regiment of the Continental Line." He notes that this Lodge became Union No. 5 under the Grand Lodge of Delaware.

A Lodge at Christiana Ferry (Wilmington) became No. 14 on Pennsylvania's roster on December 27, 1769. (Later Washington Lodge No. 1 in Delaware.) Among its members was Gunning Bedford, Jr., who Green praised highly. His daughter claimed he was an "Aide-de-Camp to General Washington," and he may have been, although Heaton doesn't list him as such. He was a "member, Continental Congress, 1783-85. Delegate to the Federal Constitutional Convention of 1787, and a leader in having Delaware the first state to ratify the Constitution on December 7, 1787."

Green's account of Bedford's eloquence in the Constitutional Convention is worth preserving:

> . . .Bedford was frequently on the floor arguing the many questions confronting the Convention. Bedford fought strenuously the efforts of the larger states to base representation in both houses of Congress on population. An early decision was made that the states should be proportionally represented in the first branch of Congress. The small states then endeavored to obtain an equal voice in the second branch. The argument continued for several weeks. Finally on June 30, 1787, Bedford made a bold and celebrated speech. He referred to South Carolina as puffed up with the possession of her wealth and Negroes. He

pointed to Georgia as a diminutive state with an eye to her future wealth and greatness. Turning to Massachusetts, Virginia and Pennsylvania, he said that in every vote they had been actuated by their numbers, wealth and ambition for power. He exclaimed, "Gentlemen, I do not trust you. If you possess the power, the abuse of it cannot be checked. You dare not dissolve the confederation; if you do the small States will find some foreign ally of more honor and good faith who will take them by the hand and do them justice."

The speech threw the Convention into a turmoil. One after another, the delegates of the large states rebuked Bedford. Argument continued until July 16, when the provision was adopted whereby each of the states was accorded equal representation in the United States Senate. Upon returning to Delaware from the Convention, Bedford used all his eloquence, ability and strength in having his state ratify the Constitution.

Bedford was born in 1747; died in 1812. He was first buried in the graveyard of the Presbyterian Church of Wilmington; later he was reinterred on the grounds of the Masonic Home in Wilmington.

Jacob Broom was the other member of Washington Lodge to be a Signer of the Constitution of the United States.

A Lodge at Dover was warranted by Pennsylvania on August 26, 1775. It was in existence for 12 years. Green states: "During the twelve years of its existence, 106 men became members and no other lodge in Delaware contributed so many members who distinguished themselves in the Revolutionary War."

David Hall was one of these. Another was Dr. James Tilton who served throughout the war as a surgeon. Of his service, beginning in 1779, Green wrote:

> . . . The army's efficiency was almost paralyzed by the great number of men sent to the hospital with typhus fever. This dreaded disease was about to extinguish the last glimmering flame of the glorious American cause of freedom.
>
> Upon the broad shoulders of Surgeon Tilton rested the future of our country. Here were sick soldiers, who because of little and poor food, crowded quarters and depressed spirits were susceptible to a deadly germ—

a germ that was killing off rapidly more men than the bullets of the enemy had done. Tilton organized a new system of hospital care. He broke up the large hospital and constructed small log huts to accomodate only six patients. These huts were roughly built so that there was ample ventilation through the crevices. In the center, on the clay floors, fireplaces were constructed with a smoke hole in the roof. Upon the burning logs in the fireplaces was thrown creosote. With the ventilation, the draft hole and the nascent creosote acting as a germicide, the idea produced satisfactory results and the epidemic was stopped. General Washington wrote to Tilton on September 9, 1780, expressing his gratitude for the meritorious labors performed. He operated a hospital at Williamsburg, Virginia, during the Yorktown campaign.

When the Delaware State Medical Society was incorporated on February 3, 1798, Tilton was chosen as the first president. With the outbreak of the War of 1812, the government appointed him Surgeon-General of the United States Army.

Robert Kirkwood, another member of the lodge at Dover, "saw action in thirty-two battles." Many of these were in the South. Allen McLane was a Lieutenant in Colonel Caesar Rodney's regiment. Rodney wasn't a Mason, but he was one of the real heroes in the drama for the signing of the Declaration of Independence. McLane "developed into one of Washington's finest scouts." According to Green's account, McLane was one of the outstanding, but unsung heroes of the war. His scouting (many would call it "spying") provided Washington and his generals with the details they needed for several successful battles.

Pennyslvania granted a warrant to "Lodge No. 33" to meet, "in alternate years in New Castle and in Christiana Bridge. It is now St. John's Lodge No. 2. Joseph Israel was the first Worshipful Master of this Lodge, and Green relates an amazing story concerning his blood brother, Israel.

After the Battle of Brandywine, Israel was captured and taken aboard the British frigate *Roebuck*. The British offered him a sizeable sum for his cattle, but "Israel declared that he would sooner drive his cattle as a present to General

Washington then receive thousands of dollars in British gold for them." The story by Green continues:

> The British commander ordered his men to seize and slaughter his cattle. Israel's young wife, seeing the sailors rowing ashore, sensed their purpose and ran to the meadows, cast down the bars and aided by her dog, began driving the cattle into the marsh. When the sailors arrived, she was told to stop or be shot. She told them to "fire away" and continued driving the cattle. They fired but not one ball grazed her. The British returned to the ship empty handed. That night, on ship, Israel was tried. From the evidence, a verdict for an ignominious death was certain. He defended himself as well as he could and at the conclusion of the trial made a sign of the Craft. Surprisingly, the haughty bearing of the British officers changed. The Tory witnesses were reprimanded for seeking to harm so honorable a gentlement. Presents were prepared for his heroic wife and he was escorted ashore and set at liberty.

Kensey Johns, Sr., a member of this Lodge married the daughter of the Governor of Delaware on April 30, 1784. "George Washington attended the wedding," said Green, "and was reported to have been in high spirits for he not only kissed the bride, but 'stood upon the hearthstone and kissed the pretty girls as was his want.'"

On June 6, 1806, four lodges met in Wilmington to form a Grand Lodge. "The work was completed the following day. Three of the lodges, No. 14 at Wilmington, No. 23 at New Castle, and No. 96 at Newark, were chartered by the Grand Lodge of Pennsylvania. The fourth, No. 31 at Laureltown, was chartered by the Grand Lodge of Maryland."

Ten

NEW JERSEY AND NEW YORK

IT was to New Jersey that the first known Freemason came to the New World to reside. John Skene arrived with his wife and several men who were also members of Aberdeen Lodge, Scotland. Alphonse Cerza, writing in *Colonial Masonry*, notes that the booking agent who "arranged passage on the vessel *Henry and Francis*" was the Master of the Lodge. He also notes that the other Masons who arrived with Skene returned home within a year. And the trip had been sponsored by "the Earl of Perth, a Freemason, John Forbes, a Freemason, and others."

Gould's *History* records: "George Harrison was appointed Provincial Grand Master of New York, June 9, 1753, and was *publicly installed* by his predecessor on December 26, 1753. He granted a warrant for a Lodge at Newark May 13, 1762, and for a Lodge at Princeton, Dec. 27, 1763. Oliver Ellsworth, afterwards Chief Justice of the Supreme Court of the United States, was one of the charter members of the latter. Both of these Lodges ceased to exist before the close of the war of the Revolution, but it cannot be ascertained when, as their records have been lost."

Actually, "Harrison" should be spelled "Harison." That's the way he preferred it. Cerza agrees that the Lodge at Newark, now St. John's No. 1, appears to be the first Lodge chartered in New Jersey. The Lodge was instituted at the Rising Sun Tavern on May 13, 1761, and the following day Passed three Entered Apprentices! The following day these three, plus one more, were Raised Master Masons! The Lodge met for five straight days.

The second lodge warranted was named Temple Lodge; the third was St. John's of Prince Town (now Princeton). Gould gives the date as "Dec. 27, 1763"; Cerza records it as "December 27, 1765"; so does Tatsch.

December 27, 1765 must be correct. Seven Masons wrote to Jeremiah Gridley for a warrant on September 24, 1765. One of those signing the request was Richard Stockton. He was to be one of the Masonic Signers of the Declaration of Independence. During the War for American Independence he was taken prisoner by the British. He died at the age of 50 in 1781.

The Provincial Grand Lodge of Pennsylvania wasn't idle in New Jersey. It warranted Baskingridge Lodge in 1767. Tatsch records: "The Lodge first met at White's Tavern, which served as General Lee's headquarters in December, 1776, where he was taken prisoner by the British."

Throughout the war Freemasons and their lodges suffered in New Jersey. Only two lodges were known to be in existence when a group of Masons gathered to form a Grand Lodge. Twenty-six met in New Brunswick on December 18, 1786, and elected David Brearley, Chief Justice of New Jersey, Grand Master. On January 20, 1787, the Grand Lodge officers were installed, and five dispensations for new lodges were granted.

Ossian Lang covered the early history of Freemasonry in New York in his book by the same name, published in 1922. Lang was an educator, public servant, historian, and world traveler. For 30 years he was the Grand Historian for the Grand Lodge of New York. His Preface opened by stating: "The object of the following pages is to give in simple language a general survey of the historic development of Freemasonry in the State of New York." This he proceeded to do (if only other historians would try to do the same!).

His comments about some of the claims by writers of Masonic history are worth noting. "The oldest well authenticated lodge in America was a St. John's Lodge known to have been at work in Philadelphia, in 1730, and presumably it could trace its existence to an even earlier date," Lang wrote, and he added:

Benjamin Franklin became a member of it, in 1731, was elected Junior Grand Warden, in 1732, and Grand Master, in 1734. As he published, in 1734, a reprint of the Anderson Constitutions of 1723, he must have been fully aware of the Regulations adopted in 1721. Quite evidently he never doubted the regularity of his Grand Lodge, though he was not so sure whether this would be "countenanced" abroad, and he admitted as much, when he wrote, a few months after his election as Grand Master, that the Fraternity in Philadelphia, "seems to want the sanction of some authority derived from home to give the proceedings and determinations of our Lodge their due weight." Nevertheless, the "Pocket Companion for Free Masons," printed at Dublin, in 1735, includes in its list of Lodges the following item:

"116. The Hoop, in Water Street, in Philadelphia. 1st Monday."

Thus it would seem that in Ireland at least the Lodge was recognized as Masonic.

No historian has driven home this point that St. John's Lodge in Philadelphia (1730) is the oldest well authenticated Lodge in America more emphatically. But to cement his conclusion he drives in a few more nails by showing that Chetwode Crawley and William J. Hughan, two English historians, agree with him.

Lang makes another point that is still argued in some quarters:

> The "immemorial" Lodges, whether working in England, Ireland, Scotland, or anywhere else, were considered "regular" provided they were in possession of a copy of the Old Constitutions; otherwise they were irregular, whether they met before or after 1717. After the Grand Lodge system was established firmly enough to enforce regulations defining lawful Masonic practice, the situation changed gradually.
>
> The proposition has been advanced repeatedly that Lodges which met before June 24, 1721, were "entirely regular," but *not after that date*. This would be true if it were not for the fact that the Regulations of the Grand Lodge of England, adopted in 1721, were intended only for the Metropolitan district of London and Westminster.

The fact that the Regulations commended themselves to
Masons elsewhere and acquired, in the course of time,
universal validity, does not make their authority binding
until they were known and accepted elsewhere. The old
Lodge at York kept right on working despite the London
regulations. So did the Lodges in Ireland and Scotland.
Grand Lodges were established at York, Dublin, Munster
and Edinburgh, without leave from London or anywhere
else.

Lang is of the opinion that there must have been Freemasons
in the Colony of New York or Daniel Coxe wouldn't have been
appointed Provincial Grand Master for *New York, New Jersey
and Pennsylvania*. His assumption is based upon the wording of
Coxe's deputation: "Whereas, application has been made unto
us by our Rt. Worshipful and well beloved Brother, Daniel
Coxe, of New Jersey, Esq'r., and by several, other brethren,
free and accepted Masons, residing and about to reside in the
said Provinces of New York, New Jersey and Pensilvania, that
we should be pleased to nominate and appoint a Provincial
Grand Master of the said Provinces."

The next Provincial Grand Master to be appointed for New
York was Captain Richard Riggs. His appointment took effect
on November 15, 1737. Less than two weeks later a "letter to
the editor" appeared in the New York *Gazette:*

> Mr. Bradford: There being a new and unusual sect or
> Society of Persons of late appeared in our native Country,
> and from thence spread into some other Kingdoms and
> Common Wealths, and at last has extended to these parts
> of *America*, their Principle, Practices and Designs not be-
> ing known, nor by them published to the World, has been
> the reason that in Holland, France, Italy and other Places
> they have been supprest. All other societies that have ap-
> peared in the World have published their Principles and
> Practices, and when they meet set open their Meeting-
> house Doors, for all that will come in and see and hear
> them, but this Society called FREE MASONS, meet with
> their Doors shut, and a Guard at the outside to prevent
> any approach near to hear or see what they are doing. And
> as they do not publish their Principles or Practices, so they
> oblige all their Proselytes to keep them secret, as may

appear by the severe Oath they are obliged to take at their first admittance. Which Oath is as follows, viz.:

"I, A.B., Hereby solemnly Vow and Swear in the Presence of Almighty God, and this Right Worshipful Assembly, that I will Hail and Conceal and never Reveal the Secrets or Secrecy of Masons or Masonry, that shall be revealed unto me; unless to a true and Lawful Brother, after the due examination, or in a just and Worshipful Lodge of Brothers and Fellows well met.

"I further more Promise and Vow, That I will not Write them, Print them, Mark them, Carve them, or Engrave them, or cause them to be written, Printed, Marked, Carved, or Engraved on Wood or Stone, so as the Visible Character or Impression of a Letter may appear, whereby it may be unlawfully obtained.

"All this under no less Penalty than to have my Throat cut, my Tongue taken from the Roof of my Mouth, my Heart pluck'd from under my left Breast, then to be buried in the Sands of the Sea, the Length of a Cable Rope from Shore where the Tide ebbs and flows twice in 24 Hours, my Body to be burnt to Ashes and be scatter'd upon the Face of the Earth, so that there shall be no more Remembrance of me among Masons. So help me God!"

The anonymous writer of the letter to the editor had copied a portion of Samuel Pritchard's *Masonry Dissected* printed in England beginning in 1730. Several printings followed rapidly after the first. So, the writer wasn't being truthful; he knew the "secrets" of Freemasonry. He also knew there were, and are, no secrets.

The next known article in the New York *Gazette* appeared on January 22, 1739:

Brethren of the Ancient and Honorable Society of Free and Accepted Masons are desired to take notice that the Lodge for the future will be held at the Montgomerie Arms Tavern on the first and third Wednesdays of every month. By order of the Grand Master.

CHARLES WOOD, Secretary.

Another notice appeared on September 24, 1739, for a meeting to be held in the same tavern. Nothing further is known about Freemasonry in New York until 1753. On June 9 of that year George Harison was appointed Provincial Grand Master. He lost no time in "setting the Craft to work" as this announcement in the New York *Mercury* notes:

> The members of the Provincial Grand Lodge of Free and Accepted Masons in New York, are desired to meet at the Kings Arms Tavern, on Wednesday, the 19th of December, on business of importance. By order of the Grand Master.
>
> H. GAINE, Secretary.

The proceedings of the meeting for the Festival of St. John the Evangelist were recorded and published by the *Mercury* on December 31, 1753:

> On Thursday last a Grand Lodge of the Ancient and Worshipful Fraternity of Free and Accepted Masons, a Commission from the Honorable John Proby, Baron of Craysfort, in the Kingdom of Ireland, Grand Master of England, appointed George Harison, Esquire, to be Provincial Grand Master, was solemnly published, we hear, to the universal satisfaction of all the brethren present, after which, it being the festival of St. John the Evangelist, service at Trinity Church. The order to which they proceeded was as follows:
>
> First walked the Sword Bearer, carrying a drawn sword; then four stewards with White Maces, followed by the Treasurer and Secretary, who bore each a crimson damask cushion, on which lay a gilt Bible, and the Book of Constitution; after these came the Grand Wardens and Wardens; then came the Grand Master himself, bearing a trunchion and other badge of his office, followed by the rest of the brotherhood, according to their respective ranks—Masters, Fellow Crafts and 'Prentices, to about the number of Fifty, all clothed with their jewels, aprons, white gloves and stockings. The whole ceremony was conducted with the utmost decorum, under a discharge of guns from some vessels in the harbor, and made a genteel appearance.
>
> We hear they afterwards conferred a generous donation of fifteen pounds from the public stock of the Society to be expended in clothing for the poor children belonging to our charity school; and made a handsome private contribution for the relief of indigent prisoners. In the

evening, by the particular request of the brethren, a comedy, called "The Conscious Lovers," was presented in the Theatre in Nassau Street to a very crowded audience. Several pieces of vocal music, in praise of the Fraternity, were performed between the acts. An epilogue suitable to the occasion, was pronounced by Mrs. Hallam, with all grace of gesture, and propriety of execution, and met with universal and loud applause.

Query: Whether the performance of public and private acts of beneficence, such as feeding the hungry and clothing the naked, be most correspondent to the Genius of Christianity, or to the Institution of the Prince of Darkness?

Lang gives Harison credit for the growth of Freemasonry during the time he was Provincial Grand Master. He notes that the *Mercury* covered the Festival in 1758. The Festival of 1767 involved St. John's, Trinity, Union, and King Solomon's Lodges. Trinity Church was the cite. The New York *Gazette* carried this account on January 2, 1768:

On Tuesday last being St. John's Day, by desire of His Excellency, Sir Henry Moore, a Charity Sermon was preached at Trinity Church, in this city. The Rev. Dr. Auchmuty, Rector of Trinity delivered a most excellent discourse upon the occasion, to a polite and numerous audience. Several Lodges of the Ancient and Honorable Society of Free and Accepted Masons, properly decorated, attended divine worship. The collection was very considerable, the Members of Hiram Lodge alone contributed one hundred pounds—a considerable relief at this inclement season to the poor of this City, many of whom have been in the greatest distress.

Sir John Johnson succeeded Harison. Although he was appointed in 1767, he wasn't installed until 1771. He only warranted one Lodge, St. George's at Schenectady, and that on September 14, 1774. "Sir John being a Tory of the Tories, he appointed Dr. Peter Middleton, Deputy Grand Master, and devoted his energies to the Royalist cause."

Middleton issued two warrants: to St. John's Regimental and Military Union. The latter was American Union Lodge which Middleton wouldn't let operate in New York except under his warrant!

The St. John's Lodge was warranted as No. 2 in 1757, but it's now No. 1. This is the Lodge that provided the Bible for the oath of office for the first President of the United States. Union Lodge was in existence in 1767, but how much earlier is not known. Robert R. Livingston was Worshipful Master of this Lodge in 1771. On April 18, 1771, he constituted Solomon's Lodge as acting Grand Master by authority of Harison.

No. 2 on the roster of New York is Independent Royal Arch Lodge. It was warranted by Harison on December 15, 1760. Harison issued a warrant on February 17, 1769, according to Lang, for King David's Lodge in New York City. He notes that Moses M. Hays was the first Master, and the Lodge was composed "entirely of Jewish Brethren." The warrant and Lodge transferred to Newport, Rhode Island. It was one of the lodges that greeted President Washington in 1790, and received a reply from him to its welcome.

"The records of the Lodges constituted in the State, above the Harlem River," wrote Lang, "are far more satisfying than those of the Lodges in the City of New York." He records four of these as having survived the war: Mount Vernon, No. 3, at Albany, which had been Union No. 1; St. Patrick's No. 4 at Johnstown; Master's No. 5 at Albany; and St. George's No. 6 at Schenectady.

Mount Vernon Lodge claims it is the oldest Lodge in New York. Here's the reason: The Grand Lodge of Ireland chartered Lodge No. 74 in 1737 for the Second Battalion 1st Royals, First Regiment of Foot Guards. This battalion served in Nova Scotia, and moved to Albany in 1758. Many prominent men of Albany were initiated into Masonry by this Lodge. When it was ordered to other duty, it left a copy of its Irish warrant so the Masons in the area could continue work. The copy reads:

> We, the Master, Warden and Brethren of a Lodge of Free and Accepted Masons, No. 74, Registry of Ireland, held in the second Battalion Royal, adorned with all the honor, and assembled in due form, Do hereby declare, certify and attest, that Whereas, our body is very numerous by the addition of many new members, merchants and

inhabitants of the city of Albany, they having earnestly requested and besought us to enable them to hold a Lodge
during the absence from them and we knowing them to be
men of undoubted reputation and men of skill and ability
in Masonry, and desirous to promote the welfare of the
Craft: We have, therefore by unanimous consent and
agreement, given them an exact copy of our Warrant as
above, and have properly installed Mr. Richard Cartright,
Mr. Henry Bostwick and Mr. Wm. Ferguson, as Assistant
Master and Wardens of our body, allowing them to set and
act during our absence, or until they, by our assistance,
can procure a separate WARRANT for themselves from
the GRAND LODGE IN IRELAND.

Given under our hands and seal of our Lodge in the City
of Albany, the eleventh day of April, in the year of
MASONRY, 5759, and in the year of our LORD GOD
1759.

JOHN STEADMAN, *Secretary*
ANIAS SUTHERLAND, *Master*
CHARLES CALDER, *Senior Warden*
THOMAS PARKER, *Junior Warden*

The Lodge continued to work, according to Lang, under this
document until February 21, 1765. It then received a warrant
from Harison and became Union Lodge No. 1. It wasn't until
January 6, 1807, that this Lodge became Mount Vernon Lodge
No. 3 on the roster of the Grand Lodge of New York.

With the end of the War for American Independence came
problems in an attempt to form an independent Grand Lodge
in New York. The "Antients," or as Lang preferred to call it, the
"Atholl Grand Lodge," had gained control of Masonry. Lodge
No. 169 of "Antient York Masons" followed the British Military
forces from Boston to New York. It called a convention of the
Lodge on January 23, 1781. Twenty-nine representatives from
seven lodges attended. The convention became a Grand Lodge,
and the Reverend William Walter was elected Grand Master.
The act was sanctioned by the "Ancient" Grand Lodge, with
"the Most Noble Prince, John, Duke of Atholl," Grand Master,
proclaiming "the New Lodge duly constituted, No. 215." But it
was still considered a Provincial Grand Lodge.

At the first meeting held on December 5, 1782, the "Lodges which were represented surrendered their warrants and received them again as coming from the Provincial Grand Lodge of New York."

The Grand Lodge adopted a peculiar resolution on January 3, 1783:

> A Modern Master Mason, known to be such, may be healed and admitted into the mysteries of the Ancient Craft, in the manner determined upon this evening, and that the same be recommended to the several Lodges under this jurisdiction, of which the several Masters and Wardens present, are desired perfectly to understand, and communicate the same to their respective Lodges.

With the end of the war, the British and their sympathizers left New York. With them went Grand Master Walter. During a meeting on February 4, 1784, Robert R. Livingston, Chancellor of the State of New York, was elected Grand Master. The Atholl Provincial Grand Lodge had seen its final days.

The new Grand Master called an emergency meeting on June 2, 1784. His goal was to bring "Moderns" and "Ancients" under the same banner. And he succeeded! Even so, harmony didn't prevail.

The "country lodges" were unhappy about the numbering of the lodges. They were also unhappy because all but one of the Grand Lodge officers were "city Masons." St. John's Lodge wanted the rank to be reevaluated. This was referred to a committee. But the Grand Lodge determined that "No Lodge can exist in this state but under the jurisdiction of the Grand Lodge." Lodge No. 210 decided it wasn't going to become a part of the Grand Lodge until it heard from the Grand Lodge of England as to the legality of the Grand Lodge of New York.

Prompt and emphatic was the reply:

> That the dues of Lodge No. 210 be paid in twenty days and they acknowledge the supremecy of this Grand Lodge, otherwise have their names erased from the books and be reported to the different lodges in the state.

"The independence and supremacy of the Grand Lodge was settled," wrote Lang. The Lodge paid its dues! And on September 3, 1788, the seal was ordered changed to read "Grand Lodge of New York."

But the rivalry between the "country" and "city" lodges would continue. While this wasn't confined merely to New York, it did lead to a more violent clash here. In 1823 the "city" lodges broke away and formed another Grand Lodge. About 100 "country" lodges remained loyal to the lawful Grand Lodge; about 31 "city" lodges continued their rebellion.

Finally, on June 6, 1827, they reunited, and on the 7th there was an enthusiastic meeting with Stephen Van Rensselaer being elected Grand Master. The name was changed to "The Grand Lodge of the Most Ancient and Honorable Fraternity of Free Masons of the State of New York."

Eleven

RHODE ISLAND, CONNECTICUT, NEW HAMPSHIRE

A MASON named J. L. Gould, of Connecticut, wrote in 1868, in a "Guide to the Chapter": "The earliest account of the introduction of Masonry into the United States is the history of a Lodge organized in Rhode Island, A.D. 1658, or fifty-nine years before the Revival in England, and seventy-five years before the establishment of the first Lodge in Massachusetts."

Gould used as his source Reverend Edward Peterson's *History of Rhode Island*, published in 1853, which had this account:

> In the spring of 1658, Mordecai Campennell, Moses Peckeckol, Levi, and others, in all fifteen families, arrived at Newport, from Holland. They brought with them the three first degrees of Masonry, and worked them in the house of Campennell, and continued to do so, they and their successors, to the year 1742.

This account came from a scrap of paper found in the garret of Hannah Hull, a distant relative of Gould's, after she had died in 1839. Gould quoted the dilapidated paper as reading: "Ths ye" (day and month not readable) 165 (6 or 8) "Wee met att ye House off Mordecai Campunall and affter Synagog Wee gave Abm Moses the degrees of Maconrie."

At least this "paper" didn't claim "the three degrees of Masonry" were conferred. As far as can be determined, there were two degrees, at most, prior to the Grand Lodge era. Unfortunately, this document couldn't be found. This caused Henry W. Rugg, D.D., in his *History of Freemasonry In Rhode Island*, to write:

Evidently no great reliance could be given to such a scrap of paper even were its genuineness assured. It lacks the support of corroborative evidence. In this connection the writer may mention the fact that he participated with Bros. W. S. Gardner and Thos. A. Doyle in a careful examination of this whole subject relating to the supposed establishment of Freemasonry in Newport about the middle of the seventeenth century, and that the results of this investigation gave absolutely no support to the tradition. It seems quite likely, reasoning inferentially, that in a thriving commerical town such as Newport was in the latter part of the seventeenth century and the early part of the eighteenth century, there should have been members of the Masonic Craft dwelling within its borders and included among its visitors. But this reasonable conjecture affords but slight support for the theory that Freemasonry was then and there organized—a Masonic Lodge established.

The first known lodge to come into existence in Rhode Island was St. John's at Newport. Thomas Oxnard, Provincial Grand Master of St. John's Provincial Grand Lodge of Massachusetts, or Boston, authorized the warrant on December 27, 1749. For some unknown reason the Worshipful Master of this Lodge withheld the warrant! The Lodge couldn't work. So, a second warrant was issued on May 14, 1753.

The Lodge was authorized to confer the first two degrees— only. But it ignored the limitation. As a result the Lodge was ordered to show cause for disobeying the law. Evidently its explanation was good, because it was granted a charter to hold a Masters' Lodge. This was granted on March 20, 1759. A Masters' Lodge wasn't formed. Evidently St. John's at Newport continued along the course it had adopted from the beginning and conferred all three degrees.

Jeremy Gridley issued a warrant for another St. John's Lodge, this one in Providence. It was issued on January 18, 1757. The warrant specified who was to be the Worshipful Master, and he was to take "special care in chusing Two Wardens and other Officers." They were charged to take "special Care that all and every member admitted into said Lodge from time to time have been or shall be made regular

Masons." They were to obey the regulations, Constitutions, and "other Rules and instructions as shall from time to time be transmitted them." They were to "send Two Guineas for their Constitution to be paid into the Stock of the Grand Lodge in Boston. And they were to "annually keep or Cause to be kept The Feast of St. John the Baptist and dine together on that day or near that day as shall be judged most Convenient."

"According to tradition," wrote Rugg, "St. John's Lodge of Newport held its meetings during the early period of its history in the Council Chamber of the Old State House, which on this account has a special claim to the regard of the Fraternity in Rhode Island."

St. John's in Providence met in private homes, The White Horse Tavern, The Two Crowns, and later in the Council Chamber of the State House.

Before the War for Independence, both lodges became dormant. Why is not known. But Rugg believes the members stayed in touch. His reason for his belief is summed up in this account:

> . . . But even at this time of an interregnum the bond of connection between brethren was not by any means devoid of vitality. This is proven by a single fact, well attested, viz., the participation of so considerable a number of Craftsmen in the destruction of the "Gaspee," June 8, 1772. Abraham Whipple, John Brown, Silas Talbot, John Mawney, Ephraim Bowen, John Bucklin, and others conspicuous in the volunteer force that boarded the British armed schooner and caused her destruction, were Masons. Abraham Whipple, the commander of the expedition, was afterwards a captain in the Continental navy, and did excellent service.
>
> The capture of the "Gaspee," though not in itself a great achievement, for the vessel, in its pursuit of the "Hannah," a schooner commanded by Capt. Benj. Lindsay, who refused to strike his flag and sumbit to an examination, had gone ashore on Namquit Point, when the descent of the Providence patriots was so much in the nature of a surprise that the crew of the "Gaspee" had no opportunity to discharge her heavy guns against the assailants.

Commander Duddington, however, did fire his pistols at the attacking party, one of whom responded with a musket shot, inflicting a wound upon Lieut. Duddington. Then a surrender was made; the crew set ashore, and vessel burned. The capture of the "Gaspee" has importance as being the first combat and interchange of shots between hostile forces representing the British Government and the American Colonies. That the Masons of Providence, under the leadership of the brave and patriotic Abraham Whipple, were promient in the affair, is not at all to their discredit, and may be referred to as evidence that they were in close and sympathetic touch as brethren even though their Lodge was then in a dormant condition.

In contrast to the affair that would turn Boston Harbor into a giant teapot a year later, the names of those taking part in the *Gaspee* affair were known and widely circulated. To this day no one knows for certain who comprised the "Mohawk Indians" who dumped the tea.

Governor Jabez Bowen, a member of the Providence Lodge, asked John Rowe, Provincial Grand Master in Massachusetts, for a dispensation to reopen the Lodge. Bowen was appointed Worshipful Master on June 15, 1778, and the Lodge resumed labor.

King David's Lodge arrived in Newport in 1780 under the leadership of Moses M. Hays. The earliest record of the Lodge is interesting:

"From the East Cometh Light"

Whereas we, Moses M. Hays Grand Elect Perft Sublime Dept. Inspector Gen'l of Masonry Prince of the East & & & by a warrant under the hand & seal of our truly and well beloved Brother George Harrison Esq. Grand Master & & & is authorized, empowered to form and establish a Lodge by the name of King David's Lodge, No. 1 & whereas we having found several true and lawful Brethren here desirous of becoming members thereof have accordingly convened for that purpose at a room convenient for holding a Lodge this evening, June 7th 1780 and in Masonry 5780, and after having appointed the following Brethren to the Office for this night affix to their respective names, Viz. Moses M. Hays, Master; Moses Seixas, Sen.

Warden; David Lopez, Jun. Warden; Jeremiah Clarke Treasurer; Henry Dayton Secretary; Solo. A. Myers, Deacon.

The Lodge was opened in due form after which the Master informed the Lodge that Robert Elliot; John Handy; Peleg Clarke and Daniel Box were Modern Masons, but were truly desirous to be Initiated into our Ancient Fraternity and that they were worthy thereof; they were all accordingly entered as Apprentices and afterwards passed to Fellow Craft.

June 10, 1780 Moses M. Hays elected Master. Brothers Robert Elliott, John Handy, Peleg Clarke and Daniel Box were raised to the Sublime Degree of Master Mason.

This turned out to be an illustrious group of Freemasons. Moses Hays later became Grand Master of Masons in Massachusetts. Moses Seixas and Peleg Clarke became Grand Masters in Rhode Island.

The Lodge in Providence prospered under the leadership of Jabez Bowen who was its Worshipful Master from 1778 to 1790. In the meantime, King David Lodge was active, but evidently concerned about the first Lodge in Newport. So, on September 20, 1790, King David's proposed:

> That a Committee be appointed to confer with the members of the First Lodge in Newport and to request them to revive their Lodge, when this Lodge will cease their existence and become members thereof; and when they acceded thereto to make immediate arrangements and cause measures to be taken accordingly for effecting the purpose without delay.

Moses Seixas was the instigator of this beautiful act of Brotherly Love. It's certainly an example the Freemasons of today could, and should, follow.

On October 19, 1790, the committee reported:

> . . . they have had the conference and in consequence thereof the said First Lodge of Free and Accepted Masons in Newport is this evening revived under full force and authority, and that they had unanimously declared the R. W. Master the Worshipful Wardens and all the members of this Lodge to be members of that Lodge to all intents and purposes whatsoever. Whereupon it is unanimously

voted and resolved that, for the sake of harmony and
Brotherly love, the Lodge shall cease its existence from the
closing of this present Lodge this evening, and that all
funds belonging to this lodge be placed into the First
Lodge of Free and Accepted Masons, on their engaging
that the business unfinished in this Lodge be completed by
that, agreeably to the arrangements made by this Lodge:
and futhermore that they guarantee and assume responsibility of all doings and transactions of this Lodge from
the date of its existence until its period this evening.

* * *

Business being completed with the utmost harmony and
Brotherly love and the Brethren infinitely happy at the
reflection that during existence of this Lodge discord never
showed its glimpse within its pales, but that all was Peace,
Friendship and Love, which belonging they wish may pervade and attend them, not only into the Lodge in which
they have consolidated themselves, but in all their social
enjoyments, and that in due time and properly clothed
they may be translated to the Heavenly Grand Lodge
where resideth the Sovereign Architect of the
Universe—Supreme Grand Master.

To add emphasis to the statement of this act of Brotherhood,
it should be noted there were but 11 members of St. John's
Lodge that absorbed 130 members of King David's Lodge.
Moses Seixas was elected Worshipful Master, and under his
guidance action was started to form a Grand Lodge.

The formation of the Grand Lodge took a strange twist. St.
John's Lodge in Newport and St. John's Lodge in Providence
agreed to the alternate election of Grand Lodge offices. The
first Grand Master was to come from Newport, the next from
Providence; the other officers were to be equally divided among
the counties involved. The Newport Lodge *elected* Chris
Champlin, Grand Master, along with other officers. The Providence Lodge *elected* its slate of officers.

Representatives of the two Lodges met in the State House in
Newport on June 27, 1791, it "being the day affixed on for the
celebration of the Feast of St. John the Baptist." Moses Seixas
presided and installed the *previously elected* Grand Lodge

officers. With the Grand Lodge organized, the members "marched in procession to Trinity Church." A collection was taken and it was ordered it "should be invested in wood, and distributed to the poor of this town during the ensuing winter."

"The Grand Lodge of the Most Ancient and Honorable Society of Free and Accepted Masons for the State of Rhode Island and Providence Plantations" had started its service to its State and country.

—CONNECTICUT—

Freemasonry was introduced into Connecticut by Massachusetts. St. John's Provincial Grand Lodge warranted Hiram Lodge in New Haven on August 12, 1750. This was the only Lodge in the Colony to be recorded on the roster of the Grand Lodge of England, "Moderns," where it was No. 143. David Wooster, who would become an outstanding patriot, was its first Worshipful Master.

The same Provincial Grand Lodge warranted several other lodges: one at New London, January 12, 1753; St. John's at Middletown, February 4, 1754; St. John's at Hartford, in 1762; Compass at Wallingford, April 28, 1769; St. Alban's at Guilford, July 10, 1771; and Union at Danbury, March 23, 1780.

Gould's *History* states that Waterbury Lodge was "put on its list" in 1765. No records remain of this Lodge except its Bylaws signed by 14 members, among them was Joel Clark, who would become the first Worshipful Master of American Union Lodge.

The same Provincial Grand Lodge chartered American Union Lodge on February 15, 1776. This Lodge remained active throughout the War for American Independence, even though many of its officers were lost in battle early in the fighting. The Lodge is still in existence! Jonathan Heart, its last military Worshipful Master, carried the charter of the Lodge to Fort Harmar, across from Marietta, Ohio, where he and his men had been sent to protect the settlers. Rufus Putnam, who had been made a Master Mason on September 9, 1779, in American Union Lodge, organized a committee to ask Heart to reopen the Lodge. He did! The first Masonic Lodge communication held in the Ohio Territory was opened on June 28, 1790. Heart was concerned about the legality of his move, but the Grand Lodges of Pennsylvania and Massachusetts assured him "Your warrant is, beyond doubt, a perfect and good one."

Gould also records: "George Harison, Provincial Grand Master of New York, under the Grand Lodge of England, chartered St. John's Lodge in Fairfield. . . in 1762; St. John's in Norwalk, May 23, 1765; Union Lodge at Greenwich, November 18, 1764, and St. John's, at Stratford, April 22, 1766.

Another source entered the picture. The Provincial Grand Lodge of Massachusetts ("Ancients") warranted Wooster Lodge at Colchester, January 12, 1781; St. Paul's at Litchfield, May 27, 1781; King Hiram at Derby, January 3, 1783; Montgomery at Salisbury, March 5, 1783; Columbia at Norwich, June 24, 1785; and Frederic at Farmington, September 18, 1787.

The "Moderns" and "Ancients" had "invaded" Connecticut in force. But there appears to have been no notice taken of this in Massachusetts, as Gould records:

> The history of the organization of Union Lodge in Danbury is curious, and shows how little division among the Massachusetts Masons was known beyond the limits of that State; the petition for that Lodge was addressed to Joseph Webb, then (January 5, 1780) Grand Master of Massachusetts Grand Lodge; it was recommended by Jonathan Hart [sic], then Master of American Union Lodge, chartered by St. John's Grand Lodge and by the Lodges at Fairfield and Norwalk both chartered by Harrison [sic] Provincial Grand Master of New York, under the Grand Lodge of England; the petition was in some manner transferred to Rowe, Grand Master of St. John's Grand Lodge, who granted the charter March 23, 1780. The Master was installed April 19, 1780, but the Lodge held a special meeting April 13, 1780, to act upon the petition of Dr. Josiah Barlett, in order that he might be initiated on the evening of the installation: Dr. Barlett afterward became a member of Massachusetts Grand Lodge, and was Grand Master of Massachusetts in 1797.

Again Gould emphasized the lack of interest in the prevailing differences in Massachusetts:

Nothing is found to indicate that any distinction between "Ancients" and "Moderns" was recognized, or even known. Of the Lodges forming the Grand Lodge, *eight* came from the Grand Lodge of England, and *four* from the Grand Lodge of Scotland, through Provincial Grand Masters or Grand Lodges appointed by, or springing from them, Hiram Lodge at New Haven being the only one that found a place on the English list; or, taking all the Lodges in the State at that time, *ten!* came from the old (not "Ancient") Grand Lodge of England, and *five* from the Grand Lodge of Scotland. Moreover, these lodges had met in convention, without discrimination, in 1783, over six years before the formation of the Grand Lodge.

James R. Case, writing in *Colonial Freemasonry,* said the Lodge at Fairfield appointed a committee in January, 1783, to write to the "Several Lodges in the State to Desire a Meeting." It wanted to discuss "Matters of Consequence," which Case assumes was the organization of a Grand Lodge.

The meeting was held in New Haven, not Fairfield. Many influential Masons "gathered about Pierpont Edwards, an ambitious lawyer, a rising politician, and a recent Master of the Lodge," Case wrote. A committee of three was appointed "to receive membership and black lists from the lodges, and to write the other states concerning the most proper measures for establishing a Grand Master for the Continent."

It's not known how many Grand Lodges were consulted, but New York replied. Case said it "recommended the election of a Grand Master and other Grand Lodge officers; suggested application to England for a charter; offered to recommend such an application, if the Connecticut grand officers elect could pass an examination in New York, or submit to receive instruction (!); and during the interim, New York promised 'every authority, support and instruction necessary and proper.'"

A special convention was called in January, 1784, at New Haven. Pierpont Edwards was unanimously elected Grand Master, and New York advised of the action. Then, James Case notes: "Here a curtain of silence descends and we grope in darkness for several years." He adds: "Possibly there was an element which objected to submission to the New York Grand Lodge. There was plenty of feeling between Yankee and Yorker."

Another convention was called and held at Hartford on May 14, 1789. A committee was named "to prepare a systematic plan for forming a Grand Lodge." Evidently it worked. The lodges met again on July 8, 1789. The Grand Lodge was "perfected."

James Case considers David Wooster the "Father of Freemasonry in Connecticut." He tells Wooster's story in *Freemasonry in Connecticut: Connecticut Masons in the American Revolution.*

Wooster was born on March 2, 1710/11. In his youth he became a successful businessman. Then, he decided to attend Yale College. (Name was changed to University in 1887.) He graduated in 1738, at the age of 28.

He returned to his business activities to have them interrupted by the War of Jenkins' Ear, 1741-43. Wooster was second in command of the Colony sloop, *Defense.* In 1742 he became Captain of the Colony's first war vessel. In 1745 he commanded a ship that carried prisoners of war from Louisbourg (Nova Scotia) to France. He spent some time in England and was commissioned a Captain in a regiment on the royal establishment to be raised in America.

Wooster's regiment was stationed at Louisbourg. While he was there a regiment arrived from Gibraltar carrying a Masonic charter. One of his fellow officers was Major Cadwallader, later Lord Blaney, and later Grand Master of Masons in England. Case notes that many New Englanders returned from Louisbourg as Masons, and could have been made Masons only there.

Wooster was empowered to form a lodge in Connecticut by St. John's Provincial Grand Lodge at Boston. The result was Hiram Lodge, now No. 1. He served as its Master for several years. From this beginning Freemasonry grew in Connecticut.

Long before the outbreak of hostilities with Great Britain he opposed the oppressive acts of Parliament. When the fighting began he was commissioned a Brigadier General and ordered to New York to observe the activities of the enemy. In September, 1775, Wooster marched with Major General Philip Schuyler into Canada. The Connecticut Yankee wasn't happy among the "Yorkers." The Canadian campaign was a disaster. Later, Wooster returned to Connecticut where he "was commissioned the first Major General of Connecticut forces in the field."

James Case relates the story of Wooster's final days:

> He was home in New Haven on leave in April, 1777, when a British fleet approached Compo Point and the alarm went out by signal fire, musket shot, church bell and mounted messenger. Arnold was also at home and the two generals rode stirrup to stirrup in pursuit of the raiders marching toward the supply depot at Danbury.
>
> Over night the British burned the military stores they found and a dozen or more houses in Danbury, and started the march back to their ships by way of Ridgefield. While Arnold dashed across country from Bethel to intercept the retreating column, Wooster was to overtake and harass the rear guard. He came up with them between Ridgebury and Ridgefield. Twice he led the attack, and as he turned to rally his men for the third and last time, he was shot down by a Tory sniper and carried off the field with a broken spine. For five days Dr. Philip Turner and Dr. John R. Watrous, among others, attended their dying Brother, but all efforts to save his life were in vain. He died on May 2nd, being laid to rest in the local cemetery, it was thought temporarily.

During the centennial of Hiram Lodge, Wooster's remains were reinterred in the Mount Moriah cemetery. A large Masonic monument identifies his final resting place.

—NEW HAMPSHIRE—

Six Freemasons signed a letter on February 5, 1735, requesting Henry Price, Provincial Grand Master of Massachusetts, to grant a warrant for a lodge in Portsmouth, New Hampshire. The petition was granted on June 24, 1735. Gould states: "Among its earlier Masters were John Sullivan, Hall Jackson, Nathaniel Adams, Thomas Thompson, Clement Storer, Edward Jennings (the first six Grand Masters of the

Grand Lodge), John Wentworth, Samuel Livermore and other leading men of their time, in the State."

Drummond, writing in Gould's *History*, is correct about the first six Grand Masters. But it took a special act to make John Sullivan one of its Worshipful Masters. On July 8, 1789, a convention met in Portsmouth for the purpose of forming a Grand Lodge. John Sullivan was elected Grand Master. The "President of the State of New Hampshire" accepted the office on July 16. It was discovered he hadn't served as a Worshipful Master. Although this would make no difference in some jurisdictions, it evidently did then in New Hampshire. St. John's Lodge agreed to elect him Master and did so on December 3, 1789. He was installed as Master on December 28; on April 8, 1790, he was installed as Grand Master.

There were, however, many interesting events that led up to this historic day. Many of them are briefly recorded in *Symbolic Freemasonry in New Hampshire* by Harry Morrison Cheney (1934).

Cheney records this from the *Proceedings* of Massachusetts dated June 24, 1735:

> About this time some Masons met at Portsmouth in the Province of New Hampshire who Pettition'd Our Rt. Worshl Grand Master Mr. Price for a Constitution to hold a Lodge there which he Granted, appointing The Rt. Worshl Bro. Mr. _____.
>
> In this year the Lodge was mov'd to the Royal Exchange Tavern in Kingstreet by Leave from the R. Worshl Grand Master for sufficient Reasons then advanc' by the Brethren.

An interesting notation is found in the same Proceedings which helps to explain discrepancies found in the early records of lodges and Grand Lodges:

> The imperfections in the Records as to Dispensations or Warrants are probably to be attributed to the fact that they were frequently granted by the Grand Master, in the interval between communications of the Grand Lodge, and no report made by him of such action. The date of the first mention in the Record is generally given, unless an earlier date has been obtained from some other reliable source.

It is doubtful that the officials in the early days of the Craft in the New World gave any consideration to dates. None of them could have envisioned the importance that would be placed on "firsts" in the ensuing years. None would have believed that dates, rather than action, would be given priority in Masonic history.

Until 1781 it appears that St. John's Lodge at Portsmouth was the only lodge in New Hampshire. But Gerald D. Foss, writing in *Colonial Masonry*, claims: "There is documentary evidence of a second lodge at work in colonial New Hampshire from 1749 to 1797." A letter dated November 14, 1797, from James Betton, is in the office of the Grand Lodge of New Hampshire. Betton "states that he came to New Hampshire in the year of Masonry 5749, that he applied to the Grand Lodge of the City of Belfast (Ireland) for permission to form Masonic lodges in the colonies, and that it authorized him by 'Warrant or Letters Patent, upon Meeting two or more brethren to form a lodge, and admit other good men into Society with us...' He says he found other good men in Windham, New Hampshire, and proceeded to form a lodge in that town." He applied to the Grand Lodge at Boston in 1752, but no reply has been found. Betton and others applied for, and received, a charter for a lodge at Windham on January 4, 1792. But the lodge was never constituted.

St. Patrick's No. 14 was authorized by the Scottish Grand Lodge of Massachusetts in 1781. It had received a petition dated March 17, 1780, from some members of St. John's Lodge. There is no evidence that it ever worked.

Also, in 1781 Vermont Lodge was warranted by Massachusetts, but it was for Vermont and not New Hampshire! The Lodge, however, met in Charleston, New Hampshire, on the other side of the Connecticut River. In spite of the turmoil over boundaries, which even President Washington had to negotiate to prevent a war, the Lodge met in New Hampshire until 1788. Many men from both sides of the river were members. On February 22, 1788, a new charter was granted for Faithful Lodge in New Hampshire. It is now No. 12 at Charlestown.

Massachusetts granted a warrant for Rising Sun Lodge at Keene on March 5, 1784. It was in this Lodge that Thomas Smith Webb, often called the Father of the American System of Freemasonry, received his degrees. On December 24, 1790, he was made an Entered Apprentice; on the 27th, he received both the Fellowcraft and Master Mason degrees. Concerning this Lodge, Cheney wrote: "Pages 105, 106, 107, of the first volume of our proceedings, have no duplication, in the blunt and severe language used, in the report of a commission, visiting Keene, on September 18, and 19, 1805, to investigate charges of gross irregularities, meriting, as the report of the commission stated, severest reprehension and unbridled censure. Things were so bad that the Lodge could not survive, and on October 4, 1805, a part of the record reads: 'Resolved, That the Grand Secretary do now break the seal of the Rising Sun Lodge's Charter, and deface the signatures; which was accordingly done.' "

The Grand Lodge had trouble with another lodge. This one was Columbian No. 2 at Nottingham. A petition for the formation of the Lodge was received on April 28, 1790. It was granted and the Lodge constituted on August 2, 1792. On December 12, 1804, by a unanimous decision, "the Master, Master elect, Wardens and brethren of the Lodge" were "convicted of unmasonic conduct and misdemeanors, and the Lodge was expelled from all privileges, immunities, and rights, as a Lodge of Free and Accepted Masons."

An appeal was asked for, granted, and the decision upheld. A request in 1806 for a restoration of the charter was denied. On January 28, 1807, "The Grand Lodge ordered 'that the seal of the late Columbian Lodge's Charter be broken, and the signatures be defaced.' "

Fortunately, these lodges were the exception. And except for the period of the anti-Masonic furor of the 1830's. Freemasonry in New Hampshire prospered.

And New Hampshire can boast of having one of the nine Freemasons who signed the Declaration of Independence as a member. This is recorded in the minutes of St. John's Lodge for January 2, 1752:

At a Lodge held at Mr. James Stoutley, this 2d Jany 5752, being the first night of the Quarter, Mr. William Whipple Proposed & by Dispensation Balloted for & Unanimously Voted to be made a member of this society.

William Whipple had been serving in the Continental Congress since 1775 before he signed the Declaration of Independence. In 1778 he declined his reelection to the Congress because he had been commissioned a Brigadier General in 1777 and became active full time with the fighting forces. He was in the Battles of Saratoga and Stillwater, and participated with Sullivan in Rhode Island.

Whipple was born January 14, 1730, in Kittery, Maine, and before he was 21 commanded a ship engaged in the European, West India, and African trade. He abandoned the sea in 1759 and became a merchant in Portsmouth, New Hampshire. He became a Freemason when he was 21. He died November 28, 1785.

Twelve

THE PROVINCIAL
GRAND LODGES

—PENNSYLVANIA—

FOR almost 30 years the only progressive Provincial Grand Lodge in the New World was that of Massachusetts. Its counterpart in Pennsylvania warranted but four lodges during its existence as a "Modern" organization. In contrast, there were close to 30 warranted by Massachusetts before it ran into opposition from the "Ancients."

Pennsylvania ran into trouble early with anti-Masonic factions in the city of Philadelphia. It began with this item in the June 16, 1737, edition of the *Pennsylvania Gazette:*

> We hear that on Monday night last, some people, pretending to be *Free Masons*, got together in a cellar with a young man, who was desirous of being made one, and in the ceremonies, 'tis said, they threw some burning spirits upon him, either accidentally or to terrify him, which burnt him so that he was obliged to take his bed, and died this morning.

The newspaper had reported the facts honestly. The legitimate Grand Lodge officers stated in the same paper their outrage "in Behalf of all the Members of St. John's Lodge, at Philad'a, the Abhorrence of all true Brethren to such Practices in general, and their Innocence of this Fact in particular." Even so, this didn't stop those who hated Freemasonry, perhaps because they didn't understand its principles, from trying to destory the Craft. They succeeded in slowing its progress.

It was 1749 before the Freemasons of Philadelphia began to revive their earlier activity. Benjamin Franklin was appointed Provincial Grand Master on July 10, 1749, by Thomas Oxnard, who had been appointed "Provincial Grand Master of North America in 1743 by Viscount Dudley and Ward," according to *Grand Lodge 1717-1967*. Drummond credits Franklin with the rebirth of Freemasonry in Philadelphia.

"At the first Grand Lodge held under this deputation," writes Drummond, "September 5, 1749, Franklin appointed his Grand Officers, and 'at the same meeting a warrant was granted to James Pogreen and others to hold a Lodge in Philadelphia.' " And, he added: "The Lodge of 1749 seems therefore not to have been a new creation, but a revival of the body over which Allen presided in 1731, and if such was the case, Franklin himself, in both instances, Grand Lodge and Lodge, served as the conduit pipe through which his anxiously sought 'authority from home' was derived."

Then there was a strange twist: "Meetings of the Prov. Grand Lodge, were regularly held until March 13, 1750, when William Allen, recorder of Philadelphia, presented a patent signed by Lord Byron, G.M. of England, appointing him Provincial Grand Master, which was duly recognized, and he then nominated Benjamin Franklin as his Deputy."

Ronald E. Heaton, writing in *Colonial Masonry*, doesn't mention Franklin as Provincial Grand Master in 1749. He writes: "The independent Grand Lodge of Pennsylvania of 1730 or earlier, 'Modern,' became a Provincial Grand Lodge of England on March 13, 1749-50, when Lord Byron, Grand Master of England, deputized William Allen Provincial Grand Master for Pennsylvania."

In a rather lengthy (for the English Grand Lodge history on Freemasonry in the New World) article on Pennsylvania, *Grand Lodge* says:

> A Patent of Appointment as P.G.M. of New York, New Jersey, and Pennsylvania was granted to Daniel Coxe in 1730. Coxe appears in the Return made in 1730 of the Lodge at the Devil Tavern within Temple Bar. The full

text of his Patent follows the Minutes of the meeting of Grand Lodge held on 21 April 1730. The appointment was for two years, and the election of a P.G.M. every other year was authorized. There is no evidence that Coxe exercised his authority. He attended Grand Lodge on 29 January 1731. He died in 1739.

William Allen was appointed P.G.M. of Pennsylvania in 1749, though presumably he had been elected in 1732 under the authority of Coxe's Patent, for he presided at a meeting of the P.G.L. in that year. Lodge No. 4 of this Modern P. G.L. applied to the Antients for a Warrant which was issued in 1758 with the No. 69. The Brethren of Lodge No. 69 then applied to the Antients for a Warrant to establish a P.G.L. This was granted by the Earl of Blessington by the issue of Warrant No. 89 in 1761. The Warrant was captured at sea by the French, a second Warrant was lost at sea, but a third dated 20 June 1764 reached Pennsylvania, and under its authority William Ball was installed as P.G.M. It was a very active P.G.L. Forty-eight Lodges are known to have been formed by it, and with its growth the Modern P. G. L. disappeared. In 1786, following the Revolution, the P. G. L. declared its independence, and the notation "Closed for ever" appears on the English Register against the No. 89.

Until it formed an independent Grand Lodge in 1786, Pennsylvania had two distinct bodies. The "Modern" group, however, was practically powerless after the "Ancients" entered the Colony. In this case the "Moderns" made a drastic mistake. So did the same body in Massachusetts.

The members of Lodge No. 4 found the "Ancient" ritual to their liking, so they adopted it. The Provincial Grand Lodge disapproved, and No. 4 was ordered to change its ways. It refused. Its warrant was revoked. The officers of No. 4 applied to the "Ancient" Grand Lodge in London for a charter. It was granted on June 7, 1758, and became No. 1 in Pennsylvania; No. 69 in England. It severed relationships with the Provincial Grand Lodge in Pennsylvania, and the other three lodges.

No. 1 then asked for a warrant for a Provincial Grand Lodge. This was approved on July 15, 1761. Lodge No. 1 became

Tun Tavern

The old Philadelphia tavern, in which the first Lodge of Freemasons was organized in North America.

Lodge No. 2, giving the Provincial Grand Lodge its original number. And from the beginning it was aggressive. Before the independent Grand Lodge was formed it warranted fifty-five lodges; eight of them Military lodges.

To the "Modern" Provincial Grand Lodge must go the credit for keeping Freemasonry alive in the Colony. But, actually, until 1751 there was no such thing as rival Grand Lodges in England. The first Lodge was St. John's which actually started work as early as 1731. The second Lodge has records beginning on December 27, 1749. "Tun Tavern Lodge" (named for its early meeting place) is known to have worked from June 28, 1749. Heaton notes that its members were composed of "seafaring and transient men, and included only a few prominent individuals, in contrast to the membership of St. John's Lodge."

Then came Lodge No. 4. William Allen, Provincial Grand Master of Pennsylvania, granted it a warrant on June 24, 1757. When this Lodge became "Ancient" and then a Provincial Grand Lodge, William Ball was *elected* Provincial Grand Master. This took place on February 12, 1760, and he served until 1782. William Adcock followed him and served until the formation of the independent Grand Lodge, when, on September 26, 1786, he was elected the first Grand Master for "The Grand Lodge of Pennsylvania, and Masonic Jurisdictions thereunto belonging."

—MASSACHUSETTS—

The Provincial Grand Lodge of Massachusetts was formed in 1733 in Boston by Henry Price. Unlike the Patent for Daniel Coxe, there was no record made in England of one for Price. No original copy of his Patent has been seen, only copies at second hand, but Melvin Johnson, who was a strong advocate of protocol in every other instance, brushes this aside:

> It has been urged that there is no account of Price's Deputation in the records of the Grand Lodge of England for 1733, and that, therefore, it was not voted by the Grand Lodge. It certainly was not voted by the Grand Lodge, for according to the regulations it was the Warrant of the Grand Master that was a deputation in those days, not a Charter or other instrument from a Grand Lodge.

Concerning Massachusetts, *Grand Lodge 1717-1967* commented:

> Henry Price was appointed P.G.M. of New England in 1733. He was born in England, a tailor by trade, and went to Boston in 1723, when he was about twenty-six years of age.
>
> Price was succeeded by Robert Tomlinson, who received a Patent of Appointment in 1736. Tomlinson was in England in 1738, and attended Grand Lodge on 31 January 1739. He died the following year, and Price assumed the office until 1743 when Thomas Oxnard was appointed P. G. M. of North America by Viscount Dudley and Ward. Oxnard served until his death in 1754, when Price again assumed office.
>
> Jeremy Gridley was appointed P.G.M. for North America in 1755, and held the office until his death in 1767, when once again Price assumed the office until John Rowe was appointed and installed in 1768. Rowe held the office until his death in 1787.
>
> The Grand Lodge of Antient Masons was formed in 1769, and Joseph Warren, who a few months previously had received a Commission from the Grand Lodge of Scotland appointing him Grand Master of Masons in Boston, was elected Grand Master. He was killed at the Battle of Bunker Hill in 1775. Following the evacuation of Boston in the spring of 1776, his body was exhumed and given a more fitting burial by the Grand Lodge on 8 April 1776. Joseph Webb was elected Grand Master in 1777, and he held office until 1782 when John Warren, a brother of Joseph Warren, was elected.
>
> In 1782 the P. G. L. declared itself 'free and independent... of any other Grand Lodge, or Grand Master in the universe.'

It makes little difference how Price's deputation came into being; he did an excellent job in promoting Freemasonry. He formed a Provincial Grand Lodge in Boston on July 30, 1733. On the same day, it appears, he authorized the formation of the First Lodge in Boston meeting at the "Sign of the Bunch of Grapes in King Street Boston, N. ENGLd." This became the second known lodge in the New World. It would remain an active spearhead for the Craft in Massachusetts.

A second lodge was organized on December 22, 1738, and named "Masters Lodge." Tatsch speculates as to what purpose this Lodge was formed. Drummond states Henry Price was its first Master and "in the first Lodge only two degrees were conferred, the third not being given in it until 1794." Johnson doesn't say why it was formed. John M. Sherman and Edwin G. Sanford, writing in *Colonial Freemasonry*, are explicit:

> On December 22, 1738, a second lodge was organized and constituted in Boston, under the name of the "Master's Lodge," with R. W. Bro. Henry Price as its first Master. This lodge had the exclusive right to confer the Master Mason degree, and its By-Laws included the statement that "no brother dwelling in this Town (is) to be admitted in this Lodge unless he be a member of one or more Regular Lodge or Lodges in this Town." The By-Laws were adopted January 2, 1738-39, and the first candidate, Brother George Moncrieff, was examined on the Fellowcraft Degree, "and being found a good Fellow-Craft to the satisfaction of the Lodge was unanimously voted in and paid 30/ for entrance and quarteridge."

The Second Lodge in Boston (actually the third, but evidently "Master's" didn't count) was organized on February 15, 1749 (or 1750, depending on which calendar is considered). It met at the Royal Exchange Tavern. Another lodge was formed less than a month later that was meeting at the White Horse Tavern, and Henry Price was appointed its Worshipful Master, but little is known about it.

During its life this Provincial Grand Lodge warranted over 40 lodges, according to Drummond. Their locations ranged widely: South Carolina, North Carolina, New Jersey, Pennsylvania, Connecticut, Rhode Island, Maryland, Nova Scotia, Quebec, Virginia, West Indies, Newfoundland, all taken by Drummond from "the official records of the G. L. of Massachusetts."

In addition, three Military lodges were warranted: the 28th Foot at Louisburgh in 1758; Crown Point, Provincial Troops, in 1764; and the most famous of all, and still in existence, American Union in 1776 (now No. 1 on the roster of the Grand Lodge of Ohio).

All went smoothly during the first 20 years for the Provincial Grand Lodge of Massachusetts. Then, in 1752 "a lodge of unknown composition" was organized and met at the Green Dragon Tavern. In 1754 it asked for a warrant from the Grand Lodge of Scotland, which was granted on November 30, 1756, but wasn't issued until 1760. In the meantime a Past Master of the Green Dragon Tavern Lodge asked the Provincial Grand Lodge in Massachusetts for recognition. Like its counterpart in Pennsylvania, it made the mistake of refusing the request.

St. Andrew's ["Ancients"] was the name of the lodge meeting in the Green Dragon Tavern. It didn't object to "Modern" Masons visiting it, in fact, it accepted several of them as affiliate members. The "Moderns"(St. John's Grand Lodge) however, wouldn't let the "Ancients" visit. Their members were even forbidden to visit St. Andrew's.

The death of Provincial Grand Master Jeremy Gridley eased the antagonism for a time. Sherman and Sanford tell the story:

> Provincial Grand Master Gridley died in 1767. A long and impressive Masonic funeral procession marched to the church, and St. Andrew's Lodge took part by special permission. The Tyler and Stewards of St. Andrew's Lodge headed the procession followed by the members of that Lodge, the Grand Stewards, the members of the First, Second and Master's Lodge (the Third Lodge having expired), the officers of St. Andrew's Lodge, the officers of the other lodges, Past Grand Officers, the Deputy Grand Master and Grand Wardens, the Grand Tyler carrying the late Grand Master's jewel on a black cushion, and finally, the hearse, followed by the general public. One hundred sixty-one Masons took part. All were Masonically clothed, and wore their jewels of office. After the funeral, St. Andrew's Lodge reverted to its former status. Its members were still excluded from the older lodges. Henry Price again assumed the Chair until Deputy Grand Master John Rowe was confirmed as Provincial Grand Master in 1768.

The same writers explain the twelve year silence in the records of the older Provincial Grand Lodge:

> The reason for the hiatus in the records of St. John's Grand Lodge has now become clear. The Grand Secretary

at the time was Thomas Brown. He was also Secretary of the Second Lodge in Boston. His last record of the Second Lodge is dated February 16, 1775. Brother Brown remained shut up in Boston during the British occupation. After the evacuation of the town in 1776, Brother Brown, who was a Tory, sought refuge in Halifax, Nova Scotia, taking with him the record books and other Masonic property then in his possession. Grand Master Rowe wrote to Brother Brown on August 20, 1784, requesting that he return the records, and he replied on October 18 requesting compensation for the same. But it was not until late in 1797 that these records were received, which was after the death of Brother Rowe.

An outstanding Mason was appointed by the Grand Lodge of Scotland on November 14, 1757, as "Provincial Grand Master for North America and the West Indies under Scotland." He was Colonel John Young. Young had served as Deputy Grand Master of the Grand Lodge of Scotland from its inception in 1736 until 1751. Sherman and Sanford speak of Young:

> Colonel Young had been Major in the American Regi-ment in 1751, and on April 26 was appointed Brevet Lieutenant Colonel, with promise of being Lieutenant Governor of Virginia. In 1758 he commanded the 2nd Bat-talion of the 60th Regiment at the siege of Louisbourg and was appointed Lieutenant Colonel of his Regiment, with the rank of Colonel in America, on June 26, and in the campaign against Quebec in 1759, he was made Comman-dant of the 3rd Battalion. On the reduction of that city he was appointed Judge of the Police, an office in which he acquitted himself with honor. On March 20, 1761, he ex-changed into the 46th Foot, which sailed for Barbados in October, and took part in the capture of Martinique, Grenada, St. Lucia, St. Vincent and Havana. Young's name appears in the Army list for 1762 as Lieutenant Col-onel commanding the regiment, but he died in November of that year. This left the lodges in North America under the Grand Lodge of Scotland without a Provincial Grand Master at their head.

The members of St. Andrew's Lodge were unhappy with the manner in which they were being treated by the members of St. John's Grand Lodge. They decided it was time for the "An-cients" to have a Provincial Grand Lodge of their own. Unlike

St. John's, they didn't consider one lodge capable of legally forming such a Grand Lodge. So, they enlisted the aid of three others.

The others were regimental lodges: No. 58, "Ancient," in the 14th Foot; No. 322, Irish, in the 29th Foot; and No. 106, Scots, in the 64th Foot. A petition from these lodges, plus St. Andrew's, was sent to Scotland. On May 30, 1769, their petition was granted and Dr. Joseph Warren became the Provincial Grand Master. For the installation ceremonies held on December 27, Nos. 58 and 322 were represented; No. 106 had left Boston. By 1770 these two Military lodges had also been sent elsewhere. St. Andrew's Lodge *was* the Provincial Grand Lodge. Warren was appointed by George Earl Dalhousie Grand Master of Masons of Scotland as Grand Master of Masons for the Continent of America on March 27, 1773. He was the only man to ever hold such a far-reaching title.

With the death of Joseph Warren during the Battle of Bunker (Breed's) Hill, the office of the Scottish "Grand Master for the Continent of America" became vacant. His deputy, Joseph Webb, assumed the office, but didn't believe he inherited Warren's prerogatives. This was discussed at length. It was finally determined to bring representatives of all the lodges together. This was attempted on March 7, 1777.

The meeting was adjourned until the next day. Even so, only eleven Masons were present, among them only one Worshipful Master of a lodge. But they proceeded to elect Joseph Webb Grand Master "'till Friday June next." Drummond states: "Thus was formed the first sovereign Grand Lodge in this country."

Sherman and Sanford take a different view, yet they base what they wrote in *Colonial Freemasonry* on Drummond's account in Gould's *History:*

> . . . It has often been stated that Massachusetts Grand Lodge declared its independence at this meeting, but there is no record of any such declaration at that time. It is true that they acted independently of their original sponsor, the Grand Master of Scotland, but that action was a mere

assumption for practical ends and might have well been intended for a temporary expedient until such time as the military and Masonic atmosphere had cleared. The fact that at this meeting the Grand Master was elected for only three months lends credence to this view.

Five years later a committee was appointed to check into the powers of the Grand Lodge. Sherman and Sanford continue the account:

> This committee reported at length on December 6, 1782, and it is in this report that the assumption of the powers and prerogatives of an independent Grand Lodge is admitted, and the independence of the Massachusetts Grand Lodge of Ancient Masons from any other Grand Lodge, or Grand Master in the Universe is claimed. Indeed, it was resolved that the action of the Grand Lodge in March, 1777, was warranted "by the Practice of Antient Masons in all Ages of the World."
>
> There are two conspicuous words in this report worthy of special attention: *assumption* and *antient*. The action in March, 1777, is unequivocally admitted to be an act of assumption, not new in the history of Masonry; and the Grand Lodge claims exclusive jurisdiction in the Commonwealth of Massachusetts over *Antient* Masons. As has been pointed out, the "modern" St. John's Lodge was still active in the Commonwealth.

Some members of St. Andrew's didn't like what was going on. On December 16, 1782, they voted to stay with Scotland. After the peace treaty was signed with England, another vote was taken on January 22, 1784. By a vote of 29 to 23, with Joseph Webb abstaining, the Lodge decided to remain loyal to Scotland. Even so, the Grand Lodge determined to remain in existence.

The dissenting members, headed by Paul Revere, asked Scotland for a warrant to form another St. Andrew's Lodge. It was granted. This was confusing, so the name was authorized to be changed to Rising States Lodge.

Attempts were made to bring about an understanding among the opposing factions. John Cutler of St. John's Grand Lodge was the spearhead for unity. He was finally successful! On

December 5, 1791, the Massachusetts Grand Lodge appointed a committee of seven "to Confer with the Officers of St. John's Grand Lodge, upon the subject of a Compleat MASONIC UNION throughout this COMMONWEALTH and that the said Committee report as soon as may be Convenient."

St. John's appointed a like committee on January 18, 1792. The committees did their job. St. John's Grand Lodge met at the Bunch of Grapes Tavern on March 5, 1792. It chose its electors, and "appointed the candidates for the designated offices." It was then "closed in Due Form." The Massachusetts Grand Lodge met at the same time in Concert Hall. It ordered all of its bills paid, and all records, papers, regalia, and furniture to be deliverd "to the *Grand Master Elect* agreeable to the Constitution." It chose its candidates for office. Then it "Voted that this Grand Lodge be Dissolved."

John Cutler was elected Grand Master of the now united Grand Lodge of Massachusetts.

Before the turn of the century, there was unity between the "Modern" and "Ancient" Freemasons in the New World. It would be 1813 before the Old World could make this claim.

Thirteen

FREEMASONRY ON THE FRONTIER

IT'S difficult in the latter part of the 20th Century to visualize conditions in the New World in the 18th Century. The country was sparsely settled, even in the cities along the bays, ocean, rivers, and streams which provided the only easy access to civilization. The forests came up to the edge of what few towns there were. The New World was a wilderness.

When Governor Dinwiddie of Virginia sent the young Master Mason George Washington to order the French to leave his colony, Washington had to hack his way to the Ohio country. On his return, with the French refusal tucked under his jacket, he met with bitter weather. On land the horses became too weak to carry packs, so Washington, against the advice of Christopher Gist, decided to push ahead on foot. To Gist's credit he went with the young man. Among the many horrors of the return trip was a fall by Washington into an ice-choked river. He spent the night on an island in the river in a soaked jacket that froze. Yet, he suffered no ill effects.

According to Washington's Diaries, Washington returned in early 1754 as second in command of "loose, idle persons that are quite destitute of House and Home; and...many of them of Cloaths." He fashioned new ways of warfare. No one knew the logistical questions of transport and supply for this type of undertaking. No one else had ever taken raw recruits into battle. No one before him had to solve these and the many other problems of wilderness warfare.

When the English General, Edward Braddock, arrived in Virginia with orders "to drive the French off the colony's frontier," Washington was chosen to act as his eyes and ears.

Into the wilderness marched Braddock, behind his large force chopping roads and paths for the army to follow. The going was rough. *G. Washington: Master Mason* tells something of what happened:

> At a rate of about two miles per day the English force moved toward Fort Duquesne. At Washington's suggestion, the General agreed to push ahead without the wagons. The faster coverage brought them to within 10 miles of the fort on July 7. On the 8th they crossed the water to be met by a French force of 900, which included more than 600 Indians.
>
> The English were butchered. Washington had two horses killed from under him as he was fighting, and four bullets tore his clothes. The whoops of the Indians, and the sight of their scalping knives, sent the regular troops into panic. They ran. Braddock was killed, but before he died he sent Washington to bring back Colonel Thomas Dunbar with reinforcements. But Dunbar destroyed his guns and wagons and retreated to Philadelphia to set up winter quarters—in August! Washington was horrified!

Did the English have to lose? Probably not, if Braddock had listened to advice sent by Benjamin Franklin through "Captain Jack." Hervey Allen, in his historical novel on frontier days, *Bedford Village*, tells a story that's more fact than fiction.

In early summer, 1755, a "sinister figure" emerged from the forest near Frederick, Maryland. He demanded to be taken to General Braddock. The blackened-faced frontiersman was taken to Colonel Washington, who introduced him to Braddock. "This is the man whose reputation I have enlarged to you, Sir," said Washington. "Far west of the mountains, which we soon hope to cross, the cries of Indian children are stilled by the syllables of his name." Then Washington left the two alone.

The frontiersman handed the general a letter from Benjamin Franklin who urged the British Commander "strongly to retain Captain Jack as the leader of advance rangers."

"So you wish to serve his Majesty?" asked a furious Braddock.

"You have read Mr. Franklin's letter," replied Jack, having trouble keeping his reply respectful.

Turning scarlet the general shouted, "I have, Sir!" He snatched up the letter and stormed out of the tent with Captain Jack following him. "And my reply is that his Majesty's troops can do without your eminent services, and still conquer for a' that——" and he furiously waved Franklin's letter in Jack's face.

"Farewell, Sir," and Jack turned and walked away.

Later Braddock told Sir Peter Halket, "My God, Halket, you'd think *I'd* been dismissed! I'll have to instruct Colonel Washington not to bring low characters like that to headquarters."

Halket shivered, "A portent; a grisly portent from the woods."

"Nonsense! Damned impudence!" And the general threw the letter into the fire before his tent. A month later he was dead; his army destroyed.

It should be noted that three of the central characters in this affair were Freemasons: George Washington, Benjamin Franklin, and Captain Jack.

Who was "Captain Jack?" Hervey Allen said his name was originally Fenwick, "either grandson or grandnephew of that Sir John Fenwick, who, in the reign of good King William, had lost his head on the block for his fanatical loyalty to the banished James."

The remaining Fenwicks had fled to the New World and "lost themselves" in the "forests amid the Alleghenies. When, and if, they reappeared it was under different names. So, the Fenwick in question, like many others before and after him, became several characters.

When he first came out of the forest he ended up in Philadelphia. There he became an assistant to a "surgeon-barber." They had a thriving business. And it must have been during this period he met Benjamin Franklin, but where he became a Freemason isn't known. It could have been in England or Philadelphia; Allen doesn't say.

Fenwick became "Dr. John Morton," and he studied his new profession. Then, during an outbreak of "ship's fever" his boss died. Morton continued the business, and people learned to love him. He "never bled any of his patients either of gold or of the liquid in their veins." He even did something never tried before; he trained widows to be nurses.

Gossip and nurses did him in! He married a girl named Mary Caldwell. Not long after the marriage his father-in-law became ill. Morton treated him with a harmless concoction, but he died. His daughter inherited a considerable fortune. Morton's nurses spread untruths about him. They ruined his reputation. His wife finally sold her property at a considerable loss, and they moved to Maryland.

In his new home Fenwick/Morton became Dr. Caldwell and prospered. A son and daughter were born. The family was happy. Then the docter left for Baltimore to purchase supplies. Two weeks later he returned to find his village in ruins. Not a single living creature met him. He later learned "drunken Hurons and five half-breed Frenchmen" had killed and destroyed everything. His wife had been hanged and burned; "what had been a little boy was shaped like an egg"; he found the remains of his little girl suspended over the fireplace.

How the insane Caldwell/Morton/Fenwick found his way back into the wilderness he never learned. But over a period of months his mind cleared. And from the day be became rational until almost the end of his life, he had one goal—the extermination of Indians. He became a genius. On the frontier he was dreaded by Indians and loved by Whites.

For several years he continued to fight alone. He trusted no one. But gradually he began to train a small group of young hunters and woodsmen who became his followers. They were "all sons of old settlers and tried frontiersmen whom Captain Jack knew. There was a decided element of secrecy about this 'forest brotherhood' of young men. All its members were Masons," wrote Allen, "or, 'sons of the widow'. All came of families who had been harrassed by the savages. All of them spent a time of probation in training with Captain Jack." Then Harvey Allen adds:

Whether there was a password among them is doubtful. That rumor seems to have arisen from the fact that most of them were Masons. The wisdom of keeping their plans and their deeds secret, and the reputation and personal authority of Captain Jack, were all that was necessary.

Yet some kind of organization there must have been. Colonel Bouquet contributed arms, powder, and rations at least once. He knew about the "Mountain Foxes," and so did Ecuyer. In Pontiac's war Captain Jack came to stay at Bedford, probably to be near his friend Garrett Pendergrass. For many years they had been associated in one scheme or another. Jack finally built himself a cabin, not far from Bedford. There he gathered his young Foxes about him from time to time. Part of this activity may have been for Masonic reasons. Masonry was then spreading along the frontier and both Captain jack and Garrett Pendergrass were furthering it.

The Grand Lodge of Pennsylvania sent an emissary to Bedford, according to Allen, to "organize the loose 'Blue Lodge' Masonry, prevalent along the frontier and in the back country." It was to be organized "into what was then called the 'Ancient Arch' where ties were more binding, selection more particular, and higher degrees could be conferred." Hervey Allen wasn't a Freemason and wasn't familiar with Masonic terminology. The "Ancient Arch" undoubtedly meant "Royal Arch."

The emissary "was to be assisted in this work by certain officers at the fort, who had a military or travelling lodge charter under a grant to the 17th Infantry. And he was, of course, being helped by Garrett and Captain Jack, who were both Masons of high degree."

What, if anything, did American Indians know about Freemasonry when the white man began to occupy the New World? There have been many conjectures. Hervey Allen supplies another.

Allen's historical novels are built around a young frontiersman named Salathiel Albine. Late in 1763 a fellow named Captain Yates was injured and confined to bed in a garrett room in Pendergrass' trading post. Salathiel visits Yates and tells him what's going on downstairs. He mentions some of the visitors:

"Anybody else?" asks Yates.

"A man by the name of Gladwin from Philadelphy, who seems thick as thieves with Garrett and Cap'n Jack. You know, one of *those* fellows."

"How do you mean?" demanded Yates.

"Oh, you know," said Salathiel, and he made a certain gesture in sign language.

"Now where the devil did you learn *that?*" exclaimed Yates, sitting up again suddenly, despite his bad back.

"From my Shawnee uncle Nymwha in a medicine lodge on the Ohio long ago," answered Salathiel. "But I didn't know the white men had it till I saw Ecuyer and Cap'n Jack talking together that day in the captain's room at the fort."

"A medicine lodge!" said Yates. "Well, I'll be damned! Now that is a new one. Either you are a very observin' man, my friend, or—"

"Or what?" demanded Salathiel.

"Oh—maybe the Injuns *are* the lost tribes of Israel," ended Yates cryptically.

"The Reverend James McArdle thought so," replied Salathiel.

"Did McArdle know the signs? This one?" asked Yates.

"Comin' to think of it, I guess he did," said Salathiel. "Now it never struck me before, but maybe that's why the medicine men let him alone to preach and to go around pretty much as he liked. Now that's curious, isn't it?"

"My friend," asked Yates very seriously, "did you ever hear of the Masons?"

"Masons? You mean stoneworkers, builders, the kind King Solomon borrowed from Hiram of Tyre to build the Temple—in the Bible, you know?"

Now it so happened that Salathiel could not have made a better answer by asking a question if he had tried a thousand years.

"I think," said Yates, "that we'll certainly have to talk this over together, and the sooner the better. Suppose you go down stairs now and ask Garrett and Captain Jack to come up here after dinner to sit with us in my room. Bring up my dinner yourself, Sal, if you don't mind. We don't want any women pokin' in. And you might ask Mr. Gladwin, too. Hurry now! Try to get them all before anybody steps out for the evening. Tell them it's important. It *is* important, Mr. Albine, for you."

And so it proved to be.

For when Salathiel went to bed that night, or rather early the next morning, he knew that all the masons were not the subjects of Hiram King of Tyre.

James Callowhill Gladwin, a Philadelphia merchant, was in Bedford at the urgent request of Garrett and Captain Jack. The "benign-looking, grey-haired old man" had "mounted his horse at Philadelphia and had ridden by Indian-haunted roads through deserted country to the extreme border settlement of Bedford in order to spread and establish the message of brotherhood," wrote Allen. The folks in Bedford "knew he had left a comfortable home and a profitable business to do so, and that the success of his mission could be his only possible reward. Therefore, to them, there was something 'worshipful' about him."

The men who dropped in to chat with Gladwin "were of the staunchest and most trustworthy, altogether the pillars of the community. And this in a similar way was true also of the officers from the fort, who in one way or another seemed involved in the stir of what was going on. There was Captain Lewis Ourry and Dr. Boyd. There was Major Cadwalader from the militia, and several officers from Captain James Smith's Black Boys, lieutenants and subalterns. . . Some of the noncommissioned officers and soldiers seemed also to be included."

Many of the young men in Bedford and the surrounding area were talked to on equal terms by the Masons. And it was being done for a purpose, according to Allen. The frontier was extremely dangerous. Indian attacks were still prevalent—"Scalps were frequently taken within a few miles of the fort by wandering war parties. As yet only the hardiest and bravest of the settlers dared to venture anywhere alone."

The Quaker government was inclined to do nothing. "The legislature at Philadelphia, mulishly disregarding the frantic pleas of the governor and the royal army officers to vote supplies for defense, had at last been compelled to look at a wagonload of scalped and mangled corpses riotously drawn through the streets of Philadelphia past the doors of the State

House. . . The combined prayers, curses, and beseechings of
Governor Penn, General Gage, and Benjamin Franklin,
together with the petitions of angry city gentlemen and the
shouts of gathering mobs, finally prevailed."

Allen adds: "But not notably.

"Hearing that Colonel Bouquet had 'borrowed' two hundred
Virginia riflemen from that province anyway, 'Friends abstained
from voting', and a thousand militia were authorized to assemble
at Carlisle in the spring of '64."

Hervey Allen believed it was because of the unsettled conditions prevailing that Captain Jack and Garrett Pendergrass had
asked for Masonic assistance:

> It was in this condition of external war and internal con-
> fusion that Garrett and Captain Jack had determined to
> revive and strengthen the Masonic bonds which held many
> men of orderly and moderate opinions together, so that
> they could co-operate in mutual good will and common
> sense.
>
> It was not that Garrett expected his fellow Masons to
> take direct action in this or that affair or instance. The
> lodges seldom did so. Their meetings provided rather a
> means and opportunity for the discussion of problems and
> the formation of influential opinion, a solemn free discus-
> sion under the protection of an oath of secrecy.
>
> If Captain Jack, Garrett Pendergrass, and others whose
> stake in the welfare of their community was more than
> usually considerable found their own interests best served
> by promoting peace, order, and good understanding
> amongst the more solid and thinking men of their
> neighbourhood—and if the lodges they cherished and
> organized tended to make property safer and the way of
> the transgressor hard, that is only to say that they mar-
> shalled public opinion effectively on *their* side, but also to
> the general benefit of everybody except rascals and rioters.
>
> As a matter of fact that is precisely what they were
> engaged in with the able assistance of Mr. James Gladwin,
> who had had long experience in planting and propagating
> Masonry along the frontiers and throughout the western
> settlements of the old Pennsylvania border. Like other mis-
> sionaries, he was devoted to the gospel he preached and
> propagated. He had answered the call of his brethren to

come over into Macedonia and help. And he was quick to grasp the idea that, while the temporary concentration of population at Bedford brought difficulties, it also provided an unusually ripe field from which to garner grain. That prospect had in fact been the most telling argument in Garrett's letter to the brethren of the Grand Lodge at Philadelphia, asking for help.

It would appear that the solicitation of members was continued in those early days on the frontier, but that's not a fact. As Allen pointed out, Gladwin's "plan was to reorganize and straighten the Blue Lodges, or the 'Hill Lodges', as they were called at the time, because they usually met in the woods under open heaven, by starting meetings, by bringing scattered or detached Masons together, again."

His next statement would, again, make it appear that solicitation was sanctioned. They planned on "initiating a large number of new and younger men as far as the first three degrees. After the first work should be accomplished, Mr. Gladwin had in mind taking some of the more promising brethren farther along the path that led under the Ancient Arch." Even so, Allen claims, "There was no general or active solicitation. News of what was afoot was more carefully passed on from one responsible person to another. . . Not everyone was accepted. And the distinction and honour of being chosen for initiation had a telling effect."

The Lodge meetings and initiations took place in "Garrett's Garret." Throughout the winter months several Masons and young men who might become Freemasons worked in the garret. This garret had seen much use over the years. Travelers had often enjoyed the warmth from the chimney that "effectually blanketed the entire north end of the house." In "General Forbe's time some twenty-odd officers of the Virginia Line had used it quite comfortably as a dormitory."

Slowly, the garret was turned into a thing of beauty—a Masonic hall. A "panelled bench" ran "clear around three sides of the room. A low stage or platform was raised at the north end across the chimney, and on this dais was placed a wooden altar made to a design furnished by Mr. Gladwin. There were two smaller altars, or lecturns, situated opposite each other halfway down the room with a special chair behind them led into the bench. And there was also a simple but more massive chair set behind the altar on the platform." Allen continues his description:

> Mr. Gladwin produced from his kit several rolls of canvas, which proved to be oil paintings of mystical import. These, an all-seeing eye, apparently enraged by what it saw, a divine hand coming out of a cloud, grasping a compass, with a beam of light and a bolt of lightening, were hung above the platform and against the chimney face at the end of the room.
>
> But what was even more admired were three small pewter chandeliers, each containing a half dozen candles that, with due precaution against fire, Garrett had suspended on short chains from the rooftree, with tin reflectors above. The resulting illumination was truly astonishing and could only have been contrived in Philadelphia, whence the chandeliers had come.
>
> In addition to three lights about the altar, there was a seven-branch candlestick set on a special stand by the worshipful master's chair. . . .
>
> [The improvements] took many nights of long, hard labour and afternoons in the saw pit. Yet the improvement was great. The rough underside of the roof shingles was entirely concealed and the room given a smooth finished appearance, even an elegance, which completely bowled over all those who first thrust their heads up through the trap door and looked about them. Finally, the floor was painted with triangles for a border surrounding the main design, an expanse of black and white checker-board squares. . . .
>
> Instead of arriving in some rude loft, the new initiates would now seem to have been translated into the finished cavernlike abode of some powerful magician or spiritual personage, a being superior to and aloof from the wild nature without, and yet one who was always close by, lurking and immanent—for merely by ascending a garret stairs and coming through a trap door had they not found him and His worshippers at home? Only a missing password had been needed—and they had at last gained entrance to His very house.

What the Masonic work was like in the garret isn't explained by Hervey Allen. It appears the candidates spent long hours in preparation prior to their initiation. Older Masons explained the history of the Order and what was to be expected of them once they were Freemasons. On the evening seven were to be initiated, Garrett sat at dinner with them. "He told them he had been initiated when he was only eighteen at Colchester in England, according to the old York rite." And he added:

> "It is the most ancient rite of all, they say," he continued. "Some people think there has been a lodge at York ever since Constantine's time. Dr. Brandsford was a very learned man at Colchester in my day. He, it was who wrote a book about old King Cole and Queen Helena, and he was also a very high Mason. I once heard him tell my father he had seen Masonic carvings on old stones along the Tyne River, that went back into heathen times. I don't know. But what you are going to learn and see tonight is not new. It has held men together in brotherhood for ages past. All of them were not fools," smiled Garrett. "It is important we should keep on remembering in this new country what they knew at home."

Then one by one the sponsors took their candidates to the garret. "An hour later" each became "a Free and Accepted Mason."

The frontier wasn't only in Pennsylvania. As one New Englander claimed—it could be found anywhere beyond the Connecticut River. But even then it could be found east and north of the river. It was anywhere past the sites of easy access by the Atlantic, its bays, the rivers, and streams moving inland. From that part of Massachusetts, now Maine, to the Ohio River there was little but dense forests.

The spreading of Freemasonry in the New World can be attributed to Military lodges warranted by England, "Ancients" and "Moderns," Ireland, and Scotland. The warrant mentioned by Hervey Allen belonging to the 17th Infantry was No. 136 granted in 1748 by the Grand Ldoge of Ireland. There were many others. James Fairbairn Smith tells of another in his *Dateline 1764, Michigan Masonry.*

"Lodge No. 1 at Detroit was actually attached to the 60th or Royal American Foot Regiment of the British Army," writes Smith. It brought Masonry into the Northwest Territory, but it would be a century before it developed into a viable entity. However, George Harison, Provincial Grand Master of New York, issued a warrant on April 27, 1764, for Zion Lodge in Detroit.

Kentucky, a part of the Colony of Virginia, was separated from it by hundreds of miles of forest, dangerous streams, and a mountain chain that was almost impassable. Freemasons managed to conquer the wilderness and penetrated Cumberland Gap. Enough Masons resided in Lexington by 1788 for them to request a charter from the Grand Lodge of Virginia. It was granted to Lexington Lodge No. 25 on November 17, 1788. And Freemasonry began to flourish in Kentucky. In 1800 it formed an independent Grand Lodge.

It was a Military lodge that paved the way for Freemasonry in the wilds of Ohio. Settlers were trickling into the area of the Northwest Territory that would be called "Marietta." In 1785 a fort was built at the mouth of the Muskingum River to help protect them. With this protection at Fort Harmar other settlers arrived, among them several Freemasons. At the fort was Jonathan Heart, the last Worshipful Master of American Union Military Lodge. In his possession was the warrant for his Lodge. With but a little persuasion he reopened his Lodge. At its last meeting it had been closed only "to stand closed until the W. Master should call them together." This he did on June 28, 1790! Freemasonry was organized in the Northwest Territory.

The frontier moved slowly westward. As it did, so did Freemasonry. In many small settlements there could be found a little church, a little schoolhouse, and a little Masonic lodge.

Lawrence Greenleaf told the story of most of the latter in the well-known poem "The Lodge Room over Simpkins' Store.":

> The plainest Lodge room in the land was over Simpkins'
>   store,
> Where Friendship Lodge had met each month
>   For fifty years or more.
> When o'er the earth the moon, full orbed, had cast her
>   brightest beam,
> The Brethren came from miles around on horseback and
>   in teams,
> And O! what hearty grasp of hand, what welcome met
>   them there,
> As mingling with the waiting groups, they slowly mount
>   the stair.

Fourteen

A REPUBLIC IS FORMED

THE first attempt to colonize the New World occurred in 1585 when Sir Walter Raleigh founded a settlement on Roanoke Island in what he called "Virginia." A year later the colony was abandoned. But another group, including seventeen women, set up another colony. And Virginia Dare became the first English child born in the New World. When its governor returned in 1590 from England with supplies, he found the entire colony had disappeared without a trace.

In 1606 two companies were formed in England to establish settlements in Virginia. In December three ships left England for Virginia. Of the 144 passengers, only 105 disembarked in May 1607 at what was to become Jamestown. Under the command of Captain John Smith the small colony managed to survive. From this small band of men, good, bad, industrious, and lazy, grew the Colony of Virginia.

England was in dire straights after a war with Spain. This was one of the reasons it desired to colonize the New World. Unemployment was spreading; the population was growing. Something had to be done, but the resources of Great Britain were limited. It needed new sources for raw material, and it needed markets for its products. Although a precarious foothold had been established in Virginia, it would be thirteen years before an attempt was made to broaden this foothold.

This was encouraged by what was happening in Virginia. On July 30, 1619, a council met at Jamestown. It was composed of two representatives from each of the eleven settlements that had come into existence. This first representative assembly in the New World established statutes based on English common law.

Less than a year later another settlement came into existence in the New World. It was established by about 100 passengers from a small ship called the "Mayflower" and the settlement was Plymouth, Massachusetts in 1620. They had missed their original destination (Virginia). They never did receive a charter, and were swallowed up by Massachusetts Bay in 1691.

The ties with Great Britain in the American Colonies were close for over 150 years. Those who had fled to the New World for various reasons, couldn't, and didn't, completely divorce themselves from the Old World. Many of the customs were transferred to North America, even many that were considered repressive.

Freedom from repressive religion was what caused many of the earlier settlers to leave the Old World. After they had arrived in the New World and had gained control, some of the leaders became even more repressive. This was especially true in the Massachusetts Bay Colony. So much so that even if Freemasonry was known in the New World at the time, none could have been practiced under the climate then prevailing. And this gave birth to several new settlements in what would become other colonies.

Some of the colonists moved westward into the Connecticut Valley. Others moved to New Hampshire and Maine. But the latter groups continually called upon the governing bodies in Massachusetts, and finally gave up their "independence." They reacted much like those who still depended on the mother country for advice and assistance.

Not so with Roger Williams and Anne Hutchinson. Williams was banished from Massachusetts. He had vocally protested taxation for the support of religion, and compulsory attendance. The Puritan powers didn't appreciate that, so in 1635 Williams moved to what became Providence in the Colony of Rhode Island. There he was joined by Anne Hutchinson.

Williams went to England to plead for a charter. Powerful factions in Massachusetts vigorously protested. But he got it anyway. And Rhode Island became the first to develop the proposition of the complete separation of church and state.

George Calvert, the first Lord Baltimore, received a charter in 1632 to establish the Colony of Maryland. Although the rulers were Catholics, they allowed extensive freedom of religion in the Colony. As businessmen, they were more interested in profits than arguing about religion. And Maryland prospered from the beginning. A local self-government system developed which contributed to political self-sufficiency in a developing New World.

A large slice of the New World called "Carolina" was granted in 1663 to several friends of King Charles II. It was a bold slap at Spain while it was also a move towards land profits. John Locke was commissioned to prepare a constitution for Carolina that would incorporate English society in the New World. A pamphlet of unknown origin appeared in England in 1666 extolling the virtues of living in Carolina. It listed six principal reasons why the reader should make a change:

"First, there is full and free liberty of conscience granted to all" and they could "worship God after their own way." The second reason concerned "freedom from custom" for several items, but only after "four ton of any of those commodities shall be imported in one bottom."

The third notes there will be servants and slaves, and that "every man be armed with a good musket full bore, 10 lb. powder, and 20 lb. of bullet, and six months provision for all, to serve them while they raise provision in that country." But all wasn't lost for the servants. When their time had been served each of them would receive 100 acres of land, and their masters were to provide them with clothing and tools.

They were to chose their own governor and council, claimed number five. And no taxes or laws to be sanctioned "without the consent of the colony in their Assembly." The sixth reason confirmed the fifth.

The first settlement of any great size was "Charles Town" established in 1670. The differences between the northern and southern portions grew, so in 1691 Carolina was divided.

Charles II rewarded one of his brothers, the Duke of York. He gave him the colony of New Netherland, which had been taken from the Dutch. It was located between the Connecticut and Delaware Rivers, and included land known as Long Island. It didn't take long for the Duke to name his vast real estate after himself. New York was recaptured by the Dutch in 1673, but it only held it a year.

The Duke of York graciously rewarded two of the supporters of the Stuarts by giving them land between the Hudson and Delaware Rivers. New Jersey was born. Among the young men was a politician in New Jersey, a Quaker named William Penn. When Penn's father died, Charles II owed him a sizable sum. The younger Penn received a large grant of land to pay off the debt. In 1681 Pennsylvania came into being.

French explorers covered thousands of tortuous miles and claimed the Mississippi Valley for France. At the mouth of the River the French standard was planted, and the land was called "Louisiana."

With the Spaniards entrenched in Florida, and the French along the Mississippi, the English colonies were in trouble. These stretched from New England to the Carolinas, and something was needed as a buffer. Religious toleration had been won in England in 1688, so other reasons had to be improvised to get people to leave Great Britain. A Freemason named James Oglethorpe was granted a charter to empty the prisons and carry the inmates to a settlement to be called "Georgia."

England kept a firm grip on its colonies. Although each had its own governor, Oglethorpe remained subservient to the English Crown. This was true even in the two colonies where he was elected. The governor had complete control of everything in his colony. Consequently, his job was a lonely one; he was criticized by his subjects and often by the politicians at home.

Daily, the colonists in the New World became more independent of the mother country. Yet they fought along side the British during the 70 years of the French and Indian Wars, often called by varying names. These began in 1690 and ended when the English defeated the French at Quebec in 1759. And during this period English, Irish, and Scottish Military lodges brought Freemasonry even deeper into the wilds of North America.

There were sharp differences in the manner in which the inhabitants lived in the different colonies. Their philosophies and governments differed widely. But they were united by common problems, and colonists of different nationalities slowly but surely became a new breed—Americans. Just as slowly, but surely, a desire for independence was growing.

Repressive acts by Great Britain began early. In 1650 England prohibited all foreign vessels from trading with English colonies. Then English colonies were forbidden to ship their goods in foreign vessels. Later, most goods had to be shipped to England before they could be sold. An added insult called for duty to be paid at the point of shipment. The colonies were prohibited from trading with each other, except through England!

Not surprisingly, the New England colonies liked what the mother country had done. Their ships were considered English. So this area became an active trading center. The shipowners prospered and they were in an excellent position to ignore the restrictive acts. They couldn't be enforced.

The colonists were also forbidden to do any manufacturing. The raw goods were to be shipped to England for that purpose. This law, also, was impossible to enforce and the colonists were forced into disobeying the law. They had to use the abundant raw materials found in America to overcome the shipping restrictions adopted by short-sighted politicians in Great Britain.

These restrictive acts were accepted for almost a century, probably because the colonists were occupied with survival. Although the people of the New World were contributing high taxes and over two million pounds in profits and wages, England was deeply in debt. It needed more and more money, so it turned to the colonies. The restraints on manufacturing were tightened, the issuing of paper money prohibited, and new taxes imposed.

A "Writ of Assistance" was enacted by England in 1761. This gave the Crown the right to search any home or business for goods not purchased in England. James Otis, who had been made a Mason in St. John's Lodge in 1752 (and it appears he later became a member of St. Andrew's also), was the General Advocate of Massachusetts. He refused to enforce the Writ, and even made a five hour speech denouncing it. He invited the colonists to "breast any storm of ministerial vengeance that their resistance might cause." He ended his plea by stating: "To my dying day will I oppose with all the power and faculties God has given me, all such instruments of slavery on one hand, and villainy on the other." He then handed the Crown Advocate his resignation.

This took place in Faneuil Hall, Boston. It has been claimed that Faneuil Hall then became "the Cradle of Liberty." Otis would later coin the phrase "Taxation without representation is tyranny."

To enforce the new taxes and regulations a large force of British soldiers was dispatched to the colonies. To house them a "Quartering Act" came into being. It required local authorities to provide housing for the troops. Then, the Stamp Act of 1765 added fuel to the burning anger of the colonists. They weren't about to accept a tax on items that were wholly American. And the "Sons of Liberty" was born. The ladies of Rhode Island got into the act. They claimed they would refuse the attentions of any man voicing approval of the Stamp Act.

Virginia and Massachusetts politicians also voiced concern over these taxes. They felt if England could make this stick, there was no limit to the taxation it could impose. So, in May 1765, Virginia objected by adopting the "Virginia Resolves." These four Virginia Stamp Act Resolutions were presented by Patrick Henry (not a Mason) and was the beginning of his fame. It was in Williamsburg that he proclaimed: "Ceasar had his

Brutus, Charles the First had his Cromwell, and George the Third—" the Speaker cried: "Treason!"—and Henry concluded:—"may profit by their example. If this be treason, make the most of it."

The "Virginia Resolves" were widely circulated. But New Yorkers considered them too treasonable to publish. Not so in New England. They were published there without any qualms. But the New Englanders were pleasantly surprised. They had considered Virginia the most loyal of colonies to the Crown.

The Stamp Act was repealed by Parliament. It wasn't because of the outcry in the colonies. It was because of the demands of English merchants. Their business had declined drastically.

The King fired his Prime Minister, Lord Charles Rockingham. William Pitt got the job. Along with him came Charles Townshend as Chancellor of the Exchequer. Those who understood the situation in England and the colonies had hoped the latter would have nothing but a minor position. To their dismay, Pitt became seriously ill; Townshend became the power in the government. He wasted no time in levying taxes on the colonies to relieve the taxes on property in England.

In June 1767 Townshend's Revenue Act went into effect, but Townshend didn't live to see it effective. His acts worked. Smuggling was almost halted and revenue from customs soared. The Mason, John Hancock, a large Boston shipper, had his sloop *Liberty* seized for nonpayment of customs. This caused a small-scale riot. England sent more customs officials and troops to Boston.

The atmosphere was tense. Yet, on November 30, 1768, Joseph Warren, the Worshipful Master of St. Andrew's Lodge, discussed the formation of a Grand Lodge for the "Ancients" in Massachusetts. This meant he had to talk with the three Military lodges in the city: No. 58 in the 14th Foot, No. 322 in the 29th Foot, and No. 106 in the 64th Foot. Out of this discussion came the appointment of Joseph Warren as Provincial Grand Master by the Grand Lodge of Scotland on May 30, 1769.

GREEN DRAGON TAVERN
Masonic meeting place in Boston, Massachusetts, 1773.

Tension in Boston mounted daily. It reached its peak on March 5, 1770. Someone threw a snowball at a British soldier. Then several more were thrown. The soldier called for assistance. It came. An angry crowd attacked the soliders with clubs. Shots were fired and five Bostonians were felled. Samuel Adams turned the incident into a full scale massacre with his fiery oratory.

The Townshend Acts were partially repealed in 1770. Normal business relationships were somewhat restored. It appeared the crisis was ended. It was—until a June afternoon in 1772. Then, obligingly the British custom schooner *Gaspee* ran aground on a sandspit near Providence. About 150 Rhode Islanders boarded her in the dark, ordered the crew ashore, and burned the vessel to the waterline. It was one ship that would no longer interfere with the smuggling activities of the folks in Rhode Island.

Two trials were held at Newport. No criminals could be identified or produced. The Crown was angry. It was even angrier with certain men in the Virgina House of Burgesses. They argued that England had no right to hold court in Rhode Island. A short-sighted Crown ordered more restrictions placed on the colonies.

Among the restrictive acts was the placing of a threepenny tax on tea in the colonies. The East India Company was overstocked with that commodity, so England permitted it to deliver it free of all duties in Great Britain. Tempers in Boston boiled. Demands for the East India ships to be moved out of the harbor were ignored. So, on the night of December 16, 1773, "Indians" boarded the ships, threw 342 chests of tea overboard, and turned the harbor into a giant tea pot.

On the evening of the 16th St. Andrew's Lodge was scheduled to meet in its regular meeting place, the Green Dragon Tavern. It didn't. There were not enough members present. It has been claimed that the "Indians" were led by Paul Revere, the Junior Warden of the Lodge. They may have been. And there may have been many Freemasons among the "tea tossers," but so well-kept was their identity not a single name has ever been conclusively revealed.

The port of Boston was closed by the British. The news quickly spread throughout the colonies. The colonists began to arm and train in earnest. The "Minute Men" came into being.

The First Continental Congress began its meetings in Philadelphia on September 5, 1774. A Freemason from Virginia, Peyton Randolph, was chosen its President. There appeared to be little desire among the representatives for open conflict with England. Its petitions to Parliament were respectful. It did, however, adopt measures designed to coerce the Crown into repealing many of the measures it considered offensive. This brought into existence in each of the colonies committees to enforce the agreements. These committees became the powerful ruling forces.

The colonists weren't without their champions in England. One of them was Edmund Burke. He believed Parliament had the right to tax the colonies, but the right wasn't worth the cost of military suppression. Lord North had proposed exempting any colony from taxation that agreed to cover some of the expense of military occupation. Burke considered this "a method of ransom by auction." In the House of Commons on March 22, 1775, he made a lengthy plea for conciliation with America.

"I persuaded myself that you would not reject a reasonable proposition because it had nothing but its reason to recommend it," he told the members of the House. "The proposition is peace. Not peace through the medium of war; not peace to be hunted through the labyrinth of intricate and endless negotiations; not peace to arise out of universal discord fomented from principle in all parts of the empire; not peace to depend on the juridical determination of perplexing questions, or the precise marking the shadowy boundaries of a complex government. It is simple peace, sought in its natural course, and in its ordinary haunts. It is peace sought in the spirit of peace, and laid in principles purely pacific."

Events would show that he was ignored. He had also been ignored when he spoke for John Wilkes when he was imprisoned for libel for writing a political pamphlet *Thoughts on the Present Discontents.* The members of "Burke's Lodge," Jerusalem No. 44, went to the King's Bench Prison and made John Wilkes a Mason on March 3, 1769.

The second Provincial Congress of Massachusetts believed war was eminent. It met on February 5, 1775, to make preparations for such an eventuality. Fifty-three articles of war were adopted on April 5.

In Virginia Lord Dunmore suspended the Virginia Assembly. It moved to Richmond, and there in St. John's Church on March 23, 1775, Patrick Henry made a speech that would make him even more famous. In his closing remarks, according to William Wirt, he said:

> . . . we shall not fight our battles alone. There is a just God who presides over the destinies of nations, and who will raise up friends to fight our battles for us. The battle, sir, is not to the strong alone; it is to the vigilant, the active, the brave. Besides, sir, we have no election. If we were base enough to desire it, it is now too late to retire from the contest. There is no retreat but in submission and slavery! Our chains are forged. Their clanking may be heard on the plains of Boston! The war is inevitable—and let it come!! I repeat it, sir, let it come!!
>
> It is vain, sir, to extenuate the matter. Gentlemen may cry, peace, peace; but there is no peace. The war is actually begun! The next gale that sweeps from the north will bring to our ears the clash of resounding arms! Our brethren are already in the field! Why stand we here idle? What is it that gentlemen wish? What would they have? Is life so dear or peace so sweet as to be purchased at the price of chains and slavery?
>
> Forbid it, Almighty God—I know not what course others may take; but as for me, give me liberty, or give me death!

Henry was more prophetic than he could have realized. War was only days away. General Thomas Gage had learned through his spies there was a large store of military supplies at Concord. Secretly, he made plans to destroy them. However, he couldn't get away from the alert eyes of the Patriots in

Boston. They knew something was afoot, but didn't know exactly what. Messengers were posted to wait for a signal from the old North Church.

The signal was flashed from the Old North Church by a Freemason. Whether it was Robert Newman, a member of St. John's Lodge or John Pulling, Jr., a member of St. Andrew's, is uncertain. But one of the two sent Paul Revere of St. Andrew's Lodge, along with William Dawes and Samuel Prescott, to warn the villagers the British were on their way by land to Concord and Lexington.

On April 18, 1775, the force of 700 redcoats started their march. At dawn on the 19th they arrived at Lexington to find a body of militia blocking their way. A nervous finger pulled a trigger (whose no one knows); the British fired, then charged with bayonets. Eight dead and ten wounded Minute Men were left on the ground as the militia fled and the British marched on to Concord. There they destroyed what stores had not been removed by the Americans.

Couriers sped throughout the colonies spreading the word of the fighting at Lexington and Concord. The same rallying cry was heard as it would for Fort Sumter and Pearl Harbor years later. From all the New England colonies volunteers arrived to form a ring around Boston. Ethan Allen and Benedict Arnold, a Freemason, took a force of militia and seized the British forts of Ticonderoga and Crown Point. They took back more military stores than had been lost at Concord.

The Second Continental Congress met on May 10, 1775. Events had forced a change in its direction. Now war was an actuality. Military problems had to take priority. Among its first acts was the selection of a Commander-in-Chief of the Continental Forces. The logical choice was the Virginia Mason, George Washington. He had had more actual experience in warfare than anyone in the colonies. He was elected unanimously on July 15. He accepted the following day. A week later he was on his way to Boston where the Battle of Bunker (Breed's) Hill had been fought.

The contribution made by Washington to the First Continental Congress is not recorded. Patrick Henry noted: "If you speak of eloquence, Mr. Rutledge of South Carolina is by far the greatest orator, but if you speak of solid information and sound judgement, Colonel Washington is unquestionably the greatest man on that floor."

It is reported that Washington was an imposing figure in The Congress. He wore his military uniform and sword proudly on his six foot two inch frame. He was active and at ease socially. It appears that he did not gamble, but he was available for teas and other social gatherings. His opinions were sought after. His judgments were considered sound.

The Second Continental Congress had been called into session on May 9, 1775. The delegates received a warm welcome to Philadelphia. But the reception for the Mason, John Hancock, and Samuel Adams, now fugitives from the British, was overwhelming. They had become the first real heroes of the Revolution. Benjamin Franklin, the Mason, had just returned from London and was amazed to find "all Americans from one End of the 12 United Provinces to the other, busily employed in learning the Use of Arms." He was also surprised at "the Unanimity." He would soon learn there wasn't much unanimity. *G. Washington: Master Mason* states:

> Washington expected to "fall" during the war. And well he might have such expectations. Some historians claim a third of the colonists were Tories; it would appear this was an underestimation. At any rate, it was evident that not even half were wholeheartedly in favor of a revolution. There certainly was no unity. Each colony was first of all for itself; this wouldn't change when they became States— at least not for the first 200 years. The Congress couldn't decide what should be done (no Congress would, at least during the first 200 years).
> Historians differ widely over the circumstances that had brought the colonies to the point where they would fight a war with Great Britain. And well they might. No two colonies were exactly alike economically, politically, or even religiously. Each had something to lose in a break with England. There appeared to be little to gain, except to be

taxed by representatives of their own choosing. But whatever the cause, or causes, the black clouds of war had lowered.

The Battle of Bunker (or Breed's) Hill was lost before it began. A working party was sent out on the night of June 16, 1775, to fortify Bunker Hill. For some unknown reason it decided to entrench Breed's Hill. This was a tactical blunder, for these exposed works could much more easily be cut off by a British landing on the neck in their rear.

Even so, the British expected the "rabble in arms" to flee at the first sign of the red-coated regulars. The "rabble" didn't. They shocked the English by holding their fire until the white of their eyes was visible. The British ranks were decimated. They fell back to regroup, then attacked again. Again, the Americans held their fire until the enemy was at close range. The fire was again devastating. Reinforcements were sent from the British ships. On the third attack the English were successful, but mainly because the Patriots had run out of ammunition. And the retreat was surprisingly orderly. The British lost 1,054; the Americans about 440.

Among the Americans killed was Dr. Joseph Warren, the Grand Master of the Scottish Grand Lodge in Massachusetts. Although he held the rank of general, he chose to fight as a private. As President of the Massachusetts Provincial Congress he had reported on the Battles of Lexington and Concord. He ended his report by stating: "We sincerely hope that the Great Sovereign of the universe, who so often appeared for the English nation, will support you in every rational and manly exertion with these colonies for saving it from ruin, and that, in a constitutional connection with the mother country, we shall soon be altogether a free and happy people."

George Washington took command of the Continental Forces in July. He set out immediately to create an army, and found it a formidable task. There was no discipline; enlistments were short and men were much more interested in the home front than the fighting front. Even so, Washington was able to mount a two-pronged attack on Canada which started in September, 1775.

Brigadier General Richard Montgomery, a Mason, with a small force, left from Ticonderoga for Montreal. Colonel Benedict Arnold, a Mason, along with riflemen under the command of Captain Daniel Morgan of Virginia, went up the Kennebec River and through the wilds of Maine with orders to take Quebec. This proved to be one of the most horrendous marches ever to be attempted. But Montgomery captured Montreal on November 13; Arnold, with a depleted force, crossed the St. Lawrence River on the same day. The force scaled the cliffs and encamped on the Plains of Abraham outside Quebec. On December 30 a blizzard raged and the Amercans attacked. They were repulsed. Montgomery was killed. Arnold was wounded. Still he kept up a seige hoping for reinforcements. Few arrived. By the middle of July the Americans were back at Ticonderoga.

In the meantime Washington had kept pressure on the British in Boston. On March 4, 1776, he moved onto Dorchester Heights. There he emplaced the heavy artillery Henry Knox, a Mason, had captured at Ticonderoga in the winter, hauling it over rugged and icy terrain.

Washington next fortified Nook's Hill. On March 17 the British marched away leaving behind a large array of stores and weapons. The Canadian defeat was balanced.

Cries by the Colonists for a declaration of independence from Great Britain were becoming more vocal. But there were still many with influence opposed to breaking away from the mother country. Pennsylvania had instructed its delegates to the Second Continental Congress to oppose independence. The statement ended by saying: "Though the oppressive measure of the British Parliament and administration have compelled us to resist their violence by force of arms, yet we strictly enjoin you that you, in behalf of this colony, dissent from and utterly reject any proposition, should such be made, that may cause or lead to a separation from our mother country or a change in the form of this government."

Rhode Island, however, early in May 1776 declared its independence. Massachusetts asked each town to voice its sentiments. The choice was overwhelmingly for independence.

Virginia adopted a Declaration of Rights on June 12, 1776. It later became the basis for the Bill of Rights in the Constitution of the United States. On the 29th it adopted a Constitution which served as a model for other State Constitutions.

On June 7, 1776, Richard Henry Lee (not a Mason, but considered by many to be one) followed the instructions of Virginia and submitted this resolution:

> Resolved, That these United Colonies are, and of right ought to be, free and independent States, that they are absolved from all allegiance to the British Crown, and that all political connection between them and the State of Great Britain is, and ought to be, totally dissolved.
>
> That it is expedient forthwith to take the most effectual measures for forming foreign Alliance.
>
> That a plan of confederation be prepared and transmitted to the respective Colonies for their consideration and approbation.

One of the reasons much that happened in the Continental Congresses isn't known can be attributed to this Resolution of Secrecy Adopted By the Continental Congress, November 9, 1775, as recorded in *Formation of the Union of the American States* as quoted from *Secret Journals of the Acts and Proceedings of U.S. Congress, Vol. 1, p. 34:*

> Resolved, That every member of this Congress considers himself under the ties of virtue, honour, and love of his country, not to divulge, directly or indirectly, any matter or thing agitated or debated in Congress, before the same shall have been determined, without leave of the Congress; nor any matter or thing determined in Congress, which a majority of the Congress shall order to be kept secret. And that if any member shall violate this agreement, he shall be expelled from this Congress, and deemed an enemy to the liberties of America, and liable to be treated as such; and that every member signify his consent to this agreement by signing the same.

The thundering rendition of the Virginia resolution by Richard Henry Lee brought mixed cries. At last what had been hinted at for two years had been brought out into the open. There was elation and fear. Seven delegations agreed with the resolution; six didn't. A recess of three weeks was called, although there were those who wanted more time. And so that no time would be wasted if the resolution was to be adopted, a committee was appointed to draft a constitution.

The Constitutional Committee consisted of Thomas Jefferson, Benjamin Franklin (a Past Grand Master of Pennsylvania), John Adams, Roger Sherman (claimed by some to be a Mason, but there's no evidence he was), and Robert R. Livingston (who would become the first Grand Master of the Grand Lodge of New York). The Committee did much of its work in the second floor living room of the Graff house at 7th and Market Streets, Philadelphia, in sweltering heat. Change after change was made in the short document before it was brought to the Congress.

The oath of secrecy kept what happened during the debate from being fully known. Years later snatches were published from diaries, biographies, and autobiographies. That there was no unanimity is clear. The debate for and against independence was heated. According to Jefferson's autobiography this occurred:

> On Monday, the 1st of July, the House resolved itself into a committee of the whole and resumed the consideration of the original motion made by the delegates of Virginia, which, being again debated through the day, was carried in the affirmative by the votes of New Hampshire, Connecticut, Massachusetts, Rhode Island, New Jersey, Maryland, Virginia, North Carolina, and Georgia. South Carolina and Pennsylvania voted against it. Delaware had but two members present, and they were divided. The delegates from New York declared they were for it themselves, and were assured their constituents were for it, but that their instructions having been drawn near a twelvemonth before, when reconciliation was still the general object, they were enjoined by them to do nothing which should impede that object. They therefore thought themselves not justified in voting on either side and asked leave to withdraw from the question, which was given them. The committee rose and reported their resolution to the house.

> Mr. Rutledge of South Carolina then requested the
> determination might be put off to the next day, as he
> believed his colleagues, though they disapproved of the
> resolution, would then join in it for the sake of unanimity.

The vote was postponed until the following day, and this
paved the way for a remarkable journey by a remarkable man.
A messenger was sent to Delaware to let the third delegate,
Caesar Rodney, know he was despereately needed. He had
returned to Delaware when the Congress recessed. Tories were
creating problems and he wanted the people of Delaware to
deny the authority of the Crown. This is where he was when his
delegation in the Congress split.

When word reached him he mounted his horse and rode into
the miserable torrential rain. It had been falling all day, turning the rutted roads into swamps. This was made more horrible
by the blackness of the stormy night, making his journey extremely dangerous.

Rodney had been described by John Adams as "the oldest looking man I ever saw—tall, slender as a reed, pale; his face is not
bigger than a large apple, yet there is a sense and fire, spirit, wit
and humor in his countenance." The description doesn't say that
Rodney knew the horror and suffering of a slowly spreading cancer. It disfigured, and finally killed him in 1784, at the age of 55.
But even this hadn't dampened his burning desire for freedom.

For more than ten years before the First Continental Congress convened, he had spoken against the tyranny of Great Britain. He, along with Thomas McKean and George Read, were
chosen in 1774 as delegates from Delaware to the First Congress. They were the representatives in this, the Second Congress.

Out of the pouring rain, thunder and lightening, the painful-
ly ill Caesar Rodney staggered into Independence Hall on July
2, 1776. He had ridden 80 miles from Dover without rest. But
he was triumphant. He turned Delaware's vote to independence—making it unanimous. South Carolina and Pennsylvania had already voted in favor; New York had abstained,
but a few days later voted for independence.

Jenkin Lloyd Jones would write in 1975: "Paul Revere had a great press agent—Henry Wadsworth Longfellow. Caesar Rodney had no press agent nor was he turned to romantic imagery. But Longfellow's line, 'The fate of a nation was riding that night,' could better have been applied to the muddy gentleman from Delaware who dashed to Philadelphia."

A plaque in the Historical Society of Delaware has Rodney saying to the Congress: "As I believe the voice of my constituents and of all sensible and honest men is in favor of independence, my own judgement concurs with them. I vote for independence."

Caesar Rodney wasn't a Mason, although a nephew of his by the same name would become a member of Washington Lodge No. 1 in Delaware.

Perhaps, as John Adams claimed, July 2nd should be celebrated as the day of Independence, but Jefferson says the debates continued through July 4th and then closed. A new era was at hand. A Republic was formed.

Fifteen

PATRIOTS OF THE REVOLUTIONARY WAR

THOMAS PAINE who wrote *An Essay on the Origin of Freemasonry,* among other items, although he wasn't a Mason, summed up the period immediately following the adoption of the Declaration of Independence. The first of his patriotic tracts called *The Crisis,* invoked a responsive cord in George Washington. Late in 1776, when the cause of the Patriots was dim, he had this paper read to his troops. Paine's tract had appeared in the *Pennsylvania Journal* on December 19, 1776. His opening lines have been repeated more times than can be counted in more ways than are known:

> These are the times that try men's souls. The summer soldier and the sunshine patriot will, in this crisis, shrink from the service of his country; but he that stands it now deserves the love and thanks of man and woman. Tyranny, like hell, is not easily conquered; yet we have this consolation with us—that the harder the conflict, the more glorious the triumph. What we obtain too cheap, we esteem too lightly: It is dearness only that gives everything its value. Heaven knows how to put a proper price upon its goods; and it would be strange indeed if so celestial an article as freedom should not be highly rated.

His paper closed with a reminder of what might have, and still could happen:

> . . . By perseverance and fortitude we have the prospect of a glorious issue; by cowardice and submission, the sad choice of a variety of evils—a ravaged country—a depopulated city—habitations without safety and slavery

without hope—our homes turned into barracks and bawdy houses for Hessians, and a future race to provide for, whose fathers we shall doubt of. Look on this picture and weep over it! And if there yet remains one thoughtless wretch who believes it not, let him suffer it unlamented.

Most of 1776 had been a disaster for the Continental forces. The British had taken over New York and much of New Jersey. The Tories in New Jersey rushed to the British side. This caused Washington to write: "Instead of turning out to defend the Country and affording aid to our army, they are making their submissions as fast as they can."

Washington had been unable to make a concerted stand; he didn't have the forces necessary. He was forced to retreat into Pennsylvania. Morale was low. The Congress fled from Philadelphia in a panic. So Paine's observations came as a blessing. And Washington took advantage of the changed attitude in his troops after they had heard the paper read. The Commander had discovered there was courage and determination among his fighting forces.

General William Howe was knighted for his victory at New York. He was content to rest in New Jersey for the winter. He claimed no sane commander would fight until spring. So, Howe stationed his 14,000 men to protect New Jersey and Delaware. He permitted Cornwallis to return to England, and he settled down in the comfort of Manhattan.

General Charles Lee, on whom the Congress pinned great hopes, had been captured while enjoying the comforts of a tavern near Morristown, New Jersey. This would prove a blessing for the Patriots. John Sullivan (who would become the first Grand Master of Masons in New Hampshire) brought 2,000 of Lee's men to join Washington who determined to go ahead with a plan he had been comtemplating. He ordered three days rations cooked for the troops, then secretly informed his chief officers of his plan.

He was going to cross the Delaware River on Christmas night! On Christmas afternoon he assembled his men, had rations and ammunition passed out, and behind concealing ridges informed them of what was ahead. An officer wrote in his diary that day: "It will be a terrible night for the soliders who have no shoes. Some of them have tied old rags around their feet, but I have not heard a man complain."

A fierce, biting wind blew off the river. Huge chunks of ice were slammed along in the swift current. The conditions were appalling. Yet, Washington relied on the hardy deep-water fishermen from Massachusetts, under the command of Colonel John Glover (a charter member in 1760 of Philanthropic Lodge in Massachusetts). He and his men had taken Washington's whole army across the East River from Long Island to Manhattan—and right under the noses of the British. They had held off Howe at Pell's Point in October long enough for Washington's main body to escape to White Plains. They had proven their courage and audacity.

The crossing which was intended to be over by midnight wasn't. The horrible weather caused a physical battle on the river that took three hours longer. But the Marblehead seamen/soldiers did the job without losing a man or a gun!

In a two-pronged attack, Nathanael Greene (considered a Rhode Island Mason) and Sullivan converged on Trenton. They took the Hessians completely by surprise. The Hessians surrendered within a half hour. Forty of them were killed; 918 taken prisoner; 400 escaped because Ewing had been unable to block their escape. The Americans lost four dead and four were wounded. The guns of the Mason, Henry Knox, and the fighting of the brigade under the Virginia Mason, Hugh Mercer, had much to do with the success of the venture and the small loss of Americans.

By offering a bounty of $10 in hard money (his own!) Washington convinced part of his army to stay past the termination of their enlistments. He again crossed the Delaware on the night of December 30-31. Cornwallis had quickly gathered scattered British garrisons and confronted Washington at Trenton. Washington escaped the trap on the night of January 2, 1777, by leaving campfires burning. The next morning he whipped the British at Princeton. Then he took his troops into winter quarters in the hills around Morristown, New Jersey.

Foreign officers arrived early in 1777 to aid the cause of the Continentals. Many of them were Freemasons. Friedrich Wilhelm von Steuben and his secretary, Peter Stephen Du Ponceau who was to serve as his aide-de-camp, were Masons. Thaddeus Kosciusko came with Benjamin Franklin's recommendation and became a colonel of engineers. (In 1928 a Lodge in New York City was founded and named for him—the only Polish Lodge in the world.) Another Pole, Count Casimir Pulaski, met Franklin in France and joined Washington with Franklin's recommendation. He would become a general and serve with distinction. Whether or not he was a Mason is debatable, but a Lodge in Chicago was named in his honor, and it believes he was a member.

Then there was the Marquis de Lafayette who became like a son to Washington. There has been, and still is, speculation concerning Lafayette's Masonic membership. An exhaustive research was made for, and reported in, *Frontier Cornerstone:*

> Varying claims have been made throughout the years as to when and where Lafayette was made a Master Mason. Among these claims is one that he was made a Mason in American Union Lodge. This and other statements about him becoming a Mason in America are false.
>
> Louis Gottschalk, a biographer who spent a lifetime studying Lafayette, states in his book *Lafayette in America*, that Lafayette was a Mason before he went to America in 1777. However, no proof of this is available. His Masonic relationship prior to 1782 is unknown.
>
> George Chaytor, then Grand Master of Masons in Delaware, is credited with telling Lafayette Lodge No. 14 of Wilmington, Delaware, in 1875, that Lafayette said he was initiated at Valley Forge in the winter of 1777-78. Chaytor reported that Lafayette said Washington did not have sufficient confidence in him to entrust him with a separate command. A true or false statement that has been perpetuated throughout the years?

It's false! Two weeks before the Continental Army went into winter quarters at Valley Forge, Washington gave Lafayette an independent command.

In spite of exhaustive research, nothing has been un-covered concerning Lafayette's Masonic affiliation until his name was presented to the Lodge of St. Jean *d'Ecosse du Contrat Social.* When his name was read out, instead of the usual ballot, Lafayette was elected by "unanimous ac-climation." He sent a letter of thanks which was read at the next session of the Lodge. It wasn't until June 24, 1782, that he was able to appear in person.

Lafayette was received "with honors which were or-dinarily shown of a Mason of the highest degree." He was informed his election was distinct and one "reserved for heroes." And, actually, one for "which there have been no previous examples." He was then "permitted to take the oath of full membership *(affilie)*." He was affiliated!

Throughout the Summer of 1777, both the British and Americans employed "hit and run" tactics around Philadelphia. The British finally took the city on September 26. Shortly after-wards Howe went into winter quarters in Philadelphia: Washington did the same at Valley Forge, about 20 miles from the city.

While this was going on major fighting was taking place around the Canadian and New York border. General John Burgoyne, with a large army of British troops and Indians set out to destroy all American resistance. Down Lake Champlain sailed the British fleet. Its target was Ticonderoga. And Ticonderoga fell easily. And Burgoyne decided to take his troops overland rather than float them down Lake George. This became a nightmare. Through the wilderness, marshes, and the harrassment of the American General Schuyler, the British were able to travel no more than a mile a day.

Washington sent Generals Benedict Arnold and Benjamin Lincoln (who would become a member of St. Andrew's Lodge in Boston in 1780) to reinforce Schuyler's meager forces. Then he dispatched Colonel Daniel Morgan and his Virginia Riflemen a short time later. These men were a fortunate choice. But it was the murder and scalping of Jane McCrea, a young settler, that roused the ire of the inhabitants of the area and brought them into the fight.

New England militiamen rallied to the cause, but they still didn't trust the New Yorker, Phillip Schuyler. John Stark, who the following year would be made a Mason in Masters Lodge, Albany, was commissioned a brigadier general by New Hampshire. He and his New Englanders took up a position at Bennington in Vermont after he had refused to join the main army. Burgoyne was unlucky enough to send a large foraging party into Stark's area. On August 16 the English force was virtually wiped out. Again the British advance was held up.

Benedict Arnold was sent to reinforce Fort Stanwix. With only 950 Continentals, Arnold devised a ruse that took full advantage of the dissatisfaction and natural superstitions of the Indians. Employing a half-wit Dutchman, his clothes shot full of holes, and a friendly Oneida Indian as his messenger, Arnold spread the rumor that the Continentals were approaching "as numerous as the leaves on the trees." The Indians, who had special respect for any madman, departed in haste, scalping not a few of their Tory allies as they went, and St. Leger was forced to abandon the seige.

Burgoyne was discouraged. Bennington and Stanwix were blows he hadn't expected. He wrote: "The great bulk of the country is undoubtedly with Congress in principle and zeal; and their measures are executed with a secrecy and dispatch that are not to be equalled. Wherever the King's forces point, militia in the amount of three or four thousand assemble in twenty-four hours; they bring with them their subsistence, etc., and the alarm over, they return to their farms."

The Congress finally bowed to the New Englanders distrust of Schuyler and replaced him with Horatio Gates. Gates would become a controversial figure in the history of what happened after his appointment. His caution could have given the British a tremendous advantage. But there were others such as Arnold who "urged, begged, and entreated" him to take the initiative. He finally agreed to send Morgan's Riflemen out after the advancing British General Simon Fraser. (This may have been the Simon "Frazier" who conferred the first recorded Royal Arch Degree in the Lodge at Fredericksburg.) At the second Battle of Freeman's Farm, Fraser was killed. And it was Arnold, Morgan, and their men who turned the tide of battle. On October 17, 1777, Burgoyne surrendered.

Actually, Arnold, Morgan and their men did more than turn the tide of battle; they turned the tide of destiny for the new United States of America. With the victory at Sarotoga the Old World began to view the new country as more than an "upstart" nation. The victory armed Benjamin Franklin, America's emmissary in France, with ammunition he could use to bring the French into the war on the side of the Americans.

Benjamin Franklin was apprenticed to his brother, James, as a printer at the age of twelve. He later opened his own business and in 1730 began publishing *The Pennsylvania Gazette*. In 1733 he began publishing *Poor Richard's Almanack*, and this would make him famous. In 1734 he printed the first Masonic book published in America, Anderson's *Constitutions*.

In February, 1731, Franklin became a Freemason in St. John's Lodge of Philadelphia. In 1734 he was elected Grand Master. He served as Secretary of his Lodge from 1735-38. He was on the committee that was responsible for the erection of the first Masonic building in America which was dedicated in Philadelphia on June 24, 1755.

Franklin sold his business in 1748 to devote his life to public service. From 1757 to 1762 he represented Pennsylvania in England. He was called before the English House of Commons in 1766 and asked to explain why the Stamp Acts were so vigorously opposed in the American colonies. In 1775 he returned to America and became a member of the First Continental Congress. Immediately after he had served on the committee that wrote the Declaration of Independence, and which he signed after its adoption, he was sent to France to try to negotiate a treaty. There he was so popular, he remained until 1785.

BENJAMIN FRANKLIN
From the anonymous Painting in the National Portrait Gallery,
after the Portrait of 1782 by J. S. Duplessis.

He became active in Freemasonry in France as he had while in England. On April 7, 1778, he assisted in the initiation of Voltaire in the Lodge of Nine Sisters in Paris. And only seven months later officiated at the Masonic funeral service for Voltaire. On May 21, 1779, Franklin was elected Worshipful Master of the Lodge, serving for two years. He was also a member of the Respectable Lodge de Saint Jean de Jerusalem, and was elected honorary Master of it on April 24, 1785. He was elected an honorary member of the *Logge des Bon Amis* of Rouen, France, the same year.

Franklin was despondent when he learned that Philadelphia had been lost to the British. This despondency quickly changed to elation when he learned "General Burgoyne and his whole army" were prisoners of war. He rushed to King Louis with the news. The King, on December 6, 1777, promised to recognize the American independence. He kept his word, and two months later a formal treaty of alliance was culminated. The long, hard, perilous road to victory was paved.

Whether Franklin's Masonic connections helped in his negotiations will never be learned. Historians rarely mention Freemasonry as a force for good. Without question, though, Franklin's Masonic friends, and their love and respect for him, didn't hurt.

After Saratoga, Howe and the British forces moved into winter quarters in Philadelphia and the surrounding area. Washington marched his 11,000 man army up the Schuylkill River to a place called "Valley Forge."

The War of the American Revolution briefly describes the situation of that winter Americans have remembered:

> The name of Valley Forge has come to stand, and right-ly so, as a patriotic symbol of suffering, courage and perseverance. The hard core of 6,000 Continentals who stayed with Washington during that bitter winter of 1777-78 indeed suffered much. Some men had no shoes, no pants, no blankets. Weeks passed when there was no meat and men were reduced to boiling their shoes and eating them. The winter winds penetrated the tattered tents that were at first the only shelter.

The symbolism of Valley Forge would not be allowed to obscure the fact that the suffering was largely unnecessary. While the soldiers shivered and went hungry, food rotted and clothing lay unused in depots throughout the country. True, access to Valley Forge was difficult, but little determined effort was made to get supplies into the area. The supply and transport system broke down.

In mid 1777, both the Quartermaster and Commissary Generals resigned along with numerous subordinate officials in both departments, mostly merchants who found private trade more lucrative. Congress, in refuge at York, Pennsylvania, and split into factions, found it difficult to find replacements. If there was not, as most historians now believe, an organized cabal seeking to replace Washington with Gates, there were many, both in and out of the Army, who were dissatisfied with the Commander in Chief, and much intrigue went on. Gates was made president of the new Board of War set up in 1777, and at least two of its members were enemies of Washington. In the administrative chaos at the height of the Valley Forge crisis, there was no functioning Quartermaster General at all.

With all its horror, Valley Forge did turn into a blessing. The Mason, Baron von Steuben, was able to turn the Continentals into an army with professional competence. The Congress began to listen to the advice of Washington. They appointed a reluctant Nathanael Greene as Quartermaster General, a position he accepted only after Washington had persuaded him to do so. This brought about needed reforms in the Quartermaster and Commissary Departments.

The Prussian von Steuben, among other things, taught the Americans how to use the bayonet. The British were experts with it, and had been using it to advantage. von Steuben knew little English and had an entirely different type of soldier to deal with than ever before. He noted this in a letter he wrote to a friend in Prussia: "You say to your soldier, 'do this,' and he doeth it. I am obliged to say to mine, 'this is the reason why you ought to do it,' and then he doeth it." His good humor, though, and hearty profanity, (just about the only English he knew), kept the Continentals amused so they drilled rigorously.

The British General Howe lost his appetite for the war and resigned. Sir Henry Clinton took command. In June 1778 Clinton evacuated Philadelphia and moved to New York. At Monmouth Court House on June 27 Washington attempted to cut off the British forces. General Lee, who had been returned from captivity by the British, failed to hold his line. A furious Washington took direct control to turn what might have been a rout into a partial victory. But the British escaped during the night.

The "West" was largely ignored by the Congress, perhaps because Virginia controlled so much of it. At any rate, the Virginia Mason, George Rogers Clark, convinced Governor Patrick Henry of Virginia to let him take a force to the western outposts. The British were outfitting several Indian Tribes from posts at Niagara, Detroit, and Fort Sackville at Vincennes. Rogers' first goal was Kaskaskia on the Mississippi, about 50 miles south of St. Louis. He and his 200 "Long Knives" took it on July 4, 1778. They had flat-bedded from Virginia to free the Illinois country.

Later, Rogers learned Vincennes had been retaken by the infamous British Colonel Henry Hamilton, known as the "Hair Buyer" (a purchaser of scalps). With 127 of his backwoodsmen Rogers traveled the 180 miles back to Vincennes. It was in the depth of winter; the Wabash River was flooded and choked with ice; his men were hungry, the floods had driven game away. The last nine miles took a week to cover. For days at a time they waded through shoulder-deep icy water. Then, on February 25, 1779, Vincennes was captured. The Americans had completely surprised the British. The border settlements were at last free.

Vincennes Lodge No. 1 of Indiana celebrated this historic event 200 years later. The Virginia Craftsmen and the Grand Master of Masons in Virginia had prominent roles in the events of the week.

Savannah, Georgia, fell to Clinton's forces on December 29, 1778, and the war in the South would continue for three long years.

Washington moved into Philadelphia on December 22, 1778. There he remained until February 2, 1779. This gave him an opportunity to meet with the Pennsylvania and Military Masons. The Festival of St. John the Evangelist was celebrated on December 28 (the 27th was a Sunday). The Commander was part of the celebration.

On June 23, 1777, a committee of a Convention selected to determine if Virginia should elect a Grand Master and form a Grand Lodge, suggested George Washington be considered for Grand Master. At the Convention of October 13, 1778, when a Grand Master was elected, Washington's name wasn't mentioned. John Blair, Jr., was elected and installed on October 30, 1778. The first wholly independent Grand Lodge in America had come into existence.

American Union Lodge met at West Point on June 24, 1779, to celebrate the Festival of St. John the Baptist. Washington was part of the enormous Masonic celebration.

The war had reached a stalemate during 1779. What few skirmishes there were found both sides winning some and losing some.

The American forces went into winter quarters at Morristown, New Jersey. There American Union Lodge met on December 15. During the meeting the Lodge agreed to a proposition that George Washington be proposed as General Grand Master of the United States. According to the painting entitled "The Petition," Washington was an interested spectator at this meeting. Although the action by Americn Union may not be too surprising because its members knew Washington well, but the same proposal by the Grand Lodge of Pennsylvania five days later was because it meant it was willing to give up its sovereignty.

Washington again joined American Union Lodge for the celebration of the Festival of St. John the Evangelist at Morristown on December 27, 1779. Of all the Military lodges, British and American, American Union was foremost in keeping the atlar fires of Freemasonry burning throughout the war.

A group of Masons met in Roxbury, Massachusetts, on February 13, 1776, to form a lodge. Action was taken and Jonathan Heart was commissioned to "wait on the Right Worshipful Grand Master tomorrow." John Rowe, the Provincial Grand Master, was a Loyalist and had virtually turned control of the Provincial Grand Lodge over to his Deputy, Richard Gridley. Gridley was pleased to comply with the wishes of the soldiers and constituted "AMERICAN UNION LODGE, now erected in Roxbury, or wherever your Body shall remove on the Continent of America, provided it is where no Grand Master is appointed."

That phrasing is important. It enabled Johathan Heart to open American Union Lodge, legally, at Marietta, Ohio, on June 28, 1790. It is also important because it permitted the Lodge to meet anywhere it might be located, with the approval of the Grand Master, if any. In 1776 it met 31 times from February 13 to August 15. Exactly where can't be determined with accuracy. The minutes simply state: "At a Lodge held at the usual place. . ." The usual business was conducted and degrees conferred. Then refreshments and fellowship followed.

While the Lodge met in New York it was supposed to use another name. When it requested permission from the Provincial Grand Lodge it was told: "The American Union Lodge held by authority under the most worshipful John Rowe, Esq., Grand Master of all Masons in North America, where no special Grand Master is appointed, confirmed by the most worshipful Peter Middleton, M.D., Provincial Deputy Grand Master for the Provinces of New York, by the name of Military Union Lodge."

Only once, as far as is known, did American Union mention the other name. It was on June 24, 1776, when the Lodge, "Voted that the Utensils purchased under the American Union Lodge . . . be returned to the said American Union Lodge, and considered only as lent to the Military Union Lodge."

The American Union records only one meeting between March 19, 1777, (which was held at Mr. M. J. Croggs') and

February 15, 1779. This meeting was held "at the Widow Sanford's, near Reading Meeting House." Eighteen meetings were held there between February 15 and May 7, when the Lodge learned it would be moving back to New York.

Members of American Union were among the troops that stormed Stony Point on July 15, 1779. Among the items captured by the Americans was a chest belonging to an English Military lodge. General Anthony Wayne was called to other duty, and General Samuel H. Parsons, the second Worshipful Master of American Union, was placed in charge. He had the chest returned, along with a letter:

> West Jersey Highlands, July 23, 1779
>
> Brethren: When the ambition of Monarchs or jarring interest of contending States, call forth their subjects to war, as Masons we are disarmed of that resentment which stimulates to undistinguished desolation; and however our political sentiments may impel us in the public dispute, we are still Brethren, and (our professional duty apart) ought to promote the happiness and advance the weal of each other. Accept therefore, at the hands of a Brother, the Constitution of the Lodge Unity No. 18, to be held in the 17th British Regiment which your late misfortunes have put in my power to restore to you.
>
> I am your Brother and obedient servant,
>
> Samuel H. Parsons

Through a letter to the Grand Lodge of Pennsylvania in 1786, Unity Lodge thanked General Parsons for his kindness.

A similar event is said to have occurred. According to Robert Freke Gould in his *Military Lodges:* "The Masonic chest of the 46th, by the chances of war, fell into the hands of the Americans. The circumstance was reported to General Washington, who directed that a guard of honour should take charge of the chest, with other articles of value belonging to the 46th, and return them to the regiment."

Gould reports the 46th Foot, with warrant No. 227, Irish Constitution, claims to have a Bible on which "Washington received a degree of Masonry." Long before 1778 when the 46th landed in Massachusetts, Washington was a Freemason.

The winter of 1779-80 at Morristown was just as bitter as the one at Valley Forge. To add to the woes, General Lincoln surrendered to the British at Charleston on May 12, 1780. But Washington's problems didn't stop there. General Gates was appointed by the Congress as Commander of the Southern Army. The English wiped out his forces on August 16. Then the Congress finally came to its senses, and asked Washington to name Gates' successor. He wisely selected Generals Nathanael Greene and von Steuben to salvage the South.

Then another blow struck. John Andre', a British spy, was captured near Tarrytown, New York. When he was searched it was learned Benedict Arnold was selling out the United States. Andre' was hanged; Arnold escaped to create havoc as a British General in the South.

Washington's men went to work in the South. General Daniel Morgan destroyed Tarleton's forces at Cowpens on January 17, 1781. At Guilford Court House Green whipped Cornwallis. And Washington met with the French to make plans for destroying the British in either South Carolina or Virginia, depending on the movements of the English.

Yorktown, Virginia, proved to be the place chosen for the final major battle of the war. In Virginia Lafayette was fighting a holding battle. Washington let him know he and his main army, along with French troops and the French navy, would be joining him. With secrecy and shrewdness the Commander-in-Chief made the long trek from White Plains, New York, to Williamsburg, Virginia. Then they bottled up Cornwallis in Yorktown.

The American siege of the British ended on October 19, 1781. Cornwallis surrendered his forces. And Washington went back to New York to wait for the formal termination of hostilities. There, in Solomon's Lodge No. 1, Poughkeepsie, he enjoyed the celebration of the Festival of St. John the Evangelist on December 27, 1782.

A provisional treaty was signed in November 1782. It was March, 1783, before the details reached Washington. He

WASHINGTON'S FAREWELL TO HIS OFFICERS

Washington is shown bidding an emotional farewell to his officers at St. Fraunces Tavern in New York on December 4, 1783.

Painting by Alonzo Chappel. Photo courtesy of the Chicago Historical Society.

declared hostilities to cease on April 19, 1783—eight years to the day that the first shot was fired. On December 4, 1783, the last of the British troops left New York. On the same day Washington bid his faithful officers farewell in Fraunces' Tavern in New York City.

He surrendered his commission to The Congress on December 23. Then he rode like the wind to reach home for Christmas.

There had been no parade. There was no last review. The Continental Army straggled away on foot in little groups, just as it had come. They had to beg for food and help as they struggled along the country roads to their homes.

These men—the ill fed, ill-clothed, weary, foot-sore, unpaid—were the real heroes of the War for American Independence. Washington had said so.

The all-out war for independence had been the aftermath of the consideration and then the adoption of a Declaration of Independence. A handful of Patriots had won that war. Would the country be able to build on what they had accomplished?

Sixteen

THE STATES REBEL

A NEW nation had been created from the hells of war. But the question asked everywhere was, "Can it survive?" The continuing question would be the same for many years.

Those who had come to enjoy and appreciate independence had joined in a common cause. Together a mere handful of Patriots had beaten the most powerful armed force in the world. But even in war there had been little cooperation between the states. This had made the job of The Congress and the Commander-in-Chief in the field almost insurmountable.

With peace each state continued to consider itself a separate and independent entity. The people had suffered under a strong central government in Great Britain. They weren't about to sanction another. So each state adopted its own constitution. Each was similar. Each gave the ultimate power to the property-holding citizens of the state although some of these state constitutions were more liberal than others. Pennsylvania's gave the middle class and frontiersman control; Virginia's was considered "middle of the road"; South Carolina's gave power only to large land owners. Farmers, tradesmen, and professionals were relegated to second-class citizenship.

Early in the war the right of religious freedom was established. The Anglican Church lost its privileges and power. The abolition of slavery was a central topic in some areas, and was abolished in some states. Imprisonment for unpaid debts was terminated almost everywhere. The use of the death penalty was curtailed. The need for some form of public education was addressed. Pennsylvania and Virginia took the lead in establishing public schools. There was still no real unity of purpose, however.

Benjamin Franklin had proposed a plan of union in 1754. This had been rejected by England and the colonies. He again proposed his idea of union to the Continental Congress in 1775. This was ignored, probably because few considered independence then. The Articles of Confederation fell far short of providing any unity. This had been evident throughout the war. The good faith of the states was all The Congress could depend on. This was lacking far, far too often. The Articles hadn't been ratified until 1781, anyway.

Taxation had been one of the principal causes for the rebellion. In the Articles of Confederation the states had made certain The Congress could levy no taxes. It could ask for, or "requisition" funds. This didn't work. Eight million dollars had been "requisitioned" in 1781; about one and one-half million was paid into the coffers—and that not until January 1784.

The Congress may have had several purposes in mind when it passed a Land Ordinance on May 20, 1785. One of them was to bring in needed funds. Potential buyers had to pay $640 cash for a building site. Another purpose was to encourage settlement in the territory between the Appalachians and the Mississippi, north of the Ohio River. Virginians and Kentuckians, in particular, began moving into the new territory "by the forties and fifties." To protect them Colonel Josiah Harmar sent Jonathan Heart and his troops down the Ohio to strengthen Fort Harmar.

General Rufus Putnam, a member of American Union Lodge and who would become the first Grand Master of Masons in Ohio, met with several veterans in Boston on March 3, 1786. They decided to turn in their paper certificates (their pay for service during the war) for land in Ohio. On April 7, 1786, 48 men landed across from Fort Harmar and Marietta, Ohio, was born. A little later General Arthur St. Clair, a Mason, arrived to take over the territory as governor. And American Union Lodge resumed labor on June 28, 1790.

In the meantime, Provincial Grand Lodges, and lodges where there was no Grand Lodge, took the necessary steps to form independent Grand Lodges. Virginia had been the first on October 13, 1778. The schisms in South Carolina ended and a Grand Lodge was formed on December 27, 1783. Pennsylvania Freemasons reconciled their differences and organized an independent Grand Lodge on September 25, 1786. Georgia followed on December 16, 1786. So did New Jersey two days later.

The settlement of the Nothwest Territory was slow. Indians, supported by the British, continued to harrass the Americans. It wasn't until General Anthony Wayne defeated a large Indian force at Fallen Timbers (Ohio) in August, 1794, that occupying the area could be considered relatively safe.

In violation of the peace treaty, Britain continued to occupy Detroit using it as a base to supply the Indians who were fighting the Americans. In 1796 Americans gained control of what had been, with exceptions, an English base for almost 40 years. It was there (Detroit) that James Fairbain Smith reports a lodge was formed on April 27, 1764. The lodge "was actually attached to the 60th Foot or Royal American Foot Regiment of the British Army." Smith notes that several English Military lodges had occupied Detroit over the long period of its control.

European nations were wary of doing business in the United States; its credit rating was indeed poor. The individual states were ignoring the requests of The Congress. They were battling each other over boundaries and all types of "rights." Each state developed its own tariffs. New York was prospering; the "little states" felt they needed a central government to protect them from the profiteers.

Taxation became a problem again. In western and central Massachusetts a group of debt-ridden farmers decided to rebel. Headed by Daniel Shays, who had fought at Bunker Hill, Ticonderoga, Saratoga, and Stony Point, they closed a court at Northhampton on August 29, 1786. That kept the debtors from being prosecuted for a time. Shays was at the head of 1,200 men armed with pitchforks and staves in an attack on the Springfield arsenal on January 25, 1787. Three of his men were shot, but the others escaped.

Benjamin Lincoln, a member of St. Andrews Lodge, and who had received the sword of Cornwallis in the surrender at Yorktown, was placed in command of state troops to put down the rebellion. He did. Shays escaped to Vermont; most of the others were pardoned.

Daniel Shays was a member of Masters' Lodge in Albany, New York. He had attended American Union Lodge at West Point on June 24, 1779. He was one of the original petitioners for the formation of Hampshire Lodge in Massachusetts in 1786. This Lodge told the Grand Lodge of Massachusetts that by "a vote of said lodge, that the names of Daniel Shays, Luke Day and Elijah Day, who are members of that Lodge, be transmitted to the Grand Lodge to be recorded with Infamy in consequence of their conduct in the late Rebellion."

Shay had been sentenced to death, but he was later granted a pardon. The grievances of these men evidently had some validity. Many changes were made in the things they complained about.

Rioting took place in other states as well. Taxes and the necessity of paying debts in hard money appeared to be the major problems for individuals.

Maryland and Virginia bickered over navigational rights on the Potomac River. Mediators met at Mount Vernon. The talks evidently were successful because other states became interested in enlarging on them. So all the states were invited to meet to discuss general trade regulations. In September, 1786, only five states sent delegates to Annapolis, Maryland. In spite of the few delegates they set up a meeting for May, 1787, in Philadelphia. The Congress cooperated by issuing a call for the meeting. It specified, however, that the meeting should deal with revising the Articles of Confederation.

On April 19, 1787, the lodges in Maryland formed an independent Grand Lodge. What had been commenced in 1783 was finally consumated. New York followed on June 6, but it would be troubled with schisms in later years.

The Convention day was set for May 14, 1787. Bad weather and horrible roads kept many of the delegates from reaching Philadelphia. Washington had arrived, and visited his old friend Benjamin Franklin. Franklin planned on nominating Washington for President of the Convention, but he was ill. Robert Morris did it in his place.

On May 25, with the arrival of the New Jersey delegation, a quorum of seven states brought the Convention to order. George Washington was unanimously elected to preside. This would be, perhaps, the only unanimous vote for the next four months.

During the wait for a quorum the delegates from Virginia had drawn up a plan of action. Edmund Randolph, the thirty-three-year old Governor of Virginia and the Grand Master of Masons in Virginia, opened the discussion about the state of the union. *Documents Illustrative of the Formation of the Union of the American States* (hereafter called *Documents*) contains hundreds of pages of notes taken by delegates to the Convention. All of these were printed several years after the Constitution had been ratified. The delegates had kept their oath of secrecy until this was no longer necessary.

Among the delegates who took copious notes was James McHenry of Maryland, who would become a member of Spiritual Lodge No. 23, Maryland, on July 30, 1806. He covered at some length Edmund Randolph's remarks as to why concerted action must be taken to preserve the union: "He observed that the confederation fulfilled *none* of the objects for which it was framed. 1st. It does not provide against foreign invasions. 2dly. It does not secure harmony to the States. 3d. It is incapable of producing certain blessings to the States. 4th. It cannot defend itself against encroachments. 5th. It is not superior to State constitutions."

McHenry, and other accounts also printed later, show that Randolph expanded on each of his five points. He then added:

"Having pointed out its defects, let us not be afraid to view with a steady eye the perils with which we are surrounded. Look at the public countenance from New Hampshire to Georgia. Are we not on the eve of war, which is only prevented by the hopes from this convention."

Randolph then presented the "Virginia Plan," which consisted of 15 articles. The delegates resolved to act as "a committee of the whole" on the following day. Then it adjourned.

The following day, May 30, 1787, Randolph again took the floor. He proposed "that a national government ought to be established consisting of a supreme legislature, judi-iary and ex-ecutive" ["-" signifies missing letters in the quotation.] Elbridge Gerry of Massachusetts disagreed. And he presented an argument often heard even today: they didn't have the right to pass it, or "If we have a right to pass this resolution we have a right to annihilate the confederation." He, and others wanted it to read "federal" rather than "national."

Gouverneur Morris of Pennsylvania explained a federal government was merely a compact that depended on the good faith of the states; a national government would be "a complete and compulsive operation." He closed his explanation by suggesting: "We had better take a supreme government now than a despot twenty years hence—for come he must." The "nationalists" won.

The debate continued point by point. What the results of the months of arguments, discussions, and debates were is summed up in *The Annals of America:*

> The Virginia Plan was debated for two weeks, and on June 13 an amended version containing nineteen resolutions was reported out. The plan called for some separation of powers between legislative, executive, and judicial branches of government, but the executive was to be elected by the legislature, and a council consisting of the executive and several members of the judiciary would have the veto power. . . On June 15 William Paterson introduced the New Jersey plan, a "small state" plan amending the Articles of Confederation by giving the Congress some added powers.

After three more days of debate the delegates voted in favor of the fundamental changes envisioned by the Virginia Plan. The issues were sharply drawn; large states wanted proportional representation in the legislature; small states wanted equal representation. The Connecticut Compromise offered by Roger Sherman and backed by William Johnson, broke the deadlock: representation would be by population in the lower house and each state would have an equal vote in the upper house. Franklin, too, called for compromise. Of fifty-five delegates, only forty-two were present Sept. 17, when the Constitution was signed. No one voted against the document, but three delegates refused to sign it.

Actually, there were ten elected as delegates but who did not attend. Sixteen delegates who did attend didn't sign the Constitution. Rhode Island refused to send delegates.

William Pierce of Georgia, one of those who didn't sign the document, did make notes during the Convention. These were printed in *The American Historical Review* in 1898, and reprinted in *Documents*. Pierce wrote brief sketches of most of the delegates. Of Nicholas Gilman, a member of St. John's Lodge No. 1, New Hampshire, he wrote: "Mr. Gilman is modest, genteel, and sensible. There is nothing brilliant or striking in his character, but there is something respectable and worthy in the man—about 30 years of age."

Rufus King was an active Mason, considering his occupation and the period. He was a member of St. John's Lodge, Newburyport, Massachusetts. Pierce viewed him this way:

Mr. King is a Man much distinguished for his eloquence and great parlimentary talents. He was educated in Massachusetts, and is said to have good classical as well as legal knowledge. He has served for three years in the Congress of the United States with great and deserved applause, and is at this time high in the confidence and approbation of his Country-men. This Gentleman is about thirty three years of age, about five feet ten Inches high, well formed, an handsome face, with a strong expressive Eye, and a sweet high toned voice. In his public speaking there is something peculiarly strong and rich in his expression, clear, and convincing in his arguments, rapid and irresistible at times in his eloquence but he is not always equal. His action is natural, swimming, and graceful, but there is a rudeness of manner sometimes accompanying it. But take him *tout en semble*, he may with propriety be ranked among the Luminaries of the present Age.

Elbridge Gerry, who went on to become Vice President of the United States in 1813, may have been a Freemason. Heaton places him in the "doubtful" class, but the Gerry descendants believed he was. Pierce considered Gerry "very much of a Gentleman in his principles and manners."

William Paterson would become a Freemason on November 7, 1791, in Trenton Lodge No. 9, New Jersey. Pierce noted of him:

> Mr. Patterson [sic] is one of those kind of Men whose powers break in upon you, and create wonder and astonishment. He is a Man of great modesty, with looks that bespeak talents of no great extent,—but he is a Classic, a Lawyer, and an Orator;—and of disposition so favorable to his advancement that every one seemed ready to exalt him with their praises. He is very happy in the choice of time and manner of engaging in a debate, and never speaks but when he understands his subject well. This Gentleman is about 34 yr of age, of a very low stature.

About Benjamin Franklin, Pierce wrote:

> Dr. Franklin is well known to be the greatest phylosopher of the present age;—all the operations of nature he seems to understand,—the very heavens obey him, and the Clouds yield up their Lightning to be imprisoned in his rod. But what claim he has to the politician, posterity must determine. It is certain that he does not shine much in public Council,—he is no Speaker, nor does he seem to let politics engage his attention. He is, however, a most extraordinary Man, and tells a story in a style more engaging than anything I ever heard. Let his Biographer finish his character. He is 82 years old, and possesses an activity of mind equal to a youth of 25 years of age.

Heaton's account of John Dickinson contains this interesting note he gleaned from Sachse who noted Dickinson became a

Mason on January 11, 1780, in Lodge No. 18, Dover, Delaware, under the Provincial Grand Lodge of Pennsylvania: "Never since Appeared in Lodge." Pierce wrote of Dickinson:

> Mr. Dickinson has been famed through all America, for his Farmers Letters; he is a Scholar, and said to be a Man of very extensive information. When I saw him in the Convention I was induced to pay the greatest attention to him whenever he spoke. I had often heard that he was a great Orator, but I found him an indifferent Speaker. With an affected air of wisdom he labors to produce a trifle,—his language is irregular and incorrect,—his flourishes, (for he sometimes attempts them), are like expiring flames, they just shew themselves and go out;—no traces of them are left on the mind to cheer or animate it. He is, however, a good writer and will be ever considered one of the most important characters in the United States. He is almost 55 years old, and was bred a Quaker.

Pierce's account of Jacob Broom, unfortunately is too brief. No picture of Broom can be found. And Pierce merely says of this member of Lodge No. 14, Christiana Ferry, Delaware: "Mr. Broom is a plain good Man, with some abilities, but nothing to render him conspicuous. He is silent in public, but cheerful and conversable in private. He is about 35 years old."

James McHenry served as an assistant secretary to George Washington for two years during the war. Earlier he had served as a surgeon for the 5th Pennsylvania Battalion. In 1780 he became Aide-de-Camp to General Lafayette, serving with him throughout Virginia and at Yorktown. Pierce noted this about McHenry, then added: "He is a man of specious talents, with nothing of genious to improve them. As a politician there is nothing remarkable in him, nor has he any of the graces of the Orator. He is however, a very respectable young Gentleman, and deserves the honor which his Country had bestowed on him. Mr. McHenry is about 32 years of age."

McHenry became a Master Mason in Spiritual Lodge No. 23, Maryland, on July 30, 1806.

Daniel Carroll was a Catholic and a member of Lodge No. 16, Baltimore, Maryland. He was made a Master Mason on

May 8, 1781. On September 18, 1793, he participated, along with George Washington, in laying the cornerstone of the National Capitol. He had been a member of the Continental Congress from 1780 to 1784. Pierce noted: "Mr. Carrol is a Man of large fortune, and influence in his State. He possesses plain good sense, and is in the full confidence of his Countrymen."

Concerning George Washington, Pierce wrote:

> Genl. Washington is well known as the Commander in chief of the late American Army. Having conducted these States to independence and peace, he now appears to assist in framing a Government to make the People happy. Like Gustavus Vasa, he may be said to be the deliverer of his Country;—like Peter the great he appears as the politician and the States-man; and like Cincinnatus he returned to his farm perfectly contented with being only a plain Citizen, after enjoying the highest honor of the Confederacy,—and now only seeks for the approbation of his Countrymen by being virtuous and useful. The General was conducted to the Chair as President of the Convention by the unanimous voice of its Members. He is in the 52d year of his age.

His age was underestimated by three years. On June 24, 1784, Washington met with officers and members of Lodge No. 39 in Alexandria, Virginia, then chartered by the Provincial Grand Lodge of Pennsylvania. He had attended a meeting of the Lodge and joined the members and visitors when they went "to Jno Wise's Tavern, where they Dined & after spending the afternoon in Masonick Festivity, returned to the Lodge room. The Worshipful Master with the unanimous consent of the Brethren, was pleased to admit his Excellency Genl Washington as an Honorary Member of Lodge No. 39."

This paved the way for Washington to become a Worshipful Master. In 1786 the Provincial Grand Lodge of Pennsylvania organized an independent Grand Lodge. Lodge No. 39 was requested to apply for a new charter. Instead it asked the Grand Lodge of Virginia for one—but not until May 29, 1788, and after Washington had agreed to become Charter Worshipful Master. The charter was issued by Grand Master Edmund

Randolph on April 28, 1788, to Alexandria Lodge No. 22. In December, Washington was elected Master. On December 27, 1789, his friend Dr. Elisha Dick, who had stepped aside so his friend could serve, succeeded him.

The first Grand Master of Masons in Virginia, John Blair, Jr., was also a member of the Convention. Pierce wrote of him: "Mr. Blair is one of the most respectable Men in Virginia, both on account of his Family as well as his fortune. He is one of the Judges of the Supreme Court in Virginia, and acknowledged to have a very extensive knowledge of the Laws. Mr. Blair however, no Orator, but his good sense, and most excellent principles, compensate for other deficiencies. He is about 50 years of age."

John Blair, Jr., was made a Mason in 1762 in a lodge held at Crown Tavern, Williamsburg, Virginia. He succeeded Peyton Randolph as Worshipful Master of Williamsburg Lodge on June 7, 1774. He was Chief Justice of Virginia's Supreme Court, and would become one of the first justices of the United States Supreme Court.

Pierce wrote of Edmund Randolph: "Mr. Randolph is Governor of Virginia,—a young Gentleman in whom unite all the accomplishments of the Scholar, and the Statesman. He came forward with the postulata, or first principles, on which the Convention acted, and he supported them with a force of eloquence and reasoning that did him great honor. He has a most harmonious voice, a fine person and striking manners. Mr. Randolph is about 32 years of age."

Randolph had been an Aide-de-Camp to Washington. He had been a member of the Continental Congress from 1779-1782. He would become the first Attorney General of the United States. He would also succeed Jefferson as Secretary of State in 1794. He was made a Master Mason in Williamsburg Lodge, Virginia, on May 28, 1774. He became the Charter Master of Jerusalem Lodge No. 54, Richmond, in 1797. As third Grand Master he signed a charter for Richmond-Randolph Lodge No. 19, named in his honor.

Pierce explains why he kept sketches of these, and the other delegates, to the Constitutional Convention: "I possess ambition, and it was that, and the flattering opinion which some of my Friends had of me, that gave me a seat in the wisest Council in the World, and furnished me with an opportunity of giving these short Sketches of the Characters who composed it."

The Society of Cincinnati was formed in 1783 with George Washington as its President and General Henry Knox as Secretary. Many of its members were Freemasons. Its purpose was to provide aid for widows and orphans of those officers who had died during the war. Its membership was restriced to the officers of the Continental Army and their descendants. On July 4, 1787, Joel Barlow addressed this Society at Hartford, Connecticut.

Barlow became a member of St. John's Lodge No. 4 in Hartford six months after his speech. Where he was originally made a Mason is not known. He served as a Chaplain during the war, and was the Chaplain at the execution of Major Andre', the British spy. Within his speech on the eleventh anniversary of the adoption of the Declaration of Independence he noted:

> . . . Whatever praise is due for the task already perfomed, it is certain that much remains to be done. The Revolution is but half completed. Independence and government were the two objects contended for, and but one is yet obtained. To the glory of the present age and the admiration of the future, our severance from the British Empire was conducted upon principles as noble as they were new and unprecedented in the history of human action. Could the same generous principles, the same wisdom and unanimity be exerted in effecting the establishment of a permanent federal system, what an additional luster would it pour upon the present age! A luster hitherto unequaled; a display of magnanimity for which mankind may never behold another opportunity.
>
> Without an efficient government, our independence will cease to be a blessing.
>
> * * * * *
>
> The present is justly considered an alarming crisis, perhaps the most alarming that America ever saw. We

have contended with the most powerful nation, and subdued the bravest and best appointed armies; but now we
have to contend with ourselves, and encounter passions
and prejudices more powerful than armies, and more
dangerous to our peace. It is not for glory, it is for existence
that we contend.

Much is expected from the Federal Convention now sitting in Philadelphia, and it is a happy circumstance that so
general a confidence from all parts of the country is
centered in that respectable body. Their former services,
as individuals, command it, and our situation requires it.
But although much is expected from them, yet more is
demanded from ourselves.

Much was indeed expected of the men who labored in the
sweltering weather in Philadelphia. The day after Barlow spoke
a special committee reported its compromise to end the "war"
between the delegates of the small and large states. It was a
week or so later before the large states agreed that one branch of
government would have an equal vote; the other branch would
have votes according to population.

The impasse had been broken. Work then began on the remaining points of the Virginia Plan. After sixty votes the
delegates agreed on the method for electing the executive officer
for the country.

Slowly all the points were brought together. The legislative
branch would become The Congress. It would consist of the
House of Representatives and the Senate. The executive would
become the President. Details on voting, who could hold office,
and a multitude of other items were hammered together. The
last long argument was over how this new Constitution should
be ratified. It was finally decided that nine states would have to
approve it before it could be adopted.

On September 17, 1787, the Constitution of the United States
was engrossed on parchment. It was ready for the signatures of
the delegates. Forty-two delegates were present at the end of
the Convention. Of these, thirty-nine signed, three refused:
Gerry, Mason, and Randolph.

Battlelines were drawn. Ratification wouldn't come easily.

Seventeen

THE BATTLE FOR RATIFICATION

A STRONG central government! That's what appeared to have been the results of the deliberations in Philadelphia. That's what the rebellion had been all about—a strong central government. Fear became widespread. Much would be said for and against the adoption of the Constitution. Both sides had the support of good men.

According to *Documents* the following letter was transmitted to The President of The Congress "from The President of the Federal Convention":

IN CONVENTION, SEPTEMBER 17, 1787

Sir,

We have now the honor to submit to the consideration of the United States in Congress assembled, that Constitution which has appeared to us the most advisable.

The friends of our country have long seen and desired, that the power of making war, peace, and treaties, that of levying money and regulating commerce, and the correspondent executive and judicial authorities should be fully and effectually vested in the general government of the Union: But the impropriety of delegating such extensive trust to one body of men is evident—Hence results the necessity of a different organization.

It is obviously impracticable in the federal government of these states, to secure all rights of independent sovereignty to each, and yet provide for the interest and safety of all: Individuals entering into society, must give up a share of liberty to preserve the rest. The magnitude of the sacrifice must depend as well on situation and circumstance, as on the object to be obtained. It is at all times difficult to draw with precision the line between these

rights which must be surrendered, and those which may be
reserved; and on the present occasion this difficulty was increased by a difference among the several states as to their
situation, extent, habits, and particular interests.

In all our deliberations on this subject we kept steadily
in our view, that which appears to us the greatest interest
of every true American, the consolidation of our Union, in
which is involved our prosperity, felicity, safety, perhaps
our national existence. This important consideration,
seriously and deeply impressed on our minds, led each
state in the Convention to be less rigid on points of inferior
magnitude, than might have been otherwise expected; and
thus the Constitution, which we now present, is the result
of a spirit of amity, and of that mutual deference and concession which the peculiarity of our political situation
rendered indispensable.

That it will meet the full and entire approbation of
every state is not perhaps to be expected; but each will
doubtless consider, that had her interest been alone consulted, the consequences might have been particularly
disagreeable or injurious to others; that it is liable to as few
exceptions as could reasonably have been expected, we
hope and believe; that it may promote the lasting welfare
of that country so dear to us all, and secure her freedom
and happiness, is our most ardent wish.

With great respect, We have the honor to be, Sir,
Your Excellency's
most obedient and humble servants,
GEORGE WASHINGTON, *President.*

By unanimous Order of the Convention.
His Excellency The PRESIDENT OF CONGRESS.

On Friday Sept 28. 1787 the Constitution was submitted to
the states after this resolution was adopted:

Congress assembled present Newhampshire Massa-
chusetts Connecticut New York New Jersey Pennsylvania.
Delaware Virginia North Carolina South Carolina and
Georgia and from Maryland Mr Ross

Congress having received the report of the Convention
lately assembled in Philadelphia

Resolved Unanimously that the said Report with the resolutions and letter accompanying the same be transmitted

to the several legislatures in Order to be submitted to a convention of Delegates chosen in each state by the people thereof in conformity to the resolves of the Convention made and provided in that case.

Delaware was the first state to ratify the Constitution. It did so on December 7, 1787. For centuries the state would let the world know it considered itself "the first State." Pennsylvania followed five days later, but the fight had been difficult. New Jersey was next on December 18, 1787. Georgia approved on January 2, and Connecticut agreed on January 9, 1788.

Massachusetts accepted the Constitution on February 6, 1788. But it added suggestions: "And as it is the opinion of this Convention that certain amendments & alterations in the said Constitution would remove the fears & quiet the apprehensions of many of the good people of this Commonwealth & more effectually guard against an undue administration of the Federal Government." There followed nine suggested "alterations & provisions to be introduced into the said Constitutions." These would become the basis for the "Bill of Rights."

The President of the Massachusetts Convention was JOHN HANCOCK who had been prominent throughout the difficulties with Great Britain. Hancock had been made a Mason in Marchants Lodge No. 277, Quebec, in 1762. He affiliated with St. Andrew's Lodge in Boston on October 14, 1762. It was he who presided over The Congress when the Declaration of Independence was adopted. It is his signature that has stood out boldly throughout the years.

Vice President of the Massachusetts Convention was WILLIAM CUSHING, also a member of St. Andrew's Lodge. He studied law with another Mason, JEREMY GRIDLEY, after he had graduated from Harvard. He became Attorney General for Massachusetts; and in 1772 became a Judge of the Superior Court and was Chief Justice in 1777. He was one of the founders of the American Academy of Arts and Sciences. In 1789, Washington appointed him a Justice of the United States Supreme Court. He turned down appointment as Chief Justice in 1796. His father, NATHANIAL, was also a Mason, and fought throughout the war. After the war he moved to Ohio where he became the first Worshipful Master of Farmer's Lodge No. 20 in Belpre.

GEORGE PLATER was President of the Maryland Convention when it ratified the Constitution on April 28, 1788. He was the first Junior Warden of the lodge at Leonardtown, Maryland, when it was chartered on June 6, 1759, later serving several terms as Worshipful Master. He served from 1778-1781 in The Congress.

The eighth state to ratify was South Carolina on May 23, 1788. It also added qualifications. On June 21 New Hampshire became the ninth state to ratify, thereby making the Constitution of the United States a legal and binding document. It wanted twelve "alterations & provisions be introduced into the said Constitution."

OLIVER ELLSWORTH probably had much to do with the favorable action of the delegates to the New Hampshire Convention. He became a charter member of St. John's Lodge of Princeton, New Jersey, on December 27, 1765. He served in the Continental Congress from 1778 to 1783, and was a member of the Constitutional Convention of 1787. It was he who had the term "national government" changed in the final draft to "government of the United States." He was called away before he could sign the Constitution but he fought for its ratification.

His "open letter" to the citizens of New Hampshire on March 10, 1778, undoubtedly swayed many who opposed ratification. Much of what he wrote remains pertinent today. In his opening he stated:

> Those who enjoy the blessings of society must be willing to suffer some restraint of personal liberty, and devote some part of their property to the public that the remainder may be secured and protected. The cheapest form of government is not always best, for parsimony, though it spends little, generally gains nothing. Neither is that the best government which imposes the least restraint on its subjects; for the benefit of having others restrained may be greater than the disadvantage of being restrained ourselves. That is the best form of government which

returns the greatest number of advantages in proportion to the disadvantages with which it is attended.

Ellsworth pointed out the benefit of a strong fishery industry, navigational protection, and lumber industry for New Hampshire. He said these were of little value "until American navigation and commerce are placed on a respectable footing which no single state can do by itself."

He concluded his letter: "Let the citizens of New Hampshire candidly consider these facts and they must be convinced that no other state is so much interested in adopting that system of government now under consideration."

Virginia became the tenth state to approve the document on June 26, 1788. The delegates there didn't know of New Hampshire's action, so the debate remained stormy to the end. Patrick Henry bitterly opposed ratification. It took the power and eloquence of EDMUND RANDOLPH, who had been converted, to sway the assembly. JOHN MARSHALL, a member of Richmond Lodge No. 10 and Richmond-Randolph No. 19, argued for approval. Marshall, although he never served as a Worshipful Master, was elected Grand Master of Masons in Virginia in 1793. He would serve as Chief Justice of the U.S. Supreme Court from 1801 to 1835.

President of the Virginia Convention was EDMUND PENDLETON, a member of Fairfax Lodge No. 43, Culpepper, Virginia. He was a member of the First Continental Congress. It was he who drafted the resolution that Richard Henry Lee introduced which resulted in the Declaration of Independence. His nephew, NATHANIEL PENDLETON, fought in the war and became a major under Nathanael Greene. He became a member of Solomon's Lodge No. 1, Savannah, Georgia.

EDMUND PENDLETON, a member of Fairfax Lodge No. 43, came out of retirement to accept the presidency of the Virginia Convention. Although it was well-known that he favored ratification, the opponents probably believed he would remain quiet as the presiding officer. He didn't. He took on the giant Patrick Henry who violently opposed the adoption of the Constitution.

After Henry had completed a lengthy and impassioned speech, Pendleton turned the Chair over to someone else, and began:

> Mr. Chairman, my worthy friend has expressed great uneasiness in his mind and informed us that a great many of our citizens are also extremely uneasy at the proposal of changing our government; but that, a year ago, before this fatal system was thought of, the public mind was at perfect repose. It is necessary to inquire whether the public mind was at ease on the subject, and if it be since disturbed, what was the cause. What was the situation of this country before the meeting of the federal Convention? Our general government was totally inadequate to the purpose of its institution; our commerce decayed; our finances deranged; public and private credit destroyed. These and many other national evils rendered necessary the meeting of that Convention. If the public mind was then at ease, it did not result from a conviction of being in a happy and easy situation; it must have been an inactive, unaccountable stupor.

Point by point Pendleton slashed away Patrick Henry's arguments. In the end the proponents won.

July 2, 1788, became an historical day in the history of the United States. A resolution was submitted to The Congress:

> Congress assembled present Newhampshire Massachusetts Rhodeisland Connecticut New York New Jersey, Pensylvania Virginia North Carolina South Carolina & Georgia & from Maryland Mr Contee
>
> * * * * * * * * * * * * * * * * *
>
> The State of Newhampshire having ratified the constitution transmitted to them by the Act of the 28 of Septr last & transmitted to Congress their ratification & the same being read, the president reminded Congress that this was the ninth ratification transmitted & laid before them. Whereupon
> On Motion of Mr Clarke seconded by Mr Edwards
> Ordered That the ratifications of the constitution of the United States transmitted to Congress be referred to a comee [committee] to examine the same and report an Act to Congress for putting the said constitution into operation in pursuance of the resolutions of the late federal Convention.
> On the question to agree to this Order the yeas & nays being required by Mr Yates

Mr. Robert Yates of New York was the only one to vote "nay"; the representatives from Rhode Island were "excused."

New York approved the Constitution on July 26, 1788. Even though ratification was a reality, without the approval of this large, centrally located state implementation of the provisions of the document would have been difficult, if not impossible. GEORGE CLINTON presided over the New York Convention while he was Governor of the state.

Clinton had been a Brigadier General during the war. He would have been one of the Signers of the Declaration of Independence, but had been called to special duty by Washington at the time. He would become Vice President of the United States in 1805. He served as Worshipful Master of Warren Lodge No. 17 in New York City in 1800. At least five lodges were named in his honor. He was an uncle of DEWITT CLINTON who would serve as Grand Master of Masons in New York from 1806 to 1819.

New York wanted several additions made to the Constitution. So did North Carolina. North Carolina approved the Constitution on November 21, 1789. It had met in August, 1788, but deferred action hoping several amendments would be made. They weren't. So North Carolina suggested twenty-six items to "improve" the documents.

SAMUEL "SAM" JOHNSTON was President of the Convention. He had been active in local politics since 1759. He was the first Grand Master in North Carolina, serving from 1787 to 1792.

The Federal Government stopped all commerce between Rhode Island and the United States. So the politicians in the state finally ratified the Constitution on May 9, 1790! They did so, though, with many qualifications. They wanted twenty-one changes made immediately. And, until these changes were made, "the militia of this State will not be continued in service out of this State for a longer term than six weeks." The delegates virtually promised to obey only those provisions they believed consistent with the laws of Rhode Island.

The Congress met on September 13, 1788, and adopted a resolution ending its life:

. . . And whereas the constitution so reported by the Convention and by Congress transmitted to the several legislatures has been ratified in the manner therein declared to be sufficient for the establishment of the same and such ratifications duly authenticated have been received by Congress and are filed in the Office of the Secretary therefore Resolved That the first Wednesday in Jany next be the day for appointing Electors in the several states, which before the said day shall have ratified the said Constitution; that the first Wednesday in feby next be the day for the electors to assemble in their respective states and vote for a president; And that the first Wednesday in March next be the time and the present seat of Congress the place for commencing proceedings under the said constitution—

An important era in the history of the New World had reached a conclusion.

Eighteen

THE FORMATIVE YEARS

ON the first Wednesday of January 1789 electors were chosen to select the man who would become the leader of America. The name of GEORGE WASHINGTON was spoken everywhere. And this man was reluctant to give up the peace and tranquility of Mount Vernon. He believed tranquility was something he had earned.

Alexander Hamilton, among others, had urged Washington to accept the job if it was offered to him. He finally answered Hamilton's letter: "I should unfeignedly rejoice," wrote Washington on October 3, "in case the Electors, by giving their votes in favor of some other person" because it "would save me from the dreaded Dilemma of being forced to accept or refuse." He desired "to live and die in peace and retirement on my own farm."

His retirement would have to wait. The electors chose him unanimously. Charles Thomson, former secretary of the Continental Congress, arrived at Mount Vernon on April 14, 1789, to officially give Washington the results that had been known for two months.

Requests for special favors had been pouring in to Mount Vernon. He replied to one received from Benjamin Harrison:

> I will go the chair under no pre-engagement of any kind or nature whatsoever. But, when in it, I will, to the best of my judgement, discharge the duties of the office with that impartiality and zeal for the public good, which ought never to suffer connections of blood or friendship to intermingle so as to have the least sway on decisions of a public nature. I may err, notwithstanding my most strenuous

GEORGE WASHINGTON TAKING THE OATH OF OFFICE

The oath was administered by the Grand Master of New York, Robert R. Livingston, on the Bible supplied by St. John's Lodge No. 1, New York City.

efforts to execute the difficult trust with fidelity and unexceptionably; but my errors shall be of the head, not of the heart. For all recommendations and appointments, so far as they may depend upon or come from me, a due regard shall be had to the fitness of characters, the pretensions of different candidates, and, so far as is proper, to political consideration. These shall be invariably my governing motives.

To clear his accounts at home, Washington had to borrow five hundred pounds. He had to so something he "never expected to be driven to, that is, borrow money on Interest." Then, on April 16, he left Mount Vernon with feelings "not unlike those of a culprit, who is going to the place of his execution." The journey was long and triumphal. When he entered New York he said: "The display. . . filled my mind with sensations as painful. . . . as they are pleasing."

A year earlier, on April 28, 1788, a charter had been issued by the Grand Lodge of Virginia for Alexandria Lodge No. 22. It had been chartered by the Grand Lodge of Pennsylvania as number 39. George Washington was named first and in bold type by the Grand Master, EDMUND RANDOLPH. On December 20 Washington was elected Worshipful Master of the Lodge. So, at the time he was elected President of the United States he was Master of his Lodge.

There were other Masonic notes at his inauguration on April 30, 1789, in New York City. There was no Holy Bible available on which he could take the oath of office. General JACOB MORTON, Worshipful Master of St. John's Lodge No. 1, rushed to his Lodge to get the altar Bible. After Morton had returned to the balcony of Federal Hall on Wall Street, Washington, then, with one hand over his heart, the other on the Sacred Volume, took the oath of office as first President of the United States. The Grand Master of Masons in New York, ROBERT R. LIVINGSTON, Chancellor, administered the oath.

The new President was dressed in fine style. His suit of brown broadcloth, specially spun for him in Connecticut. Its buttons had an eagle, with wings spread, stamped on them. His stockings were white silk; his shoe buckles, silver; his hair was powdered and worn in a queue. At his side hung a dress sword.

The *Federal Gazette* of Philadelphia reported: "The impression of his past services, the concourse of spectators, the devout fervency with which he repeated the oath, and the reverential manner in which he bowed down and kissed the sacred volume—all these conspired to render it one of the most august and interesting spectacles ever exhibited on this globe. It seemed, from the number of witnesses, to be a solemn appeal to Heaven and earth at once. Upon the subject of this great and Good man, I may perhaps be an enthusiast; but I confess that I was under an awful and religious persuasion that the gracious Ruler of the Universe was looking down at that moment with peculiar complacency."

The work of creating a government began. Opinions differed among the people and the politicians. The differences would grow throughout the years as the country expanded and the population exploded. Not to be overlooked was the demand for changes to the Constitution. Promises had to be kept in this regard. Under the leadership of James Madison of Virginia, The Congress lost no time submitting twelve amendments to the states.

In its resolution it was recorded: "Congress of the United States, begun and held at the City of New York, on Wednesday the fourth of March, one thousand seven hundred and eighty nine:

> THE Conventions of a number of the States, having at the time of their adopting the Constitution, expressed a desire, in order to prevent misconstruction or abuse of its powers, that further declaratory and restrictive clauses should be added: And as extending the ground of public confidence in the Government, will best ensure the beneficent ends of its institutions:
> RESOLVED by the Senate and House of Representatives of the United States of America, in Congress assembled, two thirds of both Houses concurring, that the following Articles be proposed to the Legislatures of the several states, as Amendments to the Constitution of the

United States, all or any of which Articles, when ratified by three fourths of the said Legislatures, to be valid to all intents and purposes, as part of the said Constitution; viz

ARTICLES in addition to, and Amendment of the Constitution of the United States of America, proposed by Congress, and ratified by the Legislatures of the several States, pursuant to the fifth Article of the original Constitution.

There followed twelve suggested amendments. Of these, ten were adopted by December 15, 1791.

Two of the four signers of the resolution placing the articles before the several states were Freemasons. JOHN BECKLEY, Clerk of the House of Representatives, was a member of Williamsburg Lodge No. 6, Virginia. FREDERICK AUGUSTUS MUHLENBERG, Speaker of the House of Representatives, was a member of Lodge No. 3, Pennsylvania.

It was fortunate that a President had been chosen who had sat through the eighty-seven gruelling days of debate over the Constitution. As the Presiding officer of that Convention, Washington knew what had been discussed. He knew what the consensus of the delegates had been. Although he had to break completely new ground, he knew where many of the pitfalls were and how to avoid them. His vast knowledge gained as Commander-in-Chief throughout the war, in politics before and after the war, and as the sole owner of a thriving business in private life, became welcome assets during his eight years as head of the new government.

Washington and his commissioners began laying out the boundaries of the Federal District on March 30, 1791. They would include portions of Alexandria, Virginia, and Georgetown, Maryland, on opposite sides of the Potomac. The boundary stone was laid with Masonic ceremonies on April 15, 1791. Dr. ELISHA CULLEN DICK, Worshipful Master of Alexandria Lodge, officiated. Freemasons from other lodges were present for the occasion. Many were from Lodge No. 9 of Maryland. From the beginning of the National Capital, Freemasonry played an important role.

This role continued when the cornerstone of "The President's House" was laid. The only account of this event appeared in the *City Gazette* of Charlotte, South Carolina, on November 15, 1792. The article was the result of "a letter from a gentleman in Philadelphia"; "On Saturday the 13th inst. the first stone was laid in the south-west corner of the president's house, in the city of Washington, by the Free Masons of Georgetown and its vicinity, who assembled on the occasion. The procession was formed at the Fountain Inn, Georgetown."

Ten months later, on September 18, 1793, the cornerstone of the United States Capital was laid. JAMES HOBAN, the architect for the Capital was a Roman Catholic and also a Freemason. He and several other Masons had requested a charter from the Grand Lodge of Maryland for Federal Lodge. It was granted just days before the greatest Masonic event ever took place.

Law and order became one of the first priorities of the new government. EDMUND RANDOLPH, a Virginia Freemason, was chosen as Attorney General. John Jay became the first Chief Justice of the Supreme Court. No proof exists concerning Jay and Masonic membership, but a letter he wrote to Washington on April 29, 1779, is interesting: "The dissolution of our government threw us into a political chaos. Time, Wisdom and Perseverance will reduce it into Form, and give it Strength, Order and Harmony. In this work you are (in the style of your professions) a Master Builder, and God grant that you may long continue a Free and Accepted one."

The Freemason, HENRY KNOX, was appointed by Washington as Secretary of War. Alexander Hamilton was appointed Secretary of the Treasury. Although the painting, *The Petition*, shows Hamilton along with Washington and many other Masonic Patriots, Hamilton wasn't a member of the Craft. His son, Philip, would become a Past Master, however.

Samuel Osgood became Postmaster General; Thomas Jefferson, Secretary of State. Neither of these was a Freemason. This points out that Washington didn't surround himself with Masons, but selected the men he considered best for a particular job, regardless of their affiliations and backgrounds.

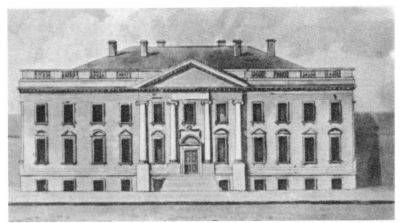

Upper: The White House or "The President's House" as first completed, from a London Print, 1807.

Lower: One of the Stones taken from the original foundation. The
  "Mason Mark" is discernible at the left side, center.

The new government took over a debt of eighty million dollars! The money had to come from somewhere. James Madison asked for a temporary tariff to keep the government going day-by-day. From the beginning, it appeared The Congress would be operating a "government by crisis," something that would continue throughout most of its history.

Was James Madison a Freemason? Ronald E. Heaton emphatically believes Madison wasn't. He quotes one Dr. Donald O. Dewey, an editor of *The Papers of James Madison* at length to prove this point. Madison did congratulate JOHN FRANCIS MERCER, Governor of Maryland, on February 11, 1795, "on your becoming a Free-Mason—a very ancient and honorable fraternity." Dewey claims this was a joke! Yet, it's strange that Madison would use the term "fraternity" as a joke; a term the uninitiated would hardly consider. But, there's no hard proof of Madison's membership. There will always be those who believe he was and those who believe he wasn't.

Alexander Hamilton, before the first year had ended, proposed a broad system of taxation. His funding plans ran into trouble. Speculators rejoiced. They rushed to purchase script, for example, that had been given to soldiers for their back pay. Purchases made at one-fourth the face value were soon after redeemed at full value. States that had paid their debts were furious; those still in debt were delighted.

Hamilton argued that the need for foreign and domestic credit necessitated a monetarily sound federal government. The need for freer trade, along with the forceful arguments of Hamilton, finally won. Even though he was often opposed by Thomas Jefferson, he continued to set the monetary policies of the government. This caused one senator to say: "Congress may go home. Mr. Hamilton is all-powerful, and fails in nothing he attempts."

Jefferson and his followers claimed what was happening in The Congress was "warping the Constitution." An exasperated Representative Fisher Ames of Massachusetts cried: "I scarce know a point which has not produced this cry, not excepting a motion for adjournment. The fishery bill was unconstitutional; it was unconstitutional to receive plans of finance from the Secretary; to give bounties; to make the militia worth having; order is unconstitutional; credit is tenfold worse."

The creators, the thinkers, had no protection for their "research and development." But this changed. On April 10, 1790, Washington signed into law a patent bill.

A permanent site for the United States capital had to be chosen. This provoked endless debates. Southerners wanted it in the South; Northerners, in the North. A compromise was finally reached. The capital was moved from New York to Philadelphia on December 6, 1790. It was understood, however, the permanent site would be on the Potomac. The act establishing a "permanent seat of government" was signed by the President on July 16, 1790.

Washington visited the site less than a year later and found the "Landholders" at odds. He met with the concerned parties, pointed out several facts, and was able to write in his diary that they "having taken the matter into consideration saw the propriety of my observations."

The President had visited the New England states, with the exception of the "foreign" Rhode Island, in 1789. The latter he visited after it had ratified the Constitution to welcome it into the fold. The members of King David's Lodge welcomed him heartily. He later wrote: "Being persuaded that a just application of the principles, on which the Masonic Fraternity is founded, must be promotive of private virtue and public prosperity, I shall always be happy to advance the interests of the Society, and to be considered by them as a deserving brother."

The President left Mount Vernon on April 5, 1791, to tour the southern states. He was welcomed everywhere by Freemasons. St. John's Lodge of New Bern, North Carolina, greeted him. So did Prince George's Lodge of Georgetown, South Carolina. Grand Master MORDECAI GIST of South Carolina, an old army friend, welcomed him to Charleston. He was welcomed to Savannah, Georgia, by Grand Master GEORGE HOUSTON.

In 1792 Washington was elected again. And once more he was confronted with a revolution. This one was in France. The politicians in American were as divided over this one as they had been over America's. Jefferson and Hamilton differed over support for the French revolution as they did over almost everything else. Political parties were being formed, something Washington was opposed to.

Washington was again inaugurated President on March 4, 1793. On April 22 he issued this proclamation:

BY THE PRESIDENT OF
THE UNITED STATES OF AMERICA

Whereas it appears that a state of war exists between Austria, Prussia, Sardinia, Great Britain, and the United Netherlands on the one part and France on the other, and the duty and interest of the United States require that they should with sincerity and good faith adopt and pursue a conduct friendly and impartial toward the belligerent powers:

I have therefore thought fit by these presents to declare the disposition of the United States to observe the conduct aforesaid toward those powers respectively, and to exhort and warn the citizens of the United States carefully to avoid all acts and proceedings whatsoever which may in any manner tend to contravene such disposition.

And I do hereby also make known that whosoever of the citizens of the United States shall render himself liable to punishment or forfeiture under the law of nations by committing, aiding or abetting hostilities against any of the said powers, or by carrying to any of them those articles which are deemed contraband by the modern usage of nations, will not receive the protection of the United States against such punishment or forfeiture; and further, that I have given instructions to those officers to whom it belongs to cause prosecutions to be instituted against all persons who shall, within the congnizance of the courts of the United States, violate the law of nations with respect to the powers at war, or any of them.

Jefferson and JAMES MONROE were opposed to the proclamation. Both believed the United States should aid France. Monroe, while Minister to France, wrote several letters to Jefferson in support of the committee's position. Then in January,

1794, Jefferson resigned. EDMUND RANDOLPH of Virginia became the Secretary of State.

John Jay was sent to England by Washington to try to strengthen trade between the two countries. He was also supposed to have the British evacuate their Northwest military posts, keep Britain from encouraging Indian attacks, and stop the seizing of American ships and seamen. Jay failed. The treaty he brought back was finally passed by the Senate, but it pleased no one.

September 18, 1793, must have been one of the most memorable days in the life of George Washington. In many respects the Federal city was the work of Washington—the builder. He had appointed the commissioners, the engineers, the surveyors, and had directed their planning and work. He had brought about an agreement between opposing factions among the land holders, saving the country millions of dollars in purchase of land. And it was the day the cornerstone of the Federal Capitol was laid.

Newspaper accounts of the ceremonies were glowing. There was "one of the grandest Masonic processions" that "took place, for the purpose of laying the cornerstone of the Capitol of the United States, which, perhaps, was never exhibited on the like important occasion." The procession was led by Alexandria Lodge No. 22 of Virginia and "Lodge No. 9" of Maryland. When the preliminaries were over "The President of the United States, and his attendant brethren, ascended from the cavazion to the east of the corner-stone, and there the Grand Master *pro tem.*, elevated on a triple rostrum, delivered an oration fitting the occasion."

The revolution in France continued and Washington learned that his close friend and Brother Mason, LAFAYETTE, had been declared a traitor and taken prisoner. He would remain one for five years, much to the distress of Washington.

Then came the "Whiskey Rebellion." Western farmers were converting much of their corn and rye into whiskey. Washington and Hamilton urged the Congress to place a moderate tax on the spirits. The farmers didn't appreciate that. Those in Pennsylvania, in particular, drove federal treasury officials away when they attempted to collect the tariff.

Washington called up the militia. Fifteen thousand rendezvoused under the leadership of the President. They marched over the mountains on October 23, 1794. The rebellion ended. No one was hurt. Those who were arrested were pardoned by Washington in July, 1795.

Washington firmly refused to allow his name to be put up for another term. He began work on his farewell address. It was a masterful piece of work. He spent considerable time in apologizing to the people for his refusal to seek a third term. He thanked them for their support throughout the years. He asked them to continue to support the Constitution—and liberty. He then added his advice for the future:

> The unity of government which constitutes you one people is also now dear to you. It is justly so, for it is a main pillar in the edifice of your real independence; the support of your tranquility at home, your peace abroad; of your safety; of that very liberty which you so highly prize. But as it is easy to foresee that, from different causes and from different quarters, much pains will be taken, many artifices employed to weaken in your minds the conviction of this truth; as this is the point in your political fortress against which the batteries of internal and external enemies will be most constantly and actively (though often covertly and insidiously) directed, it is of infinite moment that you should properly estimate the immense value of your national Union to your collective and individual happiness. . . .

He warned against political parties and those "designing men" who "may endeavor to excite a belief that there is a real difference of local interests and views." He advised his listeners to "shield yourselves against the jealousies and heart-burnings which spring from" those who spread "misrepresentations." He used many other adjectives to show his disapproval of political parties.

He asked the people to support religion and morality; to promote "institutions for the general diffusion of knowledge"; to cherish "public credit"; avoid the "accumulation of debt"; "in time of peace to discharge the debts which unavoidable wars may have occasioned, not ungenerously throwing upon posterity the burdens which we ourselves ought to bear"; "to have revenue there must be taxes; that no tax can be devised which is not, more or less, inconvenient and unpleasant."

He asked for justice for all nations. He felt there should be no such thing as a "favored" nation, but all should be treated equally by the United States. But he warned against "the insidious wiles of foreign influence," because "the jealousy of a free People ought to be constantly awake." Political connections with foreign countries should be kept at a minimum.

On October 7, 1796, Washington addressed The Congress for the last time. He stressed the need for a strong naval force, a national university, and:

> The institution of a military academy is also recommended by cogent reasons. However pacific the general policy of a nation may be, it ought never to be without an adequate stock of military knowledge for emergencies.

The Grand Lodge of Pennsylvania showed its appreciatgion of what Washington had done for his country. On December 27, 1796, a letter was drafted and approved which was sent to "the Great Master Workman, our Illustrious Br. Washington." Washington thanked the Grand Lodge in a letter written by his own hand.

In the last paragraph of a touching letter he wrote to his friend and Brother HENRY KNOX, Washington said: "As early next week as I can make arragements for it, I shall commence my journey for Mount Vernon. Tomorrow, at dinner, I shall, as a servant of the public, take my leave of the President Elect, of the foreign characters, heads of Departments, &ca. And the day following, with pleasure, I shall witness the inauguration of my Successor to the Chair of government."

On March 4, 1797, John Adams, the new President, wrote to his wife Abigail: "A solemn scene it was indeed, and it was made more affecting to me by the presence of the General, whose countenance was as serene and unclouded as the day. He seemed to enjoy a triumph over me. Methought I heard him say 'Ay! I am fairly out and you are fairly in.' "

Adams would quickly learn he was right—he was in!

Nineteen

THE COUNTRY EXPANDS

UNLIKE GEORGE WASHINGTON, John Adams hadn't been elected to the Presidency unanimously. In fact, he barely made it. The establishment of political parties Washington had warned against had taken place. The "Federalists party" had nominated Adams; the "Democratic-Republicans" had selected Thomas Jefferson. Adams won by a mere three electoral votes. Because he came in second, Jefferson became Vice President.

The heated battle for the chief office brought back a statement made shortly after the Constitutional Convention had adjourned. As BENJAMIN FRANKLIN left the hall for the last time, a lady asked him: "Well, Doctor, what have we got, a Republic or a Monarchy?" "A Republic, madam," replied Franklin, "if you can keep it." This, plus what Washington had observed during his last years in office, had brought about much of the sound advice he gave the American people in his Farewell Address.

The two "parties" fought constantly. Adams didn't enjoy his term in office. What he proposed to The Congress was usually turned down. On the diplomatic front he fared somewhat better, but not much.

France was unhappy about the Jay Treaty the United States had adopted. France did not believe it was treated fairly. Charles Cotesworth Pickney was sent to France as Minister. The French wouldn't receive him. Adams then appointed Pickney, JOHN MARSHALL, the Virginia Mason, and ELDBRIDGE GERRY to try to obtain a treaty of friendship with France.

The French Minister Talleyrand delegated three agents who would be referred to as "X, Y, Z" to meet with the American representatives. They suggested the United States give a loan to France, along with a bribe of $240,000. This brought an angry response from Pickney: "Millions for defense but not one cent for tribute!" The Congress was just as furious. It appeared war was imminent. George Washington was asked to lead the Army; a Navy Department was established.

The Federalists in The Congress adopted harsh legislation. The Naturalization and Alien Acts were pushed through in June, 1798. An undeclared naval war began in November, 1798. The French captured the American Schooner *Retaliation.* Several naval battles followed. The frigates *United States* and *Constellation* were launched. Twelve more frigates and several other ships were ordered to be built. The new naval force brought the French to terms.

George Washington was able to return to Mount Vernon and the people he loved. But he wouldn't enjoy his final retirement long. On the night of December 12, 1799, he became ill.

Tobias Lear, who had been a friend as well as secretary to Washington, tells of Washington's last hours: "Between 2 and 3 o'clk on Saturday morning he awoke Mrs. Washington and told her he was very unwell, and he had an ague. She. . .would have got up to call a servant; but he would not permit her lest she should take cold.

"For nearly four hours he lay in the cold bedroom before a servant lighted a fire.

"It was then that Washington, with a throat so swollen he could barely talk, allowed Dr. JAMES CRAIK to be summoned. Craik rushed to Mount Vernon and was alarmed at what he found. He immediately sent for two other doctors. . . .

"Before the other doctors arrived, Craik tried having Washington gargle, but this almost suffocated him. Then he was bled once again. After Brown and Dick arrived, a consultation was held, and once again Washington was bled. . . ."

Washington knew he was going to die. He had Martha bring his wills and had her burn an old one. He gave instructions for the handling of his accounts and papers. He thanked the doctors for their help and concern. He died close to eleven o'clock on the evening of December 14, 1799.

At three o'clock on the afternoon of December 18, 1799, the large funeral procession left the house for the old family vault. Troops, horse and foot, led the procession, followed by four members of the Clergy, three of whom were Masons (THOMAS DAVIS, WILLIAM MAFFITT, and Dr. JAMES MUIR, all members of Alexandria Lodge). The body was borne by the Freemasons and Officers. These pall-bearers were all Colonels: CHARLES SIMMS, DENNIS RAMSEY, WILLIAM PAYNE, GEORGE GILPIN, CHARLES LITTLE, and Philip Marsteller. All but the laat were Freemasons. When the body arrived at the vault, the Rev. Mr. Davis read the service, and pronounced a short address.

The Masons performed their ceremonies, and the body was deposited in the vault. Dr. ELISHA CULLEN DICK, the Worshipful Master of Alexandria Lodge No. 22, conducted the Masonic ceremonies, assisted by his Chaplain, Dr. JAMES MUIR. Brooke Lodge No. 15 of Alexandria and Federal Lodge No. 15 of Washington had united with Alexandria Lodge in the ceremonies.

There was disbelief in The Congress when, on the day of the funeral, word reached it of Washington's death. Upon confirmation, it adjourned until the next day. Then JOHN MARSHALL addressed the House: "Our Washington is no more! the hero, the patriot, and the sage of America; . . . .the man on whom in times of danger, every eye turned and all hopes were placed. . .lives now only in his own great actions, and in the hearts of an affectionate and afflicted people."

President Adams wrote to the Senate: "Malice could never blast his honor, and envy made him a singular exception to her universal rule. For himself he had lived long enough, to life and glory; for his fellow citizens, if their prayers could have been answered, he would have been immortal; for me, his departure is at a most unfortunate moment. Trusting, however, in the wise and righteous dominion of Providence over the passions of men, and results of their councils and actions, as well as over their lives, nothing remains for me but humble resignation.

"His example is now complete; and it will teach wisdom and virtue to magistrates, citizens, and men, not only in the present age, but in future generations, as long as history shall read."

Adams' words proved prophetic, more so than he could have imagined. Unfortunately, his words of wisdom would be ignored by far too many who would set the policies for the country—the politicians.

Many honors were received by Washington during his lifetime. Many more memorials to his memory were established over the years. These are recorded in *G. Washington: Master Mason*.

Adams ran for the Presidency in 1800. So did Thomas Jefferson. Jefferson, the party man, had AARON BURR of New York on the same ticket for Vice President. An amazing thing happened—Jefferson and Burr received identical votes. 73, for President! Adams received 65. The House of Representatives had a difficult time choosing between the two highest vote-getters. It wasn't until after the middle of February that Hamilton swung his weight behind Jefferson, a man he hated, but respected, that Jefferson won. This would cost Hamilton his life. On July 11, 1804, Aaron Burr mortally wounded Hamilton in a duel at Weehawken, New Jersey.

Thomas Jefferson, the radical, the liberal, became a conservative almost from the moment of his inauguration. It would appear he had learned, as Washington had warned, political parties are enemies of democracy. He proclaimed: "We are all Republicans! We are all Federalists!" He quickly let the states know he believed in their rights. And he wanted governmental expenditures reduced.

He inherited an unfinished Capitol, and a Presidential house with a leaky roof, sagging floors from shrinking green lumber, and unplastered walls. The country had grown. There were now sixteen states: Vermont had been admitted to the Union on March 4, 1791; Kentucky on June 1, 1792; and Tennessee on June 1, 1796.

And there were two new Grand Lodges.

—VERMONT—

Vermont had remained a wilderness for over a hundred years after the settlements along the Atlantic had begun to progress. It did have two small forts, but until 1761 when settlers arrived to form Bennington, settlements were scarce. Soldiers tramping through the fertile land had visualized the potential of the region. With the settlement of Bennington began a long struggle between its settlers, New Hampshire and New York.

JOHN SPARGO author of *Freemasonry in Vermont* notes the presence of several Military lodges in the territory. After the surrender of Quebec on September 18, 1758, a meeting was held in Vermont. On November 18 there met members "of Lodge No. 22, of the 47th Regiment; No. 218 of the 48th Regiment; No. 245 of the 15th Regiment; No. 136 of the 43rd Regiment, working under Dispensation; No. 195 of the Artillery, working under Dispensation; No. 1 of Louisbourg Warrant. With the exception of the last named, all these Lodges operated under Irish warrants.

Other Military lodges included one stationed at Albany, and another at Crown Point.

Among the captains of Ethan Allen's "Green Mountain Boys" were three Freemasons. SETH WARNER, ROBERT COCHRAN, and JOSEPH WAIT. Warner had been made a Master Mason in St. John's Lodge No. 3 of Connecticut on September 3, 1765. So well did he fight against the "Yorkers" he became their colonel and commander in July, 1775. He was with Allen at Ticonderoga, "and in charge of the seizure of Crown Point." He shared in Sharp's victory at the Battle of Bennington.

Warner became a member of Union Lodge No. 1 of Albany in 1772. So did Robert Cochran. He, also, was at Ticonderoga and Crown Point.

JONAS FAY was a member of Master's Lodge in Albany, and one who "contributed more to the creation of Vermont as an independent State than did any other individual. And he more profoundly influenced its development in the formative years than did any other man." He worked closely with the Green

Mountain Boys. In 1777 he wrote the Declaration of Independence of Vermont. From 1777 to 1782 he was Vermont's agent in the Continental Congress. He was also a member of Vermont Lodge and Temple Lodge of Bennington.

Vermont had considered itself an indepedent state, but its efforts to become a part of the Union were in vain. New York bitterly opposed its admission. As it was "open" territory Masonically, Masons desiring to form a lodge could apply where their interests lay. Consequently, Vermont Lodge of Springfield received a charter from Massachusetts on November 10, 1781. Among its signers was PAUL REVERE, Senior Grand Warden. North Star Lodge of Manchester was chartered January 20, 1785, when Paul Revere was "D.M." Dorchester Lodge of Vergennes received its charter dated September 3, 1791, from the Provincial Grand Lodge of Canada.

Why a charter from Canada? Spargo explains that there was a "strange adventure of secret diplomacy" going on. Ethan and Ira Allen, Governor THOMAS CRITTENDEN, JOSEPH FAY AND NATHANIEL CHIPMAN were the Vermonters involved. "All except Ethan Allen were Freemasons and there is at least the possibility that he was one as tradition says." Influential Freemasons in Canada were on the other side including Provincial Grand Master Sir JOHN JOHNSON. Friendships developed. And the restoration of goodwill between the two sides may have been the primary motive.

Temple Lodge of Bennington received a charter from the Grand Lodge of Connecticut on May 18, 1793. Union Lodge of Middlebury was also chartered by the Grand Lodge of Connecticut.

Dorchester Lodge, in June, 1794, proposed a convention be held in Manchester during August to form a Grand Lodge. On August 6 representatives from three lodges met. Time was allowed for further representatives to arrive, but they didn't. It was decided to go ahead with a "form of a Constitution for a Grand Lodge" and notify the absent lodges.

On October 10, 1794, representatives from all five lodges met in Rutland. On Tuesday, October 14, the Constitution was signed and then Grand Lodge officers were elected. NOAH SMITH became the first Grand Master. JOHN SPARGO credits Dr. NATHAN BROWNSON with the leadership that resulted in the formation of the Grand Lodge. Brownson had been born in Connecticut, graduated from Yale, then went to Georgia to practice medicine. He was elected Governor of Georgia in 1781. In 1793 he visited Vermont to be with his brothers, and become a member of Northstar Lodge. Shortly after the Grand Lodge was formed he returned to Georgia.

Among the long list of Vermont Masons who served in the war noted by Spargo were: THOMAS CHITTENDEN, ENOCH WOODBRIDGE, ROSWELL HOPKINS, General SAMUEL STRONG, Colonel JOHN CHIPMAN, ISAAC TICHENOR, ANTHONY HASWELL, Colonel JOSEPH FAY, DAVID FAY, General DAVID ROBINSON, Reverend ITHAMAR HIBBARD, GAMALIEL PAINTER, and WILLIAM COOLEY. Spargo notes: "The brief outline of this representative group of pioneer Freemasons will demonstrate, better than anything else could do, both the high quality of the membership of our Fraternity from the beginning and its impressively great share in establishing and shaping the destinies of this State of Vermont."

—KENTUCKY—

CHARLES SNOW GUTHRIE in his *Kentucky Freemasonry, 1788-1978*, writes: "Kentucky was separated from Tidewater Virginia by several hundred miles of forest; dangerous, fast-flowing streams; and a nearly impassable mountain chain. Yet Freemasonry found its way across the mountains long before 1800 in the persons of explorers and settlers."

Dr. THOMAS WALKER, along with five other men from Virginia, found a gap in the mountains on April 13, 1750, according to Guthrie. On the 17th they "discovered and named Cumberland River for a Mason, WILLIAM AUGUSTUS, Duke of Cumberland and son of King George II. . . . Ultimately the name Cumberland was attached to the whole region—river, mountains, gap, plateau, town, county, college, and three or four Masonic lodges took the name."

Walker became a member of Fredericksburg Lodge in 1764. He received the Fellowcraft degree there, followed by the Master Mason degree in 1767. Where and when he became an Entered Apprentice isn't known.

In 1776 "Kentucky County was created as a separate entity within Virginia. Through 1780 more and more settlers passed into and through Kentucky." By 1790 "the population was 73,677." Among the settlers were many Freemasons. Lexington had become the most important settlement. The Lexington Masons applied to the Grand Lodge of Virginia for a charter. It was granted to Lexington Lodge No. 25 on November 17, 1788.

The first Worshipful Master was RICHARD CLOUGH ANDERSON, a captain in the Virginia Continentals. He "crossed the Delaware in the first boat at the Battle of Trenton in 1776. He also saw service at Brandywine, Germantown, and Savannah."

Paris Lodge No. 35 was chartered on November 25, 1791, by the Grand Lodge of Virginia. Georgetown Lodge No. 46 received its charter from Virginia on December 1, 1796. On December 11, 1799, Frankfort Hiram No. 57 was chartered by Virginia. Abraham Lodge received a Dispensation from Virginia on July 10, 1800. This would be the Lodge that buried GEORGE ROGERS CLARK with Masonic rites.

Lexington Lodge No. 25 asked the other four lodges to meet in a Convention on September 8, 1800, for the purpose of forming a Grand Lodge. All the lodges were represented. It was determined that a Grand Lodge for Kentucky should be formed. A letter was drafted to be sent to the Grand Lodge of Virginia outlining reasons for this action. On December 11 the Grand Lodge of Virginia heartily endorsed the action of its Kentucky lodges.

In the meantime, however, the lodges met on October 16, 1800, at Masons' Hall in Lexington. The oldest Past Master was placed in the chair. He appointed the other officers, and the business of electing Grand Lodge officers commenced. WILLIAM MURRAY of Hiram Lodge was "unanimously elected Grand Master of the Grand Lodge of Kentucky, and was immediately installed according to ancient form."

Perhaps the most famous Freemason to come out of Kentucky at that time was ROB MORRIS. He is credited with founding the Order of the Eastern Star, an organization with Freemasons, but generally considered an organization for ladies. Few appear to know that Morris turned his material over to ROBERT MACOY, the Masonic book publisher of New York. And it was Macoy who really developed the Order in Chapter form.

Among Jefferson's first acts after taking office as President was to pardon those few who were still in jail for violating the sedition laws.

For years the United States paid bribes to the Barbary States of Algiers, Morocco, Tripoli, and Tunis. This was to keep the pirates from interferring with American shipping along the coast of North Africa. The Pasha of Tripoli demanded more money in May, 1801. When he received no immediate answer, he declared war on the United States.

Commodore EDWARD PREBLE became the leader of the naval force that fought over 4,000 miles away. He had little support from The Congress, yet he and his small force brought about victory for America.

Preble had been made a Mason in St. Andrew's Lodge of Boston in 1783. In 1786 he became a member of Portland Lodge No. 17 of Portland. As a young man he fought with the Navy in the War for Independence. He sailed around the world on a merchant vessel after the war.

NAPOLEON BONAPARTE, a Freemason, gained control in France. He forced Spain to trade Louisiana for some land in Italy. ROBERT LIVINGSTON, the New York Mason, was Minister to France. Jefferson sent JAMES MONROE, the Virginia Mason, to assist Livingston in making the French an offer for New Orleans. They were stunned when they were offered the whole of the Louisiana Territory for Fifteen Million Dollars. This more than doubled the size of the United States. The cost actually amounted to about four cents per acre! On December 20, 1803, the American flag was raised over the territory.

Even before the purchase was made final, two Freemasons, Captains MERIWETHER LEWIS and WILLIAM CLARK, were commissioned to explore and map the wilderness. They started up the Missouri River on May 14, 1804. In 1805 they reached the Pacific Ocean. A year later they returned to "civilization."

Ohio became a state in 1803. A surplus in the treasury of the United States was announced. Jefferson's popularity was on the rise when he ran for a second term.

The election of 1804 was changed. The Vice President would no longer be the fellow who came in second best. Each party fielded its own ticket for President and Vice President. So, Jefferson and GEORGE CLINTON, the New York Mason, opposed C. C. Pinckney and Rufus King. Jefferson carried every state except Connecticut. Much the same thing would happen in 1808 when Jefferson supported his fellow Virginian, James Madison, for the Presidency. His running mate remained GEORGE CLINTON.

War continued to plague Europe with Napoleon causing many of the problems. The United States remained neutral, but this didn't keep the French and the British from seizing American merchantmen. In February, 1807, H. M. S. *Leopard* stopped the American frigate *Chesapeake* and removed four of her crew after shots had been fired. Angry citizens of Norfolk, Virginia, saw the tattered *Chesapeake* limp into port. Jefferson asked for an Embargo Act. The Congress gave it to him in December. No goods were to leave American ports for Europe.

New Englanders, in particular, were furious. Ships rotted at the wharves; commerce came to a standstill; a thriving smuggling trade came into existence. Before Madison took over as the fourth President in March, 1809, the Embargo Act was repealed. It was replaced by the Non-Interference Act, meaning Americans could trade with anyone but the French and British.

—DELAWARE AND OHIO—

On the Masonic "front" all was peaceful and prosperous. The Grand Lodge of Delaware was established in 1806 by lodges holding charters from the Provincial Grand Lodge of Pennsylvania. In the Ohio frontier Freemasonry had grown.

American Union Lodge, under a warrant from the Provincial Grand Lodge of Massachusetts, had been reopened at Marietta on June 28, 1790. It prospered from the beginning. On September 8, 1791, Nova Cesarea Lodge of Cincinnati received a charter from the Grand Lodge of New Jersey. It didn't go to work, however, until December 27, 1794. For some unknown reason the Worshipful Master of this Lodge returned the charter to New Jersey on December 10, 1803. Eight days later it went back to work under a dispensation from the Grand Lodge of Kentucky as Cincinnati Lodge. The Master of the "old" lodge became the Secretary of the "new" one.

The Grand Lodge of Connecticut granted a charter to Erie Lodge on October 19, 1803. On the same date the same Grand Lodge granted a charter to New England Lodge. The Lodge of Amity was awarded a charter by Pennsylvania on May 7, 1803, naming LEWIS CASS as Worshipful Master. Cass would become the third Grand Master of the Grand Lodge of Ohio and the first Grand Master of the Grand Lodge of Michigan. Scioto Lodge was added to the list by the Grand Lodge of Massachusetts on November 22, 1805.

Erie Lodge, on March 11, 1807, asked the other five lodges to send delegates to a convention to form a Grand Lodge. They met at Chillicothe, the capital, on January 4, 1808. On the 5th Grand Lodge officers were elected. RUFUS PUTNAM of American Union Lodge became the first Grand Master.

The story of the formation of the Grand Lodge of Ohio, and its history, is dramatically covered in an award-winning motion picture entitled "*Precious Heritage*", and in its history, *Frontier Cornerstone*.

Devastating news came from the frontier when General William Henry Harrison (who would prove to be an anti-Mason), Governor of Indiana Territory, moved against hostile Indians. He did it in spite of a presidential order not to march into Indian territory. Waiting for Tecumseh (Shooting Star), the great Shawnee chief, to leave on another recruiting mission, Harrison attacked. He managed to defeat a powerful confederacy at Tippecanoe Creek in November, 1811. This gave Harrison a life-long nickname. It also gave the government proof that the British were arming the Indians and encouraging their attacks on the settlers.

Among the most vocal cries for war came from HENRY CLAY of Kentucky. Speaker of the House. Clay had studied law in Virginia under the guidance of ROBERT BROOKE, the attorney general, and a Mason who had been Governor of Virginia. Clay had moved to Kentucky in 1797 to practice law. He was a member of Lexington Lodge No. 1. He would become Grand Master of Masons in Kentucky in 1820.

Another who was outraged was General ANDREW JACKSON of Tennessee. When he heard about the Battle of Tippecanoe, he wrote: "The blood of our murdered countrymen must be revenged." Jackson would be heard from again, and for many years. From 1822-24 he served as Grand Master of Masons in Tennessee.

—DISTRICT OF COLUMBIA—

By 1810 there were six lodges operating in the area of the Federal Capital. For several years there had been discussions concerning the formation of a Grand Lodge. The lodges, however, were reluctant to break their ties with the parent bodies. Finally, the Maryland lodges agreed to meet in a convention. Alexandria wished them well but wanted no part in breaking away from Virginia. Brooke Lodge of Alexandria, chartered in 1796, was willing to meet with the others.

The meeting took place on December 11, 1810. The delegates agreed it was feasible to form a Grand Lodge for the District. On January 8, 1811, a final convention was held in the lodge room of Union Lodge. Grand Lodge officers were elected, with VALENTINE REINTZEL becoming the first Grand Master. The lodges were then numbered according to seniority: Federal No. 1; Brooke No. 2; Columbia No. 3; Naval No. 4; and Potomac No. 5. Of these five, only Brooke Lodge is no longer in existence.

THE GEORGE WASHINGTON MASONIC NATIONAL MEMORIAL
Shooters Hill, Alexandria, Virginia

Concerning the Grand Lodge of the District of Columbia, HARRY L. HAYWOOD wrote in *Well-Springs of American Freemasonry:*

> . . . the brethren of America have sound reason to think of Washington as a Masonic city. Certainly, if there were such a thing in Freemasonry as cross fertilization, the city's air would be full of pollen; and its lodges would exhibit surprising growth, odd shapes, and endless mutations, because the winds blow across it continually from five rites and forty-eight Grand Jurisdictions. The Grand Masters and Grand Secretaries hold their two separate national conferences in the city every February. In the same month both the George Washington Masonic National Memorial Association and the Masonic Service Association of the United States hold their annual meetings, albeit the former holds its meeting in the extraordinary structure on Shooters Hill, just across the Potomac. A number of small, and little known Masonic side-orders, some too exclusive for more than a dozen members, take opportunity to meet in the same week.

There have been some changes in what Haywood wrote in 1953. There are now 50 Masonic jurisdictions plus Puerto Rico. No longer do the Grand Masters and Grand Secretaries meet every February in Washington. The "Masonic side-orders" do meet every February in Washington and are now referred to as the "Allied Masonic Bodies."

Haywood adds:

> Although regular Freemasonry throughout the world descended from the Medival architects of cathedrals, churches, monasteries, castles, etc., it is only in America that the Craft has erected a large number of buildings of its own of a monumental kind, and fit to stand among other masterpieces. Two of those are in Washington, or on the edge of it: The Washington Memorial which from Shooters Hill in Alexandria looks across the city; and the world-famous House of the Temple, at Sixteenth and S Streets, which contains the general offices of the Scottish Rite, Southern Jurisdiction, and its great library. The National Cathedral, which mounts toward heaven from the summit of Mt. St. Alban, and which may become America's Westminster Abbey, received support from Masons

throughout the nation from the time the Foundation purchased its 65 acres of land; and there is a Masonic section
in it.

"The cornerstone of the Washington Monument was laid in
1848" by Masons from the District, wrote Haywood. "The
Grand Lodge also conducted similar ceremonies for the Smithsonian Institute, the House Office Building, made notable by the
speech in which Brother THEODORE ROOSEVELT first used
'muck-raking,' the War College, and Continental Hall. When
the Grand Lodge laid the stone of its own Temple at Ninth and F
Streets, President and Brother Andrew Johnson walked in the
procesion."

THE WAR OF 1812

War was declared on June 18, 1812. The vote in the House
was 79 to 49; in the Senate, 19 to 13. The small majority would
prove almost disastrous from the beginning. The war effort
would be sabotaged by politicians and dissenters from the
beginning, much as happened in the Vietnam "war" 150 years
later.

Ironically, five days after the declaration, Great Britain
removed the sanctions that had troubled Americans. It was too
late. Troops were already on the move against Canada. Few expected the fighting to take long. Canada was expected to be
conquered within weeks, if not days.

General WILLIAM HULL, who was a Freemason prior to
1779, and the first Master of Meridan Lodge of Massachusetts in
1797, was called out of retirement. His experience during the
War for American Independence was needed. It was his job to
lead raw American militia in the first thrust against Canada.
This he did by way of Detroit. But Sir Isaac Brock, considered a
"brilliant military mind," and Tecumseh, pushed the
Americans back to Detroit. There, on August 16, 1812, Hull
surrendered.

Hull was court-martialed for giving up Detroit. Two who accused him of cowardice were Masons, Colonel LEWIS CASS and
General HENRY DEARBORN. Strangely, Dearborn the accuser

became president of the court-martial. Hull was found quilty and sentenced to be hanged. But he was told to go home to Newton, Massachusetts, and wait for the execution. It never came!

Fort Dearborn was evacuated on August 16. Then its occupants were massacred, every man, woman, and child, by Pottawatami Indians. The American line of defense was thrown back to the Wabash and Ohio Rivers.

Hull's nephew, Captain Isaac Hull, in command of the American frigate *Constitution*, redeemed some of the family honor. On August 19, 1812, he sighted the British frigate *Guerriere*. Ordering his men to hold their fire, he waited until less than fifty yards separated the two, then Hull told his men to "pour it into them." A short time later the British commander surrendered. The *Constitution*, soon to be called "Old Ironsides," returned to Boston with British prisoners. The crew received a hero's welcome.

The *Constitution* won several other victories. So did the *United States*, commanded by STEPHEN DECATUR, JR., a Freemason. It was he, who in 1815, after his squadron had whipped Algeria, said in a toast: "Our country! In her intercourse with foreign nations may she always be in the right; but our country, right or wrong!"

His father, STEPEHEN DECATUR, SR., had proven his courage in winning several naval battles with the French. He received his Masonic degrees in Lodge No. 16 in Maryland in 1777. In 1780 he received his Master's degree in Lodge No. 3 of Pennsylvania.

General STEPHEN VAN RENSSELAER, who would become Grand Master of Masons in New York from 1825 to 1829, attacked Queenstown Heights in the middle of October. With 200 troops he ferried the Niagara River to pave the way for the New York militia to follow. The militia refused to move from the American side of the river. Van Rensselaer resigned in disgust.

Two attacks against Canada had failed. With close to 8,000 troops Dearborn was ordered to take Montreal. He half-

heartedly tried. It was said he really "advanced backwards."
The British in Canada were heartened.

The fighting along the Niagara River disrupted the work of
the Freemasons in the area. WALLACE MCLEOD, in his *Whence
Came We?*, notes that the brethren at Niagara had broken
away from the Provincial Grand Lodge of Upper Canada in
1801, electing their own Grand Master in 1802. For twenty
years this Grand Lodge existed, then it joined its parent body.
But it was unable to meet during the war years of 1812 to 1815.

It had become clear that America had to have a "fresh-water"
as well as a "salt-water" Navy. Control of the Great Lakes was
vital. Captain Oliver Hazard Perry was put in charge of the construction of a fleet for Lake Erie. During the winter of 1812-13
he supervised the building of an American flotilla from green
local timber. Early in the summer of 1813 he began searching for
enemy craft. In September he found what he was looking for at
Put-in-Bay. In a terrible and bloody three-hour fight he and his
men won a decisive victory.

This victory was commemorated in 1912, and the Grand
Lodge of Ohio played an important role. The Grand Master
opened his Grand Lodge at "high twelve" aboard the steamer
City of Buffalo, as it steamed toward Put-in-Bay. Over 5,000
members of the Craft met the steamer and proceeded to Perry's
Memorial to lay its cornerstone. At the conclusion the Grand
Lodge was closed "in the Grand Master's rooms at the Hotel
Crescent."

—LOUISIANA—

The universality of Freemasonry was evident in Louisiana.
Prior to the outbreak of the War of 1812, its lodges had received
charters from a wide variety of sources. One lodge had been
chartered by South Carolina; one by Marseilles; two by France;
one by New York; seven by Pennsylvania; and one by the Scottish Rite of Jamaica.

On June 13, 1812, five French-speaking lodges met in New
Orleans to form a Grand Lodge. The two English-speaking
lodges in the city felt this step was premature and refused to

participate. Of the five lodges that did meet, four had been chartered by the Grand Lodge of Pennsylvania.

The Constitution of the Grand Lodge, and the election of its officers took place on June 20, 1812. It became the "Grand Lodge of Louisiana, Ancient York Masons." PIERRE FRANCOIS DUBOURG was installed as Grand Master. On July 11, he installed the remaining officers. It's interesting to note a brother of the Grand Master was Louis William DuBourg, who became the Roman Catholic Bishop of Louisiana in 1815.

For a number of years the Constitution and all *Proceedings* were written in both French and English. To prove its continuing universality, the Grand Lodge chartered lodges in many areas: Alabama, Arkansas, Cuba, Veracruz, and the Yucatan Peninsula in Mexico. Simon Bolivar, "the liberator of South America," became a favorite of the Masons of New Orleans.

—TENNESSEE—

Another Grand Lodge came out of the turmoil of war. Eight lodges working under charters from the Grand Lodge of North Carolina met for the purpose of forming a Grand Lodge. They received the blessings and assistance of the Mother Grand Lodge. Consequently, on December 27, 1813, the Grand Lodge of Tennessee became a reality.

The fighting sputtered along throughout 1813 with neither side victorious. Control of border settlements were gained and lost by both sides rapidly. "Tippecanoe" Harrison did invade Canada and at the Battle of the Thames, Chief Tecumseh, who had been nothing but trouble to the Americans, was killed. This did discourage the Indians and helped the Americans to gain control of the Northwest.

American troops under the command of Generals JACOB BROWN and WINFIELD SCOTT finally won a battle across the Niagara. On July 3, 1814, they took Fort Erie, then went up the river to Chippewa. A bayonet charge by Scott's infantry on the 5th broke through the British line. Three weeks later, at Lundy's Lane, the fiercest fighting of the war took place. About forty percent of both forces became casualties. Brown and Scott were severely wounded. The Americans withdrew to Fort Erie to fight a holding battle that cost the British several hundred lives.

JACOB BROWN was made a Mason in Ontario Lodge, Sackets Harbor, New York, in 1806. WINFIELD SCOTT received his degrees in Dinwiddie Union Lodge No. 23, Virginia, in 1805. He would go on to fight valiantly in the Mexican and other wars.

At dawn on August 19, 1814, British troops landed and marched to Blandensburg, Maryland, without any opposition. They were close to the United States capital. On the 24th, with President Madison watching, 7,000 American militia broke and ran. So did the citizens of the city. Messengers reached Dolly Madison in the White House "to bid me fly." She grabbed a full-length painting of George Washington and departed to join the others across the Potomac in Virginia.

In the evening the British put the torch to the President's House and the Capitol. Then the British slipped out of Washington. Alexandria, Virginia, surrendered on the 28th. On September 12th the British landed at North Point; its goal was Baltimore, Maryland. The next morning the fleet began bombing Fort McHenry. It continued all through the night. But, with the dawn, the American flag was still flying!

The beauty of the American flag flying in the light of dawn, gave birth to what is now the national anthem. Francis Scott Key, a prisoner on board a British ship, wrote the words that would become immortal on the back of an envelope.

The war turned around on September 11, 1814. A Mason named THOMAS MACDONOUGH did it. Macdonough commanded the twenty-six gun *Saratoga* which closed in on the British frigate *Confidence* armed with thirty-six guns. While his ship was anchored, Macdonough swung it around so all of his guns could fire into the *Confidence*. The tricky maneuver worked. The British frigate struck its colors. With the loss of this battle the British commander refused to commit his troops to a land battle. He beat a retreat to Canada.

A Flemish town named Ghent had been the scene of negotiations for months between the commissioners from Great Britain
and America. The events toward the end of 1814 brought about
the "Treaty of Ghent." It indicated that neither side had won;
but neither side had lost. The papers were signed on Christmas
Eve. The War of 1812 had officially ended. The fighting wasn't
over, however.

ANDREW JACKSON fought the British in New Orleans two
weeks after the treaty was signed. There are historians who
claim this was an unnecessary battle, but the facts refute this.
General Edward Pakenham, brother-in-law of the Duke of
Wellington (a Mason), carried in his pocket a commission that
would make him governor of the territory. In this capacity he
would have authority "over all the territory fraudulently conveyed by Bonaparte to the United States." This could have
created havoc for more than half the country. But Pakenham
lost. He was shot through the neck in the withering fire from
Jackson's forces along Rodriguez Canal. The Americans lost 20;
the British more than 2,000. "Old Hickory" had won the war's
greatest, and final, battle.

GLEN LEE GREENE, in his *Masonry in Louisiana*, covers the
Battle of New Orleans from a little known angle:

> With the war going badly, General Andrew Jackson took
> command of all American operations in the Southwest
> during the Spring of 1814. In November he seized Pen-
> sacola and then came to New Orleans on December 1,
> 1814. He was unaware that a large British fleet had sailed
> from Jamaica and that the enemy planned an assault on
> New Orleans as part of a scheme to gain control of the
> Mississippi Valley.
>
> General Jackson was a great Mason and had many
> Masonic friends in New Orleans. . . . Hence the British
> machination, which ran counter to Masonic sympathies in
> New Orleans, met with rebuffs as they sought to subvert
> the Creoles and to win over to their side the Lafittes and
> their Baratarian confederates. Edward Livingston, a
> powerful figure among Louisiana Masons, won con-
> siderable applause for his successful efforts to enlist the
> Lafittes in support of the American cause. He had

represented them as legal counsel and had won their confidence. Consequently, when Jean Lafitte received some valuable documents from a British officer, he immediately made them available to Governor Claiborne. As a result of this patriotic act, Governor Claiborne, always a staunch defender of Masonic principles, learned of the impending peril to New Orleans; thus he was the first to inform Jackson that the city was in danger of attack.

General Jackson soon learned that he could expect an army of at least ten thousand invaders. Undaunted, he hastened to improvise defenses, which consisted partly of cotton bales. Jackson leaned heavily upon Governor Claiborne, who assisted with the vital co-ordination of defense efforts. In addition, Edward Livingston served as a member of Jackson's staff. Numerous Masons manned posts of trust and grave responsiblity. In a furious artillery engagement on January 1, 1815, Jackson's forces outgunned the British. A hero of that struggle was Dominique You. One of the Baratarians, he was a Mason and was buried by the Masonic fraternity.

The crucial Battle of New Orleans occurred on January 8, 1815. General Jackson, the rugged frontiersman, marshaled a motley array of fighters—sailors, regulars, pirates, Negroes, Kentuckians, Tennesseans, Creoles, Frenchmen, and any man who would join the battle against the British. In that last major engagement of the war, the people of Louisiana, of whatever national origin, dispelled any last, lingering doubt of their patriotism and their loyalty. On that day Jackson won the most notable victory of the war....

The man who would become Grand Master of Masons in Tennessee in 1822, and the seventh President of the United States, had been born of Irish immigrants. His father died from over work from farming poor soil at the age of 29. Andrew was only two years old.

When Andrew was eight British troops pillaged and burned his village. At thirteen he became a soldier. In a skirmish with the British he was scarred for life by a saber blow. Along with his brother he was thrown into a prisoners' stockade. There he contracted smallpox. And within a year he lost both his mother and brother.

At fourteen Andrew was alone. In between fighting Indians in Mississippi and Florida, he studied law and eventually became a country judge. He learned to distrust Indians, and became infuriated when he found British markings on guns that had killed his men.

The alliance between the British and Indians in the War of 1812 did nothing to change his hatred. And this war caused him to distrust all "Easterners."

With the end of the War of 1812 a period of building, exploring, and westward travel began. The United States of America was about to become the greatest democracy the world had ever known.

Twenty

WESTWARD

THE War of 1812 has been called many things, among them the "second war for independence." It appeared to prove what the War for Independence had shown—not everyone was willing to fight or sacrifice for freedom. Far too many were willing to "let the other fellow get the job done." Far too many used the war to their own advantage by enriching their own coffers.

One man who didn't take advantage of the situation was STEPHEN GIRARD. The charter of the Bank of the United States expired in 1811. In spite of approaching financial ruin the politicians bitterly opposed rechartering the bank. Girard, one of the wealthiest merchants in the country, founded another bank for the United States, and made five million dollars of his own money available to the government. It is claimed he financed ninety-five percent of the cost of the war.

Girard became a Mason in 1778 in Royal Arch Lodge No. 3 of Philadelphia. Over the years he gave thousands of dollars to Masonic, and other, charities. Most of his fortune when he died was willed to found Girard College in Philadelphia. In his will he ordered that the students be taught no sect. He wanted them to be free to chose the religion they preferred.

—INDIANA—

In Indiana, Freemasonry took roots. DWIGHT L. SMITH, in his history of the Grand Lodge, *Goodly Heritage,* writes:

> The early history of virtually every community in Indiana follows a common pattern. First, the original white settlers forded the streams and pushed their way through the forest until they found what was to be their Promised

Land. Then, always in the same order, came the building of
cabins for residence, a church, and, a little later, a school.
Within three years, or five, or ten at the most, a Lodge of
Freemasons would be meeting, usually in a second floor
room at the village inn.

The pre-Grand Lodge era in Indiana covered a period of
only nine years. In that brief span, nine Lodges were
organized; six of them in one year alone. By 1817 every settlement that had passed the blockhouse stage in its
development, with possibly three or four exceptions, had a
Masonic Lodge. Vincennes in 1809, Madison in 1815,
Charlestown in 1816; Salem, Lawrenceburg, Corydon,
Rising Sun, Vevay and Brookville in 1817. All were
creatures of the Grand Lodge of Kentucky save Brookville,
which, by reason of location, settlement and antecedents,
had close ties with Ohio and therefore was set to work by
the neighboring Grand Lodge on the east.

On July 18, 1817, Vincennes Lodge sent out a circular to the
other lodges in Indiana. It suggested a meeting be held in Lexington to make arrangements for the formation of a Grand
Lodge. Surprisingly, all six of the Indiana lodges were
represented at the Grand Lodge of Kentucky in August, 1817.
Representatives from five of the six lodges agreed they should
meet to organize a Grand Lodge.

The conference took place at Corydon in December, 1817.
Not only did a majority of the delegates favor forming a Grand
Lodge, they adopted a far-reaching resolution: "*Resolved*, That
the several subordinate Lodges here represented do appoint one
or more delegates to meet at Madison on the second Monday in
January next, for the purpose of opening a Grand Lodge in the
State of Indiana." The vote was five to four in the affirmative.
And Smith does some speculating as to the reason.

Only delegates from four lodges were present on January 12,
1818, for the opening session in the "upstairs room of Major
Lanier's home." Representatives from the other lodges arrived
later, and "at early candlelighting" the convention proceeded.

Lodges under dispensation: Rising Sun, Switzerland, and
Harmony, were excluded from the proceedings. The following

day, January 13, 1816, ALEXANDER BUCKNER, age 32, a "distinguished lawyer," was elected Grand Master. The Grand Lodge of Indiana was born.

Many prominent men and Freemasons came out of the Grand Lodge of Indiana, but, Masonically, none ever surpassed the author of its history, DWIGHT L. SMITH, a Past Grand Master, and long-time Grand Secretary. For even a longer time he edited the jurisdiction's top-rated publication, *The Indiana Freemason.*

—MISSISSIPPI—

Kentucky also played a role in Mississippi. On October 16, 1801, it chartered Harmony Lodge at Natchez. Its first Worshipful Master was SETH LEWIS, chief justice of the territory. It was August 13, 1816, before Andrew Jackson Lodge, chartered by Tennessee, joined it. Tennessee also chartered Washington Lodge on April 19, 1817.

Mississippi became the twentieth state on December 10, 1817. Its three lodges determined it was time to form an independent Grand Lodge. On July 27, 1818, representatives met in a convention at Natchez. It wasted no time in electing HENRY TOOLEY as Grand Master. Another Grand Lodge was welcomed by its sisters in the East and South.

Relations with Great Britain improved, and in 1818 several items concerning fishing rights and war ships in the Great Lakes were resolved. The government could, and did, turn its attention to Spain and her possessions in America.

In 1810 a group of American settlers had claimed West Florida as a Republic. On Febraury 22, 1819, the United States made that act legal. For $5,000,000 Spain sold East and West Florida to the United States. Included was Spain's surrender to all claims to Oregon. The western boundary of the Louisiana Purchase was now clearly defined. But the government gave up its claim to Texas. This troubled HENRY CLAY; he wanted Texas, also.

Texas may have been one of the reasons JOEL R. POINSETT was sent on a special mission to Mexico in 1822. In 1825 he returned to Mexico as a United States Minister. While there he helped establish five Masonic lodges, whose charters were granted by the Grand Lodge of New York. These lodges later formed the Grand Lodge of Mexico.

Without realizing it, every Christmas Poinsett's memory becomes prominent. He brought back to South Carolina a plant which he developed into the *Poinsettia pulcherrima*—commonly called the "poinsetta." On his election to Deputy General Grand High Priest of the General Grand Chapter, Royal Arch Masons, he spoke of his assistance to the Mexican Masons:

> I have been most unjustly accused of extending our order and our principles into a neighboring country, with a view of converting them into an engine of political influence. In the presence of this respectable assembly of my brethren, and on the symbols of our order, which are spread around me, and the sacred book which is open before me, I solemnly aver, that this accusation is false and unfounded—and that if Masonry has anywhere been converted to any other than the pure and philanthropic purposes for which it was instituted, I have in no way contributed to such a perversion of its principles. And with the same solemnity I here declare, that if such evil council were to prevail in this country, and Masonry be perverted to political use, which God forbid, I would sever the ties, dear as they are to me, which now unite me to my brothers.

For twenty years Joel R. Poinsett was Grand High Priest in South Carolina. He was elected Deputy Grand Master of the Grand Lodge three times, but was prevented from becoming Grand Master because he served as Secretary of War from 1837 to 1841.

The independence of Mexico and the South American countries was a primary concern of President JAMES MONROE. In his annual message to The Congress and American citizens in 1823 he made this clear. He warned all nations to stop attempting to colonize Hispanic-American nations. He wanted no European system in the hemisphere. His doctrine would remain in force for almost one hundred fifty years. Then a small country called Cuba wiped it out.

—GENERAL GRAND CHAPTER—

The General Grand Chapter, Royal Arch Masons, came into being in 1798 when chapters from New England and New York met to form the "Grand Royal Arch Chapter of the Northern States of America." A few months later State Grand Chapters were formed in Rhode Island (March 12, 1798); Massachusetts (March 13, 1798); New York (March 14, 1798); and Connecticut (March 17, 1798). The name was changed a couple of times, then in 1806 it became the "General Grand Chapter of Royal Arch Masons of the United States of America."

DE WITT CLINTON was elected General Grand High Priest in 1816; THOMAS SMITH WEBB, called the "Father of the American Rite of Freemasonry," became his deputy. The "United States" was dropped from the name in 1954 when several foreign Grand Chapters joined. Today it is called the "General Grand Chapter, Royal Arch Masons, International." It has an award-winning film, "The Saga of the Holy Royal Arch of Freemasonry," which tells its story.

—U.S. SUPREME COURT—

The United States was enjoying a peaceful period. Even the politicians were cooperating with one another. It was called an "Era of Good Feelings." But not everyone was happy. The Supreme Court, under the leadership of the Chief Justice, JOHN MARSHALL, was ruling in many delicate areas. The Court was helping to establish a strong central government, but doing it under a strict interpretation of the Constitution.

Marshall wrote the decision in the case of *McCulloch vs. Maryland* which has been termed his greatest. In 1819 Maryland said it could, and would, tax any branch of the Bank of the United States established in the state without permission. The Supreme Court denied a state the right to tax an agency of the federal government.

John Marshall was elected Grand Master of Masons in Virginia in 1793, although he had never served as a Worshipful

THOMAS SMITH WEBB
"Father of the American Rite of Freemasonry"

Master. In spite of his busy schedule he remained an active Mason. He presided over Richmond Lodge No. 10, on October 30, 1824, at the request of the Worshipful Master, for the purpose of receiving the MARQUIS DE LAFAYETTE. JOHN DOVE, Worshipful Master of Richmond Randolph Lodge No. 19, and a Past Master of Richmond Lodge No. 10, and Grand Secretary, officiated at the Masonic rites for the burial of Marshall on July 9, 1835.

The original Supreme Court consisted of a Chief Justice and five Associates. Of these original six, two, WILLIAM CUSHING of Massachusetts and JOHN BLAIR of Virginia, were Freemasons. A list of Supreme Court Justices compiled by Ronald Heaton through 1968 shows there have been 96. Of these, thirty-five are known to be Freemasons: HENRY BALDWIN, HUGO L. BLACK, JOHN BLAIR, SAMUEL BLATCHFORD, HAROLD H. BURTON, JAMES F. BYRNES, JOHN CATTON, THOMAS C. CLARK, JOHN H. CLARKE, WILLIAM CUSHING, WILLIAM O. DOUGLAS, OLIVER ELLSWORTH, STEPHEN J. FIELD, JOHN M. HARLAN, ROBERT H. JACKSON, JOSEPH R. LAMAR, JOHN MARSHALL, STANLEY MATHEWS, SHERMAN MINTON, WILLIAM H. MOODY, SAMUEL NELSON, WILLIAM PATERSON, MAHLON PITNEY, STANLEY F. REED, WILEY B. RUTLEDGE, POTTER STEWART, NOAH H. SWAYNE, WILLIAM H. TAFT, THOMAS TODD, ROBERT TRIMBLE, WILLIS VAN DEVANTER, FREDERICK M. VINSON, EARL WARREN, LEVI WOODBURY, and WILLIAM B. WOODS.

Since 1968 seven Justices have been added to the Court; none of them a Freemason.

Over the years changes were made in the number of Justices on the Court, but in 1869 the number was set at a Chief Justice and eight Associate Justices. It has remained at this number to the present day.

THURGOOD MARSHAL was appointed to the Supreme Court in 1967 and is a Prince Hall Freemason.

—MAINE—

During the first two years of the 1820s, three Grand Lodges were formed; Maine in 1820; Alabama and Missouri in 1821.

Organized Freemasonry began in what was to become the State of Maine in 1762 when it was part of Massachusetts. Even before Maine was admitted to the Union as the twenty-third state on March 15, 1820, the Freemasons had taken steps to organize an independent Grand Lodge. There were thirty-one lodges (two had ceased to exist). One had been chartered by the "Modern" Provinicial Grand Lodge of Massachusetts, one by the "Ancient," or Scottish, Grand Lodge, the others by the United Grand Lodge of Massachusetts.

Portland Lodge sent a circular letter to the other lodges in Maine asking them to send representatives to Portland on October 14, 1819. Only one Lodge, Eastern, wasn't represented on that date, but it later approved the actions of the convention. SIMON GREENLEAF was elected President, and a "memorial" was addressed to the Grand Lodge of Massachusetts.

The Grand Lodge of Maine was organized on June 1, 1820, when the Governor of the State, WILLIAM KING, was elected Grand Master. He appointed Simon Greenleaf as his Deputy Grand Master. It would be Greenleaf, and not King, who would be remembered by the Freemasons of Maine throughout the years. On June 24 the officers of the Grand Lodge were installed by the Grand Master and his officers of the Grand Lodge of New Hampshire. For some unexplained reason the Grand Lodge of Massachusetts wasn't represented.

Many great men would give their allegiance to the Grand Lodge of Maine throughout the years, but none would become, Masonically, more prominent than JOSIAH HAYDEN DRUM-MOND, the most outstanding Masonic scholar and jurist of his day. And none would be thought of more affectionately than the author of its early history, RALPH J. POLLARD.

—MISSOURI—

The three founding lodges of the Grand Lodge of Missouri were chartered by the Grand Lodge of Tennessee. These were Missouri, Joachim, and St. Charles. The only survivor of these three is Missouri Lodge. Representatives from these lodges met on February 22, 1821, in St. Louis. Although only four men were present, a committee to draft a constitution was appointed, and the date of April 23, 1821, set for the next meeting. At this "convocation" THOMAS F. RIDDICK was elected Grand Master. The Grand Lodge officers were installed on May 4, 1821.

A father and son team did much to enhance Freemasonry, not only in Missouri but throughout the Masonic world. RAY V. DENSLOW authored several Masonic books and represented American Freemasonry overseas after World War II. WILLIAM R. DENSLOW, his son, will always be remembered for his *10,000 Famous Freemasons*. No Masonic researcher can work without this four volume set in his library.

When the people of Missouri applied for statehood in 1818 the fight for political power between the North and the South came into the open. Although the two sections were almost equally populated—the North had 105 Representatives in the House; the South, 81; the Senate was even. A New York Representative moved that Missouri be admitted, but without slavery. This passed the House. It lost in the Senate.

Southerners claimed The Congress couldn't impose conditions on states. But conditions had been imposed on Ohio, Indiana, and Illinois under the Northwest Ordinance. The political fight continued throughout 1819. Then the first of what would be forty years of compromises passed. Slavery would be permitted in Missouri, but prohibited beyond north of 36° 30' latitude. This compromise brought Maine into the Union on March 15, 1820. But it wasn't until August 10, 1821, that Missouri was admitted.

—ALABAMA—

From Kentucky came the first charter for a lodge in Alabama. From that date, August 28, 1812, until the Grand Lodge was formed, fourteen more lodges received charters: seven from Tennessee, two from Georgia, two from North Carolina, one from South Carolina, and one other from Kentucky. Nine of these lodges organized the Grand Lodge of Alabama on June 16, 1821.

The 1824 campaign for the Presidency found John Quincy Adams opposing two Freemasons, HENRY CLAY and ANDREW JACKSON. No candidate received a majority of the electoral vote, so the contest was passed to the House of Representatives. Henry Clay had finished a poor third, but he threw his support to Adams, and Adams was elected. Then Clay was appointed Secretary of State. That caused an uproar. Cries of corruption were prevalent.

The closeness of the election didn't help Adams. He was unable to accomplish much during his term in office. Jackson and his supporters started planning the 1828 campaign early.

As civilization was moving slowly westward, and Freemasonry along with this movement, uncivilized acts were about to take place in the East.

Twenty-one

PERSECUTION

ANDREW JACKSON had resigned his seat in the Congress after his defeat in the presidential election. He did it to work toward the election of 1828. At the time he didn't know that he, and all Freemasons, would have a new element to battle. And the battles were not confined only to the political arenas.

For over a decade Freemasons were persecuted, vilified, and all but crucified. The cause was aided by the unthinking act of a few Masons in a small New York town called "Batavia."

The man was William Morgan. There are claims that Morgan was born in Culpepper, Virginia, on August 7, 1774, but there's no proof that this is true. Throughout his lifetime he remained a man without property or a ready means of support. He boarded wherever his work happened to be. This proved to be the case even after he married Lucinda Pendleton in 1819. (Morgan's marriage has been proven.) He appears to have been a brick-mason, and may have learned this trade in Hap Hazard, Virginia.

Early in his life, it is claimed, Morgan moved to Kentucky, but returned to Virginia to work on the Orange County Court House. Again, there's no proof. His movements have been recorded showing he was in Richmond, Virginia, in 1821; he then went to Canada; in 1823 to Rochester; in 1824 to Batavia, New York. The Canadian and Batavia portion of his "travels" have been proven.

Morgan has been described by almost all who knew him as "low down white trash"; "an habitual liar"; "worthless"; "drunkard." He did have one champion, Samuel D. Green who claimed "Captain Morgan" was everything others said he wasn't. But everything Greene claims becomes suspect when he gave Morgan the title of "Captain," saying he had earned it in the War of 1812. Nothing in the records of the War Department shows any service by Morgan.

JOHN C. PALMER, writing about "Morgan and Anti-Masonry" in *Little Masonic Library*, notes:

> Somewhere between these extremes, the truth lies. Let us say that the evidence justifies the opinion that Morgan was a shiftless itinerant, a rolling stone that gathers no moss; more or less fond of his drink; without any considerable schooling, yet with some natural gifts; else he would not have been welcomed into so many lodges as visitor to assist in the conferring of degrees, or as speaker and entertainer at special Masonic functions. He must have been a man of presentable appearance, of plausible manner and speech; else he could not so have imposed on staid, intelligent men of unblemished reputation. That he soon wore his welcome out, evidences his lack of substantial character. His arrests for debt, aside from the charges used to get him into the hands of those who were determined to drive him from the country, were numerous and unquestioned. His idleness and improvident habits often left his family in sore straits which were relieved by grants from the Masonic charity funds.
>
> His Masonic relations are strangely clouded. The record is clear that he was exalted to the Royal Arch degree. . . . But no records have ever been found to indicate where he received the degrees required to make him eligible for the Royal Arch.

Western Star Chapter No. 35, Royal Arch Masons, at LeRoy, New York, exalted William Morgan on May 31, 1825. Shortly thereafter a movement was started to form a chapter in Batavia. Morgan signed the petition for the new chapter. His name was later crossed out for some unknown reason. This made him angry. Then early in 1826 he entered into a partnership with one David C. Miller, proprietor of a newspaper called the *Republican Advocate*.

Miller claimed he was an "Entered Apprentice Mason." He announced in his newspaper "There will be issued from the press in this place, in a short time, a work of rare interest to the uninitiated, being an exposition of Ancient Craft Masonry, by one who has been a member of the institution for years." This created an uproar in the community.

Why? Expose's of Freemasonry were nothing new. Samuel Prichard's *Masonry Dissected* had been published in 1730. It was widely circulated in the New World as well as the Old. For years it was the only information available to legitimate Freemasons and the public about the workings of the Craft. Varying versions of it became prevalent. In France dozens of so-called expose's were circulated.

In 1760 came *Three Distinct Knocks* by "W—O—V—n," a fellow who wouldn't give his name but claimed to be a "member of a lodge in England at this Time." It would appear the author had a grievance against someone in authority. But the booklet did contain some interesting information not normally printed concerning Freemasonry. Two years later another expose' was published in England. It was called *Jachin and Boaz.* Its author didn't care to reveal his name either. He was simply listed as "a GENTLEMAN belonging to the Jerusalem Lodge; a frequent Visitor at the Queen's Arms, St. Paul's Church-Yard; the Horn, in Fleet-street; Crown and Anchor, Strand; and the Salutation, Newgate-street." He certainly was a well-traveled Mason.

Although these works are, today, trivial, they weren't then. The Freemason of the 18th Century was seeking information about his Craft. The same is true today, even though thousands of volumes and periodicals are available.

A Freemason who wasn't satisfied with the meager amount of information available about Freemasonry began looking deeper into the inner workings of the Craft. This man was WILLIAM PRESTON an Englishman who began his long search for Masonic information in 1762 when he became a Freemason. In 1775 his *Illustrations of Masonry* was published. An authentic account of the lectures and ceremonies of the Fraternity became available. The book was widely circulated. It inspired an American Mason named THOMAS SMITH WEBB to write his version of *Illustrations of Masonry* or *Freemasons' Monitor*. He said he had tried to make Preston's work more suitable for Americans.

Other Masonic books followed quickly. William Morgan's announcement of his intent to publish another book should have created no problems in Batavia, or anywhere else. Perhaps it was the man, and his mannerisms, that caused the uproar, rather then the announcement. He was evidently just what those who described him said he was. That is, if this item that appeared in *The Ontario Messenger* of Canandaigua, New York, on August 9, 1826, can be believed:

Notice and Caution

If a man, calling himself William Morgan, should intrude himself on the community, they should be on their guard, particularly the MASONIC FRATERNITY. Morgan was in this village in May last, and his conduct while here and elsewhere calls forth this notice. Any information in relation to Morgan can be obtained by calling at the Masonic Hall in this village.

Morgan is considered a swindler and a dangerous man. There are people in this village who would be happy to see this Captain Morgan.

Several other papers quoted this item. One exception was the *Republican Advocate* published by Morgan's partner, David C. Miller.

On September 10, 1826, a small fire was found in Miller's printing office, and was quickly extinguished. The next day William Morgan was arrested by Holloway Hayward, constable of Canandaigua, New York, accompanied by five men. A tavern keeper had accused Morgan of stealing a shirt and cravat. In court, Morgan proved they were loaned to him. Upon his release, he was arrested again for a debt of $2.68!

Morgan couldn't put up the security necessary for his release, so he was put in jail. Amazing! And unconstitutional. But in the State of New York a judgment for six cents that couldn't be paid meant imprisonment.

On the following evening, September 12, the jailer's wife accepted payment of Morgan's indebtedness and released him.

She didn't know who the benefactor was, and neither does anyone else. Morgan was seen to enter, either peacefully or forcibly, a closed carriage that held several other people. It is said he was coveyed to Fort Niagara, about one hundred miles away, and there confined in an unused powder magazine. It appears he remained there until September 19, and then disappeared forever.

Governor DE WITT CLINTON, a Past Grand Master of Masons in New York, took action. On October 4, 1826, he asked all citizens to cooperate with the authorities. On the 26th he offered a reward for the recovery of Morgan, or the apprehension of those responsible for his disappearance. On March 19, 1827, he raised the reward to $2,000 for finding Morgan, or "if murdered, that the perpetrators might be brought to condign [suitable] punishment."

JOHN C. PALMER claims several men were brought to trial for the abduction and served time in prison. Dr. WILLIAM L. CUMMINGS of Syracuse, New York, a noted Masonic historian, made a lifetime seach for information concerning the Morgan incident. He noted: "No proof of Morgan having been murdered has ever come to light and no one has ever been brought to trail on that charge—and but a single arrest was made. The prisoner was discharged in a few days, without examination."

WILLIAM PRESTON VAUGHN, in his *The Antimasonic Party* published in 1983, writes:

> . . . In November [1826] a grand jury at Canandaigua indicted four men, including Cheseboro [Nicholas, Master of Master's Lodge at Canandaigua], who had handled the Batavia-Cananaigua end of the abduction. They were tried in the latter town in January 1827, and on the advice of their attorneys, three of the accused pleaded quilty to "conspiracy to kidnap," claiming no knowledge of Morgan's later whereabouts. Kidnapping was still classified as a misdemeanor in New York. The three were sentenced to two years, three months, and one month, respectively, in the Canandaigua jail. . . . The fourth defendant, sometimes described as a "notoriety seeker," received a three-month term.

The light sentences and the abrupt end to the trial shocked the spectators, and 200 witnesses were released to trudge home through the snow. As Thurlow Weed later declared, the acquittals did not restore public confidence but instead implicated Freemasonry more deeply. . . . Shortly after the Canandaigua trial had concluded, the first Antimasonic conventions, held at LeRoy and Lewiston, asked for a strengthening of the laws relating to kidnapping and requested appointment of a special counsel to conduct the Morgan trials.

These trials dragged on for five years, 1826-1831, but produced few convictions. Some twenty grand juries were called, fifty-four Masons were indicated, thirty-nine were brought to trail, and ten received convictions and jail terms ranging from thirty days to twenty-eight months. . . . Of the ten convicted, only six were involved with Morgan's abduction. Four were punished for illegally moving David C. Miller from Batavia. . . .

Although Vaughn finds there never has been any evidence to support any of the wild claims of the anti-Masons, he concludes "Morgan was probably murdered by misguided Masons."

HAROLD V. B. VOORHIS writing for *Ars Quatuor Coronatorum*, London, England, and its Transactions, Volume 76, 1963, told the story of the Morgan Affair. He based his arti cle"almost entirely on the work of R. W. Bro. Dr. Wm. L. Cummings . . . whose vast researches on 'The Morgan Affair' are known to be 'true and trusty.'" Within his article he noted:

A meeting, destined to become the first of a series of anti-Masonic sessions, was held in Batavia on 25th September, 1826, to determine what had become of Morgan. Another was held on 4th October, and by now there were loud accusations that the Freemasons had murdered Morgan.

The excitement over Morgan's disappearance was now so great that everyone seemed to have forgotten about the exposure which had started the whole affair.

For an interesting "theory" on what happened to William Morgan see Voorhis' article Vol. 2 of the *Little Masonic Library*.

An advertisement was placed in the *Republican Advocate* on October 14, 1826, which read:

Expose'

JUST PUBLISHED
and for sale at the Advocate Office
THE FIRST PART OF
MASONRY UNVEILED
Containing a full exposition of the secrets and ceremonies
of that "ancient and honourable" institution
FREE MASONRY
"God said let there be light, and there was light"
The remaining part is now in press and will shortly be
published.

14th October

The book was published. Copies are still to be found.

An anti-Masonic convention was held at Seneca, New York, on January 13, 1827. Others quickly followed. Many churches prohibited Freemasons from occupying their pulpits. A convention of Baptist churches held at Milton, New York, denounced Freemasonry. And this was just the beginning.

The body of a drowned man was discovered in Lake Ontario, about forty miles from Niagara, on October 7, 1827. The verdict at the inquest was accidental drowning. After the body was interred, Morgan's wife and a delegation of Batavians led by Miller, among them Thurlow Weed, a publisher and politician, arrived on the scene. They had the body disinterred, then claimed it was that of Morgan.

How this could have been believed is a mystery. The corpse had a heavy beard and a full head of hair. No body covered in water for over a year would have this, or be recognizable. This didn't disturb the politician, Thurlow Weed. He had the corpse shaved and hairs thrust into its ears and nostrils before the second inquest began. On his deathbed Weed testified that this body was good enough for his political operations at the time to be Morgan! And this was but the beginning of the lies and distortions Weed would invent.

The publicity brought friends of Timothy Munroe of Clark, District of Newcastle, Upper Canada, to the scene. Munroe had been thrown into the water from a rowboat on September 24,

1827, and disappeared. His widow, Sara, went to Oak Harbor and described precisely the clothing worn by her husband, along with certain marks by which he could be identified. The Coroner's jury reversed its earlier decision. It determined the corpse was that of Munroe.

The presidential election of 1828 was a heated affair. AN-DREW JACKSON was a prominent Freemason who wouldn't bow to the anti-Masonic fanatics. Although he won the election, Weed and his type of politician found the anti-Masonic vote encouraging. They believed they had a weapon to use in future elections. And they did have one.

In New York, the Anti-Masonic candidate for governor received 33,335 votes in 1828. In 1830 the Anti-Masonic Party candidates came within 8,000 votes of being elected.

Freemasonry throughout the country was drastically hurt. The stories of the horrors those who remained true to the Craft had to endure are prevalent. To tell the full story would take a full-size volume.

In New York, where the trouble began, there were about 480 lodges in 1827, with some 20,000 members. In 1830 the lodges numbered 82; the membership, 3,000.

Every historian who has covered the decade of the anti-Masonic venom notes that it was most vicious in Vermont. JOHN SPARGO, author of *Freemasonry in Vermont,* believed the Morgan incident "only stirred up and revivified an old movement that had been quiet and dormant for the greater part of two decades, following a long period of savage and unreasoning frenzy." He adds this observation:

> Antagonism to Freemasonry first appeared in Vermont as a religious ferment. By a large part of the organized Christians of early Vermont, Freemasonry was considered as unchristian in its essential character. This seems strange, especially in light of the extent to which, not by precept only, but by practice no less surely, the Fraternity seemed to be what it professed to be, the handmaiden of religion.

Spargo cites several examples of Freemasonry assisting various churches throughout the state. He then points out many instances of churches of varying denominations condemning Freemasons and Freemasonry. He adds:

> The early records of many of our Vermont churches contain similar accounts of antagonism to Freemasonry, proving that Anti-Masonic feeling was widespread and intense in Vermont long before the Morgan episode. It was centered in our churches and expressed in religious discrimination and persecution. Families were divided by the fierce passions roused. Father disowned sons and never spoke to them again. Churches were torn by dissension and controversy. Men who had been companions and friends were estranged by senseless hate. Yet there was worse to come. The appearance of the Washington Benevolent Societies added fuel to the flames of bigotry and intolerance.

> The first Washington Benevolent Society was formed in New York in 1808. It was a secret society with avowed fraternal and charitable objectives, but its main purpose was to be the fighting arm of the Federalist party in its struggle against the strongly entrenched Jeffersonian party, then sometimes called the Republican party and at other times the Democratic party. As early as 1790 numerous radical clubs and societies, more or less secret in character, appeared.

> They were bitterly hostile to Washington's administration and to the Federalist party. They were enthusiastic supporters of Jefferson. They intensified the bitterness of the conflict between the two parties.

This society had been formed to oppose the "Tammany Society," according to Spargo. The latter had been formed to gain political control of New York. The rituals and charges of the Washington Benevolent Society were based "largely upon Freemasonry." Because of this and the unMasonic activities of this secret society, Spargo believed Freemasonry suffered. But by 1818 "things had become fairly quiet." Open "hostilities ceased, but the fire was only smouldering; it was not extinguished. The smouldering embers needed no more than a breeze to quicken them into flaming again. The Morgan episode furnished the breeze."

The lodges in Vermont gradually ceased to function. From 1836 to 1845 none met at all. Even the Grand Lodge ceased to meet—formally, but by resolution adopted in 1836, the Grand Master, Grand Secretary, and Grand Treasurer were to meet biennially. Technically, this would keep the Grand Lodge alive. On January 14, 1846, several members and Grand Lodge officers met in Burlington. After much discussion, the Grand Lodge was called to order and Grand Lodge officers elected.

The Grand Lodge of Michigan was formed on June 27, 1826, in Detroit. The following day LEWIS CASS, the third Grand Master of Masons in Ohio, was elected the first Grand Master of Masons in Michigan. In the beginning there were five lodges. During 1827 several dispensations were issued for new lodges. Then the anti-Masonic craze hit the Territory of Michigan. JAMES FAIRBAIN SMITH writes: "In the midst of such times as these, a meeting of the Grand Lodge was held some time in the year 1829, the exact date unknown, and it was resolved to suspend all Masonic work until the excitement should be allayed. The lodges were asked to suspend labor, and all promptly acceded to the request except the plucky Stony Creek Lodge."

Smith writes of a Masonic hero, DANIEL B. TAYLOR, Tiler of Stony Creek Lodge:

> On Lodge nights, as soon as the stage arrived bringing the mail, he would get his newspaper and wend his way to the lodge room. On arriving there he would light a candle, place it in the window and then sit down to read. If no one else came, Brother Taylor waited the usual time 'to close the lodge.' Then he would blow out the candle, lock the door, and go home.

Until the Grand Lodge was revived in 1840, Taylor kept the light of Freemasonry blazing in Michigan.

RALPH J. POLLARD writes:

> The effect of the Anti-Masonic movement on the Maine Lodges was paralyzing. Candidates ceased to apply for the degrees. Members ceased to pay their dues. The indifferent, the timid, and the weak deserted the Fraternity in droves.

The Maine Lodges fell into three classes. A few collapsed without a battle, and surrendered their Charters to the Grand Lodge. . .

On the other hand, there were some Lodges, which, through thick and thin, maintained their organization, elected officers, and transacted business. These were usually Lodges possessing substantial funds. The two Portland Lodges were in this class. . . .

Most of the Lodges, however, neither surrendered their Charters nor maintained an active existence. They simply became dormant. Some faithful brother retained custody of the Charter, jewels, and records. The hall was closed, and all meetings were discontinued. The Lodge went to sleep, like a hibernating bear, until the dark night was past and a new day dawned.

The Maine Grand Lodge continued to meet each year. It transacted its business, dispensed its charity, and elected its officers, "although on one occasion not a single subordinate Lodge was represented."

In 1830, 30 lodges were represented at the annual Grand Lodge communication; in 1831, 20; 1832, 16; 1833, 10; 1834, 7; 1835, 6; 1836, 4; 1837, 1; 1838, 4; 1839, 4; 1840, 6; 1841, 2; 1842, none.

Conditions began to improve. In 1843 five lodges were represented; in 1844 there were 19. Freemasonry in Maine was back to stay.

A "large number of citizens" of the State of Rhode Island signed a "memorial" asking the General Assembly to investigate "the designs, principles and practices of Freemasons, believed to be adverse to religion and morality, subversive of civil government, and incompatible with all the social and civil virtues." In the same year, 1831, the second convention of the Anti-Masonic Party was held in the state.

A special committee of the Assembly conducted an investigation. The final report contained over 200 printed pages. This report "was a substantial exoneration of the Fraternity in Rhode Island from all the criminal charges brought against it," writes HENRY W. RUGG, D.D. But because of the public outcry, the committee recommended: "This Committee cannot but come to the conclusion that Masons owe it to the community, to themselves, and to sound principles, now to discontinue the Masonic institution."

The General Assembly adopted this report. But the Grand Lodge courageously responded on August 27, 1832:

> *Resolved,* That we are of the opinion that no good can result, either to the public or to Masons, by adopting their recommendation—that in our view the clamorous leaders of Anti-Masonry care not whether we meet in Lodges or Chapters; it is not the Institution of Masonry they are contending against: that is merely the pretence; political favor is the object.
>
> *Resolved,* That we regret the present state of society; but are of the opinion that our duty is plain, which is that we manifest a determination peacefully to adhere to our institution through evil as well as good report.

Along with Massachusetts and Connecticut, Rhode Island Masons issued a declaration of its principles. The declaration concluded: "Should the people of this country become so infatuated as to deprive Masons of their civil rights, in violation of their written Constitutions, and the wholesome spirit of just laws and free governments, a vast majority of the Fraternity will still remain firm, confiding in GOD and the rectitude of their intentions, for consolation, under the trials to which they may be exposed."

To its shame, the General Assembly of Rhode Island bowed to the anti-Masons. It repealed the charters of several lodges, thereby proving the dangers of incorporating Masonic lodges. So, in 1834, the Grand Lodge suggested its lodges give up their civil charters. It stated, however: "We wish it to be distinctly understood by all our Masonic brethren, either at home or abroad, that the civil charters had no connection with the Masonic charters; that the Grand Lodge retains its Masonic powers as heretofore, and that its members have not relinquished their rights as citizens to assemble peacefully together or to associate as Masons. To avoid the operation of the law referred

to as it respects the Grand Lodge, its charter has been surrendered to the General Assembly, by doing which we have
disarmed our enemies and the Legislature of all rights to visit us
or interfere with our concerns, so long as we remain quiet and
peaceable subjects, and conform to the constitutional laws of
the land."

The civil charter of the Grand Lodge was surrendered on
March 17, 1834. Notably, it was restored by the General
Assembly on April 4, 1861. And, although several lodges were
for all purposes dormant during the anti-Masonic period, not a
single lodge gave up its *Masonic* charter.

Rugg records many Freemasons who deserved the plaudits of
their brethren for their courage during those trying years. One
of them was mentioned by the Grand Master in 1870:

> Rev. GEORGE TAFT, D.D., died at Pawtucket,
> December 11, 1869, aged 78 years. He was throughout his
> long life a devoted Mason and faithful Christian pastor.
> He it was, who, in the dark days of anti-Masonry, pro-
> claimed the sentiment, "Masonry and religion—what God
> hath joined together, let no man put assunder." In those
> dark and trying times, when Masons faltered and were
> afraid to declare themselve such, he openly avowed his
> connection with the institution, and would travel long
> distances to attend and read the funeral service over a
> deceased Mason. He marched through the streets of his
> village in Masonic clothing amid the jeers of the populace;
> but when he went to his grave, the places of business in
> that same village were closed, the bells of the churches of
> all denominations tolled his requiem, while a large con-
> course of citizens thronged his church and with weeping
> eyes and saddened hearts, mourned the good man
> departed.
>
> The funeral service of the church was read by Right
> Rev. Bishop Clarke, assisted by several clergy, and the
> Masonic burial office was read at the grave by myself.
> Learning that it was his wish to be buried with Masonc
> honors, I deemed it my duty to attend and give to one who
> had so honored our institution, the highest honors left for
> us to pay him.

Another was one who gave testimony before the special committee of the General Assembly in 1831:

> I, CHRISTIAN M. NESTELL, ornamental painter and gilder, a resident of Providence, am a mason and still adhere to masonry. I have taken the following regular degrees, viz.: entered apprentice, fellow craft, master mason, mark mason, past master, most excellent master, royal arch, royal master, select master, super excellent master, knight of the red cross, knight of malta, and knights templars of the order of St. John at Jerusalem. . . .
>
> In attaching myself to the masonic institution, as in the taking of the foregoing degrees, I was previously impressed with a favorable opinion of the institution; which impression led me, of my own free will and accord, to solicit the recommendation of my friends to enable me to obtain them. I never knew it to be the duty or practice of masons, to use any exertions towards soliciting the accession of members. As a man and a mason I consider my duties to my Creator paramount to all other duties; and I feel willing to testify and declare in truth and sincerity, under a solemn oath, that I have never taken an oath or obligation, that I consider can in any wise interfer or conflict with the duty I owe my country. Neither has any of my obligations or promises made in masonry, ever given my brethren any right, or power, to execute, or inflict any penalty upon me beyond expulsion.
>
> The invocation attached to each degree I have always understood to be between my Creator and myself, should I ever willingly, or knowingly, disclose unlawfully the vital secrets of freemasonry. The internal secret forms and ceremonies attached to each degree, I view as a species of private property, which I have justly and lawfully purchased, and which I never will consent to yield up to any man, or body of men, who are not as justly and lawfully entitled to the same as I am myself, even were my life and property to be the forfeiture.
>
> I consider the prominent object of freemasonry is to promote the best interest of mankind. Every mason is bound to alleviate the distress of all worthy brethren no matter whether they originated in the immediate vicinity in which he resides, or sprung from the remotest corners of the earth. I have been a mason eleven years; have held an office in all the masonic bodies of this place, and have served two years

in the first office in the gift of the lodge in this town, during which period I never knew a call for relief refused a worthy brother, his widow or orphan. . .

In taking the several degrees attached to each body, I was distinctly informed previously to taking my obligations, that they were not to interfere with my religion, politics, or my allegiance to my God or my country. I never was led, or influenced by them, to confer a favor on a mason, to the injury of one who was not a mason.

The moral precepts which masonry inculcate, have been a great stimulus in teaching me to render every man his just due without distinction. The secret forms and ceremonies of each degree, with their true explanations, are calculated to fix and impress the mind with correct principles of morality; they are also designed to unite and conciliate true friendship among men, which friendship would never have otherwise existed.

We have secrets which our obligations bind us sacredly to conceal; by them we are enabled to distinguish true brethren from imposters, and if we were not under these obligations to keep them from bad men, they would soon become common and of no intrinsic value by their subversion. I have never regretted the taking of the degrees in masonry and if there were any more to be conferred, I should ask to obtain them. They have been the means of introducing me to many valuable friends and the study of each degree has had a tendency to strengthen and improve my memory, with many other advantages, which has proved more than a renumeration of the whole amount I ever paid to obtain them.

As regards my masonic ties to those brethren who compose the masonic family, I am bound to them as far as truth, honor and justice will warrant, and no farther. I am not to screen them from the arm of the law, cloak their iniquities, render them assistance to the detriment of myself or family; nor am I to enter into plots or conspiracies against the government of the country in which I live; but feel myself bound by the precepts of masonry, to be a peaceable, quiet citizen of the place in which I reside, and to patiently submit to the legal authority thereof.

I am ready to confess we have some immoral and disorderly members among us; but I do know it be the duty of each member of the body where such belong to complain

of them, and have them admonished and exhorted to refor-
mation, and should this gentle means fail, we then have
recourse to expulsion, and thus forever withdrawing from
them our fellowship as masons.

I consider it my duty as a mason, to so live and conduct
myself as to avoid becoming a subject of reproach, and use
my endeavors to preserve unsullied the reputation of the
institution. I hold myself not accountable for the depreda-
tions said to be committed on the body of William
Morgan, by those who have passed through our solemn
ceremonies; if it be true that this outrage was committeed
by such, and they had become so wretchedly depraved as
to trample on the laws of God and man, they, and they
alone, on proof of guilt, are culpable; and agreeable to the
laws of our country, have forfeited their existence.

Surprisingly, the anti-Masonic ground swell was mild in the
South. This leads to the belief that those historians who considered the anti-Masonic craze a political adventure were correct. That it was an "eastern" plot appears to be proven. The
fact that Michigan and Illinois Masonry suffered can be attributed to their ties with the East.

Charles McCarthy's "The Antimasonic Party" is perhaps the
best treatise on the subject even though it was written in 1902.
He concluded the opposition to Freemasonry evolved from
several factors. Many of the opponents were envious of the
"wealthy, influential" and "aristocratic men" who were
Freemasons. There were religious "leaders" who desired much
more influence in some political party. Some politicians were
seeking a cause, no matter what or who was harmed, to get
themselves elected. Religion, bias, and politics gave the anti-
Masons their strength. But this strength was confined, mainly,
to the rural areas.

The leaders of the Anti-Masonic Party were shrewd, if
unscrupulous, politicians. Chief among them were Thurlow
Weed and William H. Seward of New York, and Thaddeus
Stevens of Pennsylvania. Their doctrine was widely spread
through the approximately 141 anti-Masonry newspapers that
sprang up during the "crusade." But every conceivable public
platform was utilized to spread their venom. The public square,

JOSEPH SMITH, THE MORMON PROPHET
Organized The Mormon Church, or The Church of Jesus Christ of
Latter-Day Saints, which is its full and official title, on April 16, 1830.

the political arena, clubs, organizations, and churches were employed. Nothing, not even the pulpit, was considered sacred.

The first national convention of the Party was held in Philadelphia in 1830. Delegates from nine states attended. William Wirt was nominated for the Presidency in 1832. His opponents were Freemasons, HENRY CLAY of Kentucky and ANDREW JACKSON of Tennessee, both Past Grand Masters. Vermont was the only state the party of the anti-Masons carried. But in 1835 it did elect the Governor of Pennsylvania. Its 1836 candidate, Joseph Pitner, was defeated for the Presidency. The Party died before the 1840 election.

Perhaps it's coincidental that The Church of Jesus Christ of Latterday Saints, or more often called, the Mormon Church, was organized during the tumultuous days of anti-Masonry. In New York, and elsewhere, the degrees of Freemasonry were mimicked in public squares and other places where the public congregated. It has been claimed that much of *The Book of Mormon* is based on what is purported to be Masonic ritual.

This Church was organized on April 6, 1830, at Fayette, Seneca County, New York, by Joseph Smith, Oliver Cowdery, David Whitmer, and Peter Whitmer, Jr.

MERVIN B. HOGAN was made a Blue Friar in 1976. (This is a society of Masonic authors to which one is selected each year.) For his paper he presented "Mormonism and Freemasonry: The Illinois Episode." Within it he read "The Articles of Faith of the Church of Jesus Christ of Latter-day Saints, then noted:

> It is clearly evident to anyone who acquaints himself with this creed that there are no conflicts or incompatibilities whatsoever between the teachings, theology, and dogma of Mormonism and the philosophy, principles and tenets of universal Freemasonry.
>
> The history of the various relationships, and the continuing involvements between Mormonism and Freemasonry for practically a century and a half fall naturally into two separate and essentially unrelated experiences. Each historical episode is as sharply independent of the other as the two geographical and political entities, or Grand Masonic jurisdictions, of Illinois and Utah.

Each of these fascinating accounts of Masons, people, events, declared and hidden ambitions, as well as emotional, biased motivations, are lengthy, complex, and all too frequently only sketchily recorded.

Hogan believes Freemasonry and Mormonism have much in common. The enemies of both tried to eliminate them. "Surely," said Hogan, "with that simultaneous background, it must be readily acknowledged that Mormonism and Freemasonry are so intimately and inextricably interwoven and interrelated that the two can never be disassociated." Both "presents and teaches its most profound truths symbolically by means of its temple ceremonies to those candidates it deems worthy and qualified to receive that instruction," he later adds.

He was the only Freemason, and perhaps the only outsider, to be allowed access "to the vast primary resources within the Historical Archives of the Mormon Church in Salt Lake City." His paper, and later enlarged account appearing in Volume II of the *Little Masonic Library,* is based on his research in the archives. He concludes that the Grand Lodge of Utah is wrong in barring Mormons from membership in Utah lodges.

The Grand Lodge of Utah did not agree with Hogan's conclusions until 1984 when it removed its prohibition against Mormons.

During the height of the anti-Masonic period two Grand Lodges were formed, both in the South.

On July 9, 1830, the Grand Lodge of Florida was formed. Texas won its independence from Mexico in 1835. In 1836 it became a republic with the Mason SAM HOUSTON as President. On May 11, 1838, Houston installed ANSON JONES as the first Grand Master of Masons in Texas. The Grand Lodge was born—the story of Texas Freemasonry had begun.

Twenty-two

THE JACKSON ERA

THE "Easterners" had been defeated in the election of 1828. The roughhewn "Old Hickory" had gained control of the government of the United States. His victory had been overwhelming.

Daniel Webster was gloomy on inauguration day. He said of the bustling crowd: "They seem to think the country had been rescued from some dreadful danger." "Western informality" had taken over the White House and Capitol.

A somber ANDREW JACKSON, sorrowing over the recent death of his wife, emerged from the Indian Queen Tavern. He was a contrast in his mourning clothes from the gaily dressed crowds as he walked down Pennsylvania Avenue. The eager crowds forced Jackson to climb over a wall and enter the Capitol through the basement.

After the Mason, Jackson, was sworn in by the Mason, JOHN MARSHALL, he mounted his horse and rode to the White House. The crowds followed him right into the building. The official guests were brushed aside, and even the furniture wasn't spared. Many condemned the over-enthusiasm, but at least one reporter wrote: "It was a proud day for the people." Then he added: "General Jackson is *their own* president."

The "Westerners" were happy, but not for long. Their belief that he would be partial to their interests soon turned to disappointment.

As Senator, Jackson had supported bills to improve roads and canals for the interior. As President, he advocated those projects that benefited two or more states. He vetoed a bill for $150,000 that would finance the building of a road in Kentucky only. He approved the expenditure of funds to extend the Cumberland Road running west from Maryland through Pennsylvania, Ohio, Indiana, and Illinois. He made it clear the national interest must come before local causes.

The Cherokees remained a powerful force in Georgia. Although the federal government recognized their property rights, Georgia had annexed their lands in 1828. Jackson suggested the tribes move across the Mississippi where they would be granted new lands. The Cherokees refused and asked the Supreme Court of the United States for assistance. It was denied. Then Samuel A. Worcester, a missionary, entered the case and entered the matter in his name. JOHN MARSHALL then ruled the Georgia law was unconstitutional. When Jackson was asked what could be done he is reported to have roared: "John Marshall has made his decision, now let him enforce it." The Indians moved.

Just before Jackson was elected President, Freemasonry played an important role in what would become the life-blood of western settlement. The Grand Lodge of Maryland met in Baltimore on July 4, 1828, to lay the cornerstone for the Baltimore and Ohio Railroad. Grand Masters from Pennsylvania and Virginia participated in the Masonic ceremonies. After Jackson had been sworn in, Maryland Masons opened the Baltimore and Susquehanna Railroad on August 8, 1829.

Forty years later the continent was united. The tracks of the Union Pacific and the Central Pacific Railroads were joined with a golden spike at Promontory Point, Utah. WATSON N. SHILLING, Worshipful Master of Weber Lodge No. 6 of Utah sent the news to the world via telegraph: "The last rail is laid, the last spike driven."

The news was important to many, but especially LELAND STANFORD, one of the owners of the Central Pacific. Stanford's name has been perpetuated in Stanford University, founded by him; and by Leland Stanford Lodge No. 784, Chico, California.

Jackson and his Vice President, John C. Calhoun, seldom agreed on the issues confronting the country. Calhoun was bitterly opposed to tariffs. He claimed the North was making the South pay exorbitant prices for its manufactured goods. Then, too, the tariffs had forced Europe into levying duties against southern raw materials. He claimed the "tyranny" of the majority could be nullified by the constitutional right of each state to not accept the unconstitutional acts of The Congress. He was paving the way for a war thirty years later.

The Calhoun problem wasn't eased any when Jackson told his Secretary of War and friend from Tennessee, JOHN HENRY EATON: "If you love Margaret Timberlake, go and marry her." He did. It was claimed her late husband cut his throat because of her affair with Eaton. Her great beauty didn't endear her, either, to the wives of the members of the Cabinet. The attack against Margaret was led by Mrs. Calhoun. In fact, the latter ordered the President out of her house when he asked her to visit Margaret, better known as Peggy, socially. The Eaton affair finally resulted in a practically new Cabinet.

The tariffs were reduced in 1832, but the South wasn't appeased. South Carolina nullified the tariffs and prohibited their collection after February 1, 1833. If force was used, the state declared it would secede. Jackson answered by sending General WINFIELD SCOTT, a Mason, to take command of the federal forces in the South. On December 10, 1832, the President stated: "I consider. . . the power to annul a law of the United States, assumed by one State, incompatible with the existence of the Union."

He added: "To say that any State may at pleasure secede from the Union is to say that the United States is not a nation." He concluded: "Disunion by armed force is treason. Are you really ready to incur its guilt?" Old Hickory won. Not another state went to the defense of South Carolina. But the Mason, HENRY CLAY, introduced one of the first of the compromise bills in the Senate. It called for a gradual reduction in the tariffs. Jackson's restraint and Clay's compromise calmed the crisis.

In a letter Jackson wrote to John Coffee he proved prophetic: "The nullifiers in the south intend to blow up a storm on the slave question. . . be assured these men would do any act to destroy this union and form a southern confederacy."

The Mason, ANDREW JACKSON, was opposed by the Mason, HENRY CLAY, in the presidential election of 1832. When the votes were counted, Jackson had 217 electoral votes to 49 for Clay. Nicholas Biddle had been Clay's running mate. He was also president of the United States Bank which Jackson heartily distrusted. President Jackson refused to recharter the bank. With four years yet to stay open, Biddle tightened credit throughout the country. This caused a serious recession. It wasn't until Biddle was forced to relieve the credit situation that the recession ended.

More than a recession was taking place in Texas. Thousands of Americans had moved West. Many of them had settled in Texas, then under the rule of Mexico. Relations between the two countries had been friendly for a number of years, then they deteriorated. They worsened when General Antonio Lopez de Santa Anna seized control of the central government in the summer of 1832. Santa Anna was reported to be a Freemason, but one writer claimed if he was, he was a bad Mason as well as a bad Mexican.

STEPHEN F. AUSTIN, a Freemason and a friend of Mexico, endeavored to bring about better relations with the Mexican government. For his efforts he was ordered arrested by Santa Anna. He spent the next eighteen months in a Mexican jail. Texans were outraged. And in 1834, Santa Anna declared himself dictator of Mexico. He ordered the garrison at Anahuac strengthened, refusing all requests for conciliation. A handful of Texans, led by a Freemason named WILLIAM B. TRAVIS, attacked and forced the Mexican garrison to surrender. Travis would later be killed at the Alamo.

—TEXAS—

While political affairs in Texas were going from bad to worse, many of the Freemasons in the territory wanted

Masonry to be active. JAMES D. CARTER, in his *Masonry in Texas*, reported an account written by Dr. ANSON JONES, who would become the first Grand Master of Masons in Texas:

> In the winter of 1834-35, five Master Masons, who had made themselves known to each other, consulted among themselves, and after various interviews and much deliberation, resolved to take measures to establish a Lodge of their Order in Texas.
>
> This resolution was not formed without a full appreciation of its consequence to the individuals concerned. Every movement in Texas was watched at that time with jealousy and distrust by the Mexican Government, and already had its spies and emissaries denounce some of our best citizens as factionists and disaffected persons; already were the future intended victims of despotic power being selected. It was well known that Freemasonry was particularly odious to the Catholic priesthood, whose influence in the country at the time was all-powerful. . . all fears of personal consequences were thrown aside, and a resolution to establish a Lodge. . . was adopted. . . .
>
> At 10 o'clock in the morning of a day in March, 1835, was held the first formal Masonic meeting in Texas as connected with the establishment and continuance of Masonry in this country. . . . It was concluded to apply to the Grand Lodge of Louisiana for a Dispensation to form and open a Lodge, to be called Holland Lodge, in honor of the then Most Worshipful Grand Master of that body, J. H. Holland.

John M. Allen carried the Dispensation from New Orleans, but didn't reach Texas until just before the Battle of San Jacinto. On the prairie he delivered the papers to Anson Jones. Jones carried them throughout the battle.

The Texans declared their indepedence on March 2, 1836. Twenty-two of the 59 delegates, according to Carter, were Freemasons. DAVID C. BURNET was elected President; LORENZO DE ZAVALA, Vice President; JAMES COLLINSWORTH, Secretary of State; THOMAS J. RUSK, Secretary of War; and each of these was a Freemason. SAM HOUSTON was elected commander-in-chief of all Texas land forces.

On March 6, 1836, the day Houston gathered his small force, the tiny garrison in San Antonio was massacred. Less than two hundred men under the leadership of Colonel WILLIAM B. TRAVIS had been under siege for weeks. They had taken refuge behind the stout walls of a mission called "the Alamo." On February 24 Travis had let the world know the Texans were determined "to sustain myself as long as possible and die like a soldier who never forgets what is due to his own honor and that of his country. VICTORY OR DEATH."

Twice on the 6th the entire Mexican army stormed the Alamo and was thrown back by the small American force. On the third attack the Mexicans breached the walls and annihilated the handful of men still alive. Travis and Davy Crockett were among the last to be killed. Other Freemasons killed at the Alamo, according to Carter, included JOHN C. CLARKE, ALMARON DICKENSON, JAMES BONHAM, and JAMES BOWIE.

Houston and his small force retreated before the Mexican advance. But about three o'clock in the afternoon of April 21, 1836, the command was given to attack at San Jacinto. The Mexicans weren't prepared for a battle, and within thirty minutes they were routed from the field. By the following morning almost the entire Mexican force was either killed or captured. The Texans lost two killed; twenty-three wounded, six of whom died. Carter lists 151 Freemasons among the Texas forces taking part in the Battle of San Jacinto.

Santa Anna escaped. But on April 22 he was found and captured. Concerning him, President Jackson wrote to Sam Houston:

> His person is still of much consequence to you. He is the pride of the Mexican soldiers, and the favorite of the priesthood. While he is in your power, the difficulties of your enemy, in raising another army, will continue to be great. The soldiers of Mexico will not willingly march into Texas, when they know that their advance may cost their favorite general his life. Let not his blood be shed, unless imperious necessity demands it as a retaliation for further Mexican massacres. Both wisdom and humanity enjoin this course in relation to Santa Anna.

Texas asked for admission to the United States. The request was rejected! But the United States did, however, recognize the

Republic of Texas. During the life of the Republic, each of its four Presidents and Vice Presidents were Freemasons: Samuel Houston and MIRABEAU B. LAMAR; LAMAR AND DAVID G. BURNET; HOUSTON AND EDWARD BURLESON; ANSON JONES AND KENNETH L. ANDERSON. Ten served as Secretary of State—each a Freemason. The other officials and members of the Congress were predominately Masons.

On September 22, 1837, the Grand Lodge of Louisiana chartered its second Lodge in Texas, Milam No. 40. A third Lodge, McFarland No. 41, was chartered on the same day. These two, plus Holland, met in a convention on December 20, 1837, and resolved to establish a Grand Lodge. At Houston on April 16, 1838, ANSON JONES was installed Grand Master by SAM HOUSTON.

Texas became the twenty-eighth state admitted to the Union in 1845. In the same year, on June 8, ANDREW JACKSON died. Another era had ended.

Twenty-three

FREEMASONRY ORGANIZES IN THE WEST

BETWEEN 1838 and 1851 seven new Grand Lodges were organized. The westward movement of Freemasons increased dramatically. The benefits of the Louisiana Purchase of 1803, and the courage of the early explorers were paying off. Trailbreakers hewed their way through the wilderness on foot and horseback. Eastern and Southern homesteaders followed in their footsteps.

"The cowards never started and the weak died on the way," noted more than one who reached the west coast. There were only two ways to go—by wagons drawn by horse or ox, or by boat. Often a combination of both were used. Even so, the travel was primitive. The boats were small and uncomfortable. Roads were non-existent. Trails were difficult to break and the wilderness, mountains, and deserts were obstacles to overcome.

—ARKANSAS—

More than one person has exclaimed while flying west: "How—how did those courageous men and women ever make it!"

At Arkansas Post in 1819 a Masonic lodge was formed. Little is known about this lodge or Freemasonry in Arkansas for almost twenty years. Was it because of the anti-Masonic period? However, on November 21, 1838, a convention was called to order in Little Rock by four lodges for the purpose of forming a Grand Lodge. These were Washington Lodge No. 82

with a Tennessee charter, Morning Star Lodge No. 42 and Western Star No. 43, with charters from Louisiana and Mt. Horeb which held a dispensation from Alabama. A constitution was written, and on November 27, 1838, Grand Lodge officers were elected and installed.

—ILLINOIS—

Western Star Lodge in Illinois was granted a charter on June 2, 1806, by the Grand Lodge of Pennsylvania. Its historian would report: "That little band of brethren furnished the State its first Governor, one United States Senator, two Supreme Court Justices, four State Senators, twelve national representatives, and many other State and Federal officers."

Laurence Lodge was chartered by Kentucky in 1815. In 1820 Tennessee chartered Libanus Lodge. Missouri chartered Olive Branch, Sangamo, Union, and Eden Lodges in 1822. Albion received a dispensation from Indiana in the same year.

Representatives from these lodges met at Vandalia in December, 1822, to organize a Grand Lodge. Then a strange thing happened. A Grand Lodge communication was held in January, 1827—then the Grand Lodge disappeared!

Freemasonry appeared again when Kentucky granted a dispensation for a lodge at Quincy on August 31, 1835. In 1840, four lodges with Missouri charters, and two with charters from Kentucky, organized the present Grand Lodge of Illinois. And it wasn't long before it ran into trouble.

In 1839, Mormons had purchased land in Illinois and named the village "Nauvoo." There the religion's founder, Joseph Smith, operated a grocery store. The Masons among Smith's followers petitioned the Grand Lodge of Illinois for a dispensation for a lodge. The Grand Master personally instituted the Lodge at Nauvoo on March 15, 1842. Six months later, the Grand Master suspended its charter. This new Lodge had "raised" or "made" 256 candidates! Of five Mormon lodges given dispensations by Illinois only Rising Sun Lodge No. 12 of Montrose, Iowa ever received a charter.

According to Haywood: "After the Mormons split, the mother group remained in Illinois, and later made its capital in Independence, Mo.; many of its members have been Masons ever since. The other groups, led by Brigham Young, carried bitter memories of Masonry with them to Utah, became violently anti-Masonic, and have been so ever since." Mervin B. Hogan doesn't agree with this assessment. He believes there is no anti-Masonry among the leaders of the Church of Latter Day Saints.

The Grand Lodge of Utah prohibited members of the Mormon Church from membership in Utah Masonic lodges until 1984. Other Grand Lodges have had no such prohibition.

—WISCONSIN—

The French discovered what was to become Wisconsin in 1634. With its proximity to two of the Great Lakes and a great river, the Mississippi, the French moved into the area in large numbers. Many of its cities would forever carry French names. In 1760, after the Seven Years War between the French and the English, it came under the control of the British. It became part of the United States in 1783, included in the Northwest Territory in 1787. Wisconsin was admitted to the Union in 1848.

A Masonic lodge was established in Green Bay in 1824 under a charter from the Grand Lodge of New York. Seventeen years later a lodge at Mineral Point was granted a dispensation from Missouri. And from Missouri came Melody Lodge on January 10, 1843. Kilbourn Lodge was granted a charter from Illinois on June 12, 1843.

These last three lodges met at Madison in a convention to form a Grand Lodge on December 18, 1843. BENJAMIN T. KAVANAUGH was elected Grand Master. In spite of its rugged climate and country, it continued to prosper throughout the years. It would become one of the most charitable of all Grand Lodges.

—IOWA—

The Grand Lodge of Missouri became the mother of the Grand Lodge of Iowa. On October 20, 1841, it approved charters for Des Moines Lodge and Iowa Lodge. Dubuque and

IOWA MASONIC LIBRARY
Cedar Rapids, Iowa

Courtesy of the Iowa Masonic Library

Iowa City Lodges received charters from the same source on October 10, 1843. However, while the last two Lodges were working under dispensations, they met with the two chartered Lodges on May 10, 1843, in Iowa City. It was decided a Grand Lodge should be formed. But it wasn't until the convention of January 2, 1844, that a constitution was adopted and Grand Lodge officers elected. On the 8th, Oliver Cock was installed as Grand Master.

The Congress passed an act on July 3, 1838 which formed Iowa into a Territory. President Van Buren appointed Robert Lucas of Ohio as Governor of the Territory. Along with Lucas came Theodore S. Parvin as his private secretary. Both were Freemasons, and both were active in forming the first Masonic lodge in the Territory.

After the formation of the Grand Lodge, Parvin lost no time in starting a Masonic library. His plans were endorsed by the Grand Lodge during its first annual communication with an appropriation of five dollars! From this five dollars came the first Masonic library in the country. It erected the first building anywhere in the world exclusively for use as a library in Cedar Rapids, Iowa. It continues to be one of the most excellent ones and in recent years constructed a beautiful new edifice.

Perhaps because of the library, Iowa has produced some of the Masonic literary greats. JOSEPH E. MORCOMBE, JOSEPH FORT NEWTON, D.D., CHARLES C. HUNT, JACOB HUGO TATSCH, and HARRY LEROY HAYWOOD, are among these greats. Even the lady who saved Macoy Publishing & Masonic Supply Co., Inc. during the depression got her start in the literary field at the Iowa Masonic Library. Miss Vee Hansen was Tatsch's private secretary when she was a young girl. Later she joined him at Macoy Publishing Company in New York. When the owner and officers of the company died in rapid order, she took over the business in 1945. Today it remains the largest publisher of Masonic books.

—MICHIGAN—

Why the Grand Lodge of Michigan ceased its short-lived work in 1829, is unknown. Haywood believes it was "unfortunate to have such a Grand Master as Lewis Cass." Haywood felt "the anti-Masonic influence and Lewis Cass' bowing to it" had much to do with its dissolution. Others note that Cass was a politician. Politics was his life, much more important than anything else. However, Cass was an active Freemason in Ohio. He helped form its Grand Lodge and served for three years as its third Grand Master. In Michigan he worked to establish its Grand Lodge and did serve as the first Grand Master of Michigan.

On June 2, 1841, lodges from Mt. Clemens and Pontiac, which had received dispensations from the former Junior Grand Warden, met with Stoney Creek Lodge—the only one that had not stopped working. During this meeting, held in Detroit, a committee was selected to gather all records concerning the Grand Lodge. It was then "Resolved, that we do now proceed to the election of officers of the Grand Lodge of Michigan." LEVI COOK was elected Grand Master. Cook refused to serve!

Following the lead of Michigan's most bitter opponent, the Grand Lodge of New York, with one exception (the Grand Lodge of Ohio), no Grand Lodge would recognize the reorganized Grand Lodge. It continued to work, however. New lodges were chartered and old ones revived.

Three lodges: Detroit, Zion, and Oakland received new charters from New York. James Fairbain Smith notes: "The minutes of Detroit show that its plans to reorganize Grand Lodge were beginning to bear fruit." It sent a notice to the foregoing lodges requesting a convention be held "at Masonic Hall in the City of Detroit at 10 o'clock a.m. on the third Thursday of August for the purpose of forming a constitution and reorganizing the Grand Lodge for the State of Michigan."

Smith, in his *Dateline 1764*, writes:

> It must be remembered that a Past Master of Detroit Lodge was already Grand Master of Masons of Michigan's revived Grand Lodge; thus, on December 17, 1844, the Grand Lodge was reorganized and Brother John Mullett, who was already Grand Master of the revived Grand Lodge, was named to the same office in the reorganized

Grand Body. Elisha Smith Lee, also a Past Master of Detroit Lodge, was named as Grand Secretary and Levi Cook as Grand Treasurer.

December 17, 1844, was an extremely important day for Michigan Freemasonry, for on that day it was agreed to dissolve the revived Grand Lodge of Michigan for the purpose of reorganizing Masonic work in Michigan, that it might stand in its true fraternal relations with other Grand Jurisdictions.

The fact that the reorganized Grand Lodge was in reality the revived Grand Lodge—that the same Grand Master and official personnel presided over the fortunes of both—that the subordinate lodges of each were the same—that they met in the same room on the same day and at the same hour and transacted their business—that the reorganized Grand Lodge used the effects of the old—made no difference, since Masonic usage and custom had played its part and tradition and precedent had been maintained.

The historian for the Grand Lodge of New York is silent as to the reasoning behind its refusal to recognize the Grand Lodge of Michigan. New York was having problems enough of its own without interfering with outsiders. It was again fighting a schism within its own ranks. It took the efforts of JOHN W. SIMONS and ROBERT MACOY to bring about a reunion of St. John's Grand Lodge and the regular Grand Lodge in 1850. So, why did it bitterly oppose the revival in Michigan in 1841?

—CALIFORNIA—

"On January 19, 1848, near Coloma, California, James W. Marshall discovered yellow metallic flakes in the millrace of Sutter's Mill," wrote EDWIN N. STANSEL in *1850-1975, A History of Grand Lodge of Free and Accepted Masons, State of California.*

"In spite of efforts to suppress it," he continued, "the discovery triggered an unprecedented transcontinental migration. The 'Gold Rush' was on. Thousands came overland across prairie, mountains and desert. Many seafarers sailed around Cape Horn, while others waded through jungles of the Isthmus of Panama and boarded waiting ships bound for California. The population of San Francisco jumped from 900 to 20,000 in one year."

Stansel noted that many Freemasons who migrated West carried with them dispensations to form lodges. Traveling Lodges were formed, but most of their records have been lost. Missouri did charter the first known lodge in California on May 10, 1848. The charter was carried overland by Peter Lassen, and it wasn't until October 30, 1849, that Western Star Lodge No. 98 was organized. Its birthplace was in the Lassen Trading Post, Benton City. In 1851 it moved to Shasta, and there it remained.

Delegates met on April 5, 1850, in the Masonic Hall in Sacramento City. Connecticut Lodge No. 75, Western Star No. 98, New Jersey and Benicia Lodges Under Dispensation were represented. They agreed a Grand Lodge should be formed. Notices were printed in the newspapers of Sacramento and San Francisco calling for a convention to convene on April 17, 1850. It's interesting to note that the building in which this meeting was held, and in which the Grand Lodge was formed, had its second story occupied by "participants in the world's oldest profession."

CHARLES GILMAN, a San Francisco attorney, presided over the convention held on April 17, He had Masonic officiating experience, having served as Grand Master in New Hampshire and again in Maryland, the latter from 1842 to 1848. A committee was appointed to draw up a constitution. It was adopted on the 19th. JONATHAN DRAKE STEVENSON was elected Grand Master. He was installed by Gilman. It was noted the Grand Lodge came into being on the 75th anniversary of the beginning of the "Revolutionary War, at Concord, April 19, 1775."

—OREGON—

Haywood, in his *Wellsprings of American Freemasonry* writes:

> From its beginning in Independence, Missouri, to its end in Oregon, the Trail made its way among Indians, belonging to almost all the Indian peoples, but it was those in Wyoming and Idaho that most emigrants had in mind

when they said "Indians." These "Indians" are not to be
confused with the civilized Pueblos in New Mexico; or
with the Six Nations in the East; or with the Civilized
Tribes in Indian Territory.

The Indians along the middle portions of the Trail were
savages, and it is useless for lovers of the Indians to try to
conceal the fact, as it would be useless for a white man to
try to conceal the fact that the savages who murdered at
the orders of Al Capone were white men. During the 18
annual migrations between 1841 and 1859, when 300,000
emigrants followed the Trail, some 30,000 men, women
and children died, and the savages were responsible direct-
ly or indirectly for a large number of them. The traces of
the long memory of living a generation among *savages. . .*
are still alive in Oregon in general, and in Oregon Territory in particular.

The Freemasons in the Territory of Oregon were scattered
widely. Consequently, this notice was placed in the *Oregon
Spectator* of Oregon City on February 5, 1846: "The members
of the Masonic fraternity in Oregon Territory are respectfully
requested to meet at the City Hotel in Oregon City, on the 21st
inst. to adopt some measure to obtain a charter for a lodge."

Seven Freemasons met at the appointed time and signed a
petition to be sent to Missouri for the formation of Multnomah
Lodge. The request had to be sent overland by private
messenger. The Grand Lodge of Missouri granted the request
on October 17, 1846. It had to be delivered, however, and it
wasn't until April, 1848, before a wagon train set out for
Oregon from St. Joseph. Then it was held up "near Omaha by
hostile Indians until the party was augmented by a large wagon
train from Ohio."

Then, notes JOHN C. WILKINSON in *History of the Grand
Lodge of A.F. & A.M. of Oregon,* the bearer of the charter
learned gold had been found in California. He decided to head
there, and turned the charter over to Joseph Kellogg, who was
with the Ohio wagon train. It was finally delivered in Oregon
on September 11, 1848!

The Grand Master in California issued a dispensation to form
Willamette Lodge in Portland on July 5, 1850. Twelve days

later the Lodge went to work. On November 27, 1850, the Grand Lodge of California granted the Lodge a charter. A dispensation was also granted by California for the formation of a lodge at Lafayette. Lafayette Lodge was chartered on May 9, 1851.

On September 13, 1851, delegates from these lodges attended a convention to form a Grand Lodge. The meeting was held in the Masonic hall at Oregon City. A constitution was adopted on the 15th and BERRYMAN JENNINGS was elected Grand Master.

From 1849 to 1979 Oregon Freemasonry provided 22 governors, two of whom, STEPHEN CHADWICK and EARL SNELL, served as Grand Master. Perhaps the best known of these governors was MARK O. HATFIELD who became a United States Senator.

—PRINCE HALL MASONRY—

CHARLES W. MOORE of Massachusetts published *Freemasons Monthly Magazine* for several years. In his issue of July 1, 1848, in writing about "African Grand Lodge" he used the term "Prince Hall Grand Lodge." He was referring to a man and an episode that took place in 1775. JOSEPH A. WALKES, Jr., in *Black Square and Compass*, records the event:

> It is generally accepted that Freemasonry among Blacks in the United States began with the initiation of Prince Hall and fourteen other "free" Blacks in Lodge No. 441, Irish Constitution, attached to the 38th Foot, British Army garrisoned at Castle Williams (now Fort Independence), Boston Harbor on 6 March 1775, the Master of the Lodge being one Sergeant J. Batt (or J. T. Batt or John Batt). . . .
> It is claimed that when the British Army left Boston, that Hall was left a "permit" to meet as a Lodge, but apparently not to confer degrees. Masonic authorities agree that this was how Africian Lodge No. 1 was organized, and that Prince Hall later petitioned the Mother Grand Lodge of the world, England, for a warrant that was issued on September 29, 1784, for African Lodge No. 459.

Concerning the same incident, CHARLES H. WESLEY writes in *Prince Hall, Life and Legacy:*

> John Batt, a Sergeant in the 38th Foot Regiment was in charge of the initiation. He had enlisted in the British

army in 1759 and later joined the American army. This regiment had been stationed at Antigua, Guadalupe and Martinique. Some black men in these islands were recruited for its ranks and were sent first to England, then to Nova Scotia and to the English colonies in America. It is probable that Prince Hall knew some of these soldiers and they were brought into close contacts, and the initiation was undertaken.

On January 4, 1824, Africian Lodge petitioned the Grand Lodge of England for permission to confer the degrees of Royal Arch Masonry. It had been doing this for some time, anyway, because several of the petitioners had "been regularly Exalted to the Sublime Degree of Royal Arch Masons." The letter was evidently ignored as no reply can be found. This isn't surprising. The United Grand Lodge of England probably wasn't too fond of the Royal Arch. Until the union of the "Ancients" and the "Moderns" in 1813, the "Moderns" wouldn't recognize the Royal Arch.

At any rate, three years later African Lodge notified the world on June 26, 1827, it was "free and independent of any lodge from this day." This statement would cause Prince Hall Masonry no end of difficulties in the years to follow. As the organization pleaded with the Masonic world for recognition as the legitimate Freemasonry among blacks, this statement, among others, was used as ammunition by those opposed to all black Masonry.

Prince Hall Masonry has had problems from the beginning to the present day with black Grand Lodges that are clandestine in every respect. To assist Prince Hall Masonry, MELVIN M. JOHNSON of Massachusetts, then Sovereign Grand Commander of the Scottish Rite, Northern Jurisdiction, headed a movement he described as "an adventure in understanding in which the areas of good will be sympathetically explored in an informal and unofficial meeting." Johnson received the approval of his Grand Council.

A committee was appointed by the Grand Master of Masons in Massachusetts in 1946 to investigate the matter. The original charter for African Lodge No. 459 from the Grand Lodge of England was removed from its vault, examined and found to be genuine. As a result a report was made to the Grand Lodge of Massachusetts and sent to all of its lodges. The report was adopted on March 12, 1947. The Chairman of the Committee noted: "I think it appropriate to say that your Committee of Past Grand Masters had relatively little difficulty in agreeing as to the legitimacy of Prince Hall Freemasonry, but did encounter some real perplexities when it came to phrasing their conclusions, for they felt that the subject matter is potentially controversial and that a wrong emphasis, however well intended, might harm the very ones whose interests we have at heart."

It did! Because of the unfavorable reaction to the acknowledgment of legitimacy, but not recognition, the action of the Massachusetts Grand Lodge was recinded on June 8, 1948.

Prince Hall Freemasonry has grown over the years. Many of its leaders have reached the heights in industry, government, law, education, and all of the professions. They, and their organization, have been recognized for their work for their communities and the country. Governor Endicott Peabody of Massachusetts Proclaimed September 13, 1964, as "Prince Hall American Day." This was one of many before and after. An organization over two hundred years old, composed of at least one-half million men, cannot be ignored.

Twenty-four

MANEUVERING IN THE
POLITICAL ARENA

THE war with Mexico ended on February 2, 1848, with the signing of the Treaty of Guadalupe. The Rio Grande became the boundary with Texas. Much of Colorado, all of Utah, Nevada, New Mexico, Arizona, and California became the property of the United States.

The power of gold brought California leaping into statehood. The Territories of Oregon and Washington prospered beyond the dreams of those who suffered on the long, dangerous trail heading westward. In the montainous west discoveries were made that helped fill-up more empty spaces. The nation had expanded with an explosive bang.

Other explosions were taking place in the political arena. The Northern states were insisting the territory won from Mexico be free of slavery. The Southern states claimed they would secede if slavery was excluded. Into the fray marched HENRY CLAY, defeated for the Presidency, but back in the Senate. He had claimed he "would rather be right than President," and he again endeavored to calm the troubled seas. He had been successful with the Missouri Compromise in 1820. Could he succeed again?

An historian named Clement Eaton claimed the Mexican War is what eventually caused the controversy which led to the Civil War. Actually, it wasn't the Mexican War in itself, but a political maneuver by a then little known politician from Pennysylvania.

DAVID WILMOT, a Democratic Congressman, was searching for a way to gain the support of the voters in his district in 1846. He thought he had found the means when Polk's administration asked for two million dollars to buy additional land from Mexico. Wilmot tacked a rider onto the request which would bar the institution of slavery from any lands gained from Mexico. This "Wilmot Proviso" gained him the recognition he sought. It also destroyed the work of the moderates on both sides of the issue, even though the rider never was adopted.

David Wilmot, a member of Lodge No. 108, Towanda, Pennsylvania, went on to take a leading part in the formation of the Republican Party in 1854. He filled a vacancy in the U.S. Senate from 1861 to 1863. He was one of the members of the peace convention in 1861. Lincoln rewarded him in 1863 by appointing him to the U.S. Court of Appeals.

The Presidential election of 1848 found Zachary Taylor, the hero of the Mexican War, running on the Whig ticket. Martin Van Buren was nominated by the Free Soil Party; LEWIS CASS by the Democrats. Van Buren took enough votes away from Cass for "Old Rough and Ready" to win the election.

Zachary Taylor, as President of the United States, was present for the laying of the cornerstone in Richmond, Virginia of the equestrian statue of George Washington by the Grand Lodge of Virginia on February 22, 1850. Taylor was asked if he was a Freemason. He said he wasn't, but would have been had time and circumstances permitted. "I would do so now, but have got to be too old," he added.

Taylor urged the politicians to compromise; to admit California to the Union as a free state, the others to be organized into territories with no reference to slavery. Senator John C. Calhoun of South Carolina vehemently opposed the whole idea. He felt the South had suffered the wrongs and insults of the North long enough. He and his followers wouldn't yield, even if it meant dissolving the Union.

Senator Henry Clay of Kentucky, now 72 years old, stepped forward once again. He suggested that California be admitted as a free state, and the territory acquired from Mexico become United States territories with no mention of the "peculiar institution." There was more to his proposed compromise, and the debates continued into the spring.

Calhoun, too weak to speak, was carried into the Senate on March 4, 1850. His speech was read by another to a packed gallery as he made his last plea for the South (he would die in less than a month). He bitterly opposed any compromise. Three days later Daniel Webster supported Clay's plan. On the 11th of March William H. Seward of New York, a bitter anti-Mason, spoke to a nearly empty chamber. He wanted the South to know there was a "higher law" than the Constitution.

Zachary Taylor died on July 9, 1850. Millard Fillmore succeeded him. The politicians were intensely interested in what he would do. It was well known that he leaned toward antislavery, but it was also well known that he despised Seward. The answer wasn't long in coming. Webster was appointed Secretary of State. Along with him a cabinet that favored compromise. During August and September, laws were passed generally favorable to Clay's plan. They were signed into law. Clay's Compromises of 1850 was complete.

The Grand Lodge of the District of Columbia laid the cornerstone of the extension of the Capitol on July 4, 1851. Millard Fillmore, who once described Freemasonry as "organized treason" was present. After he had examined the stone, he pronounced it laid. He then turned and said, "The Most Worshipful Grand Master of the District of Columbia will now please examine the stone and see that it is *well laid*. Fillmore also attended the Masonic laying of the cornerstone at the Buffalo State Asylum for the Insane in September, 1872. He had evidently learned his earlier evaluation of the Craft was not accurate.

A series of fictional stories took the North by storm in 1851. Within the pages of an abolitionist magazine, *The National Era*, appeared a story about slavery. The following year the series became *Uncle Tom's Cabin, or Life Among the Lowly.*

The author was Harriet Beecher Stowe. About her, *200 Years,* has this account:

> Mrs. Stowe's firsthand knowledge of her subject was slight. She had lived for eight years in Cincinnati across the Ohio River from the slave state of Kentucky, but only once, it appears, had she visited that state and then only for a few days. Moreover, conditions in Kentucky were not at all like the Deep South locale of her story. At one time during the writing she had to ask a former slave what a cotton plantation looked like.
>
> *Uncle Tom's Cabin* is wordy, given to long exposition, and loaded with improbable coincidences, but it is a powerful indictment of slavery, and it had an electric effect on the nation. . . .

How successful was she? Several years later President Lincoln met her and asked: "Is this the little woman who made this big war?"

— MINNESOTA —

In the midst of the turmoil another Grand Lodge was born. Minnesota became a Territory by an act of The Congress on March 3, 1849. On April 28, according to RALPH TURTINEN, author of *More Than Bricks and Mortar,* the first issue of *The Minnesota Pioneer,* the Territory's first newspaper appeared. On May 26 this notice appeared: "Members of the Masonic Fraternity, in and near St. Paul, intend to meet together in a room over the Pioneer office on Thursday evening next, May 31st, at six o'clock."

The result was a request for a dispensation from the Grand Lodge of Ohio, which was granted on August 8, 1849.

A dispensation was authorized by Wisconsin for St. John's Lodge in Stillwater on October 12, 1850. Cataract Lodge received a dispensation from Illinois in 1851. These three lodges subsequently received their charters, and steps were taken to form a Grand Lodge.

On February 24, 1853, a constitution was adopted and ALFRED E. AMES was elected Grand Master.

Senator STEPHEN A. DOUGLAS of Illinois introduced a measure to organize the territories of Nebraska and Kansas, giving them the power to decide whether or not they wanted slavery. This, if adopted, would do away with the Missouri Compromise. Fury was unloosened in the North. But Douglas won. This broke up the Whig Party. From it was established the Republican and Know-Nothing Parties.

Douglas was made a Master Mason in Springfield Lodge No. 4, Illinois, on June 26, 1840. He was a member of the Illinois Supreme Court in 1841. He served in the U.S. House of Representatives from 1843-47, when he was elected to the Senate. He was defeated for the Presidential nomination in 1856 by another Freemason, JAMES BUCHANAN. During 1858 he entered a series of debates with Abraham Lincoln. These brought an unknown Lincoln into national attention. In 1860, Lincoln defeated him for the Presidency. Buchanan died on June 3, 1861, and was buried with Masonic rites. When a monument was dedicated to his memory in Chicago on September 6, 1866, President ANDREW JOHNSON, also a Mason, was present for the Masonic service.

—KANSAS—

Kansas became a troublesome spot. Southerners were given free transportation to farm and fight there. Not to be outdone, Northerners did the same. The clergyman, Henry Wade Beecher, went a step further. He preached a sermon urging "free-soil" settlers to go to Kansas, and well armed, because "one Sharp's rifle will have more moral influence upon slaveholders than a hundred Bibles." Rifles then became known as "Beecher's Bibles."

BEN W. GRAYBILL in *History of Kansas Masonry* writes of the struggle:

> Thousands of easterners left their comfortable homes to go to Kansas to prevent the expansion of slavery. Hundreds were unable to cope with the hardships and returned home. Drouths, grasshoppers and countless other irritants were certainly justified reasons for surrendering their high principles for the comfort of their families. Timber was scarce, so the early settlers were forced to make their homes in tents, primitive log cabins, sod houses or "hay tents." Transportation was limited. You could walk, ride

horseback, travel by wagon or the occasional stage lines operating between military posts such as Fort Leavenworth, Fort Riley and Fort Scott. Those who remained were sincere men, dedicated to a cause and possessing the fortitude to challenge their opponents. The pro-slavery advocates were, to a great extent, just as sincere and dedicated to their cause. . . .

Graybill added: "It is a credit to the resident Masons that they were willing to overlook their political differences and establish an independent Grand Lodge at a time when this critical schism existed." During the year 1854, three lodges: Grove, Smithfield, and Leavenworth, received dispensations from Missouri. These lodges were chartered in 1855, but Grove became Kansas Lodge; Smithfield became Smithton.

It took three attempts, but these three lodges finally met in a convention to form a Grand Lodge for Kansas. The meeting was held at Leavenworth on March 17, 1856. A constitution and bylaws were adopted and RICHARD R. REES was elected Grand Master.

JAMES CHRISTIAN, the first Worshipful Master of Lawrence Lodge, was asked in 1888 to relate his experiences. (This was important as the records of the Lodge had been destroyed when Quantrill raided Lawrence on August 21, 1863.) He noted the bitter feelings existing between the anti and pro-slavery people of the area. "During the year 1856," he said, "owing to the troubles, our lodge seldom met; it was almost impossible to get the members together. I often at our monthy meetings, went along the streets, saw the officers or some of the members, told them that I would appoint them to such or such an office, then I would write up the records as though we had a regular meeting, with all officers in their places, when in reality there was no one present but myself. This I did for months at a time to save our charter, and make the proper showing to the Grand Lodge."

CHARLES ROBINSON, who would become the first Governor of Kansas when it became a state in 1861, was made a Master Mason in Lawrence Lodge No. 6 on July 21, 1859. Three years earlier he was the "free-state" governor. As such he was seized and jailed, along with several others. This, and other incidents, brought pro-slavery elements into the town. Shots were fired, the hotel fired at with cannon, so was the home of Robinson. In all, much property was damaged and one man was killed accidently. The "Sack of Lawrenceville" went into the history books. Northern politicians had a field day discussing "Bleeding Kansas."

No blood had been spilled at Lawrenceville, but plenty was spilled by John Brown, four of his sons (he had 20 children), and two other men. Two days after the incidents at Lawrenceville they went to a small settlement on Pottawatomie Creek. There they shot and then hacked to death five men and boys who were Southern sympathizers.

Pro-slavery forces attacked Brown's headquarters at Osawatomie. At least a dozen men were slain and many wounded before Brown's forces fled. Ambushes, shootings, burnings, and ransacking became a way of life in Kansas.

JOHN BROWN, the abolitionist, was made a Master Mason in Hudson Lodge No. 68, Ohio, on May 11, 1824. In 1826 he moved to Pennsylvania, and along with many others during the anti-Masonic craze, renounced Freemasonry. With help from Massachusetts abolitionists, Brown seized the government arsenal at Harper's Ferry, then in Virginia, in 1859.

Grand Master LOVE S. CORNWELL of Missouri told his Grand Lodge in 1856: "It will be well, my brethren, for us to look at the great mission of Masonry, and learn our duty. Masonry requires of its devotees, 'that they be peaceable and quiet subjects of the country in which they reside; never be concerned in plots and conspiracies against the government, but to conform cheerfully to its laws. . . . Where, then, is the Mason who will disregard those wholesome tenets of our institution?"

"Through the kindness and under the protecting care of overruling Providence," said Grand Master R. R. REES of Kansas, "we are permitted to assemble once again in Grand Communication, and though the past Masonic year has been one of turmoil, or contention, and of angry conflict in the outer world, yet peace and quietude have reigned within the retirement of our Sanctum."

The Grand Lecturer of Kansas noted: "In August, 1856, when the citizens of Lawrence and Lecompton met only at the point of the bayonet, [I] went to Lawrence for the purpose of instituting the lodge and installing the officers at that place. We saw numbers of armed men, and heard a number of prisoners who had been arrested for encroaching on the bounds of a *Corps de'armee*, and without that universal passport, which Masonry gave us, we certainly would have shared the prisoner's tent. But we were not molested or insulted in our peaceful mission, and the brethren received us hospitably and parted with us fraternally."

The Territorial Governor of Kansas was frightened by events he couldn't control, so he resigned. JOHN W. GEARY was asked to leave the retirement he had earned and take over as Governor. He did in September, 1856. Before winter he had things under control.

John W. Geary had been "made a Mason at sight" on January 4, 1847, in Pennsylvania, later affiliating with Philanthropy Lodge No. 225, Greensburg, Pennsylvania. He commanded a regiment in the Mexican War of 1846 as a lieutenant colonel. He became the first commander of the City of Mexico. In 1849 he was appointed the first postmaster of San Francisco, and affiliated with California Lodge (now No. 1) and was its first secretary. In 1850 he became the city's first mayor. He retired to Pennsylvania in 1852. He served as a general during the Civil War. After the fall of Savannah he saved the Masonic temple and earned the gratitude of the inhabitants of the city.

The comparatively new Republican Party expected to win the election of 1856. The Democratic Party was badly split; the Whig Party had fallen apart. JOHN C. FREMONT became the Republican organization's choice for the Presidency; JAMES BUCHANAN the choice of the Democrats. By a small margin Buchanan won.

The abolitionists gained a martyr while the campaign was at its height. Charles Sumner, an anti-Mason from Massachusetts, delivered a blistering speech in May, 1856, lasting for two days. His principal targets were Senator Andrew Butler of South Carolina and Stephen Douglas of Illinois. His venom angered even those who were opposed to slavery. And Sumner would have remained unpopular if Butler's nephew had not beaten Sumner over the head in the Senate two days later. It took Sumner three years to recover enough to reenter the Senate chambers.

A slave named Dred Scott added fuel to the fire. He had been taken North by his master. After they returned to Missouri the master died. Scott, or someone for him, sued for his freedom on the grounds he had been in a free state. The Supreme Court ruled against Scott on March 6, 1857. This further crumbled the Missouri Compromise.

During the "off-year" election of 1858 two oratorial giants faced each other in Illinois. Senator Stephen Douglas, "the Little Giant" met his opponent Abraham Lincoln, "the Rail Splitter," in a long series of debates. Douglas won back his senate seat, but in defending himself against Lincoln, he lost support he needed from the South to win the Presidency.

—NEBRASKA—

"The early pioneer and the pioneer Freemason were often one and the same person," said FRANCIS E. WHITE, Grand Secretary of the Grand Lodge of Nebraska in 1907. They sought a mutual bond and found it in "the mystic tie that binds us all in a common brotherhood," he added.

A two-story trading post at Bellevue was the site for the first Masonic Lodge in Nebraska. In 1854 Illinois granted Nebraska Lodge a dispensation to go to work. Its first "ballot box" consisted of an empty pickle jar; the "ballots" were stones for a favorable vote—bullets were "to perform the 'dark colored' service." It received its charter in 1855.

Missouri granted Giddings' Lodge a dispensation on May 10, 1855; it was chartered on May 26, 1856. On June 3, 1857, Capitol Lodge in Omaha City was chartered.

"These weak lodges," wrote GEORGE W. ROSENLOF in *Masonry in Nebraska,* with not a mile of railroad within one-hundred miles or more and not a telegraph line anywhere near; and with hostile Indian tribes roaming over its barren plains, joined hands to form the Grand Lodge of Ancient Free and Accepted Masons of Nebraska." This took place on September 23, 1857, with ROBERT CARREL JORDAN being elected Grand Master.

—WASHINGTON—

The Grand Lodge of Oregon chartered Olympia, Steilacoom, Grand Mound, and Washington Lodges between 1852 and 1857. These four met in a convention in Olympia on December 6, 1858, to consider the formation of a Grand Lodge for Washington. A constitution was adopted on the 8th and THORTON F. MCELROY was elected Grand Master.

John Brown seized the federal arsenal at Harpers Ferry on October 16, 1859. And he quickly learned he could expect no support from the slaves he had come to set free. During the seige, Brown lost ten of his men, including two of his sons. Refusing to admit he was insane, Brown was convicted of treason and hanged on December 2. "John Brown's body" began marching along!

The political conventions of 1860 brought forth STEPHEN DOUGLAS, JOHN BELL of Tennessee, and JOHN C. BRECKINRIDGE of Kentucky, three Freemasons. The young Republican Party nominated Abraham Lincoln. Lincoln ended up with a vote higher than the combined vote of his opposition.

The stage had been set for a crumbling house to fall.

Twenty-five

WAR

ABRAHAM LINCOLN had defeated three Freemasons for the Presidency in 1860 with an electorial vote of 180. Not a single one of these votes came from a Southern state. His opponents had gathered 123 votes. The three, however, had received almost one million more popular votes out of four million six hundred thousand votes cast.

JAMES BUCHANAN, a Past Master of Lodge No. 43, Pennsylvania, had endeavored to appease all sides during his term as President of the United States. An example of his temperament throughout the only four years he agreed to serve occurred on February 22, 1860. He joined the Grand Lodge of the District of Columbia in the dedication ceremonies of the equestrian statue of Washington. Holding the gavel said to have been used by George Washington at the laying of the cornerstone of the Capitol, he stated:

> I perform this act of pious devotion, not in the name of the people of the North, of the South, the East or the West—not in the name of those who dwell on the waters of the Atlantic, or of the far Pacific, but in the name of the whole American people, united one and indivisible, now and forever. May the God of our fathers preserve the Constitution and the Union for ages yet to come. May they stand like the everlasting hills, against which the tempest from every quarter of the heavens shall beat in vain. In a word, may they endure as long as the name of Washington shall be honored and cherished among the children of men. May Washington City, which he founded, continue throughout many generations to be the seat of government of a great, powerful, prosperous and united Confederacy.

Should it ever become a ruin by a dissolution of the Union, it will not, like the ruins of Balbic and Palmyra, be merely a monument of the vanity of human greatness, but it will teach the lesson to all the dwellers upon earth, that our grand political experiment has failed and that man is incapable of self-government. May such a direful disaster to the human race be averted, and in the language of SOLOMON, at the dedication of the Jewish Temple, "May the Lord our God be with us as he was with our fathers. Let him not leave us or forsake us." May this be the prayer of all present, and may each one return to his home in heart more determined to do his whole duty to God and his country, than when we assembled here today.

Buchanan's speech was interrupted repeatedly by prolonged applause. At least most of the people from all over the country present agreed with his sentiments. As he noted there, throughout his term he favored compromising the differences between political entities. He, along with the vast majority of Freemasons, were attempting to prevent a violent conflict.

As noted in *House Undivided:* "The complete story about the acts of Freemasons, in lodges and as individuals, during the trying years prior to the outbreak of hostilities, will never be learned . . . . for until recent years much that could have been written was not." The book, however, does cover a cross-section of Freemasonry's attempts to prevent a holocaust.

South Carolina seceded from the Union on December 20, 1860. Yet, like his predecessor HENRY CLAY, JOHN J. CRITTENDEN, a Kentucky Freemason, didn't want to see the country torn apart. He submitted a parcel of compromises to the Senate. They were turned over to a Committee of Thirteen. The Republicans on the committee, with the endorsement of Lincoln and his "let there be no compromise" statement, killed the compromises. Even the New York *Tribune* called Crittenden's work "the most considerate and conciliatory" proposal of "our opponents."

The radicals of the North and South had won. The people of the United States had lost.

Mississippi seceded on January 9, 1861. Florida, Alabama, Georgia, and Louisiana followed quickly. Texas seceded on

February 1, although SAM HOUSTON had vigorously opposed the action. On February 4, 1860, representatives from these states met in Montgomery, Alabama. The Confederate States of America was born. On February 18, Jefferson Davis was sworn in as President of the new "country."

On the first day, February 4, the seceding states met, another meeting rarely mentioned by historians took place. Twenty-one states, at the invitation of Virginia, met in Washington to try to save the Union. Only one Northern state, New Jersey, agreed to support compromises that would have prevented bloodshed.

Lincoln's opposition to compromise was bolstered by his Republican Party. It was the minority party, and anything its leaders could do to improve its position they would do. The threat to the country of political parties that George Washington had warned against was again raising its ugly head. It would throughout the history of the United States, at least through 1983. Within the political climate of opposing parties in 1860, there was no hope for peace.

After his inauguration Lincoln took it upon himself to proclaim he would "hold, occupy and possess" all government property. The following day he ordered a shipload of troops to land at Fort PICKENS, on an island off the coast of Florida. The order of March 5 was delayed for some unaccountable reason. It wasn't carried out until shortly after another fort had been fired upon.

The focus of attention was centered on an island fort in a harbor at Charleston, South Carolina. There Major ROBERT ANDERSON, a member of Mercer Lodge No. 50 of New Jersey faced Confederate troops. The Confederates were under the command of Anderson's Brother Mason and one time pupil at West Point, General PIERRE GUSTAVE TOUTANT BEAUREGARD.

When it was learned that Lincoln was sending supply ships to Fort Sumter, Jefferson Davis was urged to attack. ROBERT TOOMBS, a member of Lafayette Lodge No. 23 of Georgia told the Confederate President: "The firing on that fort will inaugurate a civil war greater than any the world has yet seen. . . it is suicide, murder, and you will lose us every friend at the North."

Davis didn't agree with Toombs. And at 4:30 in the morning of April 12, 1861, Beauregard opened fire on Fort Sumter. During the next afternoon, Anderson lowered the American flag and his troops left the fort. The War Between the States had begun. Five days later, Virginia joined the Confederacy. Her western counties, however, refused to join their mother state. They seceded. Later they formed the State of West Virginia. This proved a paradox. Lincoln claimed states couldn't secede from the Union, but he approved the secession of counties from a state.

North Carolina was the last state to join the Confederacy. The border states of Kentucky, Maryland, Delaware, and Missouri stayed with the Union. The difficulties encountered within those states have been chronicled in several volumes.

The aged WINFIELD SCOTT, a member of Dinwidde Union Lodge No. 23, Virginia, was the first commander of the Federal forces (Robert E. Lee had turned down the offer and joined the South). After the debacle at Bull Run, when Union troops outnumbered Southern troops almost three to one, Lincoln replaced Scott with GEORGE B. MCCLELLAN.

McClellan, a member of Willamette Lodge No. 2 in Oregon, immediately started the long task of building an army from civilians. During the winter of 1861-2 he miraculously did build what appeared to be a real fighting force. He believed, as did many Northerners, that one more battle would end the rebellion.

—COLORADO—

While McClellan was building an army, the Freemasons of what was to become Colorado began building a Grand Lodge. It had started in 1858 when gold was discovered in the Pikes Peak region of the Rocky Mountains. Quickly "hurriedly-formed wagon trains" departed "from Missouri river outposts" for the 700-mile, month-long journey to the area. Men of all descriptions were among the gold-seekers. Several of them were Freemasons.

Centennial Celebration notes: "Many members of the craft responded to the sudden challenge of the frontier. And having been forced to associate with adventurers of dubious backgrounds during the tedious overland journey, upon arrival in the new country they quickly sought the company of their brethren. Within ten days after the founding of the first permanent settlement at Auraria, at the junction of Cherry Creek and the Platte, the first informal assemblage of seven Masons was held in what was to be the Territory and then the State of Colorado."

The Reverend JOHN M. CHIVINGTON wrote: "On May 8, 1860 I arrived in Denver, published an appointment, and preached the following Sunday in the Masonic Hall. HENRY ALLEN founded a Masonic Lodge in Colorado long before there was a church or school."

The first Masonic Temple was built in 1859 at "Gregory Gulch, forty miles northwest" of Auraria "in the High Rockies." Nearly 100 Masons leveled the ground with ox teams dragging in logs for the 'Temple.' " During the meetings, "four Masons armed with rifles and revolvers stood on guard, one at each corner of the Temple and one at the outer door also." Surprisingly, "there were over 200 visiting brethren whose names were entered upon the 'Journal' or 'roll of Visitors' as it was called at that first meeting. A meeting was held once each week for over three months."

The Grand Lodge of Kansas granted a dispensation for the formation of Auraria Lodge, and forty attended its first regular communication on October 1, 1859. Kansas also granted a dispensation for Golden City Lodge on January 21, 1860. Then Chivington arrived with blank dispensations from the Grand Lodge of Nebraska. This resulted in the formation of Summit and Rocky Mountain Lodges. On December 20, 1860, Nevada Lodge received a dispensation from Kansas.

Three of these Lodges, Golden City, Summit and Rocky Mountain, had received charters. After Colorado became a Territory in February, 1861, these Lodges took steps to form a

Grand Lodge. This was accomplished on August 2, 1861. John M. Chivington was elected Grand Master.

McClellan's new army just might have proved correct those who believed one more battle would end the war, if Lincolon hadn't become frightened. In March, 1862, McClellan set out for Richmond, the Capital of the Confederacy. His plan was to ferry his troops down the Chesapeake Bay, landing at the tip of the Virginia peninsula. As he advanced the 70 miles toward Richmond, the 40,000 troops he left in Washington were to march overland to join him on the outskirts of Richmond. As McClellan advanced, the Confederates under General Joseph E. Johnston slowly fell back. On May 31 the Union forces had reached Fair Oaks, about nine miles from the Capital. And Johnston counter-attacked.

During the fighting at Fair Oaks, Johnston was seriously wounded. Robert E. Lee was quickly appointed to take his place. McClellan was driven back to the James River. The reinforcements McClellan had expected never arrived. Lee, even before he had taken over Johnston's command, saw to that.

With McClellan marching up the peninsula, Lee sent Thomas "Stonewall" Jackson to frighten the President of the United States. Jackson, with a small force, slipped through the Shenandoah Valley toward Washington. McClellan's reinforcements were kept busy fighting five losing battles against Jackson's men. Over 50,000 Federal troops were kept occupied around Washington instead of Richmond.

Lincoln blamed McClellan for not taking Richmond. He replaced the General with two others, Henry Halleck and John Pope. Pope didn't last long. It appears he was the only man Lee actually despised. Orders were issued to Jackson and Longstreet to "suppress" Pope. They did. On August 30, at the Second Battle of Bull Run, Pope's troops were sent fleeing to Washington. Pope was sent off to fight Indians. McClellan would be called upon to save the Union.

It happened at Antietam Creek, near Sharpsburg, Maryland. Here the bloodiest battle of the war was fought. Over 23,500 men were killed or wounded on that September 17, 1862, the most ever lost in a single day of fighting.

McClellan, who had been fired by Lincoln after the Richmond affair, took charge and managed to keep the Federal troops from being routed. Even so, when the Northerners were exhausted and waited for reserves, Robert E. Lee, with no reserves at all, withdrew. Too late, the Federal forces chased the Southerners.

The retreat of the Confederates from Maryland gave Lincoln the opportunity he had been seeking. On September 22, 1862, he issued a draft of a Proclamation which said, as of January 1, 1863, all slaves in those states in "rebellion" shall be free. Although Lincoln became known as the "Great Emancipator," he actually freed no one. No slave was freed in any state or territory over which Lincoln presided.

Once again Lincoln fired McClellan. This time he was replaced by Ambrose Burnside, who protested he wasn't the best man for the job. At Fredericksburg on December 13, 1862, he proved he was right. He sent wave after wave of Federal troops against heavily fortified Confederate forces. Over 13,000 Union soldiers were lost, while the Southerners lost less than 5,000. GEORGE PICKETT, a member of Dove Lodge No. 51, Virginia, wrote his wife the "brilliant assault. . . was beyond description. . . we forgot they were fighting us, and cheer after cheer went up all along our lines." Even the Confederates had to admire the bravery of their enemy.

Lincoln replaced Burnside on January 25, 1863, with Joseph Hooker, making him the fifth commander of the Army of the Potomac.

Hooker marched into Virginia stating he hoped God would have mercy on Lee, "for I will have none." Outnumbered by two to one, Lee chose to make a stand in a tangled wooded area along the Rappahannock River near Fredericksburg. The place was soon to be called "the Wilderness." And Hooker was soundly defeated. The victory was perhaps Lee's greatest, but it was cost-ly. Stonewall Jackson was mortally wounded by his own men.

General George Gordon Meade became the Commander of the Army of the Potomac on June 28, 1863. Three days later advance forces of Meade's and Lee's met at a market town called "Gettysburg." For three days the opposing sides fought bitterly. The fighting was culminated on July 3, when George Pickett, at the head of 15,000 Confederates, charged up Cemetery Ridge. Some reached the top, but were hurled back. The Southerners had lost.

The following day, July 4, Vicksburg surrendered to Ulysses S. Grant. For the South, the war was over. But there would be almost two more years of bloodshed.

There were battles near, at, or called Chickamauga, Chattanooga, Lookout Mountain, Orchard Knob, Missionary Ridge, the Wilderness (again), Spotsylvania Courthouse, Cold Harbor, Petersburg, Richmond, Atlanta, Sherman's march through Georgia to the sea, Appomattox. Thousands of Americans continued to be killed or maimed. But it ended abruptly on April 9, 1865, at Appomattox Courthouse, Virginia.

The role of Freemasonry and Freemasons played throughout the war is told in *House Undivided: The Story of Freemasonry and the Civil War.* It is a remarkable story of Brotherhood in action.

With the end of the fighting came cries in the north of punishment. General Grant used every effort in his means to prevent Lee and other Confederate generals from being arrested and tried for treason. The Northern politicians feared the Southern politicians would return to form a Democratic majority. This was to be prevented at all costs. So the Southern states were placed under military command.

What would have taken place had Lincoln lived is not clear. Many historians believe the people of the former Confederate states would have been treated humanely. It has been claimed that Lincoln had drawn up plans to be put into effect at the conclusion of the war. Without question, his assassination changed the course of history.

—NEVADA—

As early as 1863 an attempt was made to form a Grand Lodge for Nevada. It didn't materialize. The next attempt was started late in 1864, and on January 16, 1865, seven lodges holding California charters met in Virginia City. The lodges were: Virginia City, Excurial, Carson, Washoe, Silver City, Silver Star, and Esmeralda.

The first recognized Masonic meeting took place in Virginia City for the funeral of Captain EDW. FARIS STOREY, who had been killed in a battle with the "Pah-Ute Indians" June 2, 1860. (Haywood terms them "the Paintes, as degenerate a tribe of men as ever lived.") The first Masonic lodge, however, was established in Carson City. It was formed to assist the many traveling through the area toward the West. One of the frequent visitors to the Lodge was SAMUEL L. CLEMENTS, a reporter for the *Territorial Enterprise* at Virginia City. His first visit was recorded on February 27, 1862, when he registered as a member of Polar Star Lodge No. 99 of Missouri. If he wasn't at that time, he soon would become known as "Mark Twain."

Freemasonry was continuing to grow. The American Civil War had ended. Bitterness, discord, and "politics as usual" would continue to plague men and women everywhere.

Twenty-six

RECONSTRUCTION

IMMEDIATELY after the close of the Civil War, Major William McKinley was stationed at Winchester, Virginia. The town had changed hands over 70 times during the conflict, so feelings were mixed. Yet, when a major in the Federal forces asked for admittance in a Masonic Lodge there he was accepted.

Major WILLIAM MCKINLEY of Ohio served throughout the war in varying capacities. During the Battle of Antietam he provided men on the front lines with hot meals—the first time in history this had been done. He later said he had noted how certain men helped their wounded enemy on many occasions. He learned the reason while stationed at Winchester, Virginia.

While accompanying a Federal doctor on his rounds of the crude hospitals housing Confederates, McKinley noticed the doctor spending more time with some than others. He also saw the doctor give some of the patients money. When they stepped out of the tents he asked the doctor why he did this when he knew the money never would be repaid.

"Those men are Brother Masons," the doctor told him. McKinley asked him more questions and learned some of the lessons taught in Freemasonry. He asked the doctor how he could become a Freemason. A petition was made available from Hiram Lodge in Winchester. On May 1, 2, and 3 William McKinley received the three degrees of Masonry.

Abraham Lincoln was mortally wounded in a theatre he had not wanted to attend. John Wilkes Booth turned a rejoicing nation into one of sorrow. Although Lincoln wasn't a Freemason, Grand Masters throughout the land ordered their lodges into mourning.

The tragedy touched one man, especially, deeply. EDWIN BOOTH was the brother of the assassin. He had often said he would rather confer the Master Mason degree than "receive the plaudits of the people in the theatres of the world." His Lodge, New York No. 330, sent him a letter on June 4, 1865, offering him the sympathy of its members. He thanked the Lodge and wrote: "It has pleased God to afflict my family as none other was ever afflicted. The nature, manner and extent of the crime which has been laid at our door have crushed me to the very earth; my detestation and abhorrence of the act, in all its attributes, are inexpressible; my grief is unutterable, and were it not for the sympathy of friends such as you, it would be intolerable."

—WEST VIRGINIA—

In May, 1865, a new Grand Lodge was established. It was composed of lodges belonging to the Grand Lodge of Virginia.

Virginia, reluctantly, voted to secede from the Union on April 17, 1861, after Lincoln had called for 75,000 men to "suppress" the Confederate States. Thirty-one western counties met in Wheeling on May 13 in protest. After two weeks of bitter debate, Francis Pierpoint was elected governor of the "Restored Government of Virginia." Forty-eight counties, a year later, formed the "State of West Virginia," the legality of which is still questioned.

A convention of the Masonic lodges in West Virginia was called for December 28, 1863, to form a Grand Lodge. It was unsuccessful. So was the one called for February 22, 1864. The one held on June 24, 1864, was more successful. Grand Lodge officers were elected, but they refused to be installed. On April 12, 1865, eight lodges, all with Virginia charters, met again. WILLIAM J. BATES was elected Grand Master, along with a full slate of officers. On May 10, WILLIAM B. THRALL, a Past Grand Master of Masons in Ohio, installed the officers.

Virginia was reluctant to let its lodges go, and for almost five years resisted all overtures from the new Grand Lodge. But on December 16, 1868, the Grand Lodge of Virginia gave West

Virginia everything its lodges wanted—including permission to keep their Virginia charters.

From almost every Grand Lodge in the states that had remained loyal to the Union, messages of appreciation were sent to the Grand Lodges in the former Confederate States. As Masons returned home they related the many acts of kindness shown them while in Southern territory.

From the South, messages were sent to the North thanking the Masonic leaders who had gone out of their way to help Confederates. The instances were numerous. Two of them give an excellent example:

When Richmond fell, General GODFREY WEITZEL, a Mason, was in command. He immediately ordered the people fed and clothed, and the Richmonders soon learned they had nothing to fear. Federal troops, along side Southerners, attempted to put out the fires set by the fleeing Confederates. The Federal provost marshal placed guards about Masons Hall on Franklin Street to save it from being burned or looted. He didn't know it, but he was saving the oldest Masonic Temple in the country. It is still occupied by a Masonic Lodge and a Royal Arch Chapter. It's a testimony to the tenets and principles of Freemasonry.

Savannah, Georgia, fell to Federal forces on December 21, 1864. A mob began looting the Masonic Hall in the city. When General JOHN W. GEARY learned what was transpiring, he ordered guards placed about the Hall. In 1866 the Lodge sent him a resolution of thanks for this act, and for giving "relief to many anxious hearts."

Geary answered the resolution of thanks in 1866 while he was Governor of Pennsylvania. Within his letter he wrote: "I am entitled to no extraordinary credit or praise; for they should pervade the human heart in every circumstance of life and should be particularly prominent in every action of those connected with Freemasonry." He later added:

> We have reason to be thankful that our lives and health have been spared amid the chances and changes of the stormy period it has been our lot to witness, and for the generally increasing harmony and prosperity which seem

to prevail throughout the nation. And here I feel again justified in referring to our beloved institution, by saying that to Freemasonry the people of the country are indebted for many mitigations of the sufferings caused by the direful passions of war.

—MONTANA—

Freemasonry was organized in Montana on December 7, 1863, when Kansas granted a dispensation for Virginia City. A year later it received a charter. Montana Lodge and Helena City Lodges were chartered by Colorado on November 7, 1865. These three Lodges met in a convention at Virginia City on January 24, 1866 and on the 29th, Grand Lodge officers were elected and installed.

The war-time editor of the *Richmond Examiner*, E. A. Pollard, despised Jefferson Davis—and the North. He didn't think too highly of ANDREW JOHNSON, either, calling him, among other things, a "scrub. . . sprung from a low order of life"; and a man who "had the shallowness and fluency of the demagogue." But Pollard changed his mind. He said he changed from the day Johnson succeeded Lincoln. "The man [Johnson] who had been twitted as a tailor and condemned as a demagogue, proved a statesman, measuring his actions for the future, insensible to clamour and patient for results."

Not everyone, by far, agreed with this assessment of the President. The Northern politicians, in particular, hated him.

Johnson had been a tailor. He began his career at the age of ten in Raleigh, North Carolina. His education came through his own perseverance, and through the help of a man his father had saved. From his first elective office in 1828, at the age of 20, he remained in politics until his death on July 31, 1875.

In the House of Representatives on December 19, 1846, he said in a speech supporting Polk's handling of the War with Mexico: "But, sir, I care not whether right or wrong, *I am for my country always.*" Although he was a Southerner, he would not support secession: "I believe it is no remedy for the evils complained of," he said.

Andrew Johnson became a member of Greenville Lodge No. 119, Tennessee, in 1851. He was an ardent Freemason. Some who have analyzed the impeachment proceedings believe this fact helped lead to the trial.

Johnson was one of the main speakers when the Grand Lodge of Pennsylvania laid the cornerstone of the monument to be erected in the Soldiers' National Cemetery in Gettysburg on July 4, 1865.

In Masonic circles throughout the country there were pleas for a peaceful return to life as it had been. Freemasons in the North were sending funds to assist the destitute in the South. Citizens everywhere were concerned about the welfare of others. But this wasn't true within The Congress of the United States.

President Johnson noted: "Before our brave men have scarcely returned to their homes to renew the ties of affection and love, we find ourselves almost in *the midst of another rebellion.*" the politicians, with few exceptions, were demanding retaliation against the former Confederate states.

To a large audience on February 22, 1866, Johnson gave his version of what the politicians were doing:

> . . . You denied in the beginning of the struggle that any State had the right to go out. You said that they had neither the right nor the power. The issue has been made, and it has been settled that a State has neither the right nor the power to go out of the Union. And when you have settled that by the executive and military power of the Government, and by the public judgment, you *turn around and assume that they are out and shall not come in.*

Johnson pleaded with the people to stand behind the Constitution. "*I will be found standing by the Constitution as the chief rock of our safety,* as the palladium of our civil and religious liberty," he promised them.

In Masonic circles the mood was the same as the President's. Freemasons of the North continued to assist the destitute of the

South. Both sides pleaded with the citizens to forgive the horrors that had taken place, and remember the good.

Andrew Johnson followed much of Lincoln's plan in permitting the Southern states to return to the Union. From April, immediately after Lincoln's death, to December, The Congress was in recess. By the time the politicians returned to Washington in 1865, Johnson had reopened the doors and all but Texas had returned to the Union.

The radical Republicans were alarmed. They were about to lose control of The Congress. They took advantage of a rule that permitted them to pass upon the qualifications of their own members. Led by "vindictive Thaddeus Stevens of Pennsylvania" a special committee "studied the whole question of reconstruction." Those elected from the South were kept out of the legislature.

Over the objections and vetoes of the President, the Republicans forced several bills through in an attempt to bind the South. And Johnson's attempts at conciliation didn't go unrewarded in some quarters. On June 7, 1866, the University of North Carolina gave the President an honorary LL.D degree.

Johnson asked the citizens during the midterm campaigning to side with him. They didn't. The ballot was far from secret then. Each party had its own form. It is claimed the fear of reprisals gave the Radicals the victory they were seeking. The Radicals, bolstered by their gains, became even more audacious. In March, 1867, they divided the South into five military districts, each commanded by a general. The first of the Reconstruction Acts was passed. The Congress completely controlled the South. The President was powerless against the supremacy of the House and Senate.

To muffle the President, The Congress passed "the Tenure in Office Act." This was designed to prevent Johnson from discharging those appointees hostile to him. The President said it was unconstitutional; the Supreme Court, as it often did during this trying period, said nothing.

Johnson fired Secretary of War EDWIN M. STANTON, a member of Steubenville Lodge No. 45 of Ohio. The Radicals pounced on this action. A resolution of impeachment was adopted on February 24, 1868. *House Undivided* spoke of what transpired:

"That Andrew Johnson, President of the United States, be impeached of high crimes and misdemeanors in office," read the resolution of the committee on reconstruction of the House. The "high crimes and misdemeanors" were proved to be simply a disagreement with Congress over what punitive action should be taken against the South. Benjamin Butler, the Mason, joined the anti-Mason Stevens, and others, to oust the President.

The "trial" opened on March 30 and the first vote was taken on May 16. When the voting was over, it stood 35 guilty; 19 not guilty. One vote stood between Johnson and impeachment. The opposition did not give up; the Senate was adjourned for ten days; for ten days the senators who had voted against impeachment, particularly the seven Republicans, were subjected to the worst sort of pressure. "The Radical press raged and clamored, the pulpit thundered, while the practical politicians put on the pressure," wrote Robert Selph Henry in *The Story of Reconstruction.*

The impeachment trial ended on May 26 with the vote exactly the same as ten days earlier. Nineteen men had saved The Congress of the United States from performing a disgraceful act.

Congress was not through, however. It declared "the Johnson states" illegal and set up new state governments. They became so corrupt that many Northern newspapers began to realize that Johnson had not been completely wrong; too late for his salvation, but in time to save the country.

The Fourteenth Amendment to the Constitution, on which many decisions by later Supreme Courts depended, was actually never legally adopted. Although three-fourths of the States hadn't ratified it, The Congress ordered the Secretary of State to declare it adopted. He did so on July 29, 1868.

Two weeks later Thaddeus Stevens died. The archenemy of the South, and the President, had gone to "join the devil's cabinet," as more than one Southern editor proclaimed.

Understandably, Johnson wasn't a candidate for the Presidency. The Republicans nominated Ulysses S. Grant for President; SCHUYLER COLFAX of New York for Vice President.

Colfax was the radical Speaker of the House, and had become a Freemason in 1856, but he was dropped from the roll of Lebanon Lodge No. 45, D.C. on December 16, 1864. They were elected, as had been expected.

During Grant's first term all the Southern States returned to the Union. Their representatives were seated in The Congress. But the States were far from free of repression. Northern "Carpetbaggers" swarmed throughout the South. They controlled the political apparatus. And they were aided by Southern "Scalawags." The political scene was complete chaos. Many of the States went bankrupt; corruption was rampant.

For some sort of protection the Ku Klux Klan was born. Its organizer was NATHAN BEDFORD FORREST, a former general in the Confederate Army. He was a member of Angerona Lodge No. 168 of Tennessee, but dropped out about the time he became "Grand Wizard" of "the Invisible Empire." When actions got out of hand, Forrest attempted to disband the Klan before 1870. Many of the respectable men who had joined to protect their homes got out. But the organization continued to exist, and does today.

—IDAHO—

While the South was suffering under the heels of oppression, Freemasonry continued to grow in the West. Idaho's first Masonic lodge came into being two years after gold had been found near Idaho City. This Lodge, Idaho, received a charter from the Grand Lodge of Oregon on August 9, 1864. Two other lodges received charters from Oregon, and one from Washington.

On December 17, 1867, these lodges organized the Grand Lodge of Idaho. Concerning Idaho Lodge No. 1, Haywood writes in *Well-springs of American Freemasonry:*

> The lodge erected a home for itself in 1864, but lost it by fire. In the same year it erected the home which is still standing and in a fair state of preservation. It is frame, of two stories, and a two-story porch extends across the front. The old lodge room is 25 by 45 feet, and proved an ample space for the organization of the Grand Lodge. The boards

were sawed by hand. It was wholly built by hand. The Altar and pillars were hewn by hand from neighborhood trees. The maps on the 16-inch Terrestrial and Celestial Globes were carved by hand. A brother blacksmith hammered out of native silver on his anvil the square, compass, and the jewels of the officers. The scales which members weighed out gold dust for their fees and dues are still in existence. In 1920, when only seven members were left, the old lodge moved to Boise, the lodge itself having become a heirloom. Once a year the members make a pilgrimage to the old home, to confer degrees.

Corruption was wide-spread during Grant's administration. Even so, the economy in the North had improved and the voters elected him for another term in 1872. And the corruption continued. Then in 1873 came a financial panic in the North. In 1874, 23 States went Democratic in the midterm elections.

—UTAH—

It was in 1872 that the Grand Lodge of Utah was organized, but Freemasonry had entered the territory in 1858.

Federal troops under the command of General Albert Sidney Johnston, reported to be a Mason, were sent to Utah by President Buchanan. Mormons were defying the laws, and burning records of United States district courts. Haywood takes this a step further:

> Brigham Young, once he was established in Utah, planned and expected to set up his autocratic rule over a limitless inter-mountain empire embracing Utah, Montana, Idaho, Colorado, Nevada, Arizona, etc., with an outlet to the sea through a Mormonized Southern California. His "State of Deseret" was designed with that Napoleonic plan in view, and considered itself an independent nation. President Buchanan had to send troops to protect Federal officers.

The troops settled at Camp Floyd. Among them were several Freemasons. They wrote to the Grand Lodge of Missouri requesting a dispensation to form a Masonic lodge. It was granted on March 6, 1859. An account of the early days of Rocky Mountain Lodge No. 205, was given by General B. M. Thomas of Georgia and recorded in *House Undivided:*

> Our Lodge room was built of adobe brick. . . . We had
> men detailed to saw timber into plank, in the hills nearby.
> The saws worked vertically with men above and below the
> log, to alternately pull and push the saw. Our buildings
> were roofed with those planks and covered with dirt. We
> had no floor, yet in that room was generated the noble
> brotherly influences which softened the horrors of war
> throughout the length and breadth of our country. . . . The
> windows of our Lodge room were on the north and south
> sides and were very high up the walls—more for ventila-
> tion than light. . . . The dimensions were about 60 x 30
> feet, walls of adobe, covered with plank. . . .

Although the Lodge was careful about the men it elected, 162
degrees were conferred in a single year. The secretary of the
Lodge assured the Grand Lodge: "Grand Lodge cannot boast of
better material than this lodge has engrafted upon our ancient
and honorable institution." Along with the annual returns to
Missouri on December 27, 1860, the vacancy in the office of
Senior Warden was noted. HENRY HETH had resigned his commission and cast his lot with the South. On June 17, 1861, Heth
became a Colonel of Virginia Infantry. He was commissioned a
Brigadier General in January, 1862, and a Major General in
May, 1863. He, and JOHN C. ROBINSON, the first Worshipful
Master of Rocky Mountain Lodge and a Union Major General,
opposed each other during the Battle of Gettysburg.

This was the last the Grand Lodge of Missouri heard from
this Lodge. Its members soon scattered throughout the country.
But on January 25, 1866, organized Masonry returned to Utah.
A lodge at Salt Lake City received a dispensation from Nevada,
with the provision that no Mormons be received as members or
visitors. Two years later this lodge, for some unrecorded reason,
asked for a charter from Kansas. It was granted on October 21,
1868.

Montana gave Wasatch Lodge in Salt Lake City a charter on
October 12, 1869. Argenta Lodge received a charter on April 8,
1871. Then, on January 16, 1872, the Grand Lodge of Utah was
organized. And it had problems from the beginning, as Harry
L. Haywood records:

This new Grand Lodge had no place to go! Brigham Young held control of every square mile of arable land and refused grants to use it except to organized branches of his church; this automatically ruled out Masonry. When, however, the Union Pacific and Southern Pacific built a junction town named Corinne, a sufficient number of Masons came there to live to form Corinne Lodge No. 5, in 1872. Then the two railways changed their minds and moved their junction point to Ogden. The Masons moved with them, and in 1873 received there a charter for Weber Lodge No. 6.

Haywood attempts to explain why the Grand Lodge of Utah prohibited its lodges from accepting Mormons as Freemasons. He goes back to the early days of the anti-Masonic craze in 1826-28:

. . . The Joseph Smith who had the visions out of which Mormonism came, was the same New York State country boy who grew up hearing every day the words and phrases which became a kind of sacred or orthodox language of anti-Masonry. His present day followers, such of them as have any learning, are hard put to explain how so many anti-Masonic phrases of the New York State of 1825-1840 found their way into a book purported to have been written by angels! They also find it difficult to explain how the prophet who had grown up anti-Masonic became so ardent a Mason after moving to Nauvoo, Illinois, that his lodge there initiated no fewer than 256 candidates between March 15, 1842, and the following August 11th. If they weary of that puzzle they can then go on to explain why the Mormons who trekked to Utah behind Brigham Young (once a Mason) became more savagely anti-Masonic than the anti-Masons had been, and yet at the same time those who remained behind to establish their quarters at Indepedence, Missouri, continued friendly to Masonry and have been ever since.

Because Utah continues under the control of the Mormon Church, for the most part, Freemasonry remains a small jurisdiction. Yet it is strong, vigorous and well organized. Strangely enough, its Grand Lodge Temple is in Salt Lake City.

—WYOMING—

The first Masonic meeting held in Wyoming was on a rock estimated to be two billion years old. It took place on July 4, 1862, while several wagon trains were camped near Independence Rock. WALTER C. REUSSER, in his *History of the Grand Lodge of Wyoming*, writes:

> The preparation for the meeting was accomplished by building an altar of twelve large stones, to which a thoughtful and patriotic brother added the thirteenth, as emblematical of the thirteen original colonies, and the stations of three principle officers were built, similarly, of stones. . . . Brother Asa L. Brown informally opened "Independence Lodge No. 1" on the degrees Entered Apprentice, Fellow Craft, and Master Mason. Several of the brothers made short, appropriate speeches and the Tyler spoke of his reminiscences of Masonic history extending from 1821 to 1862. As the brothers had gone up the Rock provided with fluid extract of rye, sweet water, sugar and citric acid, the craft was called from labor to refreshment, a bucket of which was prepared and the brothers made impromptu toasts and responses until no further business appeared. Labor was then resumed, the lodge closed and the members of the Craft descended the Rock to resume their duties of preparing the camp for the night.

There were no jewels for the Bible, so a square and compasses was cut out of cardboard and placed on the appropriate chapter. The Wyoming Landmark Commission commemorated this meeting by placing a plaque, along with others, on the rock.

A convention was called to meet in Laramie City on December 15, 1874, "for the purpose of organizing a Grand Lodge for the territory." The lodges sending representatives were: Cheyenne, chartered by Colorado October 7, 1868; Wyoming, chartered by Nebraska June 23, 1870; Laramie, charterd by Colorado September 28, 1870; and Evanston, chartered by Colorado September 30, 1874. It was resolved "That we deem it highly expedient to organize a Grand Lodge for the Territory."

EDGAR P. SNOW was elected Grand Master, along with a full slate of officers. During the evening of December 15, 1874, the officers were installed.

—DAKOTA—

Yet another Grand Lodge came into existence before the election of 1876 and the centennial of the United States. It was the Grand Lodge of Dakota, which would twelve years later become South Dakota.

A group of Masons was granted a dispensation to form Dakotah Lodge at Fort Randall by the Grand Lodge of Iowa on April 23, 1862. Whether or not this Lodge was ever formed is not known. Iowa granted another dispensation, this one to St. John's Lodge at Yankton on December 2, 1862. Incense Lodge at Vermillion received a dispensation from Iowa on January 14, 1869. On June 7, 1871, Iowa issued a charter for Elk Point Lodge. Then interest in forming a Grand Lodge became apparent.

Another Lodge was added by Iowa on February 6, 1875, when a dispensation was granted for Silver Star. On June 3 it received its charter. On the same date, Minnehaha Lodge which had received a dispensation on July 15, 1873, received its charter, but only because of T. S. PARVIN, Iowa's Grand Secretary. He also interceded for Mount Zion Lodge on the same date. This Lodge had been granted a dispensation on February 16, 1875. In order to let it help form the Grand Lodge of Dakota, the Grand Lodge of Iowa waived the required time to work under a dispensation and granted it a charter on the same date as the other two, June 3.

The convention to form a Grand Lodge met from June 22-24, 1875, at Elk Point. On the 24th Grand Lodge officers were elected. They were installed in the Baptist Church, Vermillion, Dakota Territory, on July 21, 1875. THOMAS H. BROWN became the first Grand Master. He and the other officers were installed by Past Grand Master, and Grand Secretary, T. S. Parvin of Iowa.

The Grand Lodge of Minnesota refused to recognize the new Grand Lodge. It had chartered two lodges in the Territory, Shiloh and Bismarck. Neither of these lodges had been notified of the convention called to form a Grand Lodge. When these lodges were chartered isn't stated in either the history of South Dakota or Minnesota. When Minnesota finally recognized its sister, isn't mentioned.

Because Dakota was being ignored by Minnesota, the former adopted a resolution in June, 1878, "That the Grand Lodge of Dakota possesses sole and exclusive Masonic jurisdiction throughout the Territory of Dakota, and that no subordinate Lodge can maintain a lawful existence in said Territory without acknowledging allegiance to the Grand Lodge of Dakota."

It worked. Shiloh Lodge turned in its Minnesota charter the following year and requested one from Dakota. Bismarck did the same the next year, and became No. 16 on the roster.

The Democrats nominated Samuel J. Tilden, governor of New York and a "reformer," in 1876. The Republicans put up Rutherford B. Hayes as a compromise candidate. Tilden won the election by almost a quarter-million votes. But it was Hayes who became the nineteenth President of the United States. The Radical Republicans were not about to lose their power. They claimed there was fraud in Louisiana, Florida, and South Carolina. They even questioned an electoral vote from Oregon.

A commission of 15 was selected to determine the issue. By eight to seven it was decided Hayes had won. The deal had been swung by Southern Democrats. They agreed to the Hayes victory provided he would withdraw Federal troops from the South, and at least one Southerner was appointed to the Cabinet.

Hayes kept his word. Troops were writhdrawn from the South and the carpetbag governments fell. Reconstruction had ended, but its effects would be felt for many years. The South remained solidly Democratic until 1952 when another war hero, Dwight D. Eisenhower, ran and was elected President on the Republican ticket. It would be 100 years before a Southern Democrat was nominated for the Presidency, then James E.

"Jimmy" Carter was elected by a narrow margin. Lyndon B. Johnson didn't consider himself a Southerner but a Texan or Westerner.

—NEW MEXICO—

The movement westward that had reached a lull during the Civil War had picked up and expanded during the 1870s. This was evidenced by the number of Grand Lodges being formed in hitherto unknown territory. The last of these to be organized during the decade was New Mexico.

Before the United States had defeated Mexico, the loyalty of the inhabitants belonged to Mexico or Spain. It wasn't safe for white Americans. The land belonged to a favored few who had received large land grants from Mexico or Spain. They weren't about to give up this control easily. Although there were some Spanish Americans in the territory, "the square and compasses had to wait until the Stars and Stripes had opened the way," wrote LAMOINE LANGSTON in *A History of Masonry in New Mexico*.

It is believed the first Freemason to settle in the territory was CHARLES BENT. He and his brother built Fort Bent, a trading post, in the early 1830's. After General Stephen Kearny had gained control of the territory in 1846, Charles Bent was appointed its governor. KIT CARSON, who received his degrees in Montezuma Lodge December 26, 1854, arrived in New Mexico in 1826.

The Grand Lodge of Texas was asked for a dispensation for a lodge in the territory in 1841. What the disposition was is unknown. But on June 12, 1847, JOHN RALLS, Grand Master of Masons in Missouri, serving with the Third Regiment of Missouri Volunteers, issued a dispensation for Missouri Military Lodge No. 86. Ralls, three days later, publicly installed the officers of the Lodge at Independence, Missouri. Then they "marched 900 miles across the Kansas prairies and New Mexico mountains into Santa Fe." The Lodge received a charter from Missouri in 1847. On September 18, 1847, a meeting was held by the Lodge.

"This meeting of Missouri Military Lodge No. 86 is believed to be the first sanctioned Masonic meeting to be held in the vast expanse extending from the Missouri on the east to the Pacific Ocean and from Canada to Texas and old Mexico," wrote Langston. "The area is now occupied by thirteen separate Grand Lodges." Several other meetings were held by the Lodge during the months to follow.

Ralls, still Missouri's Grand Master, issued a dispensation for the formation of Hardin Lodge No. 87 on October 8, 1847. This Lodge was also a Military lodge. It held its last meeting on August 14, 1848. Then came the first permanent lodge, Montezuma, chartered by Missouri in 1849. "But," wrote Langston, "Montezuma Lodge recognizes May 8, 1851 as the charter date. There is no explanation of the two-year gap."

Langston added: "Seven other lodges were chartered under Missouri jurisdiction in those years before the New Mexico Grand Lodge was organized. They were Bent and Cimarron which surrendered their charters after four years; and Chapman, Aztec and Union Lodges, which, with Montezuma Lodge, were the charter lodges of the new Grand Lodge in 1877. Silver City, too, was chartered under Missouri, but refused to join with the other four when the new Grand Lodge was formed. . . . Kit Carson Lodge No. 326 was chartered at Elizabethtown, a mining town located between Eagle Nest Lake and Red River, October 12, 1869. The mines failed and the charter was arrested in 1878 by the Missouri Grand Lodge. Scarcely a trace of E'town remains today."

On August 6, 1877, eight men met in Montezuma Lodge in Santa Fe, to form the Grand Lodge of New Mexico. Langston notes that the scene they viewed in the city then wouldn't be far different than it is today. "Santa Fe is very old," he wrote. "Some have claimed that it is older than St. Augustine, Florida, once regarded as the oldest city in the nation. The palace of the Governors was built in 1610."

A constitution and bylaws were adopted on the 7th. In the afternoon officers were elected. In the evening WILLIAM W. GRIFFIN was installed as Grand Master. He then installed the other officers. SAMUEL B. AXTELL, Governor of the Territory, was the Master of Ceremonies. THOMAS B. CATRON, who would become New Mexico's first United States Senator, was appointed Grand Lecturer.

The West was on the way to being won.

Twenty-seven

EXPANSION

THE war had somewhat stopped the movement westward. But even before its end, thousands of Easterners were on the move. They traveled in every conceivable means of conveyance. The most popular was the covered wagon.

Most of the travelers started with high hopes and dreams of romance and adventure. It didn't take long for them to learn there wasn't much romance to be found. Their hopes were dashed. But there was plenty of adventure all around them.

They found many enemies that had to be conquered. There were rivers, flooded or dried up, to be crossed. Virtually impassable mountain ranges to go over. Weather was a continuing factor. There was little or no law enforcement to protect them. "Hemp justice" and pistols became a way of life. Then there were the Indians.

JAMES H. PEABODY made a trek to Colorado. In 1878 he became a member of Mt. Moriah Lodge No. 15, Canon City. He would later serve as governor of the state. His wife while a girl of "four going on five" wrote of her trip west. She recalled "the creaking and jolting of the wagon, the straining of the oxen," their odor and sweat. "The cracking of the long bullsnake whip," made an impression on her. So did the "clanking of the heavy chains when needed to keep the wheels from running over the oxen on bouncing over a steep place."

They "lumbered on through sandstorms and rainstorms, the intense heat during the day, the jolting of the wagon," she found hard to endure. She was among the fortunate. She and her family had encountered no hostile Indians.

The commander of American forces in the West, General Philip H. Sheridan, didn't blame the Indians for attacking whites. "We took away their country and their means of support," he wrote. "We broke up their mode of living, their habits of life, introduced disease and decay among them, and it was for this and against this that they made war. Could anyone expect less?"

The building of the transcontinental railroad particularly incensed several of the Indian tribes. Railroads in the east were plentiful. In the West they moved north and south. There were some 1700 miles of rough country that hadn't been bridged in 1865. This was another area for American ingenuity to conquer.

In 1866 Union Pacific in the East and Central Pacific in the West set out to beat each other. First location parties were sent to trace the line and pick off Indians, animals, or anything else that got in their way. The construction gangs followed. In the East these gangs were composed, mostly, of immigrant Irish, Southern whites and blacks. Chinese provided most of the manpower in the West.

It took just a little over three years for the 1,775 miles of track to meet at Promontory Point, Utah, on May 10, 1869. Five days later officials of the Central Pacific arrived on a special train. The Union Pacific train arrived three days later. It had been bogged down in floods. Along with the officials came a regimental band and three companies of infantry. By now there was another group described by Alstair Cooke as "a more colorful assortment of interested parties: saloon keepers, gamblers, whores, money lenders, odd-job rovers. And these, with the cooks and dishwashers from the dormitory trains, made up the welcoming party."

Governor LELAND STANFORD of California, a charter member of Michigan City Lodge No. 47, California, was there. He was given the honor of driving in the last spike—made of gold. The band stopped playing. A prayer was given. The telegraph operator, high on a pole, made connection with San Francisco and New York. "Stand by, we have done praying," he tapped out. Stanford swung at the spike—and missed. But the news reached both coasts that the spike had been driven in. New York fired a hundred gun salute. The Liberty Bell was rung in Philadelphia. The "annexation of the United States" was proclaimed in San Francisco.

Many branch lines followed. The railroad had changed the face of America. Among those who believed the changes would be great was a Congressman named JAMES A. GARFIELD. "The railroad is the greatest centralizing force of modern times," he claimed.

It was Garfield who nominated his fellow Ohioan, John Sherman, as his party's choice for President in 1880. The other faction of his party wanted Grant returned. Thirty-six ballots later Garfield was chosen as a compromise candidate.

James A. Garfield became a Master Mason in Columbia Lodge No. 30 on November 22, 1864. Magnolia Lodge No. 20 of Columbus, Ohio, had requested the Lodge to confer the degree. A year later he affiliated with Garrettsville Lodge No. 246. This was close to his home and work at Hiram College. On May 4, 1869, he became a charter member of Pentalpha Lodge No. 23, Washington, D.C.

Garfield was the last of the "log cabin Presidents." The Western Reserve Historical Society received his home, Lawnfield, and extensive library from his widow. Behind his home sits a replica of the log cabin in which he was born on November 19, 1831.

The 20th President of the United States settled one dispute. He checked the power of the state bosses. But, it was about all he had time for. On July 2, 1881, a disgruntled office seeker shot him while he was in a Washington railway station. He held onto life by a thread for weeks. Then, on September 19 he died.

This left Freemasonry in the East in an uncertain position. On January 20, 1881, PEYTON S. COLES, Grand Master of Masons in Virginia, received a hand-delivered request from The Congress which read:

I am instructed by the Joint Congressional Committee on the Yorktown Celebration, to invite the Grand Lodge of Virginia to perform the ceremony of laying the Cornerstone of the Monument to be erected at that point in October next. I am also instructed to suggest that it would be eminently proper to invite the Grand Masters of Masons of the Original Thirteen States to participate with you.

Coles answered the request immediately: "We accept the invitation, and will endeavor to do our part as becomes the patriotic occasion."

This was an important moment in the life of Freemasonry. It marked the first time the Federal government had officially recognized Freemasonry. Federal troops had only recently been removed from the South. With this request to the Grand Lodge of the former capital of the Confederacy, the Civil War could be considered concluded.

Chester Alan Arthur had become President with the death of Garfield. He wasn't a Freemason. There was concern about whether he would go along with the Yorktown plans. As had been expected, Garfield, the Mason, had accepted an invittaion to take part in the ceremonies. Would Arthur?

The fears proved groundless. The new President accepted the invitation. And he readily agreed to take part in the ceremonies.

The Grand Lodge of Virginia was convened at Yorktown on October 17, 1881. The Grand Master apologized to the many dignitaries: "It is a source of sincere regret to me that this interesting ceremony take place of necessity in a situation so remote and comparatively so inaccessible, that we are unable to extend our distinguished guests the courtesies and hospitalities for which the members of our Fraternity in this State are so justly celebrated." This condition no longer exists! Yet, one hundred years later (1981), Freemasonry took no part in the Yorktown ceremonies.

Grand Masters from all the original colonies, with the exception of Georgia, were present and participated in 1881.

The cornerstone of Victory Monument at Yorktown is not visible. It must be buried in the deep foundation.

304 FREEMASONRY IN AMERICAN HISTORY

Arthur would serve only the unexpired term of Garfield. He surprised many by doing a fine job. He brought Federal employees under Civil Service. This gave them security and helped curtail the "spoils system."

Immigration had been slowed during the Civil War. With the end of war, thousands left their native lands and sought a new life in America. By 1882 almost 800,000 were entering the United States annually. Many were disappointed with what they first encountered.

"I looked about the narrow streets of squeezed-in stores and houses, ragged clothes, dirty bedding oozing out of the windows," said one newcomer. "Ash cans and garbage cans cluttering the sidewalks. I looked down into the alley below, and saw pale-faced children scrambling in the gutter. 'Where is America?' cried my heart." She had found what could always be found in every country in the world. The ghetto would always exist. No amount of pleading or money would ever change this condition.

More than thirteen million immigrants reached America between the close of the Civil War and 1900. Most of them settled in the large metropolitan areas. The cities couldn't absorb them. The gold-paved streets they expected to find were not there. They weren't greeted with open arms, as they had expected. They were frequently rejected by those immigrants who had arrived a few years earlier.

These immigrants, and all who had preceeded them since 1607, had to make their own living. There were no welfare programs. There would be few until the 1930's. Fortunes were made and lost, but each man was free to seek his own level. There was little government interference. Bureaucrats were practically unknown.

The cities found it difficult to catch up with all the increased services necessary. But by the turn of the century they had accomplished more than could have been expected. Transportation helped. Trolley lines helped. People could settle on the outskirts of the city and ride to work. The Brooklyn Bridge was opened in 1883. It, along with many others, carried people to the suburbs.

Cultural advances were made. Libraries, museums, concert halls, civic centers, and public parks were opened. Urban life became more rewarding. The Statue of Liberty erected in the New York harbor took on some meaning.

The Grand Lodge of New York was invited to lay the cornerstone of this now world-renown statue. This historic event took place on August 5, 1884, on Bedloe's [now Ellis or Liberty] Island in New York Harbor. The cornerstone was laid in the pedestal of the "Statue of Liberty Enlightening the World."

This was the design and work of a French Freemason, FREDERIC A. BARTOLDI. He was a member of Lodge Alsace-Lorraine, Paris, which he convened to view his work, even before it was shown to the American committee. On June 19, 1884, the members of his Lodge marched in a body to review his masterpiece, the gift of the French people to the United States.

This masterful work would greet all who entered the New World by way of New York harbor. It withstood the vicissitudes of time and storm. Then it began to gradually erode. Millions of people had climbed throughout the inside, even up the arm, the torch and crown. Trips up the stairs to the torch had to be stopped because of the danger. Without drastic repairs the entire statue might have to be condemned. So, in 1983 a special committee was formed to raise funds for the work that must be done.

The continuing improvements in the railroads, also, helped ease the burden in the East. With more and more tracks being laid, people were able to move away from the eastern seaboard. Immigrants were able to find land, some even free and more suitable than what they had left behind.

The increasing chugging of locomotives helped build another revolution. This one was industrial. Within twenty years after the lines met at Promontory Point there were over 160,000 miles of railroad track throughout the country.

GEORGE PULLMAN, a member of Renovation Lodge No. 97, New York, had helped the passengers travel in comfort. In 1863 he built the first sleeping car. Dining cars were devised by him in 1868; chair cars in 1875; and vestibule cars in 1887. He founded the industrial town of Pullman, near Chicago, in 1880.

Capitalists such as EDWARD H. HARRIMAN and JAMES J. HILL put their expertise to work for transportation and industry. Harriman was an officer of several railroad and steampship companies on the east coast. He was also a member of Holland Lodge No. 8, New York. Jim Hill belonged to Ancient Landmark Lodge No. 5, Minnesota. He was better known as "Jim" Hill, "the Empire Builder of the Northwest." He started out on his father's farm, then went into business. In St. Paul he became associated with a steamboat company. Later he reorganized the St. Paul and Pacific Railroad into the St. Paul, Minneapolis & Manitoba Railway Company. He was the principal figure in the construction of the Great Northern Railway. This brought it into shipping connections with China and Japan.

American ingenuity found ways to produce steel and other products inexpensively. Oil, when it was found, and could be refined, became as valuable as gold. Another booming business was started. For over 100 years it remained an inexpensive means of heating and locomotion. A handful of Mideastern oil producing countries changed this in the 1970's. Through their monopoly they were able to raise the selling price to over thirty dollars a barrel for oil costing fifty cents a barrel to produce. It sent the world economy into chaos.

About 1,000 patents a year were issued by the United States Patent Office before the Civil War. In 1890, over 25,000 patents were approved. American "know-how" and educational opportunities were expanding tremendously.

By the turn of the century there was little difference between the life-styles of Americans in the East and West. All sections had to depend on the other for existence. Then, too, Alexander Graham Bell had invented the telephone in 1876. Communication between the sections was improved. Three years later Thomas A. Edison perfected the incandescent lamp to help light the world. Electricity had made great strides in every area.

—ARIZONA—

At the turn of the century only Oklahoma, New Mexico, and Arizona remained as territories. Of these, New Mexico had formed its own Grand Lodge. In 1882 Arizona did the same.

"This is a small community, far removed from others, an advance post of the army of civilization, fighting against barbarism, with a hostile and savage foe around, and depending on our own armed hands for safety of life and property." This was the beginning of a letter by JOHN T. ALSAP to the Grand Lodge of California. "I say it proudly, nowhere are the Constitutions of Masonry more cherished and loved, or its principles better or more nobly illustrated. The worthy distressed brother here has ever found a friendly word and helping hand." His request for a dispensation was granted and on October 11, 1866, Aztlan Lodge in Prescott was chartered.

Arizona Lodge at Phoenix was organized thirteen years later under a California dispensation. A year later, on July 1, 1880, White Mountain Lodge at Globe received a dispensation from New Mexico. From a Masonic club at Tucson came Tucson Lodge with a California dispensation on February 17, 1880. Solomon Lodge at Tombstone received a California dispensation on June 14, 1881. These lodges organized the Grand Lodge of Arizona in Phoenix in 1882.

Amazingly, when one considers the vast territory covered by Arizona, and its differing climates, these four lodges are still in existence. The State has many of the natural wonders of the world: the Painted Desert, the Grand Canyon, with the Colorado River winding through its awesome beauty, craters, petrified forests, disappearing rivers, numerous Indian villages, and dozens of other spectacular scenes.

The Grand Lodge began its centennial celebrations with the Virginia Craftsmen conferring the Master Mason degree throughout the State. The last of its work was conferred at the foot of Superstition Mountain with hundreds of Arizona Masons present.

—NORTH DAKOTA—

Freemasons traveled through Dakota Territory as early as 1804. MERRIWETHER LEWIS and WILLIAM CLARK, the leaders of an expedition to explore the Northwest, were Masons. On a high bluff overlooking the Missouri River the Grand Lodge of North Dakota erected a monument in memory of the leaders of the expedition. It was placed in 1935 near the site where they spent the winter of 1804-05.

HAROLD SACKETT POND, in *Masonry in North Dakota*, records The Grand Lodge authorized another marker in 1920. It was placed at Apple Creek, near Bismarck, and reads: "On this spot, July 31, 1863, occurred the first Masonic ceremony held in the present state of North Dakota.

"It was the funeral of Lieutenant FRED J. HOLT BEAVER, an Englishman and oxonian, and a volunteer soldier, attached to the staff of General H. H. Sibley. He was killed in a skirmish with the Indians and was buried in the rifle pits which were dug along this ridge.

"Deputy Grand Master JOHN C. WHIPPLE of Minnesota convened an emergency Masonic Lodge with Brothers A. J. EDGERTON as Worshipful Master; J. C. BRADEN, Senior Warden, and Bro. PATCH, Junior Warden, and the body of Brother Beaver was here consigned to earth with Masonic services."

On September 13, 1863, Minnesota granted a dispensation for the formation of Northern Light Lodge, composed of soldiers attached to Hatch's Battalion at Pembina. The name of the lodge was appropriate. It was situated at "the most northern point in the territory of the United States." The dispensation was renewed the following year, and the Lodge was moved to Fort Garry. It ceased work in 1869. But "it was in existence long enough to lay the foundation of Masonry not only in North Dakota, but also in the Canadian Northwest, more particularly the Province of Manitoba."

A mammoth "International Masonic Celebration" was held at Pembina on June 21, 1921. The officers and members of Northern Light Lodge No. 10 of Manitoba, wearing the jewels of the old Lodge, participated in the festivities. Northern Light Lodge No. 45 of North Dakota, chartered in 1896, wasn't represented.

The next lodge to receive a dispensation was Yellowstone. It was granted by Minnesota on January 26, 1871. It was another Military lodge and formed at Fort Buford. In 1872 it received a charter. But within three years troops were removed from the area and the lodge surrendered its charter. For various reasons a Grand Lodge marker couldn't be placed at this site until 1960.

The two lodges which Minnesota felt were ignored by the Dakota Grand Lodge were Shiloh and Bismarck. The former was chartered by Minnesota on January 14, 1874; the latter, January 12, 1876. Both Lodges lived under three Grand Lodges: Minnesota, Dakota, and North Dakota.

Shilo, as it was then named, began work in Fargo on September 2, 1872, two months before it received a dispensation on November 22, 1872. Bismarck received a dispensation in June, 1874.

Dakota Territory became North and South Dakota when they were admitted to the Union on November 2, 1889. It had been evident for some time that this would occur. So, on June 11, 1889, the Grand Lodge of Dakota considered the request from the Northern lodges to permit them to form a Grand Lodge. The approval was unanimous. It was also agreed to distribute the funds and property equitably.

On June 12 representatives of the lodges from the North met in the "Masonic Hall, Mitchell, S.D." It was resolved: "that this convention deem it expedient for the good of Masonry that a Grand Lodge be organized for North Dakota." A constitution and bylaws were adopted, and Grand Lodge officers elected. JAMES W. CLOES became the Grand Master.

The following day the Grand Lodges of South and North Dakota installed their officers in "a joint installation ceremony." Pond records what happened next:

> Following the forming of the two Grand Lodges and the election of their officers, the Grand officers of South Dakota were duly installed and invested with the jewels of

the Grand Lodge of Dakota, which were rightfully theirs. Then occurred one of the finest demonstrations of brotherly love and friendship one could possibly conceive. By prearrangement on the part of South Dakota, the Grand Officers of both Grand Jurisdictions lined up, each facing his corresponding Grand Officer, and at a given signal, the South Dakota line advanced and invested the Grand Officers of North Dakota with their respective jewels. There was not a dry eye in the room as this generous and significant ceremony was performed and no one could trust his voice to properly convey the gratitude and appreciation of the North Dakota brethren to their neighbors from the South.

"These beautiful jewels were used continuously by the Grand Lodge of North Dakota until June, 1959," continued Pond, "when they were replaced by a splendid gift of new jewels presented by Past Grand Master ARTHUR D. CUMMING of Calgary, Alberta, and the original jewels of Dakota were retired to the museum in the Grand Lodge Library.

Pond dedicated his history to WALTER LINCOLN STOCKWELL, a Past Grand Master and long-time Grand Secretary of his Grand Lodge. Stockwell was perhaps one of the best loved Freemasons in the country while he lived. Among his many accomplishments, Masonically, was his great assistance in forming The Masonic Service Association of the United States. During the early stages of its organizational meeting in 1918 he led the proponents. While many doubted the wisdom of forming such an organization, Stockwell jumped to his feet and said: "It is recorded in history that when the Constitutional Convention which met in Philadelphia in 1787 adjourned, Benjamin Franklin, then a very old man, and a representative from the great State of Pennsylvania, arose and pointing to the chair in which George Washington sat and on which is delineated, or was at that time, a half sun, with the rays, said, 'Men of America, during the long days of this Convention I have been wondering whether that was a rising or a setting sun. I am convinced that it is a rising sun.' "

When the representatives of the Grand Lodges present had voted unanimously for the MSA, *Freemasonry's Servant* records: " Walter Stockwell, as he was to do many times for the Association and for his fellow Grand Secretaries after they had united into a Conference, led the group in singing 'America.' " Stockwell did much more than that. He held the MSA together when it was at its lowest ebb. North Dakota remained among the seven Grand Lodges that didn't desert the Association.

—OKLAHOMA—

Oklahoma is unique among the Grand Lodges. It was organized in 1874 as the Grand Lodge of Indian Territory. In 1892 it became the Grand Lodge of Oklahoma Territory. In 1909 the two united.

"Oklahoma was found, founded, and settled by Indians," wrote Harry L. Haywood, "most of them belonging to Civilized Tribes: Cherokee, Chickasaw, Creek, and Seminole peoples. They largely came from Florida, Georgia, and Tennessee."

Haywood adds: "Masons, most of them Indians, living at Tahlequah, the Cherokee center, received a charter from Arkansas. The Choctaw Indians received from Arkansas a charter for Doaksville Lodge, in 1852. The Creeks received a charter from Arkansas for Mus-co-gee Lodge, in 1855. In 1852 the Cherokees received a charter from Arkansas for a second lodge. (During these formative years, and through the dreadful war period, Arkansas mothered Indian Territory, not its Grand Lodge only, but its lodges, and even individual members.)"

Twenty-eight

THE McKINLEY-ROOSEVELT ERA

THE beginning of the Twentieth Century found the Freemason from Ohio, WILLIAM MCKINLEY, beginning his second term in the White House. It also found the United States growing from coast to coast.

Money backed by gold, or money backed by silver became the political issues late in the Nineteenth Century. Those in favor of the gold standard wanted to keep the money value on an even level. The silver advocates were in favor of an increased money supply.

The nation went into a deep depression in 1893. Banks and other financial institutions began to fail by the hundreds. It would run into the thousands before the financial panic ended in 1897. In 1894 unemployment was widespread. Public works programs were demanded by "Coxey's Army," thousands of unemployed marched on Washington. This helped make the election of 1896 a lively affair.

It was lively, that is, for WILLIAM JENNINGS BRYAN, the Democrat. He strongly endorsed silver. The Republican candidate, WILLIAM MCKINLEY, sat on his front porch in Canton, Ohio. Delegates, his campaigners and well-wishers visited him.

Once again a Presidental candidate was a Freemason. William McKinley had been made a Master Mason in a Southern lodge, Hiram in Winchester Virginia, at the close of the Civil War. He had transferred his membership to Canton Lodge No. 90, Ohio. On June 2, 1868 he became a charter member of Eagle Lodge No. 431. After his death the name of this Lodge was changed to William McKinley.

The other candidate, Bryan, would become a Freemason on April 15, 1902, in Lincoln Lodge No. 19, Nebraska.

By an electoral vote of 271 to 176 McKinley won. His policies also won almost immediately. Gold was discovered in the Klondike and South Africa. The money supply was enlarged. The deflationary spiral was stopped. The Currency Act of 1900 consolidated the gold standard policy. Prosperity returned to the United States and the world.

The press had been supporting those Cubans who wanted to be free of Spanish control. Randolph Hearst was among the leaders of this coalition. In December, 1896, he sent a top reporter and artist to Cuba to report for his *New York Journal*. The artist told Hearst he wanted to leave Cuba. "There will be no war," he said. Hearst told him to stay there. "You furnish the pictures. I'll furnish the war," he promised.

President McKinley worked to prevent war. He believed the Cubans could gain their freedom through diplomatic means. He knew only too well the hells of war. Those who wanted war called the President "spineless," among the more temperate characterizations. Among them was the Assistant Secretary of the Navy, THEODORE ROOSEVELT.

War came. The *U.S.S. Maine* was mysteriously blown up in Havana harbor on February 15, 1898. Two hundred sixty Americans were killed. A reluctant President turned the situation over to The Congress for its decision. Its decision came in April with a declaration of war.

Less than two weeks after the sinking of the *Maine*, Roosevelt sent orders to Commodore George Dewey to take his fleet to Hong Kong. He ordered the fleet to "keep full coal—in the event of declaration war." He told Dewey "your duty will be to see that the Spanish squadron does not leave the Asiatic coast."

Roosevelt, the Navy man, became Roosevelt the "Rough Rider." His horseless corp gained immortality by charging up San Juan Hill. The Spaniards were quickly defeated. The remains of the Spanish fleet left Santiago Bay. Roosevelt returned to his job as Assistant Secretary.

The commander of the Rough Riders was LEONARD C. WOOD. With the end of hostilities he became military governor of Cuba. He had actually entered the service as an assistant surgeon in 1886, two years after receiving his medical degree from Harvard. In 1899 he received a law degree from the same college. He would become Chief of Staff of the Army from 1910-14, and Governor of the Philippines from 1921-27. He had received the Congressional Medal of Honor for his campaign against the Apache Indians in 1886. In 1920 he would be the Republican candidate for the Presidency. In 1916 he became a Freemason in Anglo Saxon Lodge No. 137, New York.

The United States was no longer isolated. It now was the protector of Cuba, Puerto Rico, and Guam. The Philippines would soon be added to the list. So would Hawaii. This caused McKinley to ponder: "In a few short months we have become a world power. . . . It is vastly different from the conditions I found when I was inaugurated."

Freemasonry memorialized the centennial of the death of George Washington on December 14, 1899. From the front porch of Mount Vernon President McKinley addressed the large audience:

> We have just participated in a service commemorative of the one hundredth anniversary of the death of George Washington. Here at his home, which he loved so well, and which the patriotic women of the country have guarded with loving hands, exercises are conducted under the auspices of the great fraternity of Freemasons, which a century ago, planned and executed the solemn ceremonial which attended the Father of his Country to his tomb. . . . Masons throughout the United States testify anew their reverence for the name of Washington and the inspiring example of his life. . . the Fraternity justly claims the immortal partiot as one of its members; the whole human family acknowledges him as one of the greatest benefactors.
>
> . . . . We summon his precepts, that we may keep his pledges to maintain justice and law, education and morality, and civil and religious liberty in every part of our country, the new as well as the old.

McKinley wasn't a lukewarm Mason. He often visited the lodges in the District. He was Grand Orator at the dedication of the Masonic Temple in Canton, Ohio, on June 25, 1890. On February 7, 1900, a delegation from Columbia Lodge No. 2397 of London, England, visited the White House. McKinley was presented with a certificate of membership in that Lodge. He attended a reception on May 22, 1901, in San Francisco held in his honor by California Commandery, Knights Templar. He was made an honorary member of New York Veterans' Association.

According to Margaret Leech in her *In the Days of McKinley*, he was reluctant to run for a second term. "He talked longingly to several friends during the summer of his desire to return to private life," she wrote. He told friends: "If what you gentlemen are saying implies that I am a candidate for renomination next year, I want to say to you that I would be the happiest man in America if I could go out of office in 1901."

McKinley married Ida Saxton in 1871. It wasn't long, according to Leech, before "the pleasure-seeking young woman McKinley had married had changed to a feeble, self-centered nervous invalid. Phlebitis left her a cripple who stood and walked with difficulty and pain. For the rest of her life, Ida was an epileptic, subject to frequent attacks of *petit mal*, a brief loss of consciousness, and at irregular intervals to prolonged and violent seizures."

William McKinley loved Ida deeply. He watched over her carefully, at home, and in the White House. This added to the burdensome job of the Presidency. Yet, when his party called, he agreed, although reluctantly, to seek a second term. He chose THEODORE ROOSEVELT as his running mate.

Theodore Roosevelt received his degrees in Freemasonry in Matinecock Lodge No. 806, Oyster Bay, New York. The first was conferred on January 2, 1901; the second, March 27; the Master Mason, April 24. From the beginning, he was an enthusiastic Mason.

The McKinley and Roosevelt team was elected. But the President would be able to accomplish little during his second term. Fate saw to that. September 6, 1901, the President said would be "the restful day." By trolley cars the Presidental party traveled to, and toured, Niagara Falls. In the afternoon they left for the Temple of Music where the President was to speak to more than 50,000 people attending the Pan-American Exposition at Buffalo, New York.

At four o'clock the President started greeting the long line of people who had come to shake his hand. One had another plan.

As the President extended his hand to the next in line it was abruptly struck aside and a man lurched forward firing two shots. Leon Czolgosz, an American anarchist, was quickly knocked down and subdued by many assailants. The crowd of people was stupefied. McKinley was assisted to a chair and surrounding men stood fanning him with their hats. With his bloody hands holding his breast and stomach, his whispered "My wife, be careful how you tell her—oh, be careful."

After a week of hope McKinley died early Saturday morning. September 14, 1901. Hundreds of Freemasons, including five companies of Knights Templar, escorted the body from the White House to the Capitol on the 17th. Thousands of Masons attended his funeral on the 19th.

Theodore Roosevelt was sworn in as President in Buffalo. "I will show the people at once that the administration of the government will not falter in spite of the terrible blow," he promised. "I wish to say that it shall be my aim to continue, absolutely unbroken, the policy of President McKinley for the peace, the prosperity, and the honor of our beloved country."

What kind of a President did Roosevelt make? It depends on whose viewpoint is read. Alstair Cooke, the English historian in his *America* wasn't particularly fond of the President. But, then, he wasn't fond of many of the American Presidents. He noted that until Roosevelt he hadn't mentioned one since Lincoln!

Cooke claims Roosevelt had been the choice of the oil, steel, and railroad trusts for Vice President. But when he assumed the Presidency after McKinley's assassination he determined to break the barons, or at least to put them under Congressional control.

Roosevelt didn't want any more "hyphenated Americans" either. He considered the time long past for immigrants to be used for cheap labor. It would appear his goals were lofty.

Roosevelt became a "trust buster." He promised the people a "square deal." And this promise he worked to achieve.

His intimate connections with the Department of Navy had convinced Roosevelt of the need to bridge the two oceans. He remembered the long voyage the *U.S.S. Oregon* had during the Spanish-American War. It had to travel from Puget Sound around South America to Cuban waters. It did arrive just in time to join the destruction of Cervera's fleet off Santiago. The timing was too close.

Ferdinand de Lesseps had built the Suez Canal. The French had selected him to head the building of a canal connecting the Atlantic with the Pacific. The company became defunct. Roosevelt wanted to take over the digging of the ditch.

The plans for the canal, which had actually begun in 1850, finally came to fruition in 1903. The Hay-Bunau-Varilla Treaty gave the new Republic of Panama a cash payment of ten million dollars, plus a stipulated annuity. In return, the United States was granted exclusive control of a Canal Zone in perpetuity, other sites necessary for defense, and sanitary control of Panama City and Colon. This treaty remained in force until 1978 when President James Carter and The Congress—by one vote—gave away the Panama Canal.

The building of the canal was accomplished in eight years under the control the Army. Malaria and yellow fever had to be brought under control. They were. "The Canal Zone was transformed from a pest hole to a healthy and attractive place for human habitation," says *American Military History.* "Without the splendid work of the Medical Department, it is doubtful that George W. Goethals would have had the success he did. Today, the canal stands as a lasting monument to the technical ability, discipline, and efficiency of the Army working at its best in the fulfillment of a peacetime mission. Its completion partially freed the Nation of the heavy cost of maintaining an enormous fleet in both the Atlantic and Pacific since it permitted vessels to move quickly to any point of need in either ocean."

Roosevelt was elected in his own right in 1904. He would consider one of the highlights of his term his "Greet White Fleet." He sent sixteen brightly painted warships on a mission of peace. They had white topsides and golden bows, making a spectacular display. They went around the Horn from the Atlantic to Japan. On the way home they passed the English outposts in the Indian Ocean and the Mediterranean Sea.

HENRY FORD, was made a member of Palestine Lodge No. 357, Michigan, on November 28, 1894. A degree team composed of men in overalls from Edison Illuminating Company where he worked raised him to the degree of Master Mason. In 1903 he organized the Ford Motor Company. Eleven years later he shocked the industrial world. He inaugurated a profit sharing plan for his employees. In September, 1940, when he received the 33rd degree of Scottish Rite Masonry, he said: "Masonry is the best balance wheel the United States has, for Masons know what to teach their children."

In the same year Ford organized his motor company, the Wright brothers at Kittyhawk, North Carolina, changed the world for all time. They flew the first heavier than air machine.

In 1905 Roosevelt brought the leaders of the war between Japan and Russia to a peace table in Portsmouth, New Hampshire. They signed a peace treaty. For his efforts Roosevelt was awarded the Nobel Peace Prize in 1906.

Masonically, Roosevelt continued to be unusually active for a man in his position. When the cornerstone of the Army War College was Masonically laid on February 21, 1903, he was there. On April 24, 1903, he was with the Grand Lodge of Montana when it laid the cornerstone of the north gate at Yellowstone National Park. He assisted in laying the cornerstone of the Masonic Temple at Tacoma, Washington, on May 22, 1903. Four days later he broke ground for the Masonic Temple at Spokane, Washington.

Roosevelt was with the Grand Lodge of Pennsylvania on April 19, 1906, to commemorate the 200th anniversary of Benjamin Franklin's birth. He delivered the address when the

Grand Lodge of the District of Columbia laid the cornerstone of the House of Representatives' office building on April 14, 1906. He also delivered the address at the laying of the cornerstone of a Masonic temple in the District on June 8, 1907. Again, he wore Masonic regalia when the cornerstone of Pilgrim Memorial Monument was laid at Provincetown, Massachusetts, on May 11, 1917.

Masonic lodges throughout the world found Theodore Roosevelt as one of their distinguished visitors.

WILLIAM HOWARD TAFT was Roosevelt's choice for the Presidency in 1908. He was elected. Historians haven't treated him kindly. But he had a distinguished law career prior to his election. He had practiced law at Cincinnati, Ohio, from 1883-87. He was a United States circuit judge from 1892-1900. He became the first civil Governor of the Philippines in 1901. In 1904 he became Secretary of War. Roosevelt had twice offered him an appointment as a Justice of the Supreme Court.

A year before he was a candidate for the Presidency, Taft had said he would like to be a Freemason. The Grand Master of Masons in Ohio, CHARLES S. HOSKINSON, exercised one of his prerogatives. He made Taft a Mason-at-Sight on February 18, 1909. The attendance was large. There were 14 Grand Masters from other states, 12 Ohio Past Grand Masters, 302 Worshipful Masters, and a large representation from appendant bodies present. Kilwinning Lodge No. 356 elected him to membership. This was the same Lodge to which his father and half-brother belonged.

After he had received the degrees, Taft told those present: "I am glad to be here, and to be a Mason. It does me good to feel the thrill that comes from recognizing on all hands the fatherhood of God and brotherhood of man. . . . Many years ago my father stood in the same place and expressed his love and admiration of the order."

During the balance of his life Taft participated in hundreds of Masonic meetings. Among them was the annual meeting of the George Washington Masonic National Memorial Association on February 22, 1912. He traveled with the Association to Mount Vernon to lay a wreath at the tomb of Washington. He was with the Association again in 1913, and on November 1, 1923, to help spread the cement on the cornerstone of the Memorial.

On this latter occasion he stated: "Masonry aims at the promotion of morality and higher living by the cultivation of the social side of man, the rousing in him of the instincts of charity and the foundation of the brotherhood of man and the fatherhood of God."

William Howard Taft was Chief Justice of the Supreme Court from 1921 until his death in 1930.

Evidently Roosevelt was disillusioned with Taft's work as President. He formed the "Bull Moose Party" when he couldn't get the Republican nomination in 1912. This led to the election of Woodrow Wilson.

Twenty-Nine

THE BIRTH OF THE
MASONIC SERVICE ASSOCIATION

WOODROW WILSON (not a Mason) was President of
the United States. Alstair Cooke didn't think too highly of him.
He claimed he would never have been elected if Roosevelt
hadn't split the Republican vote. "He saw himself as at least a
favorite pupil of God," claimed Cooke.

The editors of *200 Years* felt differently. "Wilson immediately
established himself as a leader for all the nation to see," they said.
He was "a master of the processes of democratic government, he
combined professorial insight with political effectiveness."

At any rate, Wilson became an integral part of history. In his
first year the Sixteenth and Seventeenth Amendments to the
Constitution were ratified. Americans began paying taxes on
their incomes, and Senators would forevermore be elected by
popular vote. The Federal Reserve System began regulating
private banks. The American Federation of Labor found a protector in Wilson. He reduced the tariff on foreign goods. He had
a busy first year.

There would continue to be busy years. Events over which no
political leader could have control would intervene. The first
event was the assassination of Archduke Francis Ferdinand of
Austria on June 28, 1914. This in itself would have had no
historical note, but there were alliances to be considered.
Austria severed relations with Serbia. Germany backed Austria.
Russia was on the side of Serbia. France, Belgium, and Great
Britain were drawn into the dispute. Europe was at war.

Wilson immediately let the world know the United States would remain neutral. Even so, from the beginning it was clear most of the citizens favored Britain, France, and Russia. German submarine attacks strengthened the country's sympathy for the Allies.

The apologies of the German government for the sinkings by their U-boats were accepted by Wilson. He kept the country out of war, and that's the rallying cry he ran under in 1916. He won re-election against Charles Evans Hughes by a close vote.

The Germans tightened their blockade of England soon after the election. Then Wilson learned Germany was endeavoring to form an alliance with Mexico and Japan. The news was released to the public in March, 1917. This intelligence, along with the sinking of three American ships, brought the President to The Congress. He asked for a declaration of war. On April 6, 1917, war was officially declared.

As with every war America had fought, or ever would fight, it was unprepared. A conscription bill was passed on May 18, 1917. Industrial mobilization was begun. What there were of American armaments were antiquated. The 55 aircraft the Army had were obsolete. Americans had to fight with Allied aircraft and use Allied weapons. The Navy, fortunately, was well equipped and manned (thanks to Roosevelt.) When its destroyers went into action they were armed with depth charges invented by a Freemason named SYDNEY N. BARUCH.

General JOHN J. "BLACK JACK" PERSHING was made Commander-in-Chief of the American Expeditionary Force. Theodore Roosevelt had recognized unusual leadership qualities in Pershing while he was serving in the Philippines. In 1906 Roosevelt took an unprecedented action. He promoted Pershing from a Captain to a Brigadier General. It became his task to turn a predominately civilian army into a fighting force within weeks.

Pershing was made a Freemason in Lincoln Lodge No. 19, Nebraska, on December 22, 1888. Later he was made an honorary member of other lodges and became a member of several appendant bodies. On September 24, 1942, he was elected to honorary membership of the Grand Lodge of Missouri. HARRY S. TRUMAN, then a Senator, presented him his certificate at Walter Reed Hospital.

It was June 1917, before a small American force arrived in Europe. It would be another year before a major force could reach the embattled Allies. This was at a time when the Germans had been able to free thousands of their men from the Russian front. In March the Bolshevik leaders had surrendered. The revolution that began in 1917 had destroyed Russia's resistance to the German invasion. It soon brought Lenin and Trotsky to power and the Russian people subjugated.

Many heroic deeds were performed by men on all sides during the war. The men in one branch of service found a romantic chord in the press and the minds of the American people. It was the air service, an independent branch of the AEF. But of the 55 planes the United States had in 1917, Pershing said: "Fifty-one were obsolete, and the other four were obsolescent."

Using cast-off French planes, American pilots soon captured the imagination of the American people. The command was sporadic, so Pershing brought in General MASON M. PATRICK, a West Point classmate, to solve the many problems. Patrick became the first Chief of the Air Corp, and did a remarkable job.

Patrick became a Master Mason in Orient Lodge No. 395, North Carolina, on November 11, 1891. His expertise was as an engineer. Among his accomplishments was the raising of the *Maine.*

Among the greatest of the American aces during the war was EDDIE RICKENBACKER, an auto racer. He started as a chauffeur for Pershing, but on August 25, 1917, transferred to the air service. Before the end of the war he was credited with shooting down twenty-one planes and four balloons. He would spend his life working with aviation, particularly with Eastern Airlines. He performed many special missions for America in World War II. He became a Freemason on June 26, 1922, in Kilwinning Lodge No. 297, Michigan.

The fighting Past Master of Grandview Lodge No. 618 of Missouri was described in *200 Years*. Battery D had "virtually destroyed the careers of three commanding officers." Then HARRY TRUMAN came along to take command. Soon after his battalion was ordered to the front. When a German night attack with heavy artillery blasted the area, Truman's troops panicked.

Truman was mounted on a horse when it fell into a shellhole. When he managed to free himself, he found his men fleeing. "I got up and called them everything I knew," he said. They returned to their positions. Truman had no further problems with them.

According to one of Truman's fellow officers, no matter how filthy the men were, Truman always looked neat and clean. "Dirt and cooties didn't seem to stick to him the way they did to the rest of us," the officer remarked. After two weeks of not having his clothes off, he still looked immaculate. "Moreover," continued the officer, "he was clean-shaven. He must have shaved with coffee, because we didn't have plain hot water."

The President, and Secretaries of the Navy and War, endeavored to establish "a high moral tone" for the armed forces. *The American Destiny* records; ". . . .Before the war, each had attempted to change traditions in his respective service in keeping with this philosophy. Baker had been appalled by the rampant prostitution and the saloons on the Mexican border during the 1916 mobilization. To him, a high rate of veneral disease was a problem to be solved, not an inevitable consequence of the massing of a large number of men away from home. He brought in a social worker, Raymond B. Fosdick, to study the problem and to recommend a solution. Old soldiers scoffed in vain."

Raymond B. Fosdick was a name that would be mentioned in Masonic circles for years, and not with affection. It was he, primarily, who kept Freemasonry from working with the armed forces overseas during the Great War.

TOWNSEND SCUDDER, a State Supreme Court Justice, and a Past Grand Master of Masons in New York, met Fosdick early in 1918. Scudder was heading a committee of Freemasons who wanted to voluntarily help establish clubs for servicemen overseas. The request was refused, then accepted, again refused, and then agreed to.

When Scudder and some of his group appeared at the passport office they were rudely refused their documents. Scudder contacted FRANKLIN D. ROOSEVELT, a Mason and an Assistant Secretary of the Navy, among others. This brought results. Every member of the Masonic commission received a written refusal for a passport, except Scudder. He heard nothing!

To Joseph P. Tumulty, Secretary to the President, Scudder went. He told the Secretary: "The Knights of Columbus seem able to obtain from the administration anything they wish, yet the Masonic Fraternity, many times more numerous, hundreds of years older, and fully as zealous to serve, has received scant consideration." Tumulty agreed to turn over to the President anything Scudder wrote.

Wilson refused to intervene. The Masonic Mission to help the servicemen overseas was dead.

From *The American Destiny*, and many other sources it is learned: "When war came, Baker and Fosdick already had a solution in mind which the President enthusiastically endorsed. The positive aspect would be the provision of wholesome recreation. The Commission of Training Camp Activities with Fosdick as chairman coordinated the Red Cross, YMCA, Knights of Columbus, Salvation Army, Jewish Welfare Board, and various other agencies. These provided libraries and huts where a soldier could go to read or write a letter or have a snack. They organized entertainments, led group singing, and tried to do all they could to make a soldier's off-duty hours pleasant."

— THE IOWA MEETING WHICH BROUGHT ABOUT THE
MASONIC SERVICE ASSOCIATION —

Among the unhappy Freemasons in the country because of being slighted by the federal government, was GEORGE L. SCHOONOVER, Grand Master of Masons in Iowa. He had received a letter from a Masonic club in France. The club wanted to know why Freemasonry wasn't represented among the service clubs overseas. Its members felt Masonry had let them down. So, Schoonover decided to take action.

A letter was sent to every Grand Lodge in the United States on October 3, 1918. Schoonover asked for a meeting of representatives of the Grand Lodges at some central point "to talk this thing over." The response was favorable. He sent another letter on November 1 requesting a meeting take place in Cedar Rapids, Iowa, from November 26 to 28, 1918.

Would this meeting bring forth Masonic unity? It was doubtful. All such meetings had been doomed. The lone exception, at least partially, was the Baltimore Convention of 1843. This convention followed recommendations adopted in 1842 when representatives of ten Grand Lodges met. There 16 of the 23 Grand Lodges were represented in Baltimore—an unusual percentage.

From this 1843 convention came many changes. An endeavor to create a uniform ritual was the primary goal. This wasn't to be. Although the ritual of each Grand Lodge was similar, there were major differences. This would continue to be the case. But other action was taken to devise "some uniform mode of action by which the ancient landmarks" might "be preserved and perpetuated." Among other things, a form of recognition, such as a dues card, was recommended. It was also suggested that all business in a lodge be conducted on the Third, or Master Mason, Degree. By 1851 this was adopted in all American Grand Lodges. The First, or Entered Apprentice, Degree had been the accepted practice.

The convention also recommended the leaders of Freemasonry meet every third year to exchange views and work toward unity in Freemasonry. This was ignored. *It would take the meeting of 1918 in Iowa to pave the way for the 1843 recommendations to become a fact.*

From the day American Union Lodge, and then the Grand Lodge of Pennsylvania, proposed George Washington as General Grand Master, there has been a fear of a General

Grand Lodge. No Grand Lodge was then, or now, about to give up its sovereignty. The Knights Templar come under a general head; so do the two Scottish Rite jurisdictions. The Grand Chapters of Royal Arch Masons are sovereign. They do have a service organization called the General Grand Chapter, International, but it exercises no control.

This fear of a General Grand Lodge was prevalent in Cedar Rapids on November 26, 1918. Even so, the representatives of the 22 jurisdictions present hadn't realized what the federal government had done to Freemasonry during the Great War. One of the primary purposes for the existence of Masonry was to be of service to mankind. This hadn't been allowed.

It became apparent early in the meeting that the excuse given by Fosdick for refusing the Masonic Mission was Masonry's lack of unity. He had claimed the government couldn't deal with 49 separate entities. The organizations permitted to go overseas each had a central organization. It was clear that Freemasonry had to find a solution.

"The Masons who have answered their country's call by donning the uniform will come back with the discovery that real religion is the religion of self-sacrifice, and they are going to come back and ask us if Masonry has any of that real religion!" claimed Schoonover. They want "Masonic Clubs, Masonic literature, Masonic fellowship. Now that the days of peace are imminent, they will need much of these. Time will drag heavily, and there will be no 'over the top' excitement."

After lengthy discussions, and speeches, a resolution was read. Before it was put to a vote, Scudder asked for permission to read two letters. The first was from a Past Grand Master in Virginia who warned the delegates about Scudder, considering "him a very unsafe leader." The second was from the Grand Master of Masons in Massachusetts. He didn't think the "time is ripe for such a meeting." He added: "There never has been a time in the history of the order when such a glorious opportunity has been offered for translating Masonic teachings into living expressions."

Scudder scoffed: "I might add, 'and therefore, let us do something.' There never was such an opportunity to translate Masonic teachings into Masonic action, and yet our brother says, do nothing. It is hard to understand." To the Grand Master's credit, he brought Massachusetts into the Association the following year.

Past Grand Master GEORGE LAWLER of Washington said: "Everywhere new starts must be made, and it is up to us. We are the fortunate men who have the opportunity to launch some scheme by which Masonry can be united into a single great force. I am willing to be one of this body to launch this new ship on new waters and take my chances that it will meet the approval of the whole Fraternity." The applause was deafening.

The 22 jurisdictions present voted unanimously to adopt the resolution to form a service organization for Freemasonry.

The following day, Captain CHARLES I. COOK of North Dakota spoke to the delegates. His story is recorded in *Freemasonry's Servant:*

> When he arrived in St. Nazaire he searched for a Masonic Club, Cook told the representatives of the twenty-two Grand Jurisdictions. He was told by the Freemasons there, "We have no time to do this Masonic work over here. Why don't the American members send us somebody to help us out? We go up and down the street there and the K.C. sign is flaunted in our faces; splendid rooms are provided for their people, and we do not see why the United States Masons cannot get over here and do something, too."
>
> Freemasons did not have much standing in the French community, according to Cook. When they decided to have a banquet, a committee went to the Hotel Commercial and made the arrangements. "Everything was lovely; the price was satisfactory; the stuff that we wanted served was available, and they were very courteous and kind."
>
> The banquet was to be held on Wednesday, but Cook said, "Monday the proprietor of the Hotel Commercial met me and told me that the banquet was all off. We were Masons and he absolutely refused to serve a banquet to Masons."
>
> Cook explained the many difficulties the Freemasons in France encountered, mainly because they did not have the

time to devote to anything but their war work. They did what they could, always expecting help from the Masons in the United States. They did not receive it and many wondered why.

"But," concluded Cook, "I hope that before the closing of this session [November, 1918] something will be perfected so we can go over there during the balance of the time that the boys are in France and give them the assistance they need."

The Grand Master of Masons in Minnesota, Captain WILLIAM N. KENDRICK, was about to go overseas. He was asked for his comments. "I made the statement to our Grand Secretary yesterday," he said, "that this feeling of mine is so strong that unless this meeting brought forth something, I was a convert to the General Grand Lodge idea.

"I feel that our failure has been due to the fact that we have forty-nine separate Grand Jurisdictions. I think all of you feel the same way, that if we had had some central organization, it matters not what you may call it, at the beginning of this war, we would have taken our place among the other organizations and done something for our boys in the army."

Several hours more of discussions took place on Wednesday afternoon, at this Iowa meeting in 1918. Then it was "*Resolved,* That there be organized the MASONIC SERVICE ASSOCIATION OF THE UNITED STATES, a voluntary association of Masonic Grand Jurisdictions of the United States of America, for service to Mankind."

The delegates were so enthused they remained in Cedar Rapids for Thanksgiving Day to add the final touches to the Constitution of the Association. They learned that the Grand Lodge of Georgia had sent a telegram stating it was joining.

"The Conference that had done more than had ever been accomplished before to unite American Freemasonry," records *Freemasony's Servant*, adjourned *sine die* at 12:50 p.m., Thursday, November 28, 1918, and the members gathered about a Thanksgiving banquet table. Although they were far away from home and loved ones, it was truly a Thanksgiving none would ever forget."

A delegation of Freemasons did finally go overseas to be of service to the armed forces.

The Masonic Service Association of the United States met again "at the eleventh hour of the eleventh day of the eleventh month of the year 1919." The place was the same, Cedar Rapids, Iowa.

During the year 37 jurisdictions had joined the Association. Thirty-four Grand Lodges were represented, 26 by their Grand Masters, at this meeting. They had learned that the leadership of Freemasonry could meet without compromising their sovereignty. This was more important than any realized at the time. From this knowledge would come "The Conference of Grand Masters of Masons in North America" six years later. Along with this would be formed "The Conference of Grand Secretaries."

The Association was off to an auspicious start. But forces were at work to destroy the harmony that then prevailed. These forces would almost succeed within ten years.

From *Freemasonry's Servant* it is learned:

> A dramatic moment in American Freemasonry took place on November 17, 1925. A Grand Masters' Conference was held in the La Salle Hotel, Chicago, Illinois, with twenty-six Jurisdictions represented by fourteen Grand Masters and other Grand Lodge officers. This Conference adopted a resolution asking the Grand Master of whatever Jurisdiction in which the Masonic Service Association held its next annual meeting to call a Conference of Grand Masters and delegates on the day before that annual meeting!

Thirty Grand Lodges were represented at the Grand Masters' Conference held in Chicago in 1926. It was held along with The Masonic Service Association. But forces were at work to destroy the Association. They almost succeeded.

A thorough study of the Association fails to reveal what forces tried to dissolve it. Nor are the reasons apparent. There were objections to the publishing of books by the organization. Seven, all excellent, were made available in 1924; two more in 1925. And steps were taken for the writing of a Masonic encyclopedia. The opposition was so great, however, everything concerning the books was sold in 1928 and eventually bought by Macoy Publishing & Masonic Supply Co., Inc.

Monthly *Short Talk Bulletins* began appearing in 1923. These would continue through the present day. Even motion pictures were employed for educational purposes. Warner Brothers and members of the Craft produced *Who Best Can Work* in 1923. *The Master Mason,* an excellent magazine edited by JOSEPH FORT NEWTON, D.D., was circulated. Stereoptican slides were made available. So were film strips. Freemasonry was finally getting needed educational programs.

Financial aid was collected and distributed for victims of calamities. These had occurred in Japan, Florida, and Mississippi. ANDREW RANDELL resigned as Executive Secretary on February 24, 1928. He died on March 14, 1931, at the age of 51. CARL H. CLAUDY was elected to succeed him. At the time only 14 Grand Lodges remained members of the Association. In 1930 this would decline to only nine.

—WILSON—LEAQUE OF NATIONS—

President Wilson continued his campaign to make the world "safe for democracy." An Armistice was signed on November 11, 1918. Three weeks later Wilson sailed aboard the *George Washington* on a diplomatic mission to Europe. Never before had a President of the United States visited Europe. This brought cries of "Wilson!" from the people of almost every country.

Wilson was seeking support for his Fourteen Points, particularly the formation of a league of nations. But with the beginning of peace talks in January, 1919, the previous enthusiasms for his proposals died. As the haggling over terms went on week after week, the demands of the Allies became more excessive. To get his "League of Nations," Wilson capitulated and acceded to demands that made no one happy.

Finally, at Versailles, on June 28, 1919, a peace treaty was signed. Germany was ordered to sign the document which fixed the entire guilt of the Great War on her. She was also ordered to pay the entire cost of the war. The way was paved for a German corporal to plunge the world into another war.

The Senate Republicans determined to wreck Wilson's League of Nations. So well were they succeeding, Wilson took a journey across the United States to plead his case. He traveled 8,000 miles in 22 days, making 37 long speeches. He collapsed from exhaustion, returned to Washington and was stricken with a stroke that almost proved fatal. The Senate killed Wilson's treaty.

With the end of the war came two amendments to the Constitution of the United States. The 18th Amendment prohibiting the manufacture and sale of intoxicating beverages was ratified on January 16, 1919. The 19th was ratified on August 26, 1920. It gave women the right to vote.

What was happening in Russia didn't go unnoticed in America. Advocates of Russian Communism had become exceedingly vocal in 1919. The Attorney General believed a Communist conspiracy had stirred up labor unrest, strikes, race riots, and bomb scares. He created a General Intelligence Division in the Justice Department. He selected J. EDGAR HOOVER to head the special section. Hoover became a Master Mason on November 9, 1920, in Federal Lodge No. 1, District of Columbia.

The Republicans went to their convention in June 1920, at Chicago, confident they would select the next President of the United States.

Thirty

DEPRESSION

THE midterm election of 1918 had found the Republicans triumphant. This brought out several candidates for the Republican Presidential ticket. Wilson's illness and defeats in the Senate, they believed, assured a Republican victory in 1920. This caused HARRY M. DAUGHERTY, a member of Fayette Lodge No. 107, Ohio, to predict the convention would be deadlocked.

As early as February Daughtery said around two o'clock in the morning, when everyone was bleary-eyed, he would "sit down at a big table" with the party leaders. "I will. . . present the name of Senator Harding to them, and before we get through, they will put him over."

Daughtery's prediction was correct. WARREN G. HARDING, a member of Marion Lodge No. 70, Ohio, broke the deadlock. Calvin Coolidge was selected as his running mate.

There were those who didn't like Harding. Among them was Andrew Sinclair who wrote *A Concise History of the United States*. He claimed Harding's "horizons were not larger than his home town or his state of Ohio." It would appear that Sinclair not only disapproved of the President but many things concerning capitalism and the United States.

Sinclair later wrote: "The shoddy administration of Harding was succeeded by the do-little rule of silent Calvin Coolidge, 'weaned on a pickle.'" He claimed Herbert Hoover "worked harder and produced more disaster than any other President." He claimed the war taxes on the rich were dissolved; that Andrew Mellon "believed in government of the rich by the rich for the rich."

Andrew Sinclair claimed too much of America's earnings was going into the hands of the few for speculation on the stock market and too little into the hands of the many to buy the goods America was producing.

How can this rationalize with his earlier statistics? A million "models of the 'Tin Lizzie' were sold each year and there were 26,500,000 vehicles on the road by 1929. "Electrical appliances, chemicals, radios, aeroplanes, the cinema, advertising, and the building trades also boomed as businesses," Sinclair mentioned.

The 29th President of the United States didn't live to complete his term in office. Scandals within his administration were prevalent. The most spectacular was known as the "Teapot Dome" affair. Albert Fall, Secretary of the Interior, and EDWIN DENBY, Secretary of the Navy, were accused of giving Edward Doheny and Harry Sinclair access to oil reserves set aside for the Navy. Only Fall was convicted of bribery.

Edwin Denby was a member of Oriental Lodge No. 240, Michigan. The Scottish Rite, Northern Masonic Jurisdiction, evidently didn't consider him quilty of misdeeds. It awarded him the 33rd degree of the Scottish Rite on September 16, 1924.

From all accounts, Harding was honest. "I have no trouble with my enemies," he told a journalist. "But my damned friends—they're the ones that keep me walking the floor at nights."

Harding took his membership in Freemasonry seriously. On August 27, 1920, he told a group of Masons at the Willard Hotel in Washington, D.C.:

> No man ever took the oaths and subscribed to the obligations with greater watchfulness and care than I exercised in receiving the various rites of Masonry, and I say it with due deliberation and without fear of breaking faith, I have never encountered a lesson, never witnessed an example, never heard an obligation uttered which could not be proclaimed to the world.

To the people of Birmingham, Alabama, who witnessed the laying of a cornerstone, he said: "I have been a better citizen for being a Mason. There is nothing in Masonry that a free, religious and just American could not be proud to subscribe to, and be a better citizen for so doing."

Harding was made an honorary member of several lodges and appendant bodies. He was scheduled to address several hundred Knights Templar in Hollywood, California, on August 2, 1923. He was deathly ill, so his secretary, GEORGE B. CHRISTIAN, a Knight, read the address Harding had written. Three hours later, Harding died.

At 2:30 in the morning of August 3, 1923, in a farmhouse in Vermont, the father of Calvin Coolidge performed the ceremony of making his son President of the United States. Coolidge had become famous when, as Governor, he broke a police strike in Boston. "There is no right to strike against the public safety by anybody, anywhere, at any time," he had stated. It was a statement that would be repeated for years.

The 30th President was able to point to the country's prosperity as an answer to his critics. Automobiles were everywhere. Hollywood was grinding out hundreds of films. The mail order business was flourishing. Wall Street had become the world's money market. Tin Pan Alley made the music the world danced to.

HENRY FORD had put the nation in motorized vehicles. On the water, steamships had practically replaced the sailing vessel. This system of propulsion had been invented by JOHN FITCH. Three months after becoming a Freemason in Bristol Lodge No. 25, Pennsylvania, on January 4, 1785, Fitch conceived the idea of steam as a means of power. He asked the Continental Congress for monetary aid, but didn't receive it. With $800 of his own money he formed a company and built a 60 ton boat. On August 22, 1787, before the representatives to the Constitutional Convention, he piloted his second boat on the Delaware at Philadelphia. He received a patent in 1791. Before he committed suicide in 1798, he wrote: "The day will come when some more powerful man will get fame and riches from *my* invention; but nobody will believe that poor John Fitch can do anything worthy of attention." He was correct. A fellow named Robert Fulton, who it is claimed stole Fitch's plans, ended up with the fame and fortune.

Under the seas submarines were traveling. Another Freemason, SIMON LAKE of Monmouth Lodge No. 172, New Jersey, built the first of these in 1897. To the surprise of many, people were traveling through the air. A far-thinking Postmaster General established airmail service in 1918. He was HARRY S. NEW, a member of Ancient Landmarks Lodge No. 319, Indiana.

From "Tin Pan Alley" came many Freemasons. Among them was IRVING BERLIN, who received his Master Mason degree in Munn Lodge No. 190, New York, on June 3, 1910. He was born in Russia on May 11, 1888, and brought to the United States in 1893. He had only two years of formal education, but the music he composed will live forever. Among his hundreds of compositions is *God Bless America*. This, along with many other songs, was donated to a foundation to help others.

Another Russian born actor-singer came to America while a baby. Asa Yoelson, better known as AL JOLSON, began his acting career at the age of 11 at the Herald Square Theater in New York City. He later traveled with circus, vaudeville, and minstrel shows. He became particularly famous for his blackface minstrel songs. He was the star of the first talking motion picture, *The Jazz Singer*. Jolson became a member of St. Cecile Lodge No. 568, New York, on July 1. 1913.

GEORGE M. COHAN, a Roman Catholic and a member of Pacific Lodge No. 233, New York, since November 16, 1905, was many things in the musical arena. He excelled as an actor, playwright, comedian, composer, and producer. He was presented a Congressional gold medal in 1940 by a Brother Mason, FRANKLIN D. ROOSEVELT.

As long as there are bands, the name of JOHN PHILIP SOUSA will be revered. He became a Master Mason in Hiram Lodge No. 10 in the District of Columbia, on November 18, 1881. He led the United States Marine Band from 1880 to 1892. Then he toured the world with his own band.

Freemasons were, and are, prominent in entertainment. WILLIAM F. CODY, better known as "Buffalo Bill," was the forerunner of the western rodeo. He was a pony express rider, a government scout during the Civil War, and a buffalo hunter for the Kansas Pacific Railroad. In a hand-to-hand fight he killed the Cheyenne Indian Chief, Yellow Hand. He was in the Battle of Wounded Knee, a place that would make headlines in the 1980s. In 1883 he began touring with his "Wild West Show." On January 10, 1871, he became a member of Platte Valley Lodge No. 32, Nebraska. He was buried with Masonic rites on Lookout Mountain, Colorado, on January 10, 1917.

WILLIAM WYLER, who would become an Academy Award-winning director, began work in motion pictures in the silent era. Wyler, a member of Loyalty Lodge No. 529, California, directed the production of *Ben Hur*, based on a story written by a general during the Civil War, LEWIS WALLACE. Wallace became a Master Mason on January 15, 1850, in Fountain Lodge No. 60, Indiana.

HENRY C. CLAUSEN writes in *Masons Who Helped Shape Our Nation:*

> The film industry, of course, is noted for its great number of Freemasons. During the 1920's, for instance, members of Pacific Lodge No. 233 of New York City were in southern California and were impressed in learning of the many Brethren in motion pictures. They suggested organizing a social club and, during its heyday, the resulting "233 Club" had over 1,700 Masons of the motion picture and theatrical industries as its members, including DOUGLAS FAIRBANKS, HAROLD and FRANK LLOYD, WALLACE BERRY and LOUIS B. MAYER. One of the outstanding patriotic activities of the Club was a gigantic "Pageant of Liberty" in the Los Angeles Coliseum on July 5, 1926 before an audience of 65,000 and employing over 2,500 actors and a chorus of 1,200. Brother TOM MIX, astride his horse, "Tony," portrayed PAUL REVERE, and Brother HOOT GIBSON was a Pony Express rider.
>
> The thousands of film artists who played in this pageant owed their employment, in large part, to a

fellow Mason, actor and inventor, JAMES E. BLACKSTONE, who patented in 1892 and 1894 the first practical moving picture cameras... GEORGE BRENT, EDDIE CANTOR, JOE E. BROWN, CHARLES COBURN, DAN DEFORE, GENE AUTRY, WILL ROGERS, ROY DISNEY... CECIL B. DEMILLE, ERNEST BORGNINE and RED SKELTON are only a few of the stars of the silver screen, radio and television who had been or are Freemasons and have found in the Craft principles that parallel the deep humanity of their theatrical profession.

Since 1913 Cecil B. DeMille was connected with motion pictures. Among his spectacular motion pictures were those based on the Holy Bible. He was also interested in aviation. He organized the Mercury Aviation Company in 1918 in Hollywood, California. His was the first airline to carry passengers on regular flights. He was a member of Prince of Orange Lodge No. 16 in New York City.

Clausen metions JAMES NAISMITH as the inventor of basketball. He was also a Past Master of Lawrence Lodge No. 6, Kansas. Many of the outstanding players in all the sports were, or are, Freemasons.

In 1924 Coolidge was elected President in his own right. He was opposed by the Democrat JOHN W. DAVIS, a member of Herman Lodge No. 6, West Virginia. The Progressive Party nominated ROBERT M. LAFOLLETTE. He had become a Master Mason in Madison Lodge No. 5 in Wisconsin in 1894. Using the slogan "Keep cool with Coolidge," the President received 382 electoral votes to 136 for his opponents.

During an extremely hot July in 1925, the eyes of the world were focused on Dayton, a small Tennessee town. A young school teacher named John T. Scopes was placed on trial for teaching the Darwinian theory of evolution. He was defended by Clarence Darrow; prosecuted by WILLIAM JENNINGS BRYAN. Bryan got his conviction, his last act, but Scopes was later released on a technicality.

Bryan had been on the political scene for over thirty-five years. He ran against McKinley in 1896 and 1900 for the

Presidency. In 1908 he was again defeated by Taft. While Secretary of State in Wilson's cabinet he negotiated thirty treaties. He died in Miami, Florida, on July 26, 1925.

In Lincoln Lodge No. 19, Nebraska, Bryan received the Master Mason degree on April 15, 1902. Later he affiliated with Temple Lodge No. 247, Miami, Florida.

Letters of a Self-Made Diplomat to His President appeared in 1927. The author was a cowboy-humorist named WILLIAM PENN ADAIR ROGERS, who preferred to be called simply "Will." His satiric wit delighted audiences for over a quarter century. He liked to remind everyone that "My ancestors didn't come over on the *Mayflower*—they met the boat." He enjoyed provoking politicians, stuffed shirts, and the latest fads. From 1916 to 1925 he starred in the *Ziegfel Follies* with some of the most beautiful young ladies in the country. He had started acting in motion pictures in 1918. Along with his friend and pilot, Wiley Post, Rogers was killed in an airplane crash in Alaska on August 15, 1935.

Will Rogers became a Master Mason in Claremore Lodge No. 53, Oklahoma, on March 13, 1906. Many of his Masonic and other memorabilia will be found in the Rogers Memorial at Clairmore, Oklahoma.

"LINDBERGH DOES IT! TO PARIS IN 33½ HOURS" read the headline in *The New York Times* on Sunday, May 22, 1927. This was the culmination of years of frustration for the young CHARLES AUGUSTUS LINDBERGH, JR. He had joined a flying school in 1922 at the age of 20, investing $500 for flying lessons. He soon became a barnstorming stuntman. In 1924 he became a second lieutenant. On April 15, 1926, he made the first air mail flight from Chicago to St. Louis. His dreams then turned to making a non-stop flight across the Atlantic to win the $25,000 prize that had been offered.

Others were considering the same thing. Among them was Admiral RICHARD E. BYRD, a member of Kane Lodge No. 454, New York. Byrd had flown over the North Pole with Floyd Bennett in 1926. In St. Louis Lindbergh found financial support.

At the same time he applied for the degrees in Keystone Lodge No. 243, St. Louis, Missouri. He became a Master Mason on December 15, 1926.

"The Spirit of St. Louis" was built in San Diego under Lindbergh's supervision. In it, on May 10, 1927, he flew from San Diego to Long Island, New York, in 21 hours 20 minutes—a record. From a rough, muddy field, at 7:52 a.m., May 20, 1927, Lindbergh took off. Thirty-three and one-half hours later he landed near Paris, France. His average speed had been 107.5 miles per hour; his altitude varied from 10,000 feet to 10.

Lindbergh returned to the United States aboard the *U.S.S. Memphis.* Miles of marching men, flying flags, and bands joined him in the most famous of New York's "confetti parades." And President Coolidge presented him with the Distinguished Flying Cross. The first solo flight across the Atlantic had made this young man an overnight hero.

War was outlawed in 1928. The "Pact of Paris" was signed by 62 nations, including Germany, Italy, and Japan. War was condemned; pacific means would be employed to settle all disputes. A Freemason had spearheaded the drive for this instrument to outlaw war forever.

FRANK B. KELLOGG was the Secretary of State who got the job done. Because he and the French foreign minister were the principle characters in this movement, the act became known as the "Kellogg-Briand Pact." For his efforts Kellogg received the Nobel Peace Prize in 1929. He had been a member of Rochester Lodge No. 21 since May 3, 1880.

After months of trying to learn the intentions of Coolidge for the Presidency reporters were rewarded. One day he announced: "I do not choose to run for President in 1928." The prospective candidates then became numerous. At the conventions Herbert Hoover was chosen by the Republicans; Alfred Smith, Governor of New York, was the choice of the Democrats.

Two days before Hoover was nominated, the stock market suffered an almost disasterous crash. It recovered. Prosperity continued, at least on the surface. The Republicans won by their third landslide in a row.

Tariff acts which had started in 1922 to protect American workers and farmers reached a crisis. International trade had been growing steadily. The tariffs caused other nations to adopt retaliatory measures. American exports diminished rapidly. A depression was on the way.

The political acts of the year 1920 would prove disasterous within a decade. The Merchant Marine Act created an industry requiring large subsidies from the American taxpayers. So did the Transportation Act. This was followed by the creation of the Federal Power Commission. It did little or no controlling of the industry. As an example, it let one man, Samuel Insull of Chicago, pyramid his holdings into thousands of communities in 30 states. His stocks were so heavily watered he went broke when the crash came in 1929. He fled the country leaving $1,000 cash, along with debts of fourteen million dollars.

The political acts of the '20s brought an end to "The Roaring Twenties" on October 24, 1929. The New York Stock Exchange exploded. The blast came five days later. Everyone was wounded.

Andrew Sinclair, in his anti-capitalistic style, wrote: "The last of the three successive Presidents of the wealthy nearly presided over the liquidation of the wealthy in America. It was a time when, as Scott Fitzgerald noted, the rich were only happy in each other's company. The rest of America had learned to hate them and their false promises. Ironically they were to be saved by the man whom they denounced as a traitor to their class, Franklin D. Roosevelt from New York, the handsome squire in a wheelchair."

The English historian, Alstair Cooke, saw the cause of the crash differently: "It became clear years too late that the torrent of liquidation was caused, not so much by the big traders and bankers—who rushed in to try to plug the flood with twenty-five million dollars—but by legions of small-timers who had no margins to speak of."

Before the crash, stock could be purchased for ten cents on the dollar. Years later this error was corrected. It would take sixty to sixty-five cents to purchase a dollar's worth of stock.

The country quickly came to a stop. Factories were idled. Buildings were left unfinished. Truckers had nothing to haul. Milk and farm products had to be dumped; there were few buyers. Well-dressed men roamed the streets begging for pennies. There had to be someone to blame. It became Herbert Hoover. He was even blamed for the "dust bowl" and other works of God.

There was little question that Hoover would be defeated in 1932. FRANKLIN D. ROOSEVELT, the Democratic nominee, won by a landslide.

Roosevelt, and his "New Deal," poured one billion dollars into the banks to save them. Six billion more went into the building industry and in loans to home-owners to prevent their evictions. Every letter in the alphabet was used to describe the agencies formed to try to stem unemployment. Created were the WPA, CCC, TVA, AAA, NRA, SEC, REA, and others.

The policies of the New Deal helped, but not enough. Soup kitchens and bread lines, what there were of them, became a daily sight throughout the country. Thousands became scavengers. The refuse of restaurants and dumps were thoroughly searched for food. Dumps became the sites for thousands of shacks built from discarded wood, flattened tin cans, and other materials. There the jobless lived in misery.

A bill was adopted early in 1933 to legalize the sale and consumption of beer and wine. The alcoholic content couldn't exceed 3.2 percent. On February 20, 1933, the twenty-first amendment to the Constitution was proposed by Congress. It would repeal the Eighteenth Amendment prohibiting the manufacture and sale of alcoholic beverages. It quickly received the endorsement of over three-fourths of the states. On December 5, 1933, it was proclaimed adopted by the President, after it had been certified by the acting Secretary of State. The bootleggers and speakeasies were put out of business.

On February 17, 1933, Roosevelt took part in the degree when his son, ELLIOT, became a Master Mason in Architect Lodge No. 519 of New York City. He did the same on November 7, 1935, when his sons JAMES and FRANKLIN D. were also made Master Masons. The President was a member of Holland Lodge No. 8, New York City.

Additional acts were adopted in 1935. Among them was the Works Progress Administration, or WPA. Then came the Social Security Act.

The country was in a little better shape in 1936 when ALFRED M. LANDON of Kansas ran against Roosevelt for the Presidency. Landon was a member of Fortitude Lodge No. 107, Kansas. Roosevelt carried every state except Maine and Vermont.

In 1937 the President, unhappy with the Supreme Court for voiding many of his programs, proposed a plan to increase the number of Justices. He dropped his "court-packing scheme" when the Court began to reverse itself. Being able to make five appointments within 30 months also helped.

On the national scene problems were expanding. Although the important nations had agreed to ban war in 1928, the agreement consisted of nothing but paper. Japan had invaded China in 1931 and set up a puppet government in Manchuria. Hitler was rearming Germany. The people in America were ignoring his actions. In Madrid, Spain, General Francisco Franco was challenging the government. He was receiving planes, munitions, and troops from Italy and Germany. The Spanish Government was receiving but little assistance, and that from Russia.

Roosevelt endeavored to awaken the isolationists in the United States to the danger America faced.

Adolph Hitler had gained control of Germany in 1933. He had demolished democracy. He dispossessed the Jews, and systematically began destroying them. Organized religion was abolished. Freemasonry in Germany, what there was left of it, had to go underground. Like the Jews, thousands of Freemasons were sent to concentration camps, or murdered.

The western world, including too many in the United States, turned their eyes away from the madman's actions. Hitler had counted on that. He seized Austria in March, 1938. As he hoped, the world did nothing. On September 29, 1938, Mussolini signed an agreement with Hitler. It gave the Italian nothing; the German everything; the world another war.

Stalin, in the meantime, was consolidating his control over Russia. He did it by purging peasants, army officers, the intellectual elite, and all others he considered dangerous to his dictatorship. His victims numbered in the millions.

Hitler's next goal was Czechoslovakia. When its President asked his French and English allies for help, he was ignored. The French Daladier and the English Chamberlain sold out the Czechs at Munich. This was supposed to purchase peace. But Winston Churchill scoffed: "You have gained shame and you will get war.'

Hitler and Stalin signed a nonagression pact on August 23, 1939. Russia was given permission to divide Poland, take over the Baltic states, and Finland. Finally, France and Great Britain took a firm stand. If the Nazis attacked Poland, France and England would go to its aid.

At 4:45 a.m., September 1, 1939, Germany attacked Poland. Two days later France and England declared war on Germany.

The depression in the United States was over. The nation's industry geared up quickly to supply its overseas friends. And that became a problem.

Thirty-one

FREEMASONRY'S HOME AWAY FROM HOME

AS it had always been, the United States was not prepared for war. Not even to defend itself. Franklin D. Roosevelt couldn't break the control the isolationists held over The Congress.

Risking impeachment, the President took steps to protect the country. A top secret project was commenced about 1940. Albert Einstein, and other scientists, informed Roosevelt it was possible to produce an awesome atomic bomb. He ordered work to be started.

It was late in the 1970s when it was learned the President had been working closely with Winston Churchill and English intelligence. The amazing story of his continuing flirtation with impeachment is found in *A Man Called Intrepid* by William Stevenson.

Sir William Stephenson, the man called "Intrepid," wrote the foreword to Stevenson's book. Within it he described the courage of Franklin Roosevelt in working with Churchill during the days of American neutrality. The American President was kept fully informed through "Intrepid" about the European situation. He noted: "Roosevelt was acutely aware that America, psychologically isolated since World War I and relying wistfully upon geographical insularity, was woefully unprepared to meet or counter the onslaught of newly developed military, propaganda, and espionage techniques."

Stephenson then added: "Only a leader who could extend his vision of national self-interest to the belief that a union of free people was the real defense against totalitarian aggressors would wager on Britain at such unattractive odds. Roosevelt was such a rare gambler."

Hitler crushed Poland in September, 1939. He and the Russians then divided the country. Millions of Poles were murdered after the fighting had ceased on both sides, particularly by Russia. Stalin then determined to take advantage of the situation. On November 30, 1939, he turned his hordes loose on little Finland. Although the Finns were outnumbered five to one, they fought the invaders to a standstill. England and France offered assistance, but they couldn't get permission to cross neutral Sweden and Norway. The Finns were skeptical of the French and British fighting ability, anyway. So, in March, 1940, the Finnish government bowed to the Russian pressure.

Norway's neutrality didn't disturb Hitler. He ordered German troops to take the country. On April 9, 1940, they struck. The country was quickly subdued, and Vidkum Quisling declared himself the Nazi's Prime Minister of Norway. On May 10, the day Winston Churchill became Prime Minister of Great Britain, the German *blitzkrieg* swept over Belgium. Rotterdam was brutally bombed on the 14th. Holland came under the Nazi heel. It didn't take long for the Jews and Freemasons to be swept up, murdered, or delivered to concentration camps for a life worse than death.

The German juggernaut easily rolled over thirty-six French, British, and Belgian divisions. A large gap was smashed through the "impregnable" Maginot line in France. The Belgians capitulated on May 28. France was fast crumbling. A really inferior German army had destroyed the Allies in weeks.

An Allied army of almost 340,000 was cut off at Dunkirk by the Germans. Historians had trouble understanding why Hitler refused to let his Panzer divisions attack. He wanted to give the Luftwaffe the opportunity to annihilate the helpless men. Stevenson, however, notes there was much more involved. British code breakers, and Ultra, one of the German's own coding devices smuggled into Britain, knew, or could guess,

Hitler's plans. The Nazi chief still expected to gain a peaceful conquest of England. And the beleaguered troops had been ordered to the beaches of Dunkirk, France.

"During most of May, Vice-Admiral Ramsey was mobilizing 848 captains among fishermen, yachtsmen, merchant seamen, and Royal Navy officers, for operation DYNAMO," Stevenson wrote. Dynamo was the code name for the Dunkirk evacuation. And from Britain came the most remarkable rescue mission in history. Boats of every description, manned by civilians of every persuasion, rescued almost all the soldiers trapped on the French Channel coast.

France surrendered on June 22, 1940. The terms were agreed to and signed at the same clearing in Compiegne forest where Foch had dictated the terms in 1918. Churchill vowed to continue to fight. He said he was determined to keep alive the embers of resistance in Europe. And he found an ally in a Frenchman named Charles de Gaulle.

In 1937 a Neutrality Act had been adopted. It was repeated in 1939. Exports were put on a "cash and carry" basis. After Dunkirk, "surplus" arms were released to England to help replace some of those lost in that evacuation. In September, fifty overage destroyers went to Britain on a "lend lease" exchange. A few days later the first peacetime military draft in American history was passed by The Congress. And cries similar to those of the '60s were frequently heard—"Hell no, we won't go." Scrap iron and steel were prohibited from being shipped to any country but England. The Japanese were angered.

A letter dated November 1, 1939, was sent to every Grand Lodge in the country. "If Freemasonry is to be permitted to take part in morale, or welfare work with the Army," it read, "the Craft must be able to speak to the War Department with a practically united voice. All, or a heavy majority of the Grand Lodges must cooperate, if they are not to be helpless, as in 1917-18. THE MASONIC SERVICE ASSOCIATION is the voice the Grand Lodges can command to speak their will."

Freemasonry had been ignored by the government during World War I. The Association that had been formed in 1918

because of that slight, wasn't about to let it happen again.
Neither were an overwhelming number of Grand Lodges and
appendant bodies. They agreed to work with the MSA.

Freemasonry's Servant records:

> The institution known as Freemasonry was one of the
> first victims of what is now called World War II. It has
> always been one of the first to be proscribed by despots.
> Men who desired to conquer the world knew that any
> agency that believed in truth and the freedom of man had
> to be destroyed before they could be successful. Hitler was
> no exception. As head of the German government he led
> the brutality that murdered Freemasons, or sent them
> underground to escape the wrath of his hirelings. "All
> Masons Jews—all Jews Masons," was the cry of the Ger-
> man regime that sent the people into a fratricidal mania
> and made them utterly ruthless. Its techniques of torture,
> massacre, and sadistic mutilations were beyond belief and
> description.

Under the guise of being friendly, a French professor and
author gained access to many Masonic libraries in the United
States, and other countries. Among the books he wrote were
George Washington, Republican Aristocrat and *Revolution and
Freemasonry.* The latter, published by Little, Brown, was
anything but historical. What he later did for the Nazis is
recorded briefly by *The New York Times* on December 5, 1946:

> Bernard Fay, former professor of American civilization
> at the College de France and writer on Franco-American
> relations, was sentenced to life imprisonment at hard labor
> today after his conviction on a charge of intelligence with
> the enemy. M. Fay has been charged with publishing
> documents and lists of the Freemasons for the Vichy (Nazi
> dominated) government. This had resulted, according to
> the prosecution, in deportation or death for thousands of
> them.

The Masonic Service Association established a Department of
Welfare in May, 1940. Several officers of the Armed Forces,
known to be Freemasons, accepted a place on the advisory
board. Immediately plans were made to open Service Centers
wherever the Association was invited to do so. The first "Home

Away from Home" was opened on February 1, 1941, in Columbia, South Carolina. It was welcomed by the War Department and the citizens. Service Centers were opened in many states, especially where there were large contingencies of Armed Forces personnel. London and Paris (after they were freed), also boasted of Masonic Service Centers.

General GEORGE C. MARSHALL, who would be made a Mason-at-Sight on December 16, 1941, addressed the Association on February 19, 1941. He congratulated the Freemasons of the country for their "willingness to serve the men and women of the Armed Forces."

Six days earlier, Senator HARRY TRUMAN took to the airwaves to inform the country what Freemasonry was doing. He noted only ten cents per member was being requested for the program. Then added:

> In these days of big money, when even billions are a matter of course and a million is small change, I might be excused if I were apologetic for the small sum asked of the two and a half millions of Freemasons of the nation. But, as a matter of fact, I am proud that the small contribution requested can go so far and do so much. I am proud because I know why it can do so much; proud that so many devoted Masons are willing to give of their time and strength, sell their goods at cost, work for nothing or for a pittance, for the love of their fellow members of the oldest Fraternal organization in the world.

In August, 1941, the draft act was about to expire. The isolationists in The Congress fought against Roosevelt's request to extend it. The House Armed Services Committee held hearings. The opponents of the draft were extremely vocal. The Army Chief of Staff, General George Catless Marshall, spoke. The renewal act passed the House 203 to 202! Three months before Pearl Harbor!

The Nazi continuing fire-bombing attacks on Great Britain failed to defeat the British. Hitler became more disgusted by the day. He determined Russia had to be conquered if England was to fall. So, on June 21, 1941, he turned on his conspirator. And the United States began supplying the Russians with food, arms and other material.

The Empire of Japan hadn't been idle. After extensive planning, and based on excellent undercover intelligence, a fleet headed out to sea. Under the command of Admiral Isoroku Yamamoto were six carriers, protected by a heavy screen of surface vessels and submarines. They managed to escape detection. And on December 2, 1941, Yamamoto received the coded message: "Climb Mount Niitaka." The attack on Pearl Harbor was given the go ahead which occurred on December 7, 1941.

Three hundred fifty-three Japanese bombers, torpedo bombers, and fighters knocked out half of the American Navy within minutes. The airforce was immobilized. Thousands were killed. Damage ran into the billions.

According to James Jones in his *WWII* no one was prepared for the Japanese attack. Those who were awake were at breakfast. Most were sleeping late because it was a Sunday. For a time the men held onto their extra half-pints of milk in spite of the explosions they were hearing. They thought someone was doing some blasting. It wasn't until the first fighter came at them with guns blazing that they realized they "were seeing and acting in a genuine moment of history."

He later noted that "feats of incredible heroism and rescue" were carried out in the harbor by men who were not prepared for a war.

President Roosevelt told a joint session of Congress the next day that December 7 was "a date that will live in infamy." The Senate voted unanimously to declare war against Japan. There was one dissenter in the House, Jeanette Rankin of Montana. On the 11th Germany and Italy declared war against the United States.

The Japanese launched simultaneous attacks against Hong Kong, Malaya, and the Philippines. Without the excuse of surprise the forces in Hawaii had, the Far East Airforce was crippled. Japanese planes destroyed half the Flying Fortresses, fifty-six fighters, and twenty-five other planes at Clark Field. This enabled the enemy to land at Luzon. Less than a month after the start of the war, Manila fell. American and Philippine troops retreated to the Bataan Peninsula.

Without air support, the British battleship *Prince of Wales* and heavy cruiser *Repulse* were sunk in Malayan waters by Japanese planes four days after Pearl Harbor. Through the Malayan jungle the Japanese marched toward Singapore. With British guns facing the sea, the invader's couldn't be stopped. Singapore fell on February 15, 1942.

Throughout the Pacific, the Japanese quickly overran what little opposition was encountered. In Burma, the British were aided by Chinese under the command of Chiang Kai-shek, whose chief of staff was the American General JOSEPH W. STILLWELL, better known as "Vinegar Joe." The troops made a valiant stand, but were cut off and had to retreat to northeast India. When asked, Stillwell told the truth: "The Japs ran us out of Burma. We took a hell of a beating!" Stillwell became a member of West Point Lodge No. 877, New York, on June 1, 1916, while he was an instructor at the Military Academy.

The commander of Armed Forces in the Philippines, General DOUGLAS MACARTHUR, was ordered to leave Bataan by the President. He did leave, reluctantly, vowing he would return. MacArthur had been made a Mason-at-Sight on January 17, 1936. His father, Arthur, had also been a Freemason. Both considered Freemasonry an exemplary organization.

WILLIAM DENSLOW, in his *10,000 Famous Freemasons* notes: "MacArthur has praised Freemasonry on many occasions." He attributes these words to the General:

> It embraces the highest moral laws and will bear the test of any system of ethics or philosophy ever promulgated for the uplift of man...its requirements are the things that are right, and its restraints are from the things that are wrong...inculcating doctrines of patriotism and brotherly love, enjoying sentiments of exalted benevolence, encouraging all that is good, kind and charitable, reprobating all that is cruel and oppressive, its observance will uplift everyone under its influence...to do good to others, to forgive enemies, to love neighbors, to restrain passions, to honor parents, to respect authority, to return good for evil, not to cause anger, not to bear false witness, not to lie, not to steal—these are the essential elements of the moral law.

General JONATHAN M. WAINWRIGHT, who would become a Freemason on May 16, 1946, in Union Lodge No. 7, Kansas, was left with the unenviable task of defending what was left of the Philippines. In early January the rations had to be cut in half. Foraging for whatever was edible became a way of life. It wasn't long before the half-starved troops composed their own song. "We're the battling bastards of Bataan," they sang. "No mama, no papa, no Uncle Sam;/ No aunts, no uncles, no nephews, no nieces;/ No pills, no planes, no artillery pieces./ —and nobody gives a damn."

They were correct. The President and the Chiefs of Staff agreed with the pre-planning done by Churchill and Roosevelt before Pearl Harbor. The war against Germany took priority. The loss of Wake, Guam, the Philippines, and all the little known names in the Pacific, were acceptable.

On the home front young men were being drafted. Young ladies were enlisting for noncombat duty. The work week was lengthened. A War Production Board took charge of industry. The American ingenuity was put to work as it never had been before. Even the greatest isolationist of all, Senator BURTON K. WHEELER, agreed that "the only thing now to do is lick the hell out of them." Wheeler was a member of Butte Lodge No. 22, Montana. He had been the Progressive Party candidate for Vice President in 1924. He had bitterly opposed all attempts by Roosevelt to arm the country before Pearl Harbor.

The Mason from Missouri, Colonel CHARLES LINDBERGH, asked to be reinstated in the Air Force. He wasn't. Roosevelt, and others, continued to be angered by Lindbergh's advice to stay out of the war with Germany. The Colonel had given the government this advice after witnessing first-hand the superior German airforce. But, as a civilian, Lindbergh became a technical advisor to the Air Force. He even flew combat missions in the Pacific.

On April 8, 1942, General Wainwright ordered the ammunition dumps destroyed at Bataan. He and a few of his men retreated to Corregidor. The main body surrendered. The men at Corregidor held out until May 6, and then had to yield. The Japanese gleefully brought in motion picture cameras to record Wainwright's surrender.

The survivors of Bataan began a "Death March" sixty-five miles to a railway junction. Those who survived were herded aboard cattle cars to be hauled to an internment camp. Thirsty, starved, and brutalized, thousands died. Among the few survivors was a young officer named HAROLD K. JOHNSON. He survived to become the Army Chief of Staff under President Lyndon Johnson. Later he would become the Director of Education and Americanism for the Scottish Rite, Southern Jurisdiction, a position he held until his death on September 24, 1983.

Something had to be done to blunt the humility of the continuing victories of the Japanese. A submarine staff officer suggested the use of Army bombers from aircraft carriers. General HENRY H. "HAP" ARNOLD, commander of the Army Air Force, asked Colonel JAMES DOOLITTLE to study the plan. He did. He determined that modified B-25 medium bombers could take off from a carrier with a bomb load of one ton.

Volunteers loaded their sixteen bombers aboard the *U.S.S. Hornet.* Each consisted of a five man crew. Under strict secrecy, the *Hornet* with its protective screen of other vessels sailed toward Japan. It had been hoped the carrier could get as close as 450 miles from Japan before the bombers took off. The sighting of a Japanese fishing ship changed that. So, on April 18, 1942, while 670 miles away, the B-25s took off one-by-one.

The bombers reached Japan undetected. In all, they spent about six minutes over their target, did little material damage, but created a morale problem for the enemy. All the planes flew away safely from the target. Of the eighty crew members, seventy-one returned, eventually, to the United States. To the persistent question: "Where did the American planes come from?" Roosevelt gleefully replied: "Shangri-la!" He was referring to the mythical Himalayan retreat found in James Hilton's novel *Lost Horizon.*

At least two of the principals in the raid over Japan were Freemasons. General Henry M. "Hap" Arnold was a member of

Union Lodge No. 7, Kansas, and had been since 1927. Colonel James H. Doolittle became a member of Hollenbeck Lodge No. 319, California, in 1918. He would receive the Congressional Medal of Honor. After the war he returned to the Shell Oil Company. In 1944, Arnold became a five-star general.

Through intercepted communications, and other means, "Intrepid" learned before the outbreak of hostilities that Hitler had discovered the atom could be split. Norway had the hard water necessary for the manufacture of an atom bomb. It also had the scientists capable of producing it.

This information was secretly conveyed to Roosevelt. He knew there was truth to the reports. Einstein had told him about the atom even earlier. Before Pearl Harbor, the President formed a small committee and supplied it with substantial funds to produce what would become an atom bomb. Fortunately for the world, the United States would be the first country to unfold the deadly weapon.

Early victims of the Japanese sneak attack were American-Japanese. The War Department urged the President to isolate all Japanese in "relocation centers." The Attorney General of California, EARL WARREN, was one of the leaders insisting they be shipped inland. Warren, a Past Grand Master of Masons in California, would, in 1953, become Chief Justice of the Supreme Court. It was 1944 before the first of the internees was freed. Many Japanese-Americans fought in Europe. They compiled a superb record for courage.

In May, 1942, a hugh Japanese fleet sailed past the Solomon Islands into the Coral Sea. Its initial destination was Port Moresby on New Guinea; the ultimate destination was Australia. An American task force with the carriers *Yorktown* and *Lexington* searched for the enemy fleet. The ships never came close. Their planes did all the fighting, with firepower from the ships endeavoring to knock them from the sky. For two days this strange battle continued. In the end, the Japanese flat-top *Shoho* and the American *Lexington* were sunk. The *Yorktown* limped back to Honolulu. But this first sea-air battle slowed the Japanese.

It was estimated that repairs to the *Yorktown* would take two months. It went back to sea in two days!

Toward the end of May another American task force went searching for the enemy. Navy cryptanalysts had broken the Imperial Navy's codes. Admiral Chester W. Nimitz learned an attack on Midway Island was imminent. Wide-ranging search plans scoured the ocean for the Japanese task force.

At dawn on June 4, 1942, Japanese planes struck Midway. The forces on the island took a severe pounding. But a scouting plane found the Japanese carriers and radioed their position.

Admiral Raymond Spruance emptied the *Enterprise* and the *Hornet* of its attack planes. Then, calculating when the Japanese planes would be refueling and rearming, the planes from the *Yorktown* were sent to the attack.

The slow, cumbersome American torpedo bombers attacked the enemy fleet valiantly but accomplished nothing. Thirty-five of the forty-one bombers were shot down. But as Japanese planes were about to take off, American *Dauntless* dive bombers plummeted toward the enemy's carriers. The flagship, *Akagi*, took two bombs that triggered explosions, tearing the ship apart. The *Soryu* was hit by three bombs, killing her engines and starting devastating fires. The *Kaga* took four hits. Her bombs and fuel exploded. Only the *Hiryu* escaped.

Planes from the *Hiryu* found the *Yorktown*, and crippled her so that she had to be abandoned. More *Dauntless* bombers were sent to find the *Hiryu*. They blasted her into a flaming mass of metal. By dawn the next day Nagumo's carrier task force had ceased to exist. Japan had suffered its first major defeat in three centuries. The citizens of the Empire wouldn't know what had happened for over a year!

Stalin was crying for a second front. The Nazi war against Russia that had begun on June 20, 1940, was proving davastating for the Russians. Ironically, the two dictators who had double crossed everyone, including themselves, were locked in deadly combat. Also, ironically, the United States had been sending supplies to Russia to bolster its defenses.

The *U.S.S. Alabama* had been launched in February, 1942. It was commissioned on August 16. I was one of the 2,400 man crew that was aboard her in Portsmouth, Virginia, which took her to Casco Bay, Maine, along with her sister ship the *South Dakota*. In March, 1943, the *Alabama* joined the British Home Fleet, and performed convoy duty to Murmansk, Russia.

From sub-zero temperatures the crew of the *Alabama* returned to Virginia to be fitted for duty in the South Pacific. In August, 1943, she went through the Panama Canal. In November and December she blasted the Gilbert Islands with her five and sixteen inch guns to aid the Marines to land with as little opposition as possible.

The second front Stalin pleaded for took the form of an Allied landing in French Morocco and Algeria. It was able to strike the German General Erwin Rommel, who had played havoc with the British in the desert war, in the rear. Until the fall of 1942, the "Desert Fox" had everything going his way. As the Royal Air Force grew stronger, however, the *Luftwaffe* was practically wiped out.

Before the invasion, General MARK WAYNE CLARK had been landed by submarine in Africa. Plans were laid for the invasion called "Operation Torch." Later he commanded the 5th Army in Italy. Clark became a Master Mason in Mystic Tie Lodge No. 398, Indiana, on December 30, 1929.

On the other side of the world General CLAIRE CHENNAULT was fighting with the Chinese. He had been working with Chiang since 1937. In 1941 he gathered a group of American volunteer fighters called the "Flying Tigers." In the summer of 1942 his command became the Fourteenth Air Force. Although the Flying Tigers had many Japanese "kills," and they and the Fourteenth kept the enemy bottled up, their greatest success was in conquering the Himalayas. They convoyed C-47 and C-46 transports over the "hump," the 20,000 foot Himalayas, keeping China supplied from bases in India. Before the end of the war over 45,000 tons a month were flown into besieged China.

Chennault was a member of League City Lodge No. 1053 of Texas. He once wrote: "You will note that my Masonic affiliations are widely scattered—from Texas to China to California. This is particularly unfortunate since I now divide my time between Louisiana and Formosa—Free China."

Admiral ERNEST J. KING, Chief of Naval Operations, fought within the council of the Joint Chiefs of Staff for stronger operations in the South Pacific. The first priority remained Europe and Hitler. But King managed to eke out a concession—a landing on Guadalcanal.

King became a member of George C. Whiting Lodge No. 22 of the District of Columbia on September 12, 1935.

Guadalcanal became the beginning of the road to Tokyo. About ten thousand men of the First Marine Division, the only trained division in the Pacific, landed without opposition on August 7, 1942. Then on the 8th and 9th the United States Navy took a whipping and left. The Japanese threw everything they had at the entrenched Marines. The Americans held. They, and the Twenty-fifth Infantry that succeeded them, quickly learned the only way to stop the enemy was to kill him. Before the Japanese evacuated in February, 1943, 24,000 of them had been killed. The American loss was 1,752.

Ferocious sea battles continued off the shore throughout the occupation of Guadalcanal. The *Enterprise* was badly damaged. The carriers *Wasp* and *Hornet* were sunk. Four destroyers and two cruisers went to the bottom with them. Then came the Battle of the Bismark Sea. On March 2 and 3 American and Australian planes knocked out eight Japanese transports, along with four destroyers. The road to Tokyo was made a little easier.

The road included dozens of little-known names: Gilbert Islands, Makin, Tarawa, New Guinea, Solomons, Rabaul, New Britain, Marianas, Eniwetok, Kwajalein, Marshall Islands, New Hebrides, Saipan, Tinian, Guam, Okinawa, Iwo Jima, and on and on. And the road went by way of the Philippines. The Navy as well as the Army wanted MacArthur to keep his promise to return to the place where the Americans had been humiliated in the early days of the war.

Tarawa was an example of what took place at these little-known dots on the map. Admiral Shibasaki boasted: "The Americans could not take Tarawa with a million men in a hundred years." There, on Betio, 300 acres of coral sand, Americans made their first amphibious assault on an enemy solidly dug in. Colonel (later General) MERRITT EDSON proudly said: "The reason we won this show was the ability of junior officers and noncoms to take command of small groups of six to eight or ten men, regardless of where those men came from, and to organize and lead them as a fighting team." Edson became a member of Olive Branch Lodge No. 64 of Vermont on February 24, 1926.

Before the Philippines could be regained, the Japanese threat from the Marshall Islands had to be eliminated. This job became the Navy's Admiral Spruance and the powerful Fifth Fleet. Within this fleet was Admiral MARC A. MITSCHER'S Task Force Fifty-eight. It consisted of five fleet carriers, four light carriers and a protecting screen of destroyers, cruisers, and BB 60, the *U.S.S. Alabama* (on which I was a Baker First Class).

Mitscher had been a member of Biscayne Lodge No. 124 of Florida since January 29, 1919. He had been connected with naval aviation since 1915. He was a pilot on the first Navy trans-Atlantic flight in 1919. In 1928 he made the first takeoff and landing on the old *Saratoga*. He was the commanding officer of the *Hornet* when Doolittle and his men took off for the first bombing raid on Tokyo.

Task Force Fifty-eight went to work on the Japanese stronghold on Truk Island in February, 1944. Hellcat fighters took care of Truk's defenses. Then the bombers took over. The enemy's "Gibraltar of the Pacific" was left in ruins.

Mitscher's Task Force sailed toward Guam and Saipan. Ozawa believed he had the Americans trapped. At dawn on June 19, 1944, he sent sixty-nine planes off in a first strike wave. A second, and stronger, group was sent to attack the carriers. American radar picked up the first wave 150 miles out. The American fighters were scrambled; the dive bombers and torpedo planes were launched. The Hellcats that had been sweeping the airfields on Guam were called in. The slaughter was unbelieveable. Japanese planes by the score were shot into the water. All of the first wave of enemy planes were destroyed. Ninety-eight out of 130 in the second wave were downed. The third and fourth waves were virtually obliterated. In all, the Japanese lost 346 planes; the Americans, 30. June 19, 1944, became known as "The Great Marianas Turkey Shoot."

The following day a scout plane picked up the First Mobile Fleet. The time was 4 p.m. The ships were at the maximum range of Mitscher's planes. Yet, this opportunity couldn't be lost. Two hundred sixteen planes were sent to attack Ozawa's fleet. Task Force Fifty-eight was ordered to steam full speed toward the Japanese to shorten the return distance for the planes.

The Americans attacked at sunset. The carrier *Hiyo* was sunk; the *Zuikaku* was heavily damaged. So was a light carrier. Twenty American planes were shot down; 65 Zeros were blasted.

It was pitch black when the planes returned to the American carrier. Mitscher ordered the fleet to turn on *all* lights, and even had flares lighted. The Admiral said if he could send his planes out, he sure could bring them back safely. Mitscher had lived up to his advance billing. In 1945 he would be rewarded by being made Chief of Naval Operations for Air.

It was another year before the road to Tokyo would end, but it would be easier from this point. Japan was beginning to lose the war.

Perhaps the men who received the least credit for the victories in the Pacific were the Seabees. They comprised the Navy's Construction Battalions. They were made up of civilian professional men—carpenters, plumbers, miners, engineers, heavy equipment operators. They were involved in every landing in the Pacific, and turned acres of jungles and ruins into landing strips and "tropical boomtowns" almost overnight. Where others said it would take months to do a job, the "CBs" did it in hours. They have been described as "soldiers in sailors' uniforms, doing civilian work for WPA wages." They were outstanding men!

For months the world had been looking toward the day the Allies would land on French soil. As the road to Tokyo had been, and would continue to be, bitter, so it was in Europe.

There was a no more anxious observer, and an actual participant, than GEORGE VI, King of England. In many respects England had been fortunate when his brother, Edward VIII, had abdicated because of his love for a woman not acceptable to the Royal Family. Edward was reported to be a Nazi sympathizer. George was anything but that. While Chamberlain and his government had given Hitler everthing he demanded, the King had worked with Churchill and those who knew what Germany was planning.

"Directors of British intelligence are confirmed in their appointments by the Crown," wrote Stevenson in *A Man Called Intrepid*. "This misleadingly modest man, [King George VI] who had stepped so hesitantly into the shoes of his brother. . . was an active participant in Britain's clandestine warfare." While the appeasers slept the King and his intelligence service worked. Among them was Greta Garbo, "a member of the Stephenson-Churchill group." Among other things, she reported there were "high-level Nazi sympathizers in Stockholm."

KING GEORGE (Alfred Frederick Arthur George of the house of Windsor) became a member of Naval Lodge No. 2612, England, in December, 1919. In 1936 he was installed Grand Master Mason of Scotland. He personally installed three other Grand Masters. He took an active part in Freemasonry throughout his lifetime. The reason is summed up by him: "The world today does require spiritual and moral regeneration. I have no doubt, after many years as a member of our Order, that Freemasonry can play a most important part in this vital need."

Because of the King, and another Freemason named WINSTON CHURCHILL, who was made a Master Mason in

Studholme Lodge No. 1591, in 1902, the plans of Hitler to conquer the world met a stumbling block. They were able to command the respect and dedication of thousands of men and women during the dark days when it appeared the British Empire would be lost. Slowly these men and women had built a team that would not be whipped.

In June, 1943, the Allies invaded Italy. On July 19 Mussolini met with the *Fuhrer* near Rimini. "Sicily must be made into a Stalingrad," Hitler told him. "We must hold out until winter, when new secret weapons will be ready for use against England." But he offered the Italian dictator no help. And while they were talking, 700 Allied planes had bombed Rome.

Mussolini called the first meeting of the Fascist Grand Council since 1939. His impassioned speech gained no support for his war effort. On the 25th, Mussolini was arrested, shoved into an ambulance, and carried to the island of Ponza.

The new Italian government tried to surrender. Bickering over terms continued for five weeks. On August 19 General Giuseppe Castellano offered to switch sides. It was September 1 before this information was sent to Eisenhower's headquarters. On September 8 the Italians announced via radio the nation had given up the fight. The German's hadn't. When Hitler learned what the Italian Government was planning, he rushed crack units into Italy.

Montgomery's Eighth Army, Mark Clark's American Fifth Army, Patton's Army, the Air Force, and the combined Allied Forces spent the winter trying to dislodge the entrenched German forces. It was June 4, 1944, before the Fifth Army marched into Rome. There, according to Clark: "There were gay crowds in the streets, many of them waving flags, as our infantry marched through the capital. Flowers were stuck in the muzzles of the soldiers' rifles and guns on the tanks. Many of the Romans seemed to be on the verge of hysteria in their enthusiasm for the American troops."

On the day Rome fell the high command in England met to decide whether to go ahead with the invasion of France. The weather was atrocious. Rain and high winds had caused one postponement. The best estimate of weather conditions was fair to poor. But the decision was made. Operation Overlord would begin June 6, 1944.

Out of the dark skies paratroopers fell on the morning of June 6. They led the thousands of men who would land on the beaches of Normandy. The Germans were shocked to find coming out of the haze at dawn a panorama of ships. Nearly 5,000 of them were spread without a break across the horizon. Within the warships were 174,000 troops and 20,000 vehicles. Ammunition and supplies couldn't be estimated. And the German General's "longest day" prophecy came true.

As darkness fell, reinforcements, guns and supplies reached the beaches. Hitler's wall had been breached.

Thousands lost their lives before the Germans finally capitulated. Countless acts of heroism would take place throughout Europe. Hundreds of volumes would be written to tell the story of the valor of the Allied fighting forces.

One of the most memorable days of the war came on August 25, 1944. Paris was liberated.

The man who deserves credit for his courage in providing at least a meager defense before the attack on Pearl Harbor wouldn't live to see his country victorious. Franklin Delano Roosevelt died at Warm Springs, Georgia, on April 12, 1945.

HARRY S. TRUMAN, a Past Grand Master of Masons in Missouri, was sworn in as President on the same day. He had to take a cram course in war problems and the politics of the day. For reasons not available, Roosevelt had chosen not to reveal the inner-workings of government to his Vice President. Truman promised, insofar as possible, to follow his predecessor's policies.

Truman, like millions of other Americans, had been working on the home front. What these men and women did should never be forgotten. Without them the Nazi would never have been defeated.

Ships were launched daily throughout the war. Tanks, vehicles, guns, clothing, ammunition of every type came off the assembly lines faster than ever before. It is estimated that American workers produced during the war 300,000 aircraft, 87,000 tanks, 320,000 artillery pieces, 12,000 war and cargo ships, 65,000 landing craft, and over forty-two billion bullets. Other supplies were uncountable. Day and night the American men and women manned the factories to help whip Hitler and Tojo.

About half the workers in war plants were women. Although many of them had never worked before, they did a tremendous job. Others worked behind the scenes as air raid wardens, in hospitals, and with agencies working for the men and women overseas.

The Masonic Service Association, unlike the years of World War I, was permitted to serve the fighting men and women. Freemasonry was able to do the work its principles called for. Its tenets were put into action through the Masonic Service Centers. Freemasons, through their Grand Lodges, contributed to the work. To help with this effort, Freemasons in Hollywood produced an excellent motion picture called *Your Son Is My Brother.*

In 1944 it was apparent that more than Service Centers were needed. Thousands of wounded were returned to the United States to fill government hospitals. JOHN D. CUNNINGHAM, the Chief Field Agent, proposed the MSA start a hospital visitation program. CARL H. CLAUDY, the Executive Secretary, greeted the proposal with enthusiasm. Through the assistance of Harry Truman, the Vice President of the United States, Generals George C. Marshall and H. H. Arnold, and Admiral Ernest J. King, members of the Advisory Committee of the Association, a trial program was started.

The work done on this Hospital Visitation Program caused it to become a permanent fixture. The Veterans' Administration Voluntary Services was established in 1946 with the assistance of the MSA. Dozens of non-profit groups continue to work with hospitalized veterans.

Throughout the United States canteens and social clubs were opened for service personnel. Top-rated entertainers could be found in them every day. Hollywood wasn't idle. More than one-fourth of the males associated with the motion picture industry went into the Armed Forces. Others appeared continuously in bond rallies. They gave free performances throughout the world. Many men and women worked with the USO in this country and overseas.

Unlike her Allies, the United States wasn't devastated by bombs and other acts of war. But the civilians were well-aware the country was at war. There were shortages of almost everything. Rationing was a way of life. New automobiles were nonexistent. Gasoline was scarce. The national speed limit was set at thirty-five miles per hour to conserve what gasoline there was. Household appliances couldn't be found. Like the servicemen and women, the civilians were anxious to have the war reach a successful conclusion.

The war was reaching a conclusion in Europe. Historians differ about its success. Stalin had demanded, and received, concessions that would keep the free world fighting a "cold war" through the present day.

As the bitter fighting began to wind down, the full horror of the Nazi regime was revealed. The concentration camps, with their now silent gas chambers and crematory ovens were uncovered. It is little wonder that as the Allies closed in on Berlin, Hitler shot himself. Mussolini didn't have that "luxury." Sixteen days after the death of Roosevelt, the Italian dictator was captured by Italian partisans. He was executed and strung up by his heels at a gas station in Milan, as was his mistress.

Admiral Karl Doenitz succeeded Hitler. On May 7, 1945, in Reims, surrender terms were signed. V-E Day had arrived.

But there was still the Japanese Empire.

When Truman assumed the Presidency he learned for the first time about the Manhattan Project. When the first, and only, test of the atom bomb was successful on July 16, 1945, at Alamogordo, New Mexico, word was immediately sent to the President. He then had an awesome decision to make.

The battle for Okinawa had been bloody. It was a forerunner of what could be expected when the Allies invaded Japan proper. Estimates of American casualties ranged to almost a million; the enemy was expected to lose four or five times that number. It was believed by many the Japanese would capitulate once the devastation of the atom bomb was felt.

On July 25 Truman ordered the airforce to "deliver its first special bomb as soon as weather will permit visual bombing after 3 August, 1945." The following day an ultimatum was given to the Japanese Empire. It was told to surrender unconditionally or face "prompt and utter destruction." The refusal was expected.

The *Enola Gay*, a B-29 bomber, of the 509th Bomb Group, Twentieth Air Force stationed on Tinian, dropped the bomb on the industrial city of Hiroshima on the morning of August 6. About 70,000 died in the blast; a like number were injured. The city was completely wiped out.

There were, and will continue to be, those who claim the atom bomb should never have been dropped. But they aren't the ones whose lives were probably spared because it was. I was aboard the *U.S.S. LST 877* enroute to Okinawa when the bomb was dropped. When the news came in I was in the radio shack. When I told the crew what had happened, the cheers were loud and clear. They were as elated as I was.

Stalin, with vulture-like quickness, got into the fray on August 8. He wasn't about to be kept away from dividing the spoils of war. Only hours later *Bock's Car*, another B-29, tookoff from Tinian in the Marianas. It carried the last atom bomb manufactured. The target was Kokura, but clouds and smoke blotted out the target, so the bomb was dropped on the alternate target—Nagasaki.

The Japanese capitulated. Aboard the *U.S.S. Missouri* in Tokyo Bay General Douglas MacArthur presided over the formal signing of the surrender documents. World War II had come to a close.

AN IRON CURTAIN DESCENDS

LESS than a year after the conclusion of the war against the Nazis Winston Churchill spoke in Fulton, Missouri. "From Stettin in the Baltic to Trieste in the Adriatic, an iron curtain has descended across the continent. Behind that line lie all the capitals of the ancient states of central and eastern Europe," he told his audience. They are "subject, in one form or another, not only to Soviet influence but to a very high and increasing measure of control from Moscow."

Again Churchill was warning the free world of future disaster. Again the free world ignored him, or called him a "warmonger."

As the months went by it became increasingly clear to most people in the free world that Communism was dangerous. The Conference of Grand Masters took note of this. In 1939 it had adopted a "Declaration of Principles" which read:

> Freemasonry is a charitable, benevolent, educational and religious society. Its principles are proclaimed as widely as men will hear. Its only secrets are in its methods of recognition and of symbolic instruction.
>
> It is charitable in that it is not organized for profit and none of its income inures to the benefit of any individual, but all is devoted to the promotion of the welfare and happiness of mankind.
>
> It is benevolent in that it teaches and exemplifies altruism as a duty.
>
> It is educational in that it teaches by prescribed ceremonials a system of morality and brotherhood based upon the Sacred Law.
>
> It is religious in that it teaches monotheism; the Volume of the Sacred Law is open upon its altars whenever a

Lodge is in session, reverence for God is ever present in its ceremonial, and to its brethren are constantly addressed lessons of morality; yet it is not sectarian or theological.

It is a social organization only so far as it furnishes inducement that men may forgather in numbers, thereby providing more material for its primary work of education, of worship, and of charity.

Through the improvement and strengthening of the character of the individual man, Freemasonry seeks to improve the community. Thus it impresses upon its members the principles of personal righteousness and personal responsibility, enlightens them as to those things which make for human welfare, and inspires them with that feeling of charity, or goodwill, toward all mankind which will move them to translate principle and conviction into action.

To that end, it teaches and stands for the worship of God; truth and justice; fraternity and philanthropy; and enlightenment and orderly liberty, civil, religious and intellectual. It charges each of its members to be true and loyal to the government of the country to which he owes allegiance and to be obedient to the law of any state in which he may be.

It believes that the attainment of these objectives is best accomplished by laying a broad basis of principles upon which men of every race, country, sect and opinion may unite rather than by setting up a restricted platform upon which only those of certain races, creeds, and opinions can assemble.

Believing these things, this Grand Lodge affirms its continued adherence to that ancient and approved rule of Freemasonry which forbids the discussion in Masonic meetings of creeds, politics, or other topics likely to excite personal animosities.

It further affirms its conviction that it is not only contrary to the fundamental principles of Freemasonry, but dangerous to its unity, strength, usefulness and welfare, for Masonic Bodies to take action or attempt to exercise pressure or influence for or against any legislation, or in any way to attempt to procure the election or appointment of government officials, or to influence them, whether or not members of the Fraternity, in the performance of their official duties. The true Freemason will act in civil life according to his individual judgment and the dictates of his conscience.

In 1947 an addition to the above was proposed. It was adopted in 1948:

> Masonry abhors communism as being repugnant of its conception of the dignity of the individual personality, destructive of the basic rights which are the Divine Heritage of all men and inimical to the fundamental Masonic tenet of faith in God.

During the first meeting of the United Nations in 1946, Bernard Baruch of the United States proposed atomic bombs be eliminated. Andrei Gromyko of Russia offered a counter proposal that left the question dangling. He knew what the others didn't. Russia had successfully stolen the atomic secrets from the United States. This was dramatically illustrated in 1949. The Soviets exploded their first bomb. The race was on.

With the defeat of the Nazi regime the truth as to what Hitler had done to Freemasonry in Europe became known. To determine what American Freemasonry could do to help their counterparts overseas, a commission was sent to Europe. It was headed by RAY V. DENSLOW of Missouri. President Truman cleared the way for them to go.

Soon after the commission reported its findings to The Masonic Service Association, over $123,000 was raised from American Grand Lodges and sent to European Freemasons. About 25,000 pounds of CARE packages were paid for by the Fraternity and sent to ten European countries. Over $75,000 was sent to the Philippines for Masonic relief work.

In 1960, CARL HEMKE of the Grand Lodge of Austria reported the Masons in his country were able to work unmolested until 1938. "But after Hitler's invasion they were prohibited at once; their temple was confiscated, and many of their distinguished members were sent to prison. . . .Freemasonry went underground and there the Freemasons fought with the resistance forces against the National-Socialist tyranny."

The report from Berlin in 1960 was thought-provoking:

> Most people know about Berlin today, about the plight of a city divided in a brutally divided country. Far less is known about the Soviet-occupied zone which surrounds Berlin, about the regime which calls itself the "German Democratic Republic."

Berliners know the misery, oppression and despair which communists have caused by imposing an alien system on German territory with force and terror, assisted always by the Soviet occupation power. Many of our countrymen, seeking freedom from this system, have escaped to West Berlin. Many others have died under it. But over one million of our fellow Berliners—in the East sector of our city—and sixteen million other countrymen in the Soviet-occupied zone of Germany must live under tyranny today.

C.M.R. DAVIDSON of the Netherlands noted: "The Grand East of the Netherlands received a severe blow in 1940, because Hitler did us the honour to forbid Freemasonry first of all. All lodge buildings, possessions and funds were confiscated; the world-famous Masonic Kloss Library, a present from Prince Frederick, was taken away to Germany."

Many German Freemasons had gone underground when the Nazis gained control of their country. Thousands of them had been interred in concentration camps, or murdered. A few, throughout the holocaust, wore a little blue flower to show they were Masons. The Nazis never learned of this secret form of recognition. Years later the United Grand Lodge of Germany adopted the blue forget-me-not as an official insignia. In 1970, The Masonic Brotherhood of the Blue Forget-Me-Not was formed to honor Masonic writers and educators. Its symbolism honored those German Freemasons who remained true to the principles of the Craft.

Freemasonry's simplicity, its dignity, and its spirituality sustain me in all that I try to do, and permit me to forget the incredible pettiness of mind that we sometimes encounter, *sustaining and enabling me to join hands with my Brethren everywhere, to do something, if it be only a little, before the end of the day, to make a gentler, kinder, and wiser world in which to live.*

—Joseph Fort Newton, D.D.

The autobiography of JOSEPH FORT NEWTON, D.D., *River of Years*, was published in 1946. Newton had been an enthusiastic Freemason throughout his life. One of his many Masonic books, *The Builders*, remains as popular today as in 1914 when it was first published. From 1916-19 he had been the minister of The City Temple in London, England. He was asked to return many times in later years, but it wasn't until World War II that he returned to London to stay for a while. He arrived before the United States had entered the war.

"As I went to and fro over England," he wrote, "I discovered a new England, new, especially, in its attitude toward my country; a desire, for the first time, to know America and its people—none, absolutely none, of the nagging, irritating Anti-American feelings I had known during the first World War." He described the feelings of the people for the help they had received after the evacuation of Dunkirk. "Again and again, all over the country, men of the home guard, with tears in their eyes, were to show me those rifles."

Toward the close of his autobiography, Newton observed:

> To have looked upon such a pageant of stupendous events, moving swiftly to a focus in a single year, is not to have lived in vain. To have had a part, however tiny, in such an overturning of history, is an unforgettable honor. The conquest of the vilest tyranny ever contrived against mankind was complete and crushing; a federated evil, militant, arrogant, cunning, unscrupulous, was utterly beaten. But something more happened—one age ended and another age began, the meaning of which we cannot yet guess. The Atomic Bomb did more than punctuate a new period in history; it may have made modern man obsolete, his forts flimsy, his fleets useless, his whole civilization too precarious to be endured.

From May, 1944, the "Army and Navy Masonic Service Center," a monthly publication of The Masonic Service Association, carried items concerning hospital visitations by its Field Agents. It was the start of such programs. They continue. In 1946, General OMAR N. BRADLEY became Administrator of Veterans Affairs for the Veterans Administration. He made it clear to The Congress before he accepted the position that he would work "for the benefit of service men and not for the purpose of providing political pork for anyone."

Bradley became a member of West Point Lodge No. 877, New York, in 1923. He fought throughout both World Wars; was Army Chief of Staff, 1948-49; Chairman of the Joint Chiefs of Staff from 1949-53.

President Truman took note of the destitute in Europe. "I believe it must be the policy of the United States to support free peoples who are resisting attempted subjugation by armed minorities or by outside pressure," he declared. This became known as "The Truman Doctrine." Based on this doctrine came the European reconstruction program, and in many circles, "The Marshall Plan."

GEORGE MARSHALL, as Secretary of State, said of his plan: "Our policy is directed not against any country or doctrine but against hunger, poverty, desperation, and chaos. Its purpose should be the revival of a working economy in the world so as to permit the emergence of political and social conditions in which free institutions can exist." He backed his words with over twelve billion dollars from the taxpayers of America.

Russian aggression brought into being the North Atlantic Treaty Organization, called NATO. It consisted of the United States, Canada, and the countries of Western Europe. It would be backed by United States arms and money. Truman hoped it "would serve to prevent World War III."

Even so, Russia continued its aggression. It took over Czechoslovakia. Then its troops blockaded Berlin. Rather than risk the war Truman wanted to prevent, the United States and Great Britain commenced a gigantic airlift. Three hundred twenty-eight days later, May 12, 1949, *The New York Times* reported from Berlin: "Just as the morning sun rose over the jagged skyline of this broken but defiant city a Soviet zone locomotive chugged wearily into the British sector hauling the first train to reach Berlin from the West in 328 days. Arrival of the train completed the relief of the city from the iron vise of the Soviet blockade."

While hundreds of men braved the elements and untenable flying conditions to relieve the besieged Berliners, HARRY TRUMAN was fighting for election to the Presidency. His opponent was THOMAS E. DEWEY of New York. Dewey was a member of Kane Lodge No. 454 of New York City. In 1940 he had stated: "I believe that, if there were fifty million Masons in the United States instead of three million, there would be no fear of any invasion of foreign ideas contrary to the spirit of religious and personal freedom of America."

Truman was the underdog. HENRY A. WALLACE, running on the Progressive Party ticket, and J. STROM THURMOND of South Carolina, running on the States Right Democratic ticket, were expected to cut heavily into the Democratic vote. Wallace had served as Vice President from 1941-45. He became a member of Capital Lodge No. 110, Iowa, on October 4, 1927 and was Senior Deacon when he went to Washington to be Secretary of Agriculture. Thurmond had served with the 82nd Airborne Division and was Governor of South Carolina while he ran for the Presidency. He was a member of Concordia Lodge No. 50, South Carolina.

Truman surprised most of the political pundits. He won the close race. He was able to laughingly hold up a copy of the *Chicago Daily Tribue* which carried a banner headline— DEWEY DEFEATS TRUMAN. Even *Life* magazine carried a picture of Dewey—the next President!

As so many politicians do, Dean Anderson, who had succeeded Marshall as Secretary of State, made a fateful statement. He announced that Formosa and Korea were outside the perimeter the United States felt obliged to defend. That brought an explosion from the Communist North Korea. Its troops, supported by Russian-built tanks invaded South Korea on June 25, 1950.

Truman acted quickly. He requested a special session of the United Nations Security Council. At the same time he ordered General DOUGLAS MACARTHUR to speed up naval and air support for South Korea.

Surprisingly, the Security Council voted to condemn the North Korean aggression. It called on all member nations to support the decision. It was, and would remain, the only time the United Nations opposed anything connected with the Soviets. The only reason it accomplished this feat was because of the absence of the Russians. They had boycotted the United Nations because it had seated Nationalist China as a member. Never again would the Russians be absent.

The Korean conflict became the first "no-win" military action participated in by the United States. The fear of a nuclear war was prevalent.

As in every previous war, the United States forces took a whipping in the early days. By August they had toughened. General WALTON H. WALKER told his forces: "There will be no more retreating, withdrawal, or anything else you want to call it." There wasn't. But Walker was to die in Korea on December 23, 1950. At the request of his wife, Star of the East Lodge No. 640, Yokohama, Japan, conducted Masonic funeral services for him. He was a member of Belton Lodge No. 166, Texas.

Truman refused to let MacArthur do anything to antagonize Red China. But Communist China entered the fight anyway. General OMAR BRADLEY, speaking for the Joint Chiefs, believed MacArthur was endeavoring to fight "the wrong war, at the wrong place, at the wrong time, and with the wrong enemy."

MacArthur, in a letter he sent to the House Minority leader Joe Martin, claimed "There is no substitute for victory." The letter was released to the press. "In effect, what MacArthur was doing was to threaten the enemy with an ultimatum," Truman responded. "I could no longer tolerate his insubordination." He relieved MacArthur of his command on April 11, 1951. MacArthur came to the United States to receive a rousing hero's welcome. He later told a joint session of the Congress: "Old soldiers never die, they just fade away." Truman reached a low ebb in public opinion polls.

General HENRY H. VAUGHAN, who had fought in both World Wars, was the military aide to President Truman. While the White House was being renovated, Vaughan discovered a stone in the rubble with what appeared Masonic markings. He reported this to Truman. A search was started to determine if there were more. More than a hundred were discovered bearing "Mason's Marks." These had been built into the original White House which had been laid with Masonic ceremonies on October 13, 1792. Truman set aside forty-nine of the stones, one for each of the Grand Lodges. These were delivered during 1953.

Truman didn't choose to run for the Presidency in 1952. He endorsed Adlai E. Stevenson. He wasn't a Mason, but his grandfather by the same name was, and had been Vice President of the United States from 1893-97. Dwight D. Eisenhower was chosen by the Republicans. By an electoral vote of 442 to 89 Eisenhower became the first Republican to win the Presidency since 1928.

The Korean "police action" ended in 1953. There was no formal treaty, only an armed truce which still exists.

Stalin died on March 5, 1953. His twenty-nine year rule had reached an end.

One of the most sensational court cases in history came to an end on June 19, 1953. Julius and Ethel Rosenberg were executed in Sing Sing Prison. The President refused to intervene. "I can only say that, by immeasurably increasing the chances of atomic war, the Rosenbergs may have condemned to death tens of millions of innocent people all over the world," he stated. Appeal after appeal had been made, and continued up to the last moment to save the husband and wife who had been convicted of turning atomic secrets over to Russia. Actually, this case didn't die with the Rosenbergs. It would continue to be raised to the present day.

The Grand Lodge of Israel was constituted on October 20, 1953, by the Grand Lodge of Scotland. It had the support of the Grand Lodges of England and Ireland. Freemasonry had been started in the area by Frenchmen during the building of the Suez Canal and in 1902, Scottish Freemasonry entered the territory. Other lodges were formed over the years. Those in existence when the Grand Lodge was formed received new charters from it.

The Supreme Court, with a nine to zero decision, banned segregation in the schools on May 17, 1954. In 1957, during his second term, Eisenhower sent troops with fixed bayonets to Little Rock, Arkansas. There they met National Guardsmen, also with fixed bayonets. The regular Army troops prevailed. Central High School in Little Rock was integrated, fortunately with no bloodshed.

The greatest news, at least on the medical front, was the perfection of a vaccine by Dr. Jonas Salk. It would eliminate the dread crippler polio forever.

SIR WINSTON CHURCHILL resigned as Prime Minister of England on April 5, 1955. He refused the offer by the Queen of a dukedom. He said he would remain a member of the House of Commons. He had refused an earldom offered by King George at the conclusion of World War II.

Hungary endeavored to throw off the Soviet yolk in October, 1956. The puppet Communist regime in the country was in grave danger of being overthrown. The military might of Russia was sent to quell the Hungarian revolt in Budapest. The tanks and troops whipped the Hungarians. The free world stood by. The United Nations did nothing. The iron curtain became more rigid.

Once again Adlai Stevenson opposed Eisenhower for the Presidency. He was beaten more severly in 1956 than he had been in 1952. The electoral vote was 457 to 73. In Russia on July 4, 1957, three Stalin supporters, including Molotov, were ousted. Khruschev was tightening his control of the Soviets. On October 4 he managed to shock the United States. A Russian satellite was sent into space to orbit the globe at 18,000 miles per hour. The United States announced on July 29, 1955, it was going to send a satellite into space. Then the Soviets followed up this victory by sending a dog into space in November.

The space age had started.

Thirty-three

EYES IN THE SKY

ALASKA became the forty-ninth state to be admitted to the Union. It occurred on January 3, 1959. Its Masonic lodges would continue to hold allegiance to the Grand Lodge of Washington for another twenty years. Hawaii became the fiftieth star in the flag of the United States on August 21, 1959. Its Freemasons continue to come under the jurisdiction of the Grand Lodge of California. Its Royal Arch Chapters, with encouragement from the California Grand Chapter, formed a Grand Chapter for Hawaii on August 6, 1976.

All countries, without admitting it, had been using air surveillance. The United States was caught lying on May 5, 1960. A "U-2", high-flying reconnaissance plane, piloted by Francis Gary Powers, was shot down over the Soviet Union. President Eisenhower claimed it was simply a weather research plane. Khrushchev proved this was an outright lie, demanded an apology and punishment for those involved. Eisenhower apologized, but refused to punish anyone.

Because of the U-2 incident, the Russians had another excuse to extend its strained relations with the United States. Anti-American feelings were running high in Japan. Indochina became even more of a critical situation. Fidel Castro, the Russian puppet in Cuba, gained in power. The cold war had heated up. The United Nations, as always, was impotent.

These conditions, and more, became rallying points for the nominee of the Democratic Party during the election campaign of 1960. John F. Kennedy of Massachusetts opposed the Vice President of the United States, Richard M. Nixon. Kennedy selected the Texan powerhouse in the Senate, Lyndon B. Johnson, as his running mate. Kennedy won. But of sixty-eight million votes cast, his margin was only 119,000. And his election was tainted by reports of wide-spread voting irregularities in Illinois (nothing new) and in Texas.

On the diplomatic front, Kennedy's programs became a disaster. The first was the "Bay of Pigs" debacle. On April 18, 1961, Cuban exiles, with the approval of the United States, landed in Cuba. The President refused to give them air support. Within three days they were killed or captured.

Kennedy visited Vienna six weeks later to meet with Khrushchev. Nothing was accomplished. But on August 13, 1961, the Russian zone of Berlin began erecting a wall to keep its German occupants from defecting to the West. The free world did nothing to stop this atrocity.

The Soviet Union continued to test the resolve of the United States. It began installing ballistic missiles, capable of carrying nuclear war-heads, on its unsinkable launching site—Cuba. Kennedy called for a blockade on October 23, 1962. Russian ships turned back before there could be a confrontation. Khrushchev offered to remove the missiles. There was an important condition attached—the United States must promise not to invade Cuba! Kennedy agreed! The Monroe Doctrine was dead.

In an attempt to contain communism in Indochina, Kennedy sent sixteen thousand American "advisors" to assist South Vietnam in 1963. This would lead to one of the greatest tragedies ever suffered by the United States.

The Soviets won the race to put a man into space. On April 12, 1961, Yuri Gagarin successfully orbited the earth. Less than a month later, May 6, the United States sent Alan B. Shepard, Jr., 115 miles into space. The next space traveler was a Freemason named VIRGIL I. GRISSOM who made his fifteen minute flight on July 21, 1961. About two weeks later the Russians countered by having a man make sixteen orbits in 25 hours 18 minutes.

An historic day for the United States took place on February 20, 1962. JOHN H. GLENN, JR., became the first American to orbit the earth. His almost five hour flight into space marked the beginning of the real space age for America.

In 1964 Glenn petitioned Concord Lodge No. 688 in Ohio for the degrees in Freemasonry. He was elected, but for varying reasons it would be fourteen years before he would become a Mason. It took place in one day, August 19, 1978, when the Grand Lodge of Ohio met in a special session. The Grand Lodge officers, headed by Grand Master JERRY C. RASOR, conferred each of the three degrees on him. He then became a full-fledged member of Concord Lodge.

The black civil rights movement, under Martin Luther King, became widespread in the early '60s. Gradually, segregation, which should have never existed, was wiped out. King would become, and remain, a controversial figure, loved by many, hated by a few.

Pope John XXIII, the head of the Roman Catholic Church for over four years, died on June 3, 1963, at the age of 81. He had been loved by Catholics and members of other religions alike. On the 21st, Paul VI was elected by the College of Cardinals. He would reign until 1978 when John Paul I would take over. He died thirty-four days later. On October 16, 1978, the present Pope, John Paul II, a Pole, was elected. Under his reign, in 1983, the long-standing Catholic opposition to Freemasonry would end. No longer would a Catholic be subject to excommunication from the Church for membership in a Masonic lodge.

Tragedy struck the country on November 22, 1963. While riding in a motorcade in Dallas, Texas, the President of the United States, John Fitzgerald Kennedy, was shot in the head by a sniper. Millions viewed the dasterdly act on television. Two days later millions more (including me) watched the accused assassin, Lee Harvey Oswald, shot and killed by Jack Ruby.

With the President's body on *Air Force One*, and his widow, Jacqueline still in blood stained clothing standing beside him, Lyndon B. Johnson took the Presidential oath.

Johnson had received the Entered Apprentice Degree in Johnson City Lodge No. 561, Texas, on October 30, 1937. Reasons for him going no farther are unclear. Until the 1850s becoming an Entered Apprentice made a man a full member of the lodge conferring the degree. During the 1850s all Grand Lodges adopted laws making the Master Mason (or Third) degree the criteria for a man to be considered a Freemason. Before then, all Masonic business was conducted in the First Degree (and still is in some foreign countries). With the adoption of the new law, business can be considered only in a Master Mason Lodge.

One of Johnson's first acts was to order the Federal Bureau of Investigation to check every aspect of the assassination. The FBI was headed by J. EDGAR HOOVER, who had become a member of Federal Lodge No. 1, District of Columbia, on November 9, 1920. He had taken over a corrupt law enforcement agency in 1924 and turned it into a highly respected bureau. But the public wanted more answers concerning the murder of the President than any agency could provide. So, on January 29, 1963, Johnson issued an executive order creating a special commission. It would take the name of the man chosen to head it, Chief Justice EARL WARREN.

Warren, a Past Grand Master of Masons in California, was joined on the Commission by two other known Freemasons. They were Senator RICHARD B. RUSSELL, a member of Winder Lodge No. 33, Georgia, and Representative GERALD R. FORD of Michigan. John Sherman Cooper, Hale Boggs, Allen W. Dulles, and John J. McCloy made up the balance of the Commission.

The Commission learned that Oswald had earned the rating of "sharp shooter" while in the United States Marine Corps. After he left the corps in 1959, he traveled to Moscow, Russia. There he remained until June, 1962, when he returned to the United States with his Russian-born wife. On April 10, 1963, he attempted to kill General Edwin A. Walker. On September 27, Oswald arrived in Mexico City and attempted to obtain permission to visit Cuba. It was refused. On October 22 he entered the

Texas School Book Depository where he had started work on October 16. He carried "a long bulky package, made out of wrapping paper and tape" into the building. He claimed he was carrying curtain rods.

Oswald's wife, along with a friend, followed the Presidential procession via television. They were shocked when they learned the President had been shot.

The Commission concluded: "The shots which killed President Kennedy and wounded Governor John Connally were fired from the sixth floor window at the southwest corner of the Texas School Book Depository." "The weight of the evidence indicates that there were three shots fired." "The shots which killed President Kennedy and wounded Governor Connally were fired by Lee Harvey Oswald." The report was exhaustive. The investigation had been long. The Commission's conclusion that no conspiracy existed would be disputed by some for years. But there could be no question about the Commission's conclusion that Jack Ruby killed Oswald two days later. Millions witnessed the act via television. Exactly why will probably never be learned.

Johnson's experience in dealing with The Congress became evident during his early days in the Presidency. In the name of Kennedy he was able to push through legislation that had been defeated year after year. His "Great Society" programs would be praised and also condemned in 1964 when they were passed, and for the next two decades.

As Vice President, Johnson had advised Kennedy not to get involved with "advisors" in Vietnam. Kennedy did. As the Presidentail candidate in 1964 Johnson promised: "We are not about to send American boys nine or ten thousand miles away from home to do what Asian boys ought to be doing." He was for peace. He painted the Republican candidate, Senator BARRY GOLDWATER of Arizona as a "warmonger"—a man who wouldn't hesitate to drop nuclear bombs on innocent people.

Patrick Anderson, in his *The Presidents' Men*, reveals the work of Bill D. Moyers in the election campaign through direction of the most viscious media attack in political history. Johnson and Moyers were of one mind—not only to defeat

Goldwater but to destroy him and all he stood for. Goldwater was a strong voice in opposition to much of the Great Society legislative program so dear to the heart of Johnson. Moyers wanted as he put it, "to hang the noose of nuclear irresponsiblity around Goldwater's neck."

Moyers instructed Doyle Dane to come up with something which would "knock Goldwater off balance." Doyle produced what came to be known as "The Daisy Girl," a one minute TV picture of a small blond child picking petals from a daisy when suddenly a giant mushroom-shaped nuclear cloud engulfed the child.

The attacks continued. "The TV campaign achieved its goal," wrote Anderson. Goldwater was put on the defensive. "Moyers savored every minute of the campaign against Goldwater." He and Johnson had destroyed their Republican adversary—for a time at least.

Goldwater, a member of Arizona Lodge No. 2, was soundly defeated in the Presidential election.

An incident occurred on August 2, 1964, in the Gulf of Tonkin that brought the United States into the Vietnam conflict in force. Three North Vietnam torpedo boats attacked the *U.S.S. Maddox.* They were driven off with no damage being inflicted. Two days later the *Maddox* and her sister ship the *Turner* were attacked. Again there was no damage. But Johnon ordered air strikes against support facilities in North Vietnam.

The President then asked The Congress for approval "to promote the maintenance of international peace and security in Southeast Asia." He got it. The Senate approved his request 88 to 2; the House, 416 to 0. The longest war in American history was begun.

There were about 23,000 military advisors in Vietnam in 1964. Johnson sent over 160,000 more in 1965. The American strength was increased by 200,000 in 1966. By 1968 there were a half a million Americans fighting a no-win war against the communist North Vietnam. The President's popularity plummeted.

The Russian-American space race was being anxiously watched by millions throughout the world. In 1962 two Russians had spent 94 and 70 hours in space. The United States countered by sending WALTER M. SCHIRRA, JR., a Freemason, into space for nine hours. L. GORDON COOPER, JR., another Freemason, spent 34 hours orbiting the earth on May 15, 16, 1963. From then until March, 1965, three more Russian craft were sent into space.

Frank Borman and James A. Lovell, Jr., were sent into space on December 4, 1965. On the 15th, Schirra and THOMAS P. STAFFORD, also a Freemason, were sent on a special mission. The two Gemini space craft were to rendezvous. One hundred eighty-five miles up, they completed their mission successfully.

American successes continued in 1966. Missions were successfully completed by six teams of astronauts. Of these, EDWIN E. ALDRIN, JR., was a Freemason.

A catastrophic fire struck at Cape Kennedy, Florida, on January 27, 1967. Three astronauts, Edward H. White, Roger B. Chafee, and VIRGIL I. GRISSOM, the latter a member of Mitchell Lodge No. 228, Indiana, were killed. They have been the only ones to sacrifice their lives in the American effort to conquer outer space.

Money was poured into the battle against poverty; yet the poor increased in numbers. Billions of dollars were legislated to help the elderly; yet the elderly appeared to be no better off than before. Civil Rights bills were passed and enforced; but there were increased riots, destroyed property and more bloodshed, than at any other time in American history. Millions of dollars went into health care; yet the cost of health care began to skyrocket and has continued its upward spiral.

The year 1968 became one of the most disastrous years in the history of the country. On January 23 the *U.S.S. Pueblo*, an intelligence gathering ship, operating off North Korea was captured by the communists. Its crew was imprisoned in North Korea and were not freed until the end of the year. On April 4 Martin Luther King was killed by a sniper. The worst riots ever followed. Rioters roamed the streets breaking windows, looting, burning, throwing "Molotov cocktails" during three days of mayhem. *The New York Times* reported in bold headlines on the 6th: "Army troops in Capital as Negroes Riot; Guard sent into Chicago, Detroit, Boston; Johnson asks a Joint Session of Congress." The nation's capital became a battle-ground. Thousands of troops surrounded government buildings. Soldiers manned every intersection. The White House was ringed by federal troops. Machine guns were mounted on the steps of the President's home. The unchecked violence reached into hundreds of cities. The minutes of a Royal Arch Chapter recorded: "The Constitution of the United States died tonight. Because Anarchy was permitted to run wild, no convocation of this Chapter could be held tonight."

The terror continued. Robert F. Kennedy, the brother of the late President, was assassinated in Los Angeles, California, on June 6. In Miami Beach the Republican Convention was mar-red by violence. Three blacks were killed in a gun fight with police. The Republican candidate, Richard M. Nixon, vowed: "The wave of crime is not going to be the wave of the future in the United States." The Democratic Convention in Chicago found more violence. National guardsmen and the police fought off mobs of protestors. Hubert Humphrey won the nomination. Johnson, his war policies denounced, had taken himself out of the race.

Richard Nixon won the Presidential election by a slim margin.

Czechoslovakia, under the leadership of Alexander Dubcek, had attempted to gain some freedom under communist rule. It was almost successful. Then Russian tanks and troops took over. The peaceful Czech revolt was quickly squashed.

The year 1968 did end on an upbeat note. Borman, Anders, and Lovell, three American astronauts, gave the United States an excellent Christmas present. They circled the moon on Christmas eve. Via television millions on earth followed their voyage. Each of them took turns reading: "In the beginning,

God created the heaven and the earth. And the earth was without form and void; and darkness rested upon the face of the deep…" Colonel Borman signed off: "Goodby, good night. Merry Christmas. God bless all of you, all of you on the good earth."

The greatest gift of all came on July 20, 1969. "The Eagle has landed!" thrilled uncountable millions of people on earth. Neil A. Armstrong and EDWIN E. ALDRIN, JR., a Freemason, became the first human beings to step foot on the moon. The Americans had beaten the Russians. They had, in fact, accomplished something the Soviets have yet to achieve.

The turbulent decade of the 60s came to an end with Americans still fighting in Vietnam the most unpopular war ever engaged in by the United States. It had been a bitter decade. Its only triumphs had appeared in the space program. This had been successful. Satellites were circling the globe. Both of the super powers now had eyes in the sky around the clock.

Thirty-four

CRISIS

THE fighting in Vietnam continued to be carried "in living color" into the living rooms of the homes in the United States. The most televised war in history gave the people a first-hand account of the hells of war. At least, they were getting an account the reporters wanted them to get. Those who cared to learn had long ago discovered the TV reporters could be completely selective in what the masses could see.

The cameras reported only from one side. Absolutely nothing was released by the communists not first thoroughly censored. This was true in every Soviet-block country. If the Russians hadn't known, they soon learned about the power of television. Riots and violent anti-war demonstrations in America proved invaluable instructors.

President Nixon ordered troops to invade Cambodia in an attempt to wipe out the Viet Cong military storehouses. He had been advised the enemy was using border areas of the neutral country as sanctuaries from which to attack American troops. This was considered an untenable situation, one to be eliminated.

Across the country cries were heard. The war was being widened the opponents claimed. Demonstrations again became wide-spread. One took place at Kent State University in Ohio that would remain in the news for years. National guardsmen fired into a group of demonstrators. Four students were killed. At Jackson State College in Mississippi police killed two students.

The space program of the United States that had been so successful it had been taken for granted ran into problems. The

moon bound Apollo 13 suffered a massive power failure on
April 13, 1970. The three member crew, John Swigert, Fred
Haise and James Lovell, was in danger of losing power and oxygen. Mission control sent the craft looping the moon on the
14th to fire its engines in an attempt to set it on an accurate
course for earth. It worked. Using power and oxygen from the
lunar module the space craft landed in the Pacific. The triumphant crew received a warm-hearted reception.

The next trip to the moon was successful in February, 1971.
So were the others in the program. The American space program had accomplished what the Russians had promised to do
but didn't.

Lieutenant William L. Calley, Jr., was convicted by a court-
martial on March 29, 1971, of "murdering" 22 Vietnamese in
1968. His "crime" took place during what was called the "My
Lai massacre." A federal court would overturn the conviction
and free Calley in 1974. His life sentence was reinstated by an
appeals court in 1975. Notably, no enemy officer was ever tried
for atrocities committed by the communists.

The Supreme Court, in a decision announced on April 20,
upheld the principle of "busing" school children to achieve
desegregation.   The opponents of the war continued to
demonstrate. Between May 2 and 5 more than thirteen thousand were arrested in the District of Columbia.

The twenty-sixth amendment to the Constitution was proclaimed ratified on July 5, 1971. All citizens eighteen years of
age or older could not be denied the right to vote.

President Nixon announced on July 15 he would take "a
journey for peace." He planned on visiting the People's
Republic of China. Later he said he would also visit the Soviet
Union. This decision must have led to an emotion-packed session of the General Assembly of the United Nations on October
26. It threw out the National Chinese government and seated
the Red Chinese. To its credit, the United States fought to keep
the Nationalists in.

Nixon arrived in Peking on February 21, 1972. The historical
visit was concluded with both governments pledging to work
toward "a normalization of relations." On May 22 he arrived in

Moscow to become the first President of the United States to ever visit Russia. An arms pact was agreed to before the journey ended. But it never became a reality.

Although American troops were being reduced in South Vietnam, the fighting became heated. During 1968 agreements were concluded between both sides that caused the Americans to stop bombing the North. The day after Christmas bombing was resumed. The United States claimed the 1968 agreements had been violated by the Viet Cong.

The bombing was stopped in less than a week. But on March 30, 1972 the North Vietnamese forces launched the biggest attacks across the demilitarized zone in years. Bombing of Hanoi and Haiphong was resumed on April 15. The enemy ports were ordered mined on May 9.

The country was stunned in 1972 by the attempted assassination of GEORGE C. WALLACE, Governor of Alabama, who was campaigning as a Democrat for the Presidential nomination. He was finding broad support on his issues of forced busing of school children and the disintegration of law and order. He won the Florida primary by a wide margin. He came in second in Wisconsin, and won in Maryland and Michigan. But before the last two results were in he had been shot while campaigning in Maryland. The wounds he suffered on May 15, 1972, would leave him paralyzed from the waist down.

Wallace had served as Grand Orator of the Grand Lodge of Alabama in 1961 while he was Governor-elect. Joseph Abram Jackson, author of *Masonry in Alabama*, considered Wallace among the best. Wallace continued in politics in Alabama, and in 1982 he was reelected Governor.

George S. McGovern, who campaigned strongly against the war, was soundly whipped by Richard Nixon for the Presidency. McGovern carried only Massachusetts and the District of Columbia. But what Nixon's enemies couldn't do to him in the polls, they did through an episode to be called "Watergate."

Peace negotiations that had appeared promising before the election broke down. Nixon wrote in his *Memoirs:* "I was

strongly opposed to breaking off the talks and resuming the
bombing unless it was absolutely necessary to compel the enemy
to negotiate." The threat of bombing made "the North Vietnamese immediately more concilliatory." Nixon wrote of his
December 14 decision: "The order to renew bombing the week
before Christmas was the most difficult decision I made during
the entire war; at the same time, however, it was also one of the
most clear-cut and necessary ones."

In his diary for December 22, Nixon took note of his media
detractors: "The election was a terrible blow to them and this is
their first opportunity to recover from the election and to strike
back." The bombing was halted for Christmas day, but Nixon
ordered it resumed more intensly on the 26th. On the 28th
Hanoi offered to go back to the negotiating table.

HARRY S. TRUMAN died on December 26, 1972. Nixon wrote:
"On December 27 Pat and I flew there to pay our respects to
him and to call on Mrs. Truman." The "there" was the Truman
Library in Independence, Missouri, where the former President's body lay in state.

Early in 1973 Henry Kissinger brought Nixon news that the
enemy and the United States had finally reached an agreement.
"On January 15 at ten o'clock in the morning all bombing and
mining of North Vietnam were stopped for an indefinite
period," Nixon wrote. On the 22nd Lyndon Johnson died. Nixon announced on the 23rd "that a settlement had been reached
in Paris and that a Vietnam cease-fire would begin on January
27. That evening he wrote:

> Dear Lady Bird,
> I only wish Lyndon could have lived to hear my an-
> nouncement of the Vietnam peace settlement tonight.
> I know what abuse he took—particularly from members
> of his own party—in standing firm for peace with honor.
> Now that we have such a settlement, we shall do
> everything we can to make it last so that he and other
> brave men who sacrificed their lives for this cause will not
> have died in vain.

Throughout the final days of the discussions for a cease-fire,
the campaign for the Presidency, and an attempt to reduce the

size of government, Nixon was haunted by an unlocked door at the Watergate apartment complex, close to the White House. There, on the night of June 17, 1972, a guard discovered a door whose lock was held back by a piece of tape. Police with pistols drawn found five burglars in the headquarters of the Democratic National Committee.

SAMUEL J. ERVIN, JR., a member of Catawba Lodge No. 17 of North Carolina, and a Senator from that state, was chosen to head the investigating committee for 1972 campaign practices. This became known as the "Watergate" committee. Nixon noted in his diary:

> An indication of the fact that we are going to have a very hard four years is Mansfield's announcement that he wants Ervin's committee to investigate Watergate. Mansfield is going to be deeply and bitterly partisan without question. The Democrats actually are starting early for their run for the White House.

The Democrats, the media, and the "liberal" element in the country who couldn't defeat Nixon at the polls, whipped him soundly in the newspapers and television newscasts.

With the end of American involvement in Vietnam, many of the men being held as prisoners-of-war were released. The first of them arrived at Clark Air Force Base in the Philippines on February 12, 1973. The historic moment was broadcast via television and will never be forgotten.

How many Freemasons served in Vietnam will never be known. The number who died or were captured cannot be determined. But of the prisoners of war who returned there were several known Masons. Among them was Captain MELVIN POLLACK, a member of Hope Lodge No. 244, New York City. He had been shot down after 78 combat missions in 1966. He spent almost six years in the "Hanoi Hilton" prison.

Major PAUL J. MONTAGUE, a United States Marine, a member of Anthony Lodge No. 200, Kansas, was a prisoner of war for five years and two weeks. Lieutenant Colonel DEWEY W. WADDALL, a member of Bremen Lodge No. 456, Georgia, was a prisoner in Hanoi for six years. He had been made a

Master Mason on October 23, 1956. On May 12, 1973, he was awarded a Life Membership scroll by Bremen Lodge.

Colonel JAMES E. BEAN of Duvall Lodge No. 6, Kentucky, was shot down on January 3, 1968, near Hanoi. He was held prisoner for more than five years.

Major JERRY SINGLETON said "the first thing he wanted to do after returning" to the United States from being a prisoner of war was to become a Mason. On June 24, 1974, he became a Master Mason in A. C. Garrett Lodge, Texas. Also becoming a Master Mason after his return was Lieutenant Colonel LEO K. THORSNESS. He became a member of Unity Lodge No. 130, South Dakota, on September 9, 1973.

Freemasonry didn't forget the men who weren't Masons upon their return. Many were honored in several ways. Among them were Lt. Commander Michael Christian and Commander Eugene Barker McDaniel. They were presented special Grand Lodge of Virginia certificates.

On top of the Watergate affair, another bomb was dropped. The Vice President, Spiro T. Agnew, was accused of "conspiracy, extortion, bribery, and tax fraud" while Governor of Maryland. Agnew protested he was innocent. As the pressure continued to build, he decided to request an impeachment proceeding. The Speaker of the House refused the request. Agnew determined to fight.

And another kind of fighting started. On Saturday, October 6, 1973, Yom Kippur, Syria attacked Israel from the north; Egypt from the south. The CIA and Israelis intelligence had been caught completely by surprise. The Arabs pushed the troops of Golda Meir into the Sinai. It became clear on the fourth day of the war that United States arms would be needed quickly if the Israelis were to survive. Nixon ordered them to be sent immediately. They weren't. The Department of Defense threw up a series of bottlenecks. This was not so with the Russians. Their airlift to Syria and Egypt had reached massive proportions.

On the same day, October 10, Agnew gave Nixon his resignation. The next day he pleaded "nolo contendre" in a Baltimore court to one count of failing to report income for tax purposes. He was sentenced to three years probation and fined $10,000.

On October 12 GERALD R. FORD was informed he was Nixon's choice for Vice President. The nation was informed via television at 9 p.m.

Ford was, and is, a member of Malta Lodge No. 465, Grand Rapids, Michigan. On December 6 he was sworn in as Vice President of the United States.

The success of the American airlift when it finally started, and military might of Israel proved too much for Syria, Egypt, and their Russian masters. A cease-fire proposal was submitted to the United Nations on October 18. Terms for stopping the war were agreed to in Moscow by the Russians and the United States—two "non-belligerents"! The fighting was supposed to stop on the 22nd, but it was the 24th before the shooting ceased.

The "shooting" at Nixon continued. Watergate wouldn't go away. Nixon wrote: "Survival matters most in politics. Washington is ruled by Darwinian forces, and if you are in serious political trouble, you cannot expect generosity or magnanimity for long." In June, 1974, it became evident the vote in the House was going to be for impeachment, even before a witness was heard. On July 27 Nixon learned he was the first President "in 106 years to be recommended for impeachment." He decided "the country simply could not afford to have a crippled President for six months." On Thursday, August 1, 1974 he decided to resign. He sent Alexander Haig to inform Ford he should be prepared to take over.

Thirty-Five

THE "HEALING" YEARS

"TRUST in the Lord with all thine heart, and lean not unto thine own understanding. In all thy ways acknowledge Him, and He shall direct thy paths," the Vice President prayed on August 1, 1974. Ford had learned earlier in the day from General Alexander Haig that the President might resign. As he lay in bed that evening he recalled the prayer from Proverbs he had learned fifty years earlier.

GERALD R. FORD, in his autobiography, *A Time To Heal*, described an emotional cabinet meeting held on the 6th. During this meeting Ford informed the President: "I wish to emphasize that had I known what has been disclosed in reference to Watergate in the last twenty-four hours, I would not have made a number of statements I made either as Minority Leader or as Vice President. I came to a decision yesterday and you may be aware that I informed the press that because of commitments to Congress and the public, I'll have no further comment on the issue because I'm a party in interest. I'm sure there will be impeachment in the House. I can't predict the Senate outcome. I will make no comment concerning this."

During a luncheon with members of the GOP Senate Policy Committee Ford heard many statements made. Among these was one by BARRY GOLDWATER, the Mason from Arizona: "I've been defending Richard Nixon for years. While he may be right legally—and on that ground I've been one of his strongest backers—the situation now is totally out of hand. We can't support this any longer. We can be lied to only so many times. The best thing he can do for the country is to get the hell out of the White House, and get out this afternoon."

Nixon didn't that afternoon, but two days later Ford received another call from Haig: "The President wants to see you." Ten minutes later the Vice President was in the Oval Office. The President wasted no time. "I have made the decision to resign," he stated. Then they discussed many of the problems facing the country.

While speaking of the economic conditions in the country, Nixon offered a piece of advice. He said "his own decision to impose wage and price controls in 1971...had been more harmful than helpful." Ford wrote: "I told him that he didn't have to worry about that. I'd lived through wage and price controls during the Korean War and again in 1971, and I was convinced they didn't work."

At nine o'clock that evening, August 8, 1974, the President told a nation-wide television and radio audience: "I shall resign the Presidency, effective at noon tomorrow."

Early the following morning Richard M. Nixon bid his staff and his Cabinet goodbye. "Always remember, others may hate you, but those who hate you don't win, unless you hate them, and then you destroy yourself," was some of the advice he left with them. Shortly before ten o'clock the Nixons and Fords walked along a red carpet toward the olive-drab helicopter, *Army One*, waiting on the White House lawn. Nixon boarded it and waved farewell.

The media that hated Nixon, and the radical liberal element in the country had accomplished what they couldn't in a free election. They helped to destroy Richard Nixon.

Gerald and Betty Ford walked into the East Room of the White House shortly before noon. Chief Justice Warren Burger, who the day before had been in the Netherlands, administered the oath of office. GERALD R. FORD, the Freemason from Michigan, became President of the United States.

The new President had been born on July 14, 1913, and christened Leslie L. King, Jr. His mother, Dorothy Gardner King and his father agreed two years later to get a divorce. She later married Gerald Rudolf Ford, who adopted her son and named him after himself. Of his stepfather, Ford wrote: "He did what he could to help others in need. He was a vestryman in church, a devoted Mason, a Shriner, and active Elk, and a strong supporter of the Boy Scouts."

The Representative holding the seat from the Fifth District in Michigan was an isolationist. Ford had learned during World War II that a strong America was necessary to discourage would-be enemies, and in 1948 Ford decided to run for a seat in the House of Representatives. Just before the election, on October 15, 1948, he married Betty Warren.

He was elected on November 2. Among the men in the House who impressed him was Richard Nixon, the man who would be responsible for Ford becoming the thirty-eighth President of the United States. Ford was also the first man chosen Vice President (when Agnew resigned that office) under the provisions of the 25th Amendment to the Constitution of the United States.

Ford selected Nelson Rockefeller to be Vice President. And it wasn't long before he changed his views about politicians. "When I was in The Congress myself, I thought it fulfilled its constitutional obligations in a very responsible way," he wrote, "but after I became President, my perspective changed. It seemed to me that Congress was beginning to disintegrate as an organized legislative body. It wasn't answering the nation's challenge domestically because it was too fragmented. It responded too often to single-issue special interest groups and it therefore wound up dealing with minutiae instead of attacking serious problems in a coherent way. Moreover, Congress was determined to get its oar deeply into the conduct of foreign affairs. This not only undermined the Chief Executive's ability to act, it eroded the separation of powers concept in the Constitution."

The "guns and butter" policies of Johnson in the sixties had caught up with the economy. Ford inherited a twelve percent rate of inflation. Wholesale prices were running at a rate of increase of more than twenty percent a year. The trade deficit was increasing; productivity was declining. And as Nixon had pointed out, his wage and price controls had helped contribute to the problem.

What Ford planned on doing about the economy or world affairs didn't interest the media during his first press conference. It wanted to know what he was going to do about Nixon. It was clear the question of Nixon was going to have to be cleared up before the President could conduct the affairs of government.

Ford wrote about the reasoning he did:

> I was very sure of what would happen if I let the charges against Nixon run their legal course. Months were sure to elapse between an indictment and trial. The entire process would no doubt require years: a minimum of two, a maximum of six. And Nixon would not spend time quietly in San Clemente. He would be fighting for his freedom, taking his cause to the people, and his constant struggle would have dominated the news. The story would overshadow everything else. No other issue could compete with the drama of a former President trying to stay out of jail. It would be virtually impossible for me to direct public attention to anything else. Passions on both sides would be aroused. A period of such prolonged vituperation and recrimination would be disastrous for the nation. America needed recovery, not revenge. The hate had to be drained and the healing begun.

Sunday morning, September 8, 1974, at eleven o'clock, President Ford told a nation-wide television audience that he did "grant a full, free and absolute pardon unto Richard Nixon for all offenses against the United States which he, Richard Nixon, has committed or may have committed or taken part in during the period from January 20, 1969, through August 9, 1974."

Ford was surprised at "the vehemence of the hostile reaction" to his decision. "Nixon's critics apparantly wanted to see him drawn and quartered publicly," Ford wrote. "They wanted a body, some broken bones or at least some blood on the floor, and their mood was mean." It was a situation that would continue, at least until 1983.

In an endeavor to counter the hue and cry of the Nixon pardon, Ford worked out a program of clemency for the Vietnam draft-doggers, those men who had skipped to Canada to avoid serving in the armed forces. Even deserters were to find their situation eased.

The "Watergate" events wouldn't go away. Nixon's top aides, H. R. Haldeman and John D. Ehrlichman, along with former Attorney General John N. Mitchell and former Assistant Attorney General Robert C. Mardian were found quilty on January 1, 1975.

In referring to the whole affair, Victor Lasky in *It Didn't Start With Watergate* asked: "But complicity in what? Precisely what is Nixon accused of doing, if he actually did it, that his predecessors didn't do many times over? The break-in and wiretapping at the Watergate? Just how different was that from the bugging of Barry Goldwater's apartment during the 1964 presidential campaign?"

The media's hostility to Nixon blew "Watergate" into hysterical magnitude. As Lasky wrote: "The aim of these partisans in nonpartisan clothing was to win the 1972 election." Past Democratic questionable acts of equal, if not greater, importance were given scant attention by commentators and the press. Jerome R. Waldie noted that the press "disliked Nixon intensely," and he doubted whether the President would have been forced out of office "if the press had not desired it."

Lasky proves many more serious events were condoned by Presidents and political parties over the years than the breaking into the Democratic headquarters at the Watergate complex.

To head off another potential "Watergate," President Ford ordered an investigation of the Central Intelligence Agency. Within this agency, as in all governmental agencies, there were and are many Freemasons. *The New York Times* accused the CIA of harassing American citizens. This intelligence gathering agency was scrutinized and made ineffectual for the next several years.

In 1973 the Arab oil producing nations had established an oil embargo. Large oil reserves had been discovered in Alaska in 1967. A pipe line to bring this oil to the other states was advocated. The environmentalists were concerned about the safety of caribou and other animals in Alaska. The welfare of people appeared to mean less to them. After a long legal fight a pipe line was finally started on March 9, 1975. There has never been a report of harm to any wildlife, but the benefits to the people of the U.S. have been enormous.

The South Vietnamese, receiving but little help from the United States, fell apart. The Viet Cong, having broken every one of the Paris Peace Accords, rapidly gained control of the South. American personnel, still there, along with as many Vietnamese refugees as possible, were evacuated from Da Nang on March 26, 1975. Conditions continued to worsen, and on April 17 Americans were evacuated from Phnom Penh, Cambodia. And "the noose tightened around Saigon."

After a harrowing period, the Americans were evacuated from Saigon on April 29, 1975. With them were 120,000 Vietnamese who had worked with or fought with American forces. The President asked The Congress for money to aid the refugees. Congress refused! It took pressure from Ford, several Governors, and George Meany, President of the AFL-CIO to change the mind of the congressional politicians. Transportation and camps were provided for the refugees. The involvement of the United States had ended. The repercussions would last for years.

On the morning of May 12, 1975 President Ford was informed the S. S. *Mayaguez* an American merchant vessel had been seized in international waters off the coast of Cambodia. The ship had been intercepted and fired upon by Communist gunboats. Troops had boarded her and taken her thirty-nine member crew captive. The President was determined to regain the ship and its crew.

The *U. S. S. Coral Sea*, an aircraft carrier was ordererd to speed toward the Cambodian coast. Aircraft from the Philippines were ordered to keep the *Mayaguez* in view. The Chinese representative in the United States refused to carry a protest message to the Cambodians. Following Presidential orders, American fighter pilots kept the ship under surveillance. It was found anchored in Koh Tang harbor. The fighters were ordered to keep any Cambodian vessels away from the ship. They were to be turned back or be sunk.

A battalion landing team of eleven hundred Marines was ordered airlifted from Okinawa to Thailand. The aircraft carrier *Hancock* was ordered to steam from the Philippines. Two marine platoons were ordered to leave the Philippines by air.

With the planes of the *Coral Sea* within striking distance, and the destroyer escort *Holt* close by, the President ordered the Marines to land on the island of Koh Tang. They ran into heavier resistance than expected, but pushed the Cambodians back. They didn't find the crew. Neither did the *Holt* when it went along side the *Mayaquez*. The planes from the *Coral Sea* were ordered to strike. They made four bombing runs in all.

The crew was missing. But at eleven P.M. Washington time the Pentagon telephoned the President. The pilot of a reconnaissance plane had found a fishing vessel fleeing toward Koh Tang. He saw caucasians waving white flags. The *U. S. S. Wilson* intercepted the fishing vessel. The crew of the *Mayaguez* was saved!

A triumphant President Ford went before television cameras and radio microphones to inform the nation the United States was no longer a sleeping giant. The press wasn't impressed. Nor was the Democratic leadership in The Congress. The President had prevented another *Pueblo* debacle, yet his critics were vehement.

The *U. S. S. Pueblo* had also been captured in international waters off North Korea on January 23, 1966 during Johnson's administration. No effort, other than protests, was made by the United States politicians to save the ship and the crew. For eleven months the crew was subjected to inhuman indignities, constant threats of facing firing squads, horrible beatings, poor or no medical treatment, and bare subsistence food.

The inaction of the Executive didn't set well with several Congressmen and Senators. Among them was EVERETT M. DIRKSEN, a member of Pekin Lodge No. 29, Illinois. "A clammy spirit of fear and timidity surrounds our efforts to regain our ship and her crew," he told the press.

Another Senator, J. STROM THURMOND, a member of Concordia Lodge No. 50, South Carolina, told the press on

February 5, 1968: "To send poorly armed surface reconnaissance ships into dangerous waters without air cover, naval escort, or emergency plans was a serious error in judgement."

The horror ended for the crew of the *Pueblo* just before Christmas. They were released to the American forces in South Korea. There they were rushed through hospitalization so they could leave on Christmas eve, making it still Christmas eve because of the International Date Line when they joined their families in San Diego, California.

The *Pueblo* "coverup" in high places over the responsibilities involved during the next several months made "Watergate" look like a minor project. But the media didn't persecute the Executive Branch in this case.

President Ford learned the *Mayaguez* rescue had been bungled. Not all the bombing waves he had ordered had been carried out. He never was satisfied with the explanations he received from the Pentagon, but decided not to pursue it. The United States had finally won a victory.

The New York Times headlined an outstanding moment on July 18, 1975: "U.S. and Soviet astronauts unite ships and then join in historic handshakes." Of the two Americans joining the Russians was the Freemason, Brigadier General THOMAS P. STAFFORD.

Years later it was learned the American *Apollo* space ship was forced to do all the maneuvering to link up with the Russian ship. The latter was not capable of doing the job. This was proven early in 1983 when another Russian ship failed to carry out its mission to link up with an orbiting sister craft. It was also learned the American astronauts were amazed to find how crude the equipment inside the Russian vessel really was.

By vetoing thirty-three bills sent to him by The Congress, President Ford was able to reduce the rate of inflation drastically. Believing he still had a job to do as President, he decided not to retire in 1977 as he had originally planned. He announced on July 8, 1975, he would be a candidate for reelection.

From the beginning the President ran into trouble. Howard H. Callaway of Georgia was selected as Ford's campaign manager. He announced that Nelson Rockefeller would be replaced as Vice President. This didn't set well with the President or Rockefeller with his many supporters. Conservatives cheered the announcement. When it was changed, the latter group was dismayed.

Then a Soviet author, critical of the Communists, wanted to visit the President. Ford considered such a meeting would be unwise. The story was leaked to the press, and a furor was raised.

And at Helsinki the President was duped by the Russians. They readily agreed to recognize and observe the principles of human rights. They also agreed not to change political boundaries by force, but only through peaceful means. The President was accussed by his detractors of selling out the United States.

To make it even tougher on himself as a candidate, in September Ford suspended grain sales to Russia. American farmers were furious. But later an agreement was reached with the Soviets and shipments were continued.

A 27-year old woman named Lynette Alice "Squeaky" Fromme tried to assassinate President Ford in Sacramento on September 5, 1975. She was a follower of the convicted murderer Charles Manson. Secret Service agents disarmed her quickly. On November 26 she was sentenced to life in prison.

In San Francisco on the 22nd of September a shot rang out from the pistol of Sara Jane Moore, 45, a civil-rights activist. Ford was shoved into his automobile with Secret Service agents on top of him. The car sped to the airport and *Airforce One.* She also was sentenced to life in prison.

The nation's 1976 bicentennial was a tremendous success. The President wrote: "Never in my wildest dreams had I imagined that I would be President of the United States on its 200th birthday." He had determined the year should be one to remember. He had been reminded that Ulysses S. Grant had taken little notice of the centennial of the nation. This wasn't to happen in 1976.

"What a busy weekend that was!" Ford wrote. "Over a five day period, I participated in the dedication of the Smithsonian

Institution's new Air and Space Museum. I spoke at the National Archives, where the Declaration of Independence, the Constitution and the Bill of Rights were on public display. I flew to Valley Forge, where George Washington and his ragged Continental Army had encamped, exhausted, out-numbered and short of everything but faith. I spoke at Independence Hall in Philadelphia, where the fifty-six framers of the Declaration of Independence had signed their names to that glorious document. Then I helicoptered to New York Harbor to watch the tall ships from thirty nations pass by majestically in Operation Sail."

Throughout the nation people prayed, celebrated, watched parades, and generally took part in rededicating the birth of the United States. Ford was convinced "the nation's wounds had been healed. We had regained our pride and rediscovered our faith and, in doing so, we had laid the foundation for a future that had to be filled with hope."

Throughout Freemasonry the bicentennial of the United States was celebrated. And not just on July 4th, but throughout the year. *The Philalethes* magazine continued its series on the early years of the country, and would continue to do so throughout 1983. Articles concerning Freemasonry and its principles were published in numerous newspapers. Macoy Publishing Company published a new book, *G. Washington: Master Mason.* Governors, Congressmen, Senators, and other leaders of the country who were Freemasons joined Grand Lodges and Grand Masters in mammoth celebrations.

The appendant bodies joined in. There were the Knights Templar; both the Northern and Southern Jurisdictions of the Scottish Rite; the General Grand Chapter of Royal Arch Masons, International; and individual Grand Chapters. The "little" Masonic bodies of the Allied Masonic Degrees during their meeting in Washington, D.C., in February took note of this historic occasion. Later, organizations such as the Order of the Eastern Star, the White Shrine of Jerusalem, and the Order of the Amaranth, which are predominately ladies' associations did their share.

The Virginia Craftsmen, a traveling Masonic Degree Team whose members wear a Confederate cavalry-type grey and gold uniform, traveled to California, Indiana, Missouri, Ohio, and South Carolina to help those jurisdictions celebrate 200 years of freedom. This team became the only such group ever to be invited by the Grand Lodge of Pennsylvania to exemplify its Masonic ritual.

Problems for the President mounted. New York City was on the verge of bankruptcy. Ford refused to bail it out until its politicians produced a fiscally responsible plan. He was having internal problems with a couple of his cabinet members. He made changes he believed necessary. These were condemned by the press. To add to the chaos, Ronald Reagan decided to challenge the President for the Republican nomination. Reagan waged a vigorous campaign. About half way through the primaries, Reagan led in delegates.

The way was paved for an unknown politician from Georgia to win the Presidency of the United States in 1977.

With all the rejoicing going on in the country, politics was still at work as usual. After a long and bitter primary battle the Republican fight ended in Kansas City. There, on the first ballot, GERALD FORD won the nomination by a close vote. After a long debate, he chose ROBERT DOLE of Kansas as his running mate. Dole is a member of Russell Lodge No. 177, Kansas.

The Democratic nomination was locked up by James Earl Carter of Georgia. He was the first Southerner since the War Between the States to be selected by either party as a Presidential candidate. Lyndon Johnson had considered himself a "Westerner" although he came from Texas.

The rhetoric became heated during the Ford-Carter campaign. Ford claimed during a "Whistle-stop" speech: "Jimmy Carter wants to divide America. Jimmy Carter will say anything anywhere to be President of the United States. He wavers, he wiggles and he waffles, and he should not be President of the United States. There was a great, great President a few years ago named Teddy Roosevelt who once said, 'Speak softly and carry a big stick.' Jimmy Carter wants to speak loudly and carry a fly swatter."

By a slim margin, Carter won the election.

Shortly before he left the Presidency, GERALD R. FORD received Royal Arch and Cryptic degrees, in the Oval Office. Throughout his political life, and particularly as President of the United States, Ford had been honored by his brethren of the largest fraternal association in the world—Freemasonry.

A plaque depicting his likeness had joined those of the other Presidents of the United States who were Freemasons. These will be found within the George Washington Masonic National Memorial. These plaques are illustrated in *G. Washington: Master Mason*. The others are George Washington, James Monroe, Andrew Jackson, James Knox Polk, James Buchanan, Andrew Johnson, James Abram Garfield, William McKinley, Theodore Roosevelt, William Howard Taft, Warren Gamaliel Harding, Franklin Delano Roosevelt, and Harry S. Truman. Many of these men had taken time from their busy schedules to work with and for Freemasonry. All were proud to acknowledge their faith in the principles for which the Order stands.

The George Washington Masonic National Memorial in which these plaques have a place of honor is situated on Shooters Hill, Alexandria, Virginia. This Memorial depicts the universality of Freemasonry. It was built by the Freemasons of the United States. It is supported by them. Although it comes under the jurisdiction of the Grand Lodge of Virginia, it is in reality the property of every jurisdiction, and every Freemason, in the United States. From it the George Washington Monument five miles away in the District of Columbia, can easily be seen.

In 1971 Charles E. White of Wisconsin responded to the welcome of the Grand Masters to the Memorial on Washington's Birthday. He paid homage to the first President, then added:

> This love that George Washington displayed has caused this ground to be hallowed in another sense. We often extol the virtues of the universality of Freemasonry. Too seldom

do we witness this universality in actuality. But here on Shooters Hill in Alexandria, Virginia, we have seen the fruits of this oneness of spirit.

In this city on February 22, 1910, William McChesney of Virginia told the representatives of eighteen Grand Lodges: "By the grace of God and the invitation of Alexandria-Washington Lodge No. 22, we are here today to form an organization which we hope will be as lasting as the memory of him whose birthday we celebrate."

You know the results. Today, sixty-one years later, we are beneficiaries of the love of our forefathers. All of Freemasonry in the United States, united to build this monument to a man, the like of which has never before been accomplished. As the Colonial soldiers rallied around George Washington to give us the greatest country the world has ever known, so the Freemasons of the country rallied around the spirit of this great and good Freemason to give us the greatest monument ever built to the memory of a man.

After President Ford's plaque had been unveiled on February 17, 1975, the day proclaimed to celebrate the birth of Washington, he thanked those present for their kindness. He then added a personal note:

The dedication of this medallion gives me a great personal pleasure and, of course, is an honor that I will always cherish.

When I took my obligation as a Master Mason—incidentally, with my three younger brothers—I recalled the value my own father attached to that order. But I had no idea that I would ever be added to the company of the Father of our Country and 13 other members of the Order, who also served as President of the United States.

Masonic principles—internal, not external—and our Order's vision of duty to country and acceptance of God as Supreme Being and guiding light have sustained me during my years of government service. Today, especially, the guidelines by which I strive to become an upright man in Masonry give me great personal strength.

Masonic precepts can help America retain our inspiring aspirations while adapting to a new age. It is apparent to me that the Supreme Architect has set out the duties each of us has to perform, and I have trusted in His will with the knowledge that my trust is well-founded....

The Memorial was the site for the Easter sunrise services of the Grand Encampment of Knights Templar on Easter Sunday, 1983. For many years this service had been conducted at Arlington National Cemetery. For some unaccountable reason, the federal government had decided sectarian services could no longer be held on government property. The George Washington National Masonic Memorial Association welcomed the Knights and other Freemasons who had been participating in these special services to their Lord. Thousands turned out for the occasion.

Thirty-six

THE CARTER YEARS

THE day, January 20, 1977, was sunny and cloudless, but windy and cold, when the out-going and in-coming Presidents went to the East front of the Capitol. Chief Justice Warren Burger administered the Presidential oath to James Earl Carter, who used the assumed name "Jimmy." The first words of the thirty-ninth President were: "For myself and for our nation I want to thank my predecessor for all he has done to heal our land."

Instead of riding in the inaugural parade, the new President, his wife Rosalynn and daughter Amy, followed by their three sons and wives, walked down the broad avenue in the bitter cold. The thousands of people lining the streets were first shocked and then joyous with cries of "They're walking!"

In his *Keeping Faith*, Carter writes of his first dramatic moment:

> "We were surprised at the depth of feeling from our friends along the way. Some of them wept openly, and when I saw this, a few tears of joy ran down my cold cheeks. It was one of those few perfect moments in life when everything seems absolutely right."

Why did he do it? To more than promote exercise, he noted. He wanted to "provide a vivid demonstration" of his confidence in the people. And to provide "a tangible indication of some reduction in the imperial status of the President and his family."

The reception of this act by the general public was decidely mixed.

In his book, Carter quoted from his diary dated January 20, 1977:

"...some of our staff asked the chef and cooks if they thought that they could prepare the kind of meals which we enjoyed in the South, and the cook said, "Yes, Ma'am, we've been fixing that kind of food for the servants for a long time.""

Carter decided frugality was to be practiced throughout his administration. "I wanted to eliminate some of the perquisities of Washington officials, beginning with my own immediate political family," he wrote. Yet, according to Clark R. Mollenhoff in *The President Who Failed:* "The large number of Georgians brought to Washington for the White House staff had to be a disappointment to those of us who believed he would carry out his pledge to cut the White House staff by one-third. (The White House staff was actually increased by more than one hundred people in the first months Carter was President....)"

The President, like all his predecessors and those who would follow, found comments leaked to the media were troublesome. Although discussions during cabinet and other meetings were closed, "we later found that most of our deliberations reached the press after each meeting, often in a highly distorted form," he wrote. "There were times when I thought that we would have been better off publishing minutes....After Watergate, it seemed that every subordinate functionary in government wanted to be Deep Throat."

As part of the "human rights" program, that would be the mainstay of the administration, on March 1, the President lifted travel restrictions on Americans to "such countries as Cuba, North Korea, Vietnam, and Cambodia."

One of Carter's first acts as President took place on January 27, 1977. He pardoned about 10,000 Vietnam draft evaders. His reasoning isn't mentioned in his book, nor is it noted in his "Chronology."

Carter soon learned that the leading newspaper in the District often exaggerated the truth. He wrote in his diary on September 1: "The Washington Post is conducting a vendetta against Bert [Lance] and has apparently ordered two front-page stories about him each day....In contrast, The New York Times didn't mention him."

Thomas Bertram (Bert) Lance was one of Carter's first appointments—Budget Director—and had long been a close friend of the President.

Lance had been accused of conducting unsavory, and perhaps illegal, banking practices in Georgia. For two months he and the President were hounded by the media. On September 20, Carter wrote in his diary: "I played tennis late in the afternoon with Bert, and he indicated to me that he wanted to resign. I didn't argue with him."

LaBelle Lance was opposed to her husband's resignation, but Carter wanted it and the resignation was accepted. According to Carter's diary, Mrs. Lance phoned the President to say that, in accepting the resignation Carter had betrayed his best friend.

The investigations continued for many months. No proof of illegality was ever produced. Carter wrote: "The ordeal was terrible for us all, and I am not even sure what lessons were taught. I am just grateful that eventually it turned out all right."

A once unbelievable deed reached its final stage on April 18, 1978. The Congress voted to give away the Panama Canal. The President justified the leadership he had provided in this fight by claiming it was clear from the treaty of 1903 that Panamanians "retained ultimate sovereignty over the Canal Zone."

What apparently the politicians overlooked is that there would have been no country of Panama, nor any canal, if it had not been for American ingenuity.

President Omar Torrijos of Panama stated publicly that "we would have started our struggle for liberation, and possibly tomorrow the Canal would not be operating any more" if the treaty hadn't been passed. This didn't help the "give-away" plan in the House. It took much "arm-twisting" on the part of the President and his supporters before Panama achieved its goal. That wasn't until September 27, 1979.

A bright note appeared in the gloom of the Panama "give-away." A Masonic Lodge in Cristobal, "Isthmus of Panama," under the jurisdiction of the Grand Lodge of Massachusetts, was saved. But it was almost lost, along with everything else in Panama.

In the 1903 treaty between the United States and Panama, a track of land was owned by the Panama Railroad Company. In 1921 the railroad sold a tract of land and a building to Sojourners Lodge, Ancient, Free and Accepted Masons. The Lodge had been constituted in 1913 by Massachusetts. The transaction was specifically authorized by an act of Congress. In 1967 a new treaty was drawn up. Within it there was a stipulation that the property of the Lodge would not be transferred to the Panamanian government. This treaty was never ratified by the Senate.

President Carter and the State Department hastened to give General Omar Torrijos of Panama everything he wanted in a 1977 treaty. This included the *only privately owned property in Panama*—that of Sojourners Lodge. The pleas of the Lodge fell on deaf ears in the State Department. The Panama government wouldn't renounce its claim to the property. So, the Lodge decided to appeal to The Congress.

A member of the Lodge, after over a week of wandering from office to office on Capitol Hill, arrived at the office of Senator ROBERT J. DOLE. He was fortunate. He met ROBERT L. DOWNEN, an assistant and legislative aide of the Senator. Downen had been a Master Councilor of Wichita Chapter, Order of DeMolay. In 1969 he had been selected as the "outstanding DeMolay in Kansas." He was then a member of Albert Pike Lodge No. 303 in Kansas. He had followed in the footsteps of his great-great grandfather, grandfather, and father. Dole, a member of Russell Lodge No. 177, Kansas, had received the 33⁰ of the Scottish Rite in 1975.

"I've just about reached the end of the line," the brother from Panama told Downen. "We know that Senator Dole is a Brother in the Craft, and he's just about our last hope in this predicament." He told Downen the full story. He then provided Dole's assistant with documents necessary to prove the claims of the Lodge. These Downen took to Dole. Dole took the matter to the Carter administration. As it had continually done, the State Department turned aside the claims of the Lodge.

A week before the crucial vote on the treaty, Senator Dole informed the President and the State Department he was going to introduce an amendment that would exclude the Lodge property. He would insist on the Senate voting on this before final ratification of the treaty. A frightened administration, for the first time, looked seriously at the matter. It feared any changes would kill the "give-away." Lawyers and diplomats within the administration went to work.

Four days before the scheduled vote, the Chief Legal Advisor of the Department produced a written guarantee from Torrijos in Panama and the Panamanian Embassy in Washington stating: "We recognize the validity of the title now held by the Sojourners Lodge, of the Ancient Free and Accepted Masons. . . .The entry into force of the Panama Canal Treaty of 1977 will not in any way impair the validity of this title." It was dated April 14, 1978.

On the 18th Senator Dole read the written guarantee into the official, permanent legislative record of the treaty in the Senate. "This commitment has been cleared with the highest authorities in the Government of Panama," he said, "so that there may be no question on this point now, or at any future date." He then withdrew his amendment. Sojourners Lodge had its legal property in perpetuity.

Both Downen and Dole were made Honorary Members of Sojourners Lodge.

Carter noted the high cost the politicians paid for abdicating their trust to the people of the United States. In the elections of 1978, six who voted for the treaties didn't run; seven were defeated; seven won. "Eleven more of the senators who supported the treaties were defeated in 1980—plus one President," Carter wrote.

In the meantime the President was working to remove all American aid to Anastasio Somoza of Nicaragua. The Somoza government fell in 1979. On September 17, 1980, Somoza was assassinated in Paraguay. Nicaragua was taken over by Marxists, whose rule, along with that of Cuba, would cause more horror for Central America.

Pope Paul VI died on August 6, 1978. The College of Cardinals elected a kindly 65 year old Cardinal Albino Luciani, who assumed the title Pope John Paul I. Ironically, he only served thirty-four days, dying on September 28. The present Pope, John Paul II, a Polish Cardinal, was elected on October 16. He would endear himself to all freedom-loving peoples throughout the world.

On May 13, 1981 Pope John Paul II was almost killed by an assassin's bullet. Subsequent investigations strongly alleged orders for his death had been handed down from the Russian hierarchy. Another attempt was made on his life in Portugal on May 12, 1982. Despite these senseless attempts, the Pope continued to travel widely speaking strongly for peace and love.

And the Pope proved his universality. Early in 1983 he removed the long standing ban on Roman Catholics becoming Freemasons. Until then Catholic men, and there have been thousands of them, who became Masons were subject to excommunication.

The President to the United States, the President of Egypt, Anwar Sadat, and the Prime Minister of Israel, Menahem Begin, spent months at Camp David, Washington, and other places, hammering out a peace settlement between Egypt and Israel. These became known as the "Camp David Accords." Few expected success. But an agreement was finally reached in 1979. Although Carter vividly described his frustrations, particularly with Begin, during the months of discussions.

Sadat proved to be a good friend of the United Staes. From all accounts he was a brave man, one who feared nothing. When the world including America, turned the deposed Shah of Iran away, Sadat took him in. For his efforts in "modernizing" his country, a band of fanatics killed Sadat along with several others, on October 6, 1981.

Shah MOHAMMED REZA PAHLEVI was described by Carter after his visit to the United States on November 15, 1977 as "a likeable man, erect without being pompous, seemingly calm and self-assured in spite of the tear gas incidents and surprisingly modest in demeanor."

Carter, as other Presidents had before, considered the Shah a strong ally. He had maintained good relations with Egypt and Saudi Arabia, and he was willing to provide Israel with needed oil in spite of the Arab boycott. At the time of the Shah's visit to Washington in November of 1977, President Carter hoped to secure his influence in support of Sadat's dramatic visit to Jerusalem.

The Shah decreed Iran a one-party state in 1975, establishing the National Resurrection Party. While he attempted to modernize his country, riots broke out and hundreds of persons were killed as his "secret police" and troops battled the demonstrators. Riots and demonstrations continued and the Shah endeavored to restore civilian government by appointing a military government.

The tear gas mentioned was used by the police in an attempt to subdue Iranian students, and their supporters, who were protesting the visit of the Shah. This happened frequently, even when the Shah wasn't in the country. Many times those attending the Grand Masters, Grand Secretaries, and Allied Masonic Degree meetings in the District of Columbia witnessed these fanatics marching through the streets. Although they were in this country at the expense of Iran, and with the support of the Shah, they protested!

He made a fatal mistake. He tried to appease his dissidents, even granting amnesty to his fiercest opponent, the Ayatollah Ruhollah Khomeini, whom he had exiled 15 years earlier. The Ayatollah had gone to Paris. There he began issuing orders to his supporters in Iran.

The problems grew worse in Iran. The opposition now had a leader, although in Paris, they could rally around. The Russian propaganda machine did "everything possible to aggravate the situation." Carter advised the Shah to continue to do everything possible to hold his country together.

General strikes were ordered by Khomeini, along with bloodshed. The Shah appointed Shahpour Bakhtiar as Prime Minister. The new leader immediately called for the Shah to leave Iran! Even so, Khomeini said he wouldn't accept anyone loyal to the Shah as a leader in Iran.

Ambassador William Sullivan was sending Carter conflicting reports, according to the President. He believed the Ambassador was carrying out the President's orders "halfheartedly, if at all." Carter ordered the Secretary of State "to get Sullivan out of Iran." Cyrus Vance wouldn't. He felt it would be "a mistake to put a new man in the country."

The Shah left Iran on January 16, 1979. This was the end of the freedom he had tried to give his countrymen, and which they had refused to accept. It also marked the end of Freemasonry in the country. Pahlevi, a Freemason, had encouraged and supported its growth in Iran. The Order of DeMolay, a Masonic youth organization, had been particularly strong. So had the Scottish Rite of Freemasonry.

According to Mohamed Heikal in *Iran: The Untold Story:*

> Khomeini's message to the Iranian people was that getting rid of the Shah was only a first step: "It is not our final victory, but the preface to victory." He called upon the army to destroy its new sophisticated American weaponry, and on the people to continue their strikes and demonstrations...As for Carter's suggestion that he should cooperate with Bakhtiar, he simply said that this was none of Carter's business.

Aboard an Air France jet Khomeini returned to Iran on February 1, 1979. Untold thousands greeted him in the streets of Tehran. The revolution began. Several of the Shah's supporters committed suicide. In the weeks to follow, thousands more were murdered in the name of Allah.

Heikal writes that "Khomeini proceeded to destroy everything connected with the Shah's regime and in this he was remarkably successful. The army had to be destroyed because it was the creation of the Shah and represented the only potential threat to the Khomeini Revolution."

Doyle McManus in *Free at Last* tells us that the Carter administration and many American firms with large interests in Iran attempted to act, after the fall of the Shah, as if nothing were amiss. Iran had been a valued regional ally, a strategic military partner, a wealthy customer and faithful source of oil.

Unemployment, which had been high under the Shah became worse under the Ayatollah. "The revolution did not take place to provide people with bread," he told Heikal.

Friends of the Shah pleaded with Carter to let the former Iranian leader into the United States. "I adamantly resisted all entreaties," the President wrote. "Circumstances had changed since I had offered the Shah a haven. Now many Americans would be threatened, and there was no urgent need for the Shah to come here."

The President believed conditions had improved during the spring and summer. The embassy staff in Iran had been greatly reduced. Americans were still urged to leave Iran. Thousands did (including my son).

The exiled Shah's health which had been declining, worsened. All of the President's advisers, according to him, thought the Shah should be admitted to the United States for medical treatment. "I was the lone holdout," he wrote. Bruce Laingen, from the embassy, however, was skeptical. He felt the Iranian government "did not have sufficient control over any of its security forces to carry out its promise" to protect the embassy if trouble erupted because of the admission of the Shah.

Henry Precht, "the Iran desk officer in Washington," according to McManus said: "We should make no move toward admitting the Shah until we have obtained and tested a new and substantially more effective guard force for the embassy. Secondly, when the decision is made to admit the Shah, we should quietly assign additional American security guards to the embassy to provide protection for key personnel until the danger period is considered over." His proposals were ignored.

The Shah entered New York Hospital on October 22 under the name of David Newsom. The demonstrations began. On November 1 Khomeini told the students to "expand with all their might their attacks against the United States and Israel, so they may force the United States to return the deposed and cruel shah."

Sunday, November 4, 1979, started out peacefully. But at 10:15 a.m. all hell broke loose. A well-rehearsed mob of "students" broke into the embassy compound. The eight Marine guards did what they could, short of killing the invaders, to hold them back. They didn't succeed. The Marines outside the compound were ordered to do nothing, but to surrender when the mob told them to.

Almost one hundred embassy employees were captured, bound, and blindfolded. MOORHEAD KENNEDY, who would become a Master Mason in Holland Lodge No. 8 in New York City when his long ordeal was over, was told, "Vietnam, Vietnam. We're paying you back for Vietnam."

Rosalynn Carter suggested to her husbnad that the United States stop buying Iranian oil. This the President ordered carried out. On November 14 he ordered Iran assets in the United States frozen. On the 17th the Ayatollah said the women and blacks who weren't American spies would be set free. Thirteen of them were later sent home.

The United States Embassy in Islamabad, Pakistan, was burned down by a mob on November 21. Two Marines were killed. Khomeini praised the killers. In Saudi Arabia the Great Mosque of Mecca was seized by fanatics. The Ayatollah claimed America was behind the desecration. United States missions in Turkey, India and Bangladesh were later attacked by Muslim hoodlums.

The American hostages were submitted to varying degrees of torture throughout their imprisonment. Meanwhile in the "civilized" world, little could be accomplished. As always, the United Nations was useless. The World Court condemned Iran, but was powerless.

The President refused to light the national Christmas tree as a symbolic gesture. Then the Russians invaded Afghanistan. The Afghans resisted the Soviets, and they would continue to keep the invaders from taking over the whole country. As another gesture of displeasure, the President refused to let American athletes compete in the Moscow Olympic games the following year.

The Shah finally made his escape to Egypt and the friendly hands of Anwar Sadat. In Cairo on July 27, 1980, Pahlevi died from the cancer he had been suffering for years. He was no longer an issue in the imprisonment of the hostages. But this issue was a sham, as Berry Rubin points out in *Paved With Good Intentions*. Americans believed that this would lead to the release of the hostages, but in this we were mistaken for "the focus had shifted from the holding of American diplomats as bargaining chips to force the return of the Shah and his money to the holding of these people as spies and enemies."

There was a bright note within the gloom. Six Americans had managed to escape the mob on November 4. They finally found refuge and protection through the Canadian Ambassador, Kenneth Taylor. A means had to be found to get them out of Iran. The airport was indeed risky, but it was the only way the Ambassador felt his plan might work. To get through the terminal and on a Swissair flight to Zurich passports would be needed. McManus tells part of the story:

> "...the Canadian Cabinet of Prime Minister Joe Clark had to vote on the plan." Canadian passports with the Americans' photographs and fictious names of Canadian technicians and businessmen were issued and with the help of the CIA contributing counterfeit Iranian visa stamps, the six Americans made their escape. The Canadian Ambassador closed his country's embassy the next day and returned home. America was jubilant and the good news was heard around the world. "Taylor was hailed a hero. In what had seemed like its darkest hour, America discovered it had a true and gutsy friend."

The Iranians were irate! What the Canadians had done was proclaimed "Illegal!" Vengence was vowed against Canada.

During the Masonic meetings in the District of Columbia in February, the Canadian Freemasons were hailed as conquering heroes. The American Masons couldn't do enough for them to show their appreciation of Canada.

Later, an excellent, and factual television motion picture was produced and viewed by millions.

The President had been endeavoring to have the imprisonment of the hostages transferred from the militants to the Iranian government. He didn't succeed, so he told Henry Precht, who had been placed in charge of the hostage situation, to call in the Iranian ambassador to the United States. Precht told the ambassador he and his diplomatic corp would have to leave the United States immediately. Carter continued the story:

> The Ambassador was angry, and told Henry that the hostages were well cared for and were under complete control of the Iranian government. . . . He looked straight at the Ambassador and said, "Bull shit!" The Iranian Ambassador stalked out of the building and complained to the American press about mistreatment and abusive language.
>
> *I wrote Henry a note, saying that one of the elements of good diplomatic language was to be concise and accurate and clear, and his reply to the Iranians proved that he was a master of this technique.*
>
> DIARY, APRIL 8, 1980

At a National Security Council meeting on April 11 the President suggested a rescue mission be carried out. Secretary of State Vance objected. On the 15th he was the only objector. On the 16th plans were made for the operation. Secret agents, according to Carter, had continued to move in and out of Iran. One, who couldn't be identified, knew where every hostage was kept. The rescue plan seemed excellent.

The rescue mission was started at 7 p.m. April 24 when sand-colored helicopters lifted off from the deck of the *U.S.S. Nimitz*. Then "Murphy's law" took over. Just about everything that could go wrong did. An unexpected sand storm disabled two helicopters. The C-130s reached the initial landing site. The remaining helicopters joined them. Then one developed hydraulic problems. With less than the required six, the mission was aborted. In the darkness a helicopter flew into a C-130. The crash and subsequent fire killed eight. Three others were burned. The latter were flown to a hospital in Texas for treatment. A memorial service for the dead was held at Arlington National Cemetery on May 9.

Cyrus Vance resigned. Edmund Muskie of Maine accepted the position as Secretary of State. The American hostages continued to be held in Iran.

Politics, as always, went on as usual in America. Edward M. "Ted" Kennedy, the Massachusetts ultra liberal, was endeavoring to win the Democratic nomination. When Kennedy announced his candidacy, Carter had claimed he would "whip his ass." He did! Ronald Wilson Reagan of California beat out his challengers and won the Republican nomination. He chose George Bush, no stranger to Washington politics, as his running mate.

Reagan won the election on November 4, 1980, by a landslide. In fact, the television newscasters projected the dimensions of his victory as early as 7:30 p.m. E.S.T. Perhaps this news brought about a positive change in the Iranian attitude toward the hostage situation. The President-elect didn't mince his words in discussing the Iranians. Among his mildest he called them "criminals"; "kidnappers"; "barbarians." It was clear that negotiations then taking place would change after the day of inauguration.

The Algerian government agreed to negotiate between Iran and the United States. Warren Christopher, a Deputy Secretary of State, did a herculean job in the last days of the negotiations. In the final analysis the return of the hostages depended upon the transfer of $7,977 billion, the amount of the Iranian funds that had been frozen in American banks. The description of Carter's last twenty-four hours in office makes dramatic reading.

The Algerians had sent two 727s to Tehran, carrying about fifty Algerian special commandos, ready for combat in case anything went wrong. The fifty-two American hostages were placed aboard one where each was greeted by an Algerian stewardess and a Swiss embassy official. Their plane began taxiing to the end of the runway. At 8:55 p.m. in Iran, 12:25 p.m. in Washington, the plane speeded up and made a quick take off.

At 12:33 p.m., no longer President, Carter learned the first plane was off the ground. Two hours later the planes had cleared Iranian airspace. The hostages were free. President

Ronald Reagan, at a formal lunch, and before television cameras, raised a glass and said: "Some 30 minutes ago, the planes bearing our prisoners left Iranian airspace, and they're now free of Iran. So we can all drink to this one—to all of us together. Doing what we all know we can do to make this country what it should be, what it always has been."

One of America's darkest periods had been brought to a conclusion.

Millions greeted the former hostages when they arrived home after their short stay in a West German hospital. The millions included world-wide televison coverage. This country had never before witnessed anything as emotional.

Their welcome continued during the months following. Many Grand Lodges paid tribute to their heroism during their 444 days of captivity.

During the 1981 Conference of Grand Masters the Commission reported: "It appears that Freemasonry in Iran may have been completely destroyed. The information which comes to the Commission is that all of the Lodges under the Grand Lodge of Iran have been closed, and Masons who were not able to escape the country have been persecuted and some of them executed. Until there is a chagne in the revolutionary government ruled by the Ayatollah Khomeini, there does not seem to be any possibility for the revival of Freemasonry in Iran."

Thirty-seven

FREEMASONRY CONTINUES A VIABLE FORCE

—ALASKA—

A Convention of Lodges holding charters from the Grand Lodge of Washington met on February 3 and 4, 1981. All nineteen of the lodges in Alaska were chartered by, and came under the authority of Washington. For over twenty years the formation of a Grand Lodge of Alaska had been discussed. But until 1976 no concerted effort had been made to break away from Washington.

With the approval of the Grand Lodge of Washington the Alaska Masonic Research Association was formed on July 25, 1976. Its primary purpose was to consider the possibilities of forming a Grand Lodge. Its conclusions were presented to the Grand Lodge of Washington. And on June 18, 1980, this Grand Lodge unanimously adopted a resolution, which in effect, stated it had "no objection to the formation of a Grand Lodge of F. & A.M. of Alaska."

The previous year the AMRA had voted to form a Grand Lodge in February, 1980, provided a majority of the Alaska lodges should approve. Ten agreed, but nine didn't. With such a slim majority it was considered wise to wait. During the year a letter-writing campaign was mounted by some of the lodges voting in the negative. The issue was in doubt when the Convention was called in 1981.

On February 3 the ten approving lodges held fast. One of the negative lodges switched its vote. That evening another, during its Stated Communication, decided to switch. It did so on the 4th. The proponents then had a twelve to seven majority. On the 5th a Constitution and Bylaws were adopted. The Code, as adopted, was almost the same as that of its Mother Grand Lodge.

There was an impressive line of officers selected to install the elected and appointed Grand Lodge of Alaska officers on February 6. The Installing Master was ROY FOSS, a Past Grand Master of the Grand Lodge of Washington. The Installing Marshal, Chaplain, and Secretary were BYRON C. JENKINS, Grand Master of Nebraska; FRANCIS D. HESS, Past Grand Master of Montana; CHARLES S. MOULTHROP, JR., Past Grand Master of Michigan.

Immediately after the installation, the Marshal read a letter which established fraternal recognition to the Grand Lodge of Alaska from its Mother Grand Lodge of Washington.

The first annual communication of the new Grand Lodge was held on February 7. The twelve former Washington lodges that had formed the new Grand Lodge were granted new charters and numbers. The other seven lodges in Alaska were granted permission to remain with Washington as long as they desired. The Grand Secretary of Alaska informed the Commission of Information for Recognition of the Conference of Grand Masters its reasoning for this unusual permission:

> Five of the negative Lodges are in the Southeast Alaska "Panhandle," where a strong feeling of apartness and difference from the rest of the State has existed since the Territory of Alaska first became populated. The people of SE Alaska look and travel south to Washington rather than north to the rest of the State. There is an historical sectionalism that will not die, and it has been intensified by the desire of the northern residents to move the State Capital north.
>
> Since one of the six SE Lodges changed its vote to join the majority, the other five are likely to join within a very few years when they see that the Alaska Grand Lodge is successful. The Alaska Masonic Code provides that each negative Lodge may retain its Washington Charter as long

FREEMASONRY IN AMERICAN HISTORY

as it wishes as long as the Grand Lodge of Washington has
no objections.

The other two negative Lodges are Adak Lodge No. 309
and Anchorage Lodge No. 221. The Adak Lodge was 100%
positive until June 1980, but suddenly changed to negative.
A phone call from Adak on February 8, 1981, indicated that
Adak Lodge is now again becoming positive and inquiring
how to join the new Grand Lodge.

It was estimated that sixty percent of the Masonic population
of Alaska had been incorporated into the new Grand Lodge.

—U.S. MILITARY LODGES IN SPAIN—

From Spain there came good news on the Masonic front. The
Commission, in the person of ROBERT L. DILLARD, JR., its
Secretary and a Past Grand Master of Masons in Texas, reported:

The United Grand Orient of Spain (Grande Oriente
Espanol Unido) through its Master, Francisco Espinar La-
fuente, and its Grand Secretary, Pascual Paricio Perez, have
asked many Grand Lodges in the United States for recognition declaring that the United Grand Orient meets all of the
Standards of Recognition, but failing to show any
legitimacy of origin. The Grande Loge Nationale Francaise,
a regular, recognized Grand Lodge, has chartered a
number of lodges in Spain within recent years, the latest being Arthur T. Weed Lodge No. 59, chartered and set to
work in Madrid in January of this year. [1983]

The United Grand Orient has issued a circular letter to
various Grand Lodges in which it is asserted that the National Grand Lodge of France has invaded the exclusive
jurisdiction in Spain of the United Grand Orient, claiming
that Spain was not "open territory." Since the old Grand
Orient of Spain, prior to the time it went into exile in Mexico, was never recognized as a regular Grand Lodge by the
Grand Lodges of the United States nor by the Grand Lodges
of England, Scotland and Ireland, Spain would be considered open territory. The National Grand Lodge in
France, therefore, acted properly in chartering lodges in
Spain.

It would appear that the most-likely possibility for the
recognizing of a regular Grand Lodge in Spain would be
through the lodges chartered by the National Grand Lodge

of France. It is the understanding of the commission that the name, "Grand Lodge of Spain," has already been reserved through the efforts of officers of the National Grand Lodge of France. The Commission cannot consider the United Grand Lodge of Spain to be regular under the legitimacy of origin of Standards referred to above.

Freemasonry had returned to Spain, legitimately, after its long absence due to the repressive acts of the dictator Francisco Franco. When he became the head of the insurgent government of Spain in 1936, following the "Spanish Civil War," one of his first acts was to ban Freemasonry. Yet, he didn't hesitate to use the tax dollars of American Freemasons to further his causes.

In February, 1982, the Commission on Information for Recognition reported to the Grand Masters that conditions were improving, Masonically, in Spain. Large numbers of the members of what was considered the illegal United Grand Orient had joined lodges chartered by the legal Grand Lodge National of France. The latter had chartered several new lodges in Spain during 1981. The way was paved for the formation of the Grand Lodge of Spain.

The historic day arrived on November 6, 1982. Masonic dignitaries from many countries arrived at the Hotel Castellana in Madrid. They were there to participate in the "consecration and constitution" of the Grand Lodge of Spain. At 4 p.m. the Grand Master and his officers of the Grand Lodge National of France opened Occasional Grand Lodge.

After the French and Spanish national anthems were played, the Grand Lodge was opened on the First Degree. Entered Apprentices and Fellowcrafts were then admitted. The distinguished visitors were received and introduced. The Grand Master of the French Grand Lodge then formed the new Grand Lodge. The Grand Master of the Grand Lodge of Spain, LUIS SALAT-GUSILS was installed.

Freemasonry had returned to a country that had witnessed the persecution of Masons over the centuries.

PHILLIP, DUKE OF WHARTON, Grand Master of the Grand Lodge of England, first established Freemasonry in Spain in

1728. Little is known about what happened in Masonic circles after that. What Masonry there was appears to have been loosely governed. It was in existence when France gained control of the government.

According to ANDRE A. G. BASSOU: "A number of our older Brethren today have lived through that tragic period and had to go into exile in order to escape imprisonment or worse if caught and proven to be Masons, the present Most Worshipful Grand Master of Spain being one of them. Their heart and memory have indelible bruises, their families suffered and friends of old were lost while some of their Brethren had to pay with their lives [because of] being Masons of our Order."

With the introduction of American military bases in Spain during the Franco regime, Freemasonry entered the country. It appears an agreement was reached in the early 1960s with the government whereby it would ignore Masonic lodges on military bases, provided they were kept on the bases. Spaniards, however, were not to be admitted as candidates. The French National Grand Lodge chartered several of these Lodges.

In July 1969, Franco chose Don Juan Carlos to become the future head of state. Franco died on November 20, 1975. Carlos was sworn in as King. He dissolved the remnants of the dictator's regime, and free elections were held in 1976. Quickly Spaniards desiring to become Freemasons traveled to France or Italy and received the degrees. A lodge composed of Spaniards was formed in Perpignan, twenty miles from the Spanish border. Gradually, and cautiously, Freemasons began working within Spain itself.

On July 2, 1982, the National Grand Lodge of France constituted a Grand Lodge in Spain. LUIS SALAT-GUSILS was chosen Grand Master. He immediately started work toward bringing the many differing Masonic bodies under one constitution. He succeeded better than expected.

In an informal, but lengthy, account of the proceedings of the constituting of the new Grand Lodge, Andrew A. G. Bassou wrote:

During that period your writer had time watching in astonishment the many several different regalia exhibited by Brethren on the Columns in the North and South: prominent amongst them were two plaid-patterned Scottish constitution aprons and sashes, with the tartan chosen by the Lodge according to Scottish regulations; there were also rounded-corners aprons with flourished-type rosettes of the Lodges under Grand Lodges members of the United Grand Lodge of Germany and the Grand Orient of The Netherlands; there were light-blue lined with silver braid Irish aprons; there were Yale blue, Royal blue or Copen blue aprons in line with the different American Grand Lodge regulations and there were the sky-blue and silver, sky-blue and gold, bright-red and gold and watered-blue regalia corresponding to the four rites practiced under the G.L.N.F., they being respectively the English Union-Promulgation, the 'Scottish' Rectified Craft, the Ancient and Acepted Craft and the French 'Modern' Traditional rites.

It was noted that the Grand Master customarily takes his Obligation "while the Lodge is opened in the Second or F.C.'s degree." Because of the number of Entered Apprentices present, it was done on the First Degree. Bassou continued his narrative:

The Obligation then pronounced was the exact French version of that prepared in 1969 for the swearing in of the first Grand Master of the Grand Lodge of Iran then consecrated by the MM.WW. Grand Masters of Scotland, France and Germany. Indeed it must be added that the whole programme was closely set on that prepared for the Iranian constitution of thirteen years before, in order to introduce as little innovation as possible in a ceremony which, everybody would agree, does not take place very often nowadays.

The Commission reported in 1983 there were ten lodges that helped consecrate the Grand Lodge of Spain (*Gran Logia De Espana*) in Madrid. Six additional lodges were chartered between then and February, 1983. A remarkable increase. The Commission concluded: "The Grand Lodge of Spain is entitled to recognition by the regular Grand Lodges of the world."

Since at least 1717 Freemasonry has proven to be a vital force in the lives of men, and consequently women. Millions of men have knelt at Masonic altars and assumed obligations to be true and faithful to God, their country, and their neighbors.

These men have ranged from the lowliest of pursuits to the loftiests. They have come from every walk of life. Presidents and Kings have met upon a common level with gardeners and judges. It has been, and remains, one of the few organizations where rank or worldly wealth has no meaning.

As long as there are men who believe in the Brotherhood of Man under the Fatherhood of God, Freemasonry will remain a viable force for all that is good in the world.

—So Mote It Be—

BIBLIOGRAPHY

ALLEN, HERVEY, *City in the Dawn*, Rinehart, N.Y., 1950.

——— *Bedford Village*, Rinehart, N.Y., 1950.

ALLEN, J. EDWARD, *Nocalore, Vol. 6*, Lodge of Research, N.C.

American Military History, Department of the Army, U.S. Gov. Prtg. Office, D.C., 1956.

ANDERSON, PATRICK, *The Presidents' Men*, Doubleday & Co., N.Y., 1968.

Annals of America, The Encyclopedia Britannica, 1968.

BORNEMAN, HENRY S. *Early Freemasonry in Pennsylvania*, Grand Lodge of Pennsylvania, 1931.

BROWN, WILLIAM MOSELEY, *Freemasonry in Virginia*, Masonic Home Press, VA.

——— Blandford Lodge No. 3, A.F. & A.M. (VA).

BURCHER, LLOYD M. AND RASCOVICH, MARK, *Burcher: My Story*, Doubleday, N.Y., 1970.

CABANISS, ALLEN, *Freemasonry in Mississippi*, Grand Lodge of Mississippi, 1976.

CARTER, JAMES D. *Masonry in Texas*, Grand Lodge of Texas, 2nd Ed. 1955.

CARTER, JIMMY, *Keeping Faith: Memoirs of a President*, Bantam Books, N.Y., 1982.

Centennial Anniversary of the Grand Lodge of Iowa of Ancient, Free, and Accepted Masons, 1844 to 1944, compiled by Ernest R. Moore, Charles C. Hunt and Earl B. Delzell.

Centennial Celebration, Grand Lodge A.F. & A.M. of Colorado, 1961.

CHENEY, HARRY MORRISON, *Symbolic Freemasonry in New Hampshire*, Grand Lodge of New Hampshire, 1934.

CLAUSEN, HENRY C. *Masons Who Helped Shape Our Nation*, AASR, SJ, 1976.

COAKLEY, ROBERT W. AND CONN, STETSON, *The War of the American Revolution*, U.S. Government Printing Office, 1974.

COIL, HENRY WILSON, *Freemasonry Through Six Centuries*, Macoy, VA., 1967.

Colonial Freemasonry, Various authors, Missouri Lodge of Research, 1974.

COMMAGER, HENRY STEELE, *The American Destiny*, Editor in Chief, "Making the World Safe for Democracy, Vol. 12, Danbury Press, 1976.

COOKE, ALISTAIR, *Alistair Cooke's America*, Knopf, N.Y., 1973.

DENSLOW, WILLIAM R. *10,000 Famous Freemasons*, Missouri Lodge of Research, 1960.

Documents Illustrative of the Formation of the Union of American States, Selected, arranged and edited by Charles C.Tansill, U.S. Government Printing Office, 1927.

FORD, GERALD R., *A Time to Heal*, Harper & Row, N.Y., 1979.

FRAIM, ROBERT, C. *Freemasonry in Delaware*, Washington Lodge No.1, Delaware, 1890.

GOTTSCHALK, LOUIS, *Lafayette in America*, University of Chicago, 1975.

GOULD, ROBERT FREKE, *The History of Freemasonry*.Its Antiquities, Symbols, Constitution, Customs, Etc., 4 vols., Yorkston Co., N.Y.

——— *Military Lodges, 1895.*

GRAND LODGE OF VIRGINIA, *Proceedings*, 1882.

Grand Lodge 1717-1967, Various authors, United Grand Lodge of England, London, 1967.

GRAYBILL, BEN W. (Forrest D. Haggard, Editor), *History of Kansas Masonry*, Grand Lodge of Kansas, 1974.

GREENE, GLEN LEE, *Masonic In Louisiana*, Grand Lodge of Louisiana.

GUTHRIE, CHARLES SNOW, *Kentucky Freemasonry, 1788-1978*, Grand Lodge of Kentucky, 1981.

HAHN, CONRAD, *A Short History of the Conference of Grand Masters of Masons in North America*, 1963, M.S.A.

HARVEY, PAUL W. *"Not Made With Hands"*, Grand Lodge of Washington, 1958.

HAYWOOD, HARRY L. *Wellsprings of American Freemasonry*, M.S.A., 1973.

HEATON, RONALD E. *Masonic Membership of the Founding Fathers*, Masonic Service Association, 1965.

———AND CASE, JAMES, R. *The Lodge at Fredericksburgh*, Heaton, PA, 1975.

HEIKAL, MOHAMED, *Iran: The Untold Story*, Pantheon Books, N.Y., 1982.

History of the United States, Illustrated, American Heritage, Fawcett Publications, N.Y., 1971.

Hornbook of Virginia History, A, Virginia State Library, 1965.

JOHNSON, MELVIN MAYNARD, *Freemasonry in America Prior to 1750*, 1916.

——— *The Beginnings of Freemasonry in America*, Doran, N.Y., 1924.

JONES, JAMES, *WWII*, Grosset & Dunlap, N.Y., 1975.

LANG, OSSIAN, *History of Freemasonry in New York*, Grand Lodge of New York, 1922.

LANGSTON, LaMOINE, *A History of Masonry in New Mexico*, 1977.

LASKY, VICTOR, *It Didn't Start With Watergate*, Dial Press, N.Y., 1977.

Leaves from Georgia Masonry, Various authors, Third printing, Grand Lodge of Georgia, 1970.

LEECH, MARGARET, *In the Days of McKinley*, Harper & Bros., N.Y., 1959.

Little Masonic Library, Various authors, 5 vols., Macoy, VA, 1977.

LYON, DAVID M. *History of the Lodge of Edinburgh No.1*.

MACKEY, ALBERT G., *History of Freemasonry in South Carolina*, Grand Lodge of South Carolina, 1861.

MCARTHY, CHARLES, "The Antimasonic Party: A study of Political Antimasonry in the United States, 1827-1840," *Annual Report of the American Historical Association for the year 1902*, U.S. Government Printing Office, 1903.

MCLEOD, WALLACE, *Whence Come We?* Grand Lodge of Canada in the Province of Ontario, 1980.

MCMANUS, DOYLE, *Free at Last*, Los Angeles Times Book, 1981.

MOLLENHOFF, CLARK R., *The President Who Failed: Carter Out of Control*, Macmillan, N.Y., 1980.

MOORE, CHARLES W., *Freemasons Monthly Magazine*, July 1, 1848.

New York Times, The, various editions 1920-1975.

NEWTON, JOSEPH FORT, D.D., *River of Years*, J.P. Lippincott, N.Y., 1946.

NIXON, RICHARD, *The Memoirs of Richard Nixon*, Grosset & Dunlap, N.Y., 1978.

PARRAMORE, THOMAS C., "Launching the Craft," Grand Lodge of North Carolina, 1975.

Picture History of World War Two, Staff editors, American Heritage, 1966.

POLLARD, RALPH J. *Freemasonry in Maine*, Grand Lodge of Maine, 1945.

POND, HAROLD SACKETT, *Masonry in North Dakota*, 1964.

PRICHARD, SAMUEL, *Masonry Dissected*, 1730, Masonic Book Club reprint.

REUSSER, WALTER C. *History of the Grand Lodge of Ancient, Free and Accepted Masons of Wyoming*, 1975.

ROBBINS, SIR ALFRED, *English Speaking Freemasonry*, with Foreword by Joseph Fort Newton, Macoy, Virginia, 1930.

ROBERTS, ALLEN E. *The Saga of the Holy Royal Arch of Freemasonry*, motion picture, General Grand Chapter of Royal Arch Masons, Int'l, 1974.

——— *Frontier Cornerstone*, Grand Lodge of Ohio, 1980.

——— *G. Washington: Master Mason*, Macoy, VA, 1976.

——— *House Undivided*, Macoy, VA, 1961.

ROBERTS, ALLEN E., *(cont.)*

——— "A Daughter of the Grand Lodge of Virginia," Virginia Research Lodge No.1777, 1959.

——— *Freemasonry's Servant*, The Masonic Service Association, MD., 1969.

"Report from London: England's 250th Anniversary," 1968, M.S.A.

ROSENLOF, GEORGE W. *Masonry in Nebraska*, Grand Lodge of Nebraska, 1957.

RUBIN, BARRY, *Paved With Good Intentions*, Oxford University Press, N.Y., 1980.

RUGG, HENRY W., D.D *History of Freemasonry in Rhode Island*, Grand Lodge of Rhode Island, 1895.

SINCLAIR, ANDREW, *A Concise History of the United States*, Viking Press, N.Y., 1967.

SINGER, HERBERT R. *New York Freemasonry*, Grand Lodge of New York, 1981.

SMITH, DWIGHT L. *Goodly Heritage*, Grand Lodge of Indiana, 1968.

SMITH, JAMES FAIRBAIRN, *Dateline 1764, Michigan Masonry*, Grand Lodge of Michigan, 1979.

SPARGO, JOHN, *Freemasonry in Vermont 1765-1944*, Grand Lodge of Vermont, 1944.

STANSEL, EDWIN N. *1850-1975, A History of Grand Lodge of Free and Accepted Masons, State of California*, Grand Lodge F. & A.M. of California, 1975.

STEVENSON, WILLIAM, *A Man called Intrepid*, Harcourt Brace Jovanovich, N.Y., 1976.

TATSCH, J. HUGO, *Freemasonry in the Thirteen Colonies*, Macoy, VA, 1929.

"Tidings From Europe," 1960, M.S.A.

TISHER, HAROLD L. *The First 100 Years*, Grand Lodge of South Dakota, 1974.

TORRENCE, C.W. *History of Masonry in Nevada*, Grand Lodge F. & A.M. of Nevada, 1944, reprinted 1975.

TURTINEN, RALPH, *More Than Bricks and Mortar*, Grand Lodge of Minnesota, 1975.

200 Years, two volumes, U.S. News and World Report, D.C., 1973.

VAUGHN, WILLIAM PRESTON, *The Antimasonic Party in the United States, 1826-1843*, University Press of Kentucky, 1983.

VOORHIS, HAROLD, V.B., *Facts for Freemasons*, Macoy, VA, 1979.

WALKES, JOSEPH A., JR. *Black Square and Compass*, Macoy, VA, 1979.

Warren Report, The, The Associated Press, 1964.

WESLEY, CHARLES H. *Prince Hall, Life and Legacy*, United Supreme Council, SJ, PHA, and Afro-American Historical and Cultural Museum, PA, 1977.

WHITRIDGE, ARNOLD, *No Compromise!*, Farrar, Straus and Cudahy, N.Y., 1960.

WILKINSON, JOHN, C. *History of the Grand Lodge of A.F. & A.M. of Oregon*, (with subsequent chapters through 1977), Grand Lodge of Oregon, 1952.

INDEX

Baltimore and Susquehanna
Railroad, 246
Bangladesh, 415
Bank of the United State, 218
Barbados, 111
Barbary States, 204
Barlow, Joel, 173-174
Bartlett, Dr. Josiah, 96
Bartoldi, Frederic A., 305
Baruch, Sydney N., 322
Baskingridge Lodge, NJ, 79
Bassou, Andre A.G., 424-425
Bataan Death March, 353
Bataan Peninsula, 350-352
Batavia, NY, 227-228, 230-231
Bates, William J., 284
Batson, Thomas, 27
Batt, John, 261
Battery D, 324
Battle of Bennington, 200
Bloody Marsh, 31-32
Brandywine, 76
Freeman's Farm, 152
Saratoga, 103
Stillwater, 103
Trenton, 203
the Thames, 213
Baxter, Roderick H., 3
Bay of Pigs, 377
Bean, Col. James E., 390
Beaufort, Duke of, 46
Beauregard, Gen. Pierre Gustave
Toutant, 276-277
Beaver, Lt. Fred J. Holt, 308
Beckley, John, 187
Bedford, Gunning, Jr., 74-75
Bedford Village, 116, 119, 120-125
Bedloe's Island, NY, 305
"Beecher's Bibles", 268
Beecher, Rev. Henry Wade, 268
Begeman, Wilhelm, 19
Begin, Menaham, 411
Beginnings of Freemasonry in America,
The, 8
Beginnings of Freemasonry in England,
The, 19
Belcher, Andrew, 23
Belcher, Jonathan, 8
Belgium, 321, 346
Bell, Alexander Graham, 306
Bell, John, 273
Belton Lodge No. 166, Tx., 373
Ben Hur, 337
Benicia Lodge, Ca., 259
Bennett, Floyd, 339
Bennington, Vt., 151

Bent, Charles, 297
Bent Lodge, NM, 298
Berlin, 364
Berlin blockade, 371
Berlin, Irving, 336
Berlin wall, 377
Berry, Wallace, 337
Betton, James, 101
Bible, 120, 268, 338, 366
Bible of St. John's Lodge No. 1, 85, 185
Bicentennial of the United States, 400
Biddle, Nicholas, 248
Bill of Rights, 142, 177, 187
Birmingham, Al., 334
Biscayne Lodge No. 124, Fl., 358
Bismarck Lodge, Dakota Territory,
295-296
Bismarck, ND, 308-309
Bismark Sea, Battle of, 357
Black, Hugo L., 223
Black Square and Compass, 261
Blackstone, James E., 338
Blair, John, Jr., 64, 157, 172, 223
Blandensburg, Md., 214
Blandford Lodge No. 3, A.F. & A.M.,
history of, 53, 57, 64-65
Blaney, Lord (Major Cadwallader),
71, 98
Blatchford, Samuel, 223
Blecher, Jonathan, 27
"Bleeding Kansas", 270
Blessington, Earl of, 106
Bock's Car, 365
Boggs, Hale, 379
Bolivar, Simon, 213
Bon Amis, Logge des, France, 153
Bonaparte, Napoleon, 204, 206, 215
Bonham, James, 250
Book of Mormon, The, 243
Booth, Edwin, 284
Booth, John Wilkes, 283
Borgnine, Ernest, 338
Borman, Frank, 382-384
Borneman, Henry S., 15
Boston Evening Post, 39
Boston, Lodge at, 30
Boston, Ma., 23, 30, 37, 42, 92, 110-111
Boston Massacre, 135
Boston Tea Party, 92, 135-136
Bostwick, Henry, 86
Botetourt Lodge No. 7, Va., 57, 67-68
Bouquet, Colonel, 119, 122
Bowen, Ephraim, 91
Bowen, Jabez, 92-93
Bowie, James, 250
Box, Daniel, 93

CARE, 368
Carlos, King Don Juan, 424
"Carolana", 20
Carolinas, 130-131
"Carpetbaggers", 290
Carr, Harry, 3
Carroll, Daniel, 170-171
Carruthers, Joseph, 49
Carson City, Nev., 282
Carson, Kit, 297
Carter, Amy, 406
Carter, James "Jimmy" Earl, 296-297, 317, 402-403, 406-419
Carter, James D., 249-250
Carter, Rosalynn, 406, 415
Cartright, Richard, 86
Case, James R., 62-63, 97-98, 99
Cass, Lewis, 206, 210, 236, 257, 265
Castellano, Gen. Giuseppe, 361
Castro, Fidel, 376
Caswell, Richard, 54
Cataract Lodge, Mn., 267
Catawba Lodge No. 17, NC, 389
Catholics, 34, 130, 170, 188, 213, 249, 336, 378, 411
Catron, Thomas B., 299
Catton, John, 223
Cedar Rapids, Ia., 256, 326, 327
Cemetery Ridge, Pa., 281
Centennial Celebration, 278
Central America, 410
Central High School, Ark., 374
Central Intelligence Agency (CIA), 390, 396, 416,
Central Pacific Railroad, 246, 301
Cerza, Alphonse, 70, 72, 78-79
Chadwick, Stephen, 261
Chafee, Roger B., 382
Chamberlain, Neville, 344, 360
Chapman Lodge, NM, 298
Charles County at Port Tobacco, Md., Lodge at, 70
Charles II, King, 130-131
Charleston (Charles Town), SC, 38, 41-42, 130, 160
Charleston, NH, 101
Charleston, SC, 276
Charlestown, In., 219
Chatanooga, 281
Chaytor, George, 149
Cheney, Harry Morrison, 100, 102
Chennault, Gen. Claire, 356-357
Cherokee Indians, 246, 311
Chesapeake (U.S. frigate), 205
Cheseboro, Nicholas, 231
Chestertown, Md., 72

Cheyenne Lodge, Wy.. 294
Cheyennes, 337
Chicago, Il., 268
Chicago Daily Tribune, 372
Chickamauga, 281
Chickasaws, 311
Chief of Naval Operations, 357
  for Air, 359
Chiefs of Staff, 352
Chillicothe, Oh., 206
China, 306, 343, 351, 356-357
China, Nationalist, 372-373, 386
China, Peoples Republic of, 386, 397
Chipman, Col. John, 202
Chipman, Nathaniel, 201
Chittenden, Thomas, 202
Chivington, Rev. John M., 278-279
Choctaws, 311
Christian, George B., 335
Christian, James, 269
Christian, Lt. Com. Michael, 390
Christiana Ferry (Wilmington), De., Lodge at, 74
Christmas, 147-148, 161, 221, 383-384, 387-388, 399,415
Christopher, Warren, 418
Church of Jesus Christ of Latterday Saints, The (see Mormons)
Churchill, Winston, 344-345, 352, 360-361, 366, 375
Cimarron Lodge, NM, 298
Cincinnati Lodge, Oh., 206
Cincinnati, Oh., 267, 319
Cincinnati, Society of, 173
Cincinnatus, 171
City Gazette, Charlotte, SC, 188
City of Buffalo (steamer), 212
City Temple, The, England, 370
Civil Rights Movement, 378, 382, 400
Civil Service, 304
Civil War, vii, 264, 274-283, 297, 303, 304, 306, 312, 337, 402
Claiborne, Gov. La., 216
Claremore Lodge No. 53, Ok., 339
Clark Air Force Base, 389
Clark Field, 350
Clark, Gen. Mark Wayne, 356, 361
Clark, George Rogers, 155, 203
Clark, Joe, 416
Clark, Joel, 95
Clark, Thomas C., 223
Clark, William, 205, 308
Clarke, Jeremiah, 93
Clarke, John C., 250
Clarke, John H., 223
Clarke, Peleg, 93

439

440

Enola Gay, 365
Enterprise, U.S.S., 355, 357
Episcopal Church, 20
Equestrian statue of Washington,
  in Washington, D.C., 274,
  in Richmond, Virginia, 265
Erie Lodge, Oh, 206
Erikson, Jerry, vii
Ervin, Samuel J., Jr., 389
Esmeralda Lodge, Nev., 282
Europe, 321, 323, 345, 354, 357, 360,
  362, 364, 366, 368, 371
European reconstruction program, 371
Evanston Lodge, Wy., 294
Ewing, Gen. James, 148
Excurial Lodge, Nev., 282
Exposes, 1, 229, 233

FABRIC ROLLS OF YORK MINSTER, 4
Fair Oaks, Va., 279
Fairbanks, Douglas, 337
Fairfax Lodge No. 43, Va., 179
Faithful Lodge No. 12, NH, 101
Fall, Albert, 334
Fallen Timbers, Oh., 164
Falmouth Lodge, Va., 64, 68
Faneuil Hall, Boston, Ma., 133
Far East Airforce, 350
Farewell Address, Washington's, 193-94,
  196
Fargo, ND, 309
Farmer's Lodge No. 20, Oh., 178
Fascist Grand Council, 361
Fay, Bernard, 348
Fay, Col. Joseph, 201-202
Fay, David, 202
Fay, Jonas, 200
Fayette Lodge No. 107, Oh., 333
Federal Bureau of Investigation (FBI),
  379
Federal City (D.C.),187, 192
Federal Gazette, Pa, 186
Federal Hall, New York City, 185
Federal Lodge No. 1, DC (15 Md.), 188,
  198, 207, 332, 379
Federal Power Commission, 341
Federal Reserve System, 321
Federal troops, 276-277, 279-280, 285,
  291, 296, 303
Federalist party, 196, 235
Federalists, 199
Fell's Point, Md., 72
Fenwick, Sir John, 117
Ferdinand, Archduke Francis, 321
Ferguson, Wm., 86

Festivals of the Sts. John, 18, 37, 44, 49,
  52, 62, 64, 66, 70, 71, 83-84, 91, 94,
  157, 160, 171
Field Agents, MSA, 370
Field, Stephen J., 223
Fifth Army, 356, 361
Fifth Fleet, 358
5th Pennsylvania Battalion, 170
Fillmore, Millard, 266
Finland, 344, 346
Finnie, Alex., 63
First Lodge in Boston, Ma., 8, 24, 27,
  108, 110
First Lodge in Newport, RI, 93-94
First Marine Division, 357
First Mobile Fleet, 359
Fitch, John, 335
Fitzgerald, Scott, 341
509th Bomb Group, 365
Florida, 217, 220, 275-276, 296, 311,
  331, 339, 383, 387,
Florida, Grand Lodge of, 244
Flud, William, 38
Flying Fortresses, 350
Flying Tigers, 356
Foch, Gen. Marshall, 347
Forbes, Gen. John, 78, 123
Force, Peter, 33
Ford, Betty Warren, 393-394
Ford, Gerald Rudolf, 379, 391-406
Ford, Henry, 318, 335
Ford Motor Company, 318
Formation of the Union of the American
  States, 142
Formosa, 357, 372
Forrest, Gen. Nathan Bedford, 290
Fort Bent, NM, 297
Fort Buford, 309
Fort Dearborn, 211
Fort Erie, 213-214
Fort Garry, 308
Fort Harmar, Ohio, 95, 126, 163
Fort Leavenworth, Ks., 269
Fort McHenry, Md., 214
Fort Niagara, NY, 231
Fort Pickens, Fla., 276
Fort Riley, 269
Fort Sackville, In., 155
Fort Scott, 269
Fort Stanwix, 151
Fort Sumter, 138, 276, 277
Fortitude Lodge No. 107, Ks., 343
46th Foot, 159
Fosdick, Raymond B., 324, 327
Foss, Gerald D., 101
Foss, Roy, 421

441

442

Germany, United Grand Lodge of, 369, 425
Gerry, Elbridge, 167, 169, 174, 196
Gettysburg, Battle of, 292
Gettysburg, Pa., 281, 287
Ghent, Treaty of, 215
Gibson, Hoot, 337
Giddings' Lodge, Neb., 272
Gilbert Islands, 356-357
Gilman, Charles, 259
Gilman, Nicholas, 168
Gilpin, Col. George, 198
Girard College of Philadelphia, 218
Girard, Stephen, 218
Gist, Christopher, 115
Gist, Mordecai, 190
Gladwin, James Callowhill, 120-124
Glenn, John H., Jr., 378
Glover, Col. John, 148
God, 367-368, 384, 392, 404-405, 426
God Bless America, 336
Goethals, George W., 317
"Gold Rush", Ca., 258
Golden City Lodge, Co., 278
Goldwater, Barry, 380, 381, 392, 396
Goodly Heritage, 218-219
Goose and Gridiron, Lodge at, 39
Gordon, James, 24
Gothic Manuscripts, 2
Gottschalk, Louis, 149
Gould, J. L., 89
Gould, Robert Freke, 24-26, 41-44, 48, 68, 70-73, 78-79, 95-96, 99-100, 159
Graeme, James, 36-37
Graff house, Pa., 143
Grand Canyon, Az., 307
Grand Lodge 1717-1967, 12-13, 29, 33, 36, 46, 56, 105-106, 108
Grand Master of Masons for the Continent of America (Scotland), 112
Grand Masters, Conference of, 209, 366, 412, 419, 421, 423
Grand Mound Lodge, Wa., 273
Grand Secretaries Conference, 209, 412
Grand Secretaries, xii
Grandview Lodge No. 618, Mo., 324
Grant, Gen. Ulysses S., 281, 289-290, 302, 400
Graybill, Ben W., 268-269
Great Britain, 8, 36, 38, 47-48, 54, 68, 80-82, 98, 117, 128-133, 135-136, 147, 152, 162-164, 177, 192, 207, 210, 220, 229, 254, 318, 321-322, 344, 346-347, 349, 351, 360-361, 371
Great Lakes, 212, 220

Great Mosque of Mecca, Saudi Arabia, 415
Great Northern Railway, 306
"Great Society", 380-381
"Great White Fleet", 318
Green, Charles E., 74
Green, Gen. Nathanael, 148, 154, 160
Green, Samuel D., 227-228
Green Bay, Lodge at, Wi., 254
Green Dragon Tavern, 110, 135
Green Mountain Boys, 200
Greene, Glen Lee, 215-216
Greenleaf, Lawrence, 127
Greenleaf, Simon, 224
Greenville Lodge No. 119, Tn., 287
Gregory Gulch, Co., 278
Grenada, 111
Gridley, Jeremiah (Jeremy), 27, 50, 79, 90, 108, 110, 177
Griffin, William W., 298
Grissom, Virgil I., 377, 382
Gromyko, Andrei, 368
Grove (Kansas) Lodge, Ks., 269
Guadalcanal, 357
Guam, 314, 352, 357-359
Guerriere (British frigate), 211
"Guide to the Chapter", 89
Guilde Lodge, England, 8
Guildhall, London, Eng., 4
Guilford Courthouse, 160
Gulf of Tonkin, 381
Guthrie, Charles Snow, 202

HABERSHAM, JOSEPH, 35
Hagarty, James, 42
Haig, Alexander, 391, 393
Haiphong, 387
Haise, Fred, 386
Haldeman, H.R., 396
Halifax, Lodge at, NC, 50
Halifax, NC, 50-51
Halifax, Nova Scotia, 111
Halket, Sir Peter, 117
Hall, David, 75
Hall, Prince, 261
Halleck, Gen. Henry, 279
Halliwell, James O., 2
Halliwell Manuscript, 2
Hamilton, Alexander, 9, 91, 99, 183, 188, 189
Hamilton, Andrew, 22
Hamilton, Col. Henry, 155
Hamilton, Frederick, 24
Hamilton, Philip, 188
Hammerton, John, 36
Hampshire Lodge, Ma., 165

443

444

445

449

Pennsylvania Grand Lodge, 31, 44, 69, 71-74, 79, 96, 104-107, 119, 123, 143, 152, 157, 159, 164, 170-171, 185, 194, 206, 213, 246, 253, 287, 318, 326, 402
Pennsylvania Gazette, The, 10, 104, 152
Pennsylvania Journal, 146
Pentagon, 398-399
Pentalpha Lodge No. 23, DC, 302
Perez, Pascual Paricio, 422
Perry, Capt. Oliver Hazard, 212
Perry, James, 43
Pershing, Gen. John J. "Blackjack", 322-323
Perth, Earl of, 78
Petersburg, Va., 53, 281
Peterson, Rev. Edward, 89
"Petition, The", 157, 188
Philadelphia, Pa., 17-18, 21-22, 25, 42, 67. 117, 121, 124, 139, 143, 147, 150, 153, 157, 165-174, 190, 302, 313, 335
Philalethes, The, vii, xiii, 401
Philalethes Society, The, vii, 48
Philanthropic Lodge, Ma., 148
Philanthropy Lodge No. 225, Pa., 271
Philippine Islands, 314, 319, 322, 350-352, 357-358, 368, 389, 397-398
Phillips, Thomas, 24
Phoenix, Az., 307
Pickett, Gen. George, 280-281
Pickney, Charles Cotesworth, 196
Pierce, William, 168-169,170
Pierpoint, Francis, 284
Pikes Peak, Co., 277
Pilgrim Memorial Monument, 319
Pinckney, C.C., 205
Pitner, Joseph, 243
Pitney, Mahlon, 223
Pitt, William, 134
Pitt County, NC, 50
Plains of Abraham, 141
Plan of Union (Coxe's), 20
Plater, George, 178
Platte Valley Lodge No. 32, Neb., 337
Plymouth, Ma., 129
Pocket Companion for Free Masons, 80
Pogreen, James, 105
Poinsett, Joel R., 221
Poinsetta, 221
Poland, 344, 411
Polar Star Lodge No. 99, Mo., 282
Polk, James Knox, 265, 286, 403
Pollack, Capt. Melvin, 389
Pollard, E.A., 286
Pollard, Ralph J., 224, 236-237
Pond, Harold Sackett, 308-310
Pontiac's war, 119

Pontiac, Lodge at, Mi., 257
Poor Richard's Almanack, 152
Pope, Col. Charles, 74
Pope, Gen. John, 279
Port Moresby, New Guinea, 354
Port Royal, Nova Scotia, 7
Port Royal Kilwinning Crosse Lodge No. 2, Va., 57, 60, 63
Port Royal Lodge, SC, 41
Portland Lodge No. 17, Me., 204, 224
Portsmouth, NH, 100, 310
Portsmouth, Va., 356
Portugal, 411
Post, Wiley, 339
Postmaster General, U.S., 188, 336
Potomac Lodge No. 5, DC, 207
Potomac River, 69, 165, 187, 190, 209, 214
Pottawatomie Creek, Ks., 270
Powers, Gary Francis, 376
Preble, Commodore Edward, 204
Precht, Henry, 414, 417
Precious Heritage, 206
Prescott, Samuel, 138
President Who Failed, The, 407
President of the United States, 174, 185, 187, 191-192, 194-196, 198-199, 204-205, 216, 221, 226-227, 245-248, 264, 266, 271-274, 276, 279, 286, 296, 302, 312-316, 318-322, 324, 333, 335, 338-340, 342, 345, 352, 362, 364, 371-372, 374-381, 383, 387,388, 393, 394, 399, 400, 402-403, 406-407, 411, 418
"President's House, The", 188
President's Men, The, 380-381
Preston, William, 229
Price, Henry, 9, 23-28, 38-39, 46, 99, 100, 107-110
Price, Mary, 27
Price, Rebecca, 27
Prince George's Lodge, SC, 41
Prince George's Lodge of Georgetown, SC, 190
Prince Hall, Life and Legacy, 261-262
Prince Hall American Day, 263
Prince Hall Grand Lodge, 261
Prince Hall Masonry, 223, 261-263
Prince of Orange Lodge No. 16, NY, 338
Prince of Wales, H.M.S., 351
Princeton, Lodge at, 78
Princeton, NJ, 149
Princeton University, 8
Prisoners-of-war, 389
Pritchard, Samuel, 1-2, 82, 229
Proby, John, Baron, 83

454

Rising Sun Tavern, 78
River of Years, 370
Roberts, Allen E., *vii-xiii*, 2, 47, 116,
 139-140, 149-150, 199, 206, 275, 289,
 310-311, 328-330, 348, 401
Roberts, Dorothy G. "Dottie", *viii, xiii*
Robinson, Charles, 269-270
Robinson, Gen. David, 202
Robinson, Gen. John C., 292
Rochester Lodge No. 21, NY, 340
Rockefeller, Nelson, 394, 400
Rockingham, Lord Charles, 134
Rocky Mountain Lodge, Co., 278
Rocky Mountain Lodge No. 205, Mi.,
 291-292
Rocky Mountains, 277
Rodney, Col. Caesar, 76, 144-145
Rodriguez Canal, La., 215
Roebuck (British frigate), 76-7
Rogers, William Penn Adair "Will",
 338-339
Rogers Memorial, Ok., 339
Rome, Italy, 361
Rommel, Gen. Erwin, 356
Roosevelt, Elliot, 342
Roosevelt, Franklin D., 325, 336,
 341-343, 345-346, 349-350, 352, 354,
 362, 364, 403
Roosevelt, Franklin D., Jr., 342-343
 James, 342-343
 Theodore "Teddy", 210, 313, 315-322,
 403
Rose, Duncan, 65
Rosenberg, Ethel and Julius, 374
Rosenlof, George W., 273
Rotterdam, 346
"Rough Riders", 313-314
Rowe, John, 28, 92, 96, 108, 110, 158
Roxbury, Ma., 158
Royal Air Force, 356
Royal Arch Lodge No. 3, Pa., 218
Royal Arch Mason, The, *xiii*
Royal Arch Masonry, *vii, xiii*, 43, 51, 63,
 119, 152, 221-222, 228, 240, 262, 285,
 327, 376, 383, 376, 383, 401
Royal Exchange Tavern, Ma., 109
Royal Exchange Tavern, NH., 100
Royal Exchange at Norfolk, Va., 56-60
Royal Navy, 347
Royal White Hart Lodge, NC, 50-52, 54
Rubin, Berry, 416
Ruby, Jack, 378, 380
Rugg, Henry W., D.D., 7, 89-90, 91-92,
 237-242
Rusk, Thomas J., 249
Russell, Richard B., 379

Russell Lodge No. 177, Ks., 402, 409
Russia, 318, 321,322
Rutledge, Edward, 139, 144
Rutledge, Wiley B., 223

Sachse, 169-170
Sacramento, Ca., 400
Sacramento City, Ca., 259
Sadat, Anwar, 411-412, 416
Saga of the Holy Royal Arch of
 Freemasonry, The, 4
St. Alban's Lodge, Ct., 95
St. Andrew's Lodge at Boston, Ma., 9,
 69, 110-111, 113, 133-135, 138, 150,
 165, 177, 204
St. Augustine, Fl., 298
St. Cecile Lodge No. 568, NY, 336
St. Charles Lodge, Mo., 224
St. Clair, Gen. Authur, 163
St. George's Lodge, SC, 41
St. George's Lodge No. 6, NY, 84-85
St. Jean d'Ecosse du Contrat Social,
 Lodge of, 150
Saint Jean de Jerusalem, Lodge de, 153
St. John's Church, Richmond, Va., 137
St. John's Grand Lodge, NY, 258
St. John's Lodge, Ma., 8, 95, 113, 133,
 138, 168
St. John's Lodge, Mn., 267
St. John's Lodge, NC, 46, 48
St. John's Lodge, NH, 100-103
St. John's Lodge, NJ, 178
St. John's Lodge, New Bern, NC, 190
St. John's Lodge, Pa., 18, 79, 104, 107,
 152
St. John's Lodge, SC, 38, 45
St. John's Lodge, Va., 68
St. John's Lodge No. 1, NC, 54
St. John's Lodge No. 1, NH, 168
St. John's Lodge No. 1, NY, 84-85, 87
St. John's Lodge No. 2, De., 76
St. John's Lodge No. 2, NC, 49-50
St. John's Lodge No. 3, Ct., 200
St. John's Lodge No. 3, NC, 49
St. John's Lodge No. 20, Md., 72
St. John's Lodge at Fairfield, Ct., 96
St. John's Lodge at Hartford, Ct., 95
St. John's Lodge at Middletown, Ct., 95
St. John's Lodge at New Bern, NC, 52
St. John's Lodge at Newport, RI, 90-91
St. John's Lodge at Norfolk, Va., 59
St. John's Lodge at Norwalk, Ct., 96
St. John's Lodge at Providence, RI, 90-91
St. John's Lodge at Stratford, Ct., 96
St. John's Lodge at Yankton, Dakota
 Territory, 295

455

457

460

West Indies, 109
West Point, NY, 323
West Point Lodge No. 877, NY, 351, 371
West Point Military Academy, 351
West Virginia, 69, 277
West Virginia, Grand Lodge of, 284-285
Western Reserve Historical Society, 302
Western Star Chapter No. 35, R.A.M.,
    NY, 228
Western Star Lodge, Ark., 253
Western Star Lodge, Ca., 259
Western Star Lodge, Il., 253
Wharton, Phillip, Duke of, 423
Wheeler, Burton K., 352
Whence Came We?, 212
Whig party, 265, 268, 271
Whipple, Abraham, 91-92
Whipple, Gen. William, 103
Whipple, John C., 308
"Whiskey Rebellion", 192-193
White, Charles E., 403-404
White, Edward H., 382
White, Francis E., 272
White Horse Tavern, Ma., 109
White Horse Tavern, RI, 91
White House, (burned), 214, 245, 312,
    315-316, 373, 383, 389, 392-293, 403,
    407
White Mountain Lodge at Globe, Az.,
    307
White Plains, NY, 148, 160
White Shrine of Jerusalem, 401
White's Tavern, 79
Whitmer, David, 243
Whitmer, Peter, Jr., 243
Who Can Best Work, 331
Wilderness, Battle of, 280-281
Wilkes, John, 136-137
Wilkinson, John C., 260
Willamette Lodge No. 2, Or., 260-261,
    277
Willard Hotel, DC, 334
William McKinley Lodge No. 431, 312
William and Mary College, 66
Williams, Roger, 129
Williamsburg, Va., 61, 67, 69, 76, 133,
    160
Williamsburg Lodge No. 6, Va., 57, 63,
    64, 65-66, 172, 187
Wilmington, NC, 48
Wilmot, David, 265
Wilson, U.S.S., 398
Wilson, Woodrow, 320-322, 325, 331,
    333, 339
Winchester Hiram Lodge No. 21, Va.,
    69, 283, 312

Winder Lodge No. 33, Ga., 379
Windham, NH, 101
Wirt, William, 137, 243
Wisconsin, 69, 254, 387, 403
Wisconsin, Grand Lodge of, 254, 267,
    403
Wood, Charles, 82
Wood, Leonard C., 314
Woodbridge, Enoch, 202
Woodbury, Levi, 223
Woods, William B., 223
Wooster, Gen. David, 95, 98-99
Wooster Lodge at Colchester, Ct., 96
Worcester, Samuel A., 246
World Court, 415
World War I, 321-332, 345, 347, 363,
    370, 371, 373
World War II, 47, 225, 323, 345-365,
    370-371, 373
"World War III", 371
Wounded Knee, Battle of, 337
Wren, Sir Christopher, 3
Wright, James, 37
Wright, Orville, 318
Wright, Wilbur, 318
Writ of Assistance, 133
Wyler, William, 337
Wyoming, 259
Wyoming, Grand Lodge of, 294
Wyoming Landmark Commission, 294
Wyoming Lodge, Wy., 294

YALE UNIVERSITY, 98, 202
Yamamoto, Admiral Isoroku, 350
Yates, Captain, 119-120
Yates, Robert, 180-181
Yellow Hand, 337
Yellowstone Military Lodge, ND, 309
Yellowstone National Park, 318
Yoelson, Asa (Al Jolson), 336
Yom Kipper, 390
York, Duke of, 131
York, Eng., 26, 125
York, Lodge at, 9, 81
York, Pa., 154
York Grand Lodge, 9
York Lodge No. 9, Va., 57
York Minster, 4
Yorktown, Lodge at, Va., 57
Yorktown, U.S.S., 354, 355
Yorktown, Va., 160, 170, 303
Yorktown campaign, Va., 76
Yorktown celebration of 1881, 303
Yorktown Lodge No. 205, Va., 69
You, Dominique, 216
Young, Brigham, 254, 291, 293

461